SKIN DEEP, SPIRIT STRONG

SKIN DEEP, SPIRIT STRONG

The Black Female Body in American Culture

Kimberly Wallace-Sanders, Editor

THE UNIVERSITY OF MICHIGAN PRESS

Ann Arbor

Copyright © by the University of Michigan 2002
All rights reserved
Published in the United States of America by
The University of Michigan Press
Manufactured in the United States of America
♾ Printed on acid-free paper

2005   2004   2003   2002   4   3   2   1

A CIP catalog record for this book is available from the British Library.

Library of Congress Cataloging-in-Publication Data

Skin deep, spirit strong : the Black female body in American culture / Kimberly
Wallace-Sanders, editor.
       p. cm.
    Includes bibliographical references and index.
    ISBN 0-472-09707-5 (alk. paper) — ISBN 0-472-06707-9 (pbk. : alk. paper)
    1. African Americans in popular culture.   2. Women in popular culture—United States.
 3. African American women—Race identity.   4. African American women—Social
 conditions.   5. Gender identity—United States.   6. Body, Human, in literature.   7. Human
 figure in art.   8. Racism in popular culture—United States.   9. United States—Race
 relations.   10. Popular culture—United States.   I. Wallace-Sanders, Kimberly, 1962–

E185.625 .S55 2003
305.48'896073—dc21   2002075016

Dedicated to my students,
who manage to get under my skin and
next to my heart in the most surprising ways.

And to my son, Isaiah Anthony Wallace Sanders,
who taught me that the body must be
loved from the inside out.

Acknowledgments

There were many torchbearers on this journey. The kind words and actions of friends, family members, colleagues, and students helped me to navigate my way through terrain that was far more challenging than I ever expected. There are moments in academic study that cause some subtle yet profound shifts in thinking. Most often these are quiet moments that occur between you and the page. If you are fortunate they also occur between you and your colleagues. I am indebted to Jeanne Bergman and Siobhan Somerville for directing me to new ways of imagining the antebellum plantation as the body politic and to Karla Holloway, Hazel Carby, bell hooks, and Susan Bordo for igniting my fierce interest in the Black female body.

The major work on this book was made possible by a Rockefeller funded grant to the Womanist Studies Consortium at the University of Georgia in 1997. Their associated faculty, Layli Phillips, Barbara McCaskill, and Velma Murray were helpful to me during my leave from Spelman College. The New York University Faculty Resource Network also supported this work; special thanks go to Phillip Michael Harper and Tricia Rose for patiently listening to my thoughts and offering much needed advice.

My editor, LeAnn Fields, has a wonderfully rare combination of wit and wisdom; she, Laurie Clark-Klavins, and Abigail Potter provided invaluable assistance to me. All of the contributors to this volume constitute an impressive group of scholars and writers; I am proud to be affiliated with them.

My Atlanta colleagues Beverly Guy-Sheftall, Francis Smith Foster, Rudolph Byrd, and Johnnetta B. Cole sustained me with generous mentoring and an unwavering faith in my abilities. Darlene Clark Hine and Ann duCille also provided tremendous encouragement to me at crucial stages of this work; both scholars continue to raise the bar of excellence so that it is never out of sight and just barely out of reach. Rosemarie Garland Thomson read and made valuable contributions to my introduction.

I extend my deep gratitude to Audree Irons and the student staff at the Spelman College Women's Research and Resource Center, especially

Acknowledgments

Shanell McGoy, who made a wonderful contribution to one of these essays simply by asking the right question. I am delighted to commend outstanding Emory graduate students Michelle Wilkinson, Jennifer Steadman, Ariel Browne, Abigail Blankner, and Andy Lowry, who made valuable contributions to the completion of this work: each has the makings of an exceptional scholar.

My true sisters of the spirit—Suzette Garland, Leslie Harris, Vanessa Jackson, Kathryn Naylor, Bethany Poindexter, and Claire Sanders—extended themselves to me in the most important ways throughout the duration of this project. Robyn Thurston Guy, Phyllis Rose, and Estelle Vaughn have sustained me with unwavering friendshiip since our Oberlin days. Atlanta artist Mary Logan bolstered my confidence when I almost gave up. Elizabeth Alexander, Nikki Finney, and Opal Moore threw lifelines of poetry to me when I needed them most.

I am grateful to my parents, Rose Hardman Wallace and Raymond Wallace, who taught me my very first lesson about my own body: that it is one small measure of who I am as a human being. Their emotional and financial support over the years has sustained my body, mind, and spirit. My brothers, Chris and Greg Wallace, have given me enormous boosts of confidence over the years. (Thanks, Greg, for leading me to a crucial insight that allowed me to take the manuscript to the post office and *just walk away.*) My grandmother Adeline Hardman let me sit on her lap long after it was appropriate, teaching me a significant life lesson about the female body and comfort. My mother and my mother-in-law, Arthrell Sanders, rescued me with unlimited child-care and last-minute proofreading, thus allowing the book to go to press on time.

I extend my most affectionate gratitude to my partner in life, Mark A. Sanders, who listened to endless discussions about this work and still managed to smile and nod encouragingly at all the right times. He is, quite simply, an extraordinary human being who makes my life richer in every moment.

I stand on this path in the footprints of my elders and in the light of my ancestors. I want to honor the memory of my late grandfather, Henry Hardman, who was fond of telling the women in my family that we had hourglass figures, *with all of the sand at the bottom.*

Grateful acknowledgment is given to the following publishers for permission to use copyrighted material.

"'Some Could Suckle over Their Shoulder,'" by Jennifer L. Morgan, *William and Mary Quarterly* 54 (January 1997): 167–92. Reprinted by permission of the Omohundro Institute of Early American History and Culture.

"Gender, Race, and Nation," by Anne Fausto-Sterling, in Jennifer Terry and

Acknowledgments

Jacqueline Urla, eds., *Deviant Bodies* (Bloomington: Indiana University Press, 1995), 19–48. Reprinted by permission of Indiana University Press.

"'The Prettiest Specimen of Boyhood,'" in Siobhan Somerville, *Queering the Color Line: Race and the Invention of Homosexuality in American Culture* (Durham: Duke University Press, 2000), 100–106. Reprinted by permission of Duke University Press. © 2000, Duke University Press. All rights reserved.

"'Coming Out Blackened and Whole,'" by Elizabeth Alexander, *American Literary History* 6 (winter 1994): 695–715. Reprinted by permission of Oxford University Press.

"What (N)ever Happened to Aunt Jemima," by Doris Witt, *Discourse* 17, no. 2 (1994–95): 98–122. Reprinted by permission of the Wayne State University Press. © Wayne State University Press.

"Mastering the Female Pelvis," by Terri Kapsalis, in her *Public Privates: Performing Gynecology from Both Ends of the Speculum* (Durham: Duke University Press, 1997), 31–59. Reprinted by permission of Duke University Press. © 1997 Duke University Press. All rights reserved.

"Black (W)holes and the Geometry of Black Female Sexuality," by Evelynn Hammonds, *differences* 6 (summer–fall 1994): 1–59. Reprinted by permission of Indiana University Press.

"The Black Look and 'the Spectacle of Whitefolks': Wildness in Toni Morrison's *Beloved*," in *SIDESHOW U.S.A.* (Chicago: University of Chicago Press, 2001), 161–85. Reprinted by permission of the University of Chicago Press.

Every effort has been made to trace the ownership of all copyrighted material in this book and to obtain permission for its use.

Contents

Contents

● ● ●
▲ ▲ ▲

Conclusion

Illustrations

Illustrations

Kimberly Wallace-Sanders

Introduction

A revolution happened in feminist discourse when race
was included as a category of analysis informing gender
identity. As a consequent, feminist visions of the body
politic were expanded. . . . As the feminist movement
progressed, discussions of the body were highlighted,
and the focus on the "politics of the body were central-
ized." . . . The black body has always received attention
within the framework of white supremacy, as racist/sexist
iconography has been deployed to perpetrate notions of
innate biological inferiority.
>—bell hooks, "Feminism Inside:
>Toward a Black Body Politics"

Mass culture, as [bell] hooks argues, produces, promotes
and perpetuates the commodification of Otherness,
through the exploitation of the black female body. In the
1990s however, the principal sites of exploitation are not
simply the cabaret, the speakeasy, the music video, the
glamour magazine; they are also the academy, the
publishing industry, the intellectual community.
>—Ann duCille, "The (Oc)cult of True Black
>Womanhood: Critical Demeanor and
>Black Feminist Studies"

More than fifteen years have passed since the Feminist Press first published the seminal work on Black Women's studies, an edited volume
brilliantly entitled *All the Women Are White, All the Blacks Are Men, but
Some of Us Are Brave.*[1] The title was suggested by Barbara Smith, who
sought to critique the limitations of both Women's studies and Black
studies. Smith says, "At that time, Women's studies was about white

women, Black studies was about Black men." Groundbreaking ideology in both fields often resulted in Black women being pushed into the cracks of obscurity. Much has changed in fifteen years; issues of racism and sexism are now much more central to both Women's studies and African American studies. The work of Black feminists like Ann duCille, Barbara Smith, Elsa Barkley Brown, Darlene Clark Hine, Deborah Mc-Dowell, bell hooks, Mae Henderson, Cheryl Wall, Beverly Guy-Sheftall, Valerie Smith, and others has been critical in this regard, as they make valiant efforts to outline a common destiny for these areas.[2] What persists is a tendency for Black studies and Women's studies to emphasize categories of identity as competitive rather than mutually cooperative or integral.[3]

In 1993 I designed undergraduate- and graduate-level courses on the Black female body and discovered that it was impossible to teach these courses using theoretical texts that ignored the intersections of both race and gender. In discourse that linked the body to larger systems of knowledge it seemed that all of the female bodies were white, all of the Black bodies male. Once again, the bodies of women of color in general, and of Black women in particular, were either excluded as a point of scholarly interest or included as a cursory afterthought.[4] There are far too many cases of this binary exclusion to name them all here, but two examples effectively demonstrate the reductive ideologies to which the essays in this volume respond.

For example, in his introduction to *The Female Body,* editor Laurence Goldstein writes: "The female body has for so long been identified as an erotic object, canonized in the nudes of high art and the sex symbols of popular culture . . . Most women would not protest John Updike's remark that 'a naked woman is, for most men, one of the most beautiful things they will ever see.'"[5]

As for Updike's remark about the naked female being one of the more beautiful sights most men will ever see, I refer him to the sad, short history of Saartjie Baartman, the South African woman considered so hideous that she was displayed by an animal trainer throughout early nineteenth-century Europe. Her story is chronicled here in detail in "Gender, Race, and Nation," by Anne Fausto-Sterling. The female body that Goldstein describes is undoubtedly that of a healthy, able-bodied, white woman, her body rendered free of any identifiable markers of class or ethnicity. Subtle and profound shifts occur in the discourse about the female body when any of those factors are altered. When the female body is also Black, for example, the descriptive runs to extremes. The bodies of Black women have not only been identified as erotic objects but have symbolized the most extreme sexuality imaginable: wild, insatiable, and deviant. One example of the erasure of race is that while the white female body has been extensively canonized in art, the Black female nude is conspicuously absent in fine art, as Lisa Collins tells us in her contribution to this book. Her work demonstrates that while the white female nude has been the subject of great artistic concern both aesthetically and academically—as Goldstein notes—there is a noticeable absence of depictions of the Black female nude.

Another example of the erasure of gender appears in the 1993 postscript to author Charles Johnson's essay "A Phenomenology of the Black Body," written eighteen years earlier.[6] Johnson comments astutely on the need to investigate many of the questions that this volume engages. Johnson writes, "I realize that my hope was to examine the black male body as a cultural object and to inquire into how it has been interpreted, manipulated, and given to us, particularly in popular culture." Johnson goes on to delineate recent representations of Black men as a cultural metaphor for the worst of human behavior. He points out that there is a repetitious characterization of Black men as the "'Negro beast'—violent, sex-obsessed, irresponsible, and stupid"—in literature and in media images from the news to music. Johnson then expands on his observation with nothing less than shocking inaccuracy, by stating quite unequivocally that "none of these cultural meanings cluster around the black *female* body." Johnson ignores the fact that Black women have historically been represented as hypersexual, ignorant, and violent female "Negro beasts," in addition to many other denigrating types including the long-suffering desexualized Mammy, the primitive Topsy, the exotic Jezebel, and the evil, emasculating Sapphire. These well-known stereotypes are of pathologized bodies that are specifically Black and female, and they are also found in literature and in media images from the news to contemporary music. When Charles Johnson writes of the "black as body," he affirms a common sexist mistake by writing about a monolithic Black body that is male, or at best, gender neutral.[7]

These exclusions are ironic when we consider the many ways in which Black women's bodies have historically symbolized a site where the vast (and largely problematic) complexities of gender and race are represented. For example, consider the ways in which American slavery, racism, and motherhood converged upon slave women's bodies, determining that their own children belonged to slave owners rather than to the mothers themselves. The most pervasive stereotypes about Black women reveal some fundamental conflicts of gender and race. For example, the stereotype of the "strong Black woman" occupies heroic standing within African American culture, yet her lack of femininity obscures her gender.

Johnson suggests that Black women "have succeeded in culturally 'defining' themselves in their own terms and not those of the racial (or gendered) Other." Yet it is precisely because Black women are very often defined as the racial *and* gendered Other that this volume is so desperately needed. *Skin Deep, Spirit Strong* builds upon this theme and provides an insightful historical context for comprehending the representation of Black female embodiment.

Each chapter in this volume constitutes an eloquent and passionate response to the previous implication that all of the female bodies are white and all of the Black bodies are male. Additionally, they reveal a struggle between constructed and projected versions of Black women's bodies as devoid of beauty, innocence, or purity and more complex representations granting Black women a full measure of humanity and selfhood. This book serves as a map acknowledging those complex representations and directing us toward possible paths leading us to an increase in the quality and the quantity of these representations.

One of the most devastating results of this aggressively consistent mythology is that contemporary Black women are trapped by this externally imposed second skin of misconception and misrepresentation. This shell is both *skin deep,* as it emphasizes the most superficial versions of Black women, and *skin tight,* as it has proved to be nearly inescapable, even in Black women's self-conception and self-representation. Shedding this illusive layer is a daunting task, yet it is an imperative one if Black women are ever to be seen and to see themselves in a more humane light. Poet Nikki Giovanni writes: "We are all imprisoned in *the castle of our skins . . .* let my world be defined by my skin and the skin of my people. / for we spirit to spirit / will embrace this world." In this movement from the confines of "skin deep" or superficial misconceptions to the celebration of a "spirit to spirit" acceptance of historic limitations, transcendence becomes not only possible, but inevitable.[8] Certainly it begins with the kind of close cultural scrutiny that these chapters undertake. Perhaps the best and most eloquent suggestion for a remedy comes from Elizabeth Alexander's reading of Audre Lorde's words.

> The implications of this thinking for questions of identity are broad. For the self to remain simultaneously multiple and integrated, embracing the definitive boundaries of each category—race, gender, class, et cetera—while dissembling their

static limitations, assumes a depth and complexity of identity construction that refute a history of limitation. For the self to be fundamentally collaged—overlapping and discernibly dialogic—is to break free from diminishing concepts of identity.[9]

This volume marks a significant step in creating that collage of Black women's corporeal existence in the United States. The metaphor of a collage of identities is especially powerful for me because my father uses collage in his artwork. From childhood I recall he used cutouts from *Ebony* and *Life* magazines, layered them on canvas, and then drizzled Elmer's glue over them in complex designs. When I asked him why he didn't try to hide the glue neatly behind the cutouts, he pointed out that when the glue dried, it was transparent; it did not obscure the pictures themselves. "The glue is part of the whole picture," he explained. These words came back to me as I thought about how the chapters here are held together by a common theme as they overlap in concepts, ideology, theories, and approaches.

The chapters in *Skin Deep, Spirit Strong* are both discernibly independent and in dialogue with each other as they address issues of identity and representation in visual, literary, and historical contexts. The volume demonstrates that when Black women stand at the center of the discussion about the female body, their bodies tell a profoundly different story about historic and contemporary American culture. The work of feminist scholars like Hazel Carby, Susan Bordo, Jennifer Terry, and many others directed us toward a cultural approach to the female body. This study builds upon that approach by concerning itself specifically with theoretical discourses on the Black female body. The authors take on the task of redirecting the current discourse about the female body that ignores or sublimates race.

This project was preceded by some inspiring work on race, gender, and corporeality.[10] My editorial intention was to design and present a conference of reflections, concepts, theories, and insights about representations of Black women's bodies in literature, history, and visual culture. The pieces included are therefore comprehensive in scope and provocative in eclectic methodological approaches, as they constitute a fundamental stepping-stone to future theories of race, gender, and corporeal reality. *Skin Deep, Spirit Strong* is clearly structured to evoke discussions and responses that will lead to necessary paradigm shifts.

The collection is both interdisciplinary and multidisciplinary, suggesting a model for scholars devoted to stimulating dialogue across disciplines. As this volume makes clear, all of the most salient discourses in post-structuralist and feminist theory are made richer and more complex when the Black female body is considered.

This volume represents an effort to chart how the simultaneous interrogation of gender, race, and corporeality shapes the construction of Black female representation. As the table of contents reveals, this volume enlists a wide variety of scholarly perspectives on, and critical approaches to, the place of Black women's bodies within the American cultural consciousness. Each chapter presents a persuasive argument for broadening the ongoing scholarly conversations about the body.

Part one sets up a framework of constructions of Black female subjectivity through history, travel narratives, and scientific racism. Beverly Guy-Sheftall's chapter informs us that in order to properly understand the history of American attitudes about the Black female form, we must begin with a close look at how both blackness and femaleness figured within the European imagination. In her look at how the Euro-American imagination has defined and manipulated Black women's sexuality, Guy-Sheftall combines historical and theoretical perspectives on art, history, and feminist theory to illuminate how "being Black and female is characterized by the private being made public."

Jennifer L. Morgan and Anne Fausto-Sterling illuminate the perspective of early European contact with the African female form, providing significant insight into the complexities of attraction and repulsion characterizing this interaction. Morgan points out how European discourse on the "monstrous" bodies of African and Amerindian women was used to justify the slave trade. Fausto-Sterling finds that these early depictions of African women became the working background of nineteenth-century racial studies.

Part two draws our attention to the symbolic power of the Black female body in visual culture and literary representations. The chapters here stress the profound consequences of narrow and predictable typecasting of the Black female form in visual mediums. This section begins with Lisa Collins's overview of the historic and contemporary representations of the Black female body in fine art. Collins notes that scholarly discussion on the unclothed Black body in art is missing from most formalist and feminist scholarship on the nude. Collins's argument moves deftly from this historical overview to an examination of recent representations of the Black female nude in the work of African American artists Emma Amos, Alison Saar, and Renée Stout. These artists work to expand the range of visual possibility "by taking the body elsewhere," thereby combining contradictory and opposing histories, concepts, and artistic practices. Lisa E. Farrington picks up this thread by taking a very detailed look at African American artist Faith Ringgold's series of paintings entitled *Slave Rape Series*. Ringgold's female figures are particularly compelling for their vulnerability, which is at first unnerving to the viewer, as it shakes the image of heroic "strong Black slave women." Through this risky yet necessary move to highlight their humanity, slave women become "real" to us in a new way. Viewers are challenged to interact with the subject first, before attempting to fully comprehend the circumstances and experiences surrounding slavery and sexual violence. Carla Williams's chapter on the history of photographic preoccupation with Black women's bodies is a troubling and significant documentation of the narrow and predictable typecasting of Black women as photographic subjects. Williams concludes that it is an especially complex task for contemporary Black women to define their own images in a holistic way that necessarily both incorporates and subverts the stereotypes, myths, facts, and fantasies that precede them. Williams reminds us that, despite the inextricable linkages between blackness and sexuality, ironically, it is taboo for Black people, especially Black women, to revel in their bodies, to enjoy expressing the sexuality that has traditionally defined them.

The relentless symbolism of Sethe's body in *Beloved* has held the attention of literary and historical scholars since the novel's publication in 1987. Rachel Adams shifts the emphasis from Sethe's body to the carnival that Sethe, Denver, and Paul D attend right before Beloved appears. Her strategy is to read the carnival's display of "racialized" and deviant bodies against *Beloved*'s embodiment and eventual disembodiment within the context of corporeal extremes. Adams reads the Black body as a "spectacle," thus linking the novel with visual aspects of the Black female bodies on display in art and photography.

Siobhan B. Somerville's study of cross-dressing and racial disguise in nineteenth-century literature frames her thorough analysis of Pauline E. Hopkins's novella *Winona*. Somerville suggests that the temporary passing and gender-bending in this novel reflect the contradictory status of nineteenth-century Black women writers at the turn of the twentieth century, when literary and political worlds were closed to them.

In "'Coming Out Blackened and Whole,'" Elizabeth Alexander pays homage to lesbian poet and activist Audre Lorde. Alexander takes on the complexity of race, gender, sexuality, class, and corporeality in her astute reading of Lorde's work. Lorde's body "becomes a map of lived experience and a way of printing suffering as well as joy upon the flesh. . . . In Lorde's work, the body speaks its own history."

Part three explores how deeply invested American culture has been in controlling Black women's bodies. Doris Witt and Terri Kapsalis confront how cultural systems of surveillance have manifested around issues of the Black female appetite and reproductive technologies. Witt identifies the intricate network of forces obsessed with Black women's bodies, first by valuing them exclusively for their ability to nurture others, then by devaluing them as unsuitable to nurture their own children. Kapsalis deftly describes the work of James Marion Sims, who invented the speculum during a prolonged period of experimentation on slave women. Sims treated several slave women for a gynecological disorder, women who endured one operation after another—all without anesthesia—while Sims perfected his surgery. Kapsalis points to how Sims's technological innovations help to reinforce institutionalized racism. Emphasizing these consequences, Evelynn Hammonds charts the evolution of contemporary feminist scholarship on sexuality through queer theory. She describes a space where Black women are both invisible and silent, finding that the "void" of Black women articulating their own sexuality is not empty at all but is, instead, full of silence. Hammonds makes the powerful suggestion that Black women "have not taken up this project in part because of their own status in the academy." I am intrigued by this overt call for more scholarly attention to Black female sexuality; I look forward to readers responding to this invitation.

The final chapter challenges readers to imagine new possibilities for future representations of Black women. In 1992 African American filmmaker Bridgett Davis set out to confront some of the most daunting and perplexing issues surrounding Black women's preoccupation with body image. In her independent film *Naked Acts,* her main character's identity is complicated by intricate issues of Black female representation within her own family, since she is a third-generation entertainer. Both cultural and familial baggage weighs heavily on the protagonist as she attempts to construct a healthy identity for herself. Davis presents her film as one example of a Black woman defining her own image. Like Faith Ringgold, Davis finds that viewers must be challenged to interact with Black women as subjects first, rather than as victims.

These authors point to ways that art, literature, theories about sexuality, public policy, and medical history interlace and interconnect with regard to bodies that are both Black and female. Clearly one volume cannot begin to fill the gap left by the absence of more specific focuses on race and ethnicity in contemporary discourse on the female body.

This introduction serves as a kind of drum roll for the chapters that follow, which constitute an impressive gathering of writings from feminist scholars and artists, teachers, poets, and visionaries. Each contributing author is a drum major for justice, a righteous warrior of words, insisting that the collage of Black womanhood be seen as a whole, bound together by a richly complex diversity.

As this book was going to press, I received an email message from Yvette Abrahams informing me that Sarah Bartmann's remains would be buried on 9 August 2002 on the banks of the river Gamtoos, where she was born. Abrahams is the project manager for "Herstory: The Return of Sarah Bartmann," at the University of the Western Cape. Bartmann's return to South Africa is significant to this volume for many reasons. Several contributors evoke Bartmann in their discussions about the perceptions of and attitudes toward African American women's bodies; Bartmann's experience represented the most pernicious "editing" of Black women's bodies and Black women's lives. Many of us feel a kinship with Bartmann and have been paying close attention to the negotiations between the South African government and the Musée de l'Homme concerning the fate of the woman known as Sarah, Sartjie, and the "Hottentot Venus."

The funeral was held in Hankey and (appropriately) coincided with national Women's Day. President Thabo Mbeki said that it was not enough to honor her death by burying her remains, but that the country had a responsibility to work toward racial and gender equality. "When that is done, then it will be possible to say that Sarah Baartman has truly come home."[11]

May this book honor Bartmann's life and celebrate her return.

NOTES

1. Gloria Hull, Barbara Smith, and Pat Bell-Scott, eds., *All the Women Are White, All the Blacks Are Men, but Some of Us Are Brave* (New York: Feminist Press, 1982).

2. This kind of list is always problematic, as it is impossible not to exclude someone of importance.

3. By extension, as a feminist activist and coeditor of *All the Women Are White, All the Blacks Are Men, but Some of Us Are Brave*, Barbara Smith succinctly points out, in the introduction to *The Truth That Never Hurts* (New York: Routledge, 1998): "Racism is what happens to black men. Sexism is what happens to white women."

4. I taught the undergraduate course, called "The Black Female Body in American Culture," at Spelman College in 1995. I taught graduate seminars by the same name at Emory University in 1996 and 1997. A list of such exclusionary works includes, but is not limited to, the following: *The Female Body* (a

collection of scholarly essays and creative work in which author Ruth Behar is the single representation of women of color), edited by Laurence Goldstein; *The Female Body in Western Culture* by Susan Suleiman; *Gender/Body/Knowledge: Feminist Reconstruction of Being and Knowing*, edited by Alison Jagger and Susan Bordo; *Volatile Body: Towards a Corporeal Feminism* by Elizabeth Grosz; *Body Politics: Women and the Discourses of Science*, edited by Mary Jacobus, Evelyn Fox Keller, and Sally Shuttleworth; "Phenomenology of the Black Body," by Charles Johnson, addressed in this introduction; the exhibition "Black Male: Representations of Masculinity in Contemporary American Art," and the catalog by the same name, edited by Thelma Golden; and "Friday on the Potomac," the introduction to *Rac(e)ing Justice, En-gendering Power,* by Toni Morrison.

5. Laurence Goldstein, introduction to *The Female Body in Western Culture* (Ann Arbor: University of Michigan Press, 1991), vii–viii.

6. Charles Johnson, "A Phenomenology of the Black Body," *Michigan Quarterly Review* (fall 1993): 519–614.

7. Johnson goes on to describe what he calls "an amazing and revolutionary feat of cultural reconstruction" that resulted in Black women taking control of their own images and in their bodies being represented as, "first and foremost, spiritual. . . . The black female body is, in fact, frequently offered to us as the original body of a humankind descended from a black Eve of Africa." The chapters included here show that the "cultural reconstruction" to which Johnson refers has not had any substantial impact on the larger culture, if in fact it existed at all. From a feminist perspective, Johnson's essay reinforces a phallocentric African American canon. He speaks of "black authors" yet refers only to male authors like Eldridge Cleaver and Claude McKay.

8. *The Selected Poems of Nikki Giovanni* (New York: William Morrow, 1996), 139.

9. Alexander, "Coming Out Blackened and Whole," this volume.

10. See: bell hooks, "Selling Hot Pussy," in *Black Looks* and "Feminism Inside: Toward a Black Body Politic"; Hazel Carby, "Policing the Black Female Body in an Urban Context"; June Jordan, "A New Politics of Sexuality"; Barbara Omolade, "Hearts of Darkness"; Lisa Jones, *Bullet Proof Diva;* and *Codes of Conduct* by Karla Holloway. Since the conception of this project new titles in related areas have been published including *Recovering the Black Female Body: Self Representations by African American Women,* edited by Michael Bennett and Vanessa Dickerson; *Killing the Black Body: Race, Reproduction and the Meaning of Liberty* by Dorothy Roberts; *Dark Continent of Our Bodies: Black Feminism and the Politics of Respectability* by E. Frances White; *The Black Female Body in Photographic History,* edited by Deborah Willis and Carla Williams; and *Stolen Women: Reclaiming Our Sexuality, Taking Back Our Lives* by Gail Elizabeth Wyatt. *The Hyper-In-Visible Woman: Black Female Bodies in Public Culture* by Deborah Grayson, is forthcoming from Duke University Press.

11. Associated Press, Friday, 9 August 2002. For additional information see the excellent documentary film *The Life and Times of Sara Baartman: The Hottentot Venus,* by Zola Masek.

PART

Beverly Guy-Sheftall

The Body Politic

Black Female Sexuality and the Nineteenth-Century Euro-American Imagination

> Any account of the nineteenth-century preoccupation
> with seeing and narrating the body needs to think about
> a long tradition of European fascination with the bodies
> of other cultures—particularly, women's bodies from
> cultures considered exotic or primitive, which are used
> to define an alluring or menacing other of Western
> "civilized" sexuality.
> —Peter Brooks, "Gauguin's Tahitian Body"

In one of the earliest Black feminist analyses of European constructions of African female sexuality and its impact on the sexual history of the United States, Barbara Omolade makes this assertion:

> The sexual history of the United States began at the historical moment when European men met African women in the "heart of darkness"—Mother Africa. They faced each other as conqueror and conquered: African women captives were considered the sexual property of the European conquerors.[1]

I began my introduction to the section entitled "The Body Politic: Sexuality, Violence, and Reproduction" in *Words of Fire* with a provocative quotation by literary critic Hortense Spillers that underscores the paucity of analyses of Black female sexuality, including by Black women scholars themselves: "Black women are the beached whales of the sexual universe,

13

unvoiced, misseen, not doing, awaiting their verb. Their sexual experiences are depicted, but not often by them."[2] Spillers's essay, the first scholarly treatise on the silences surrounding Black female sexuality, was written over a decade ago, as was Barbara Omolade's "Hearts of Darkness," which focuses on the sexual treatment of African American women, especially during slavery.

Despite the importance of discussions of the sexual history of the West, the subject of Black female sexuality has been marginalized in the new discourse on the female body, which illuminates important aspects of that history. Since the work of Omolade and Spillers, a small but growing number of essays—including Hazel Carby's "'On the Threshold of Woman's Era': Lynching, Empire, and Sexuality in Black Feminist Theory"; Lorraine O'Grady's "Olympia's Maid: Reclaiming Black Female Subjectivity"; Evelynn Hammonds's "Black (W)holes and the Geometry of Black Female Sexuality" and "Toward a Genealogy of Black Female Sexuality: The Problematic of Silence"—all provide important correctives to the invisibility of Black women in the considerable corpus of work on the cultural body or the body politic, which constitutes some of the most exciting new work within feminist theoretical discourse at the present time.[3]

I want to begin this chapter, which provides an overview of Euro-American representations of Black female sexuality, particularly during the nineteenth century, with a quotation from art historian Lorraine O'Grady, who analyzes one of the most visible and frequently studied images of a Black woman in European art, Édouard Manet's *Olympia* (see fig. 1), which was painted in 1862–63.

> The female body in the West is not a unitary sign. Rather, like a coin, it has an obverse and a reverse: on the one side, it is white; on the other, not-white or, prototypically, black. The two bodies cannot be separated, nor can one body be understood in isolation from the other in the West's metaphoric construction of "woman." White is what woman is; not-white (and the stereotypes not-white gather in) is what she had better not be. Even in an allegedly postmodern era, the not-white woman as well as the not-white man are symbolically and even theoretically excluded from sexual difference.[4]

Here O'Grady captures Western constructions of womanhood that represent Black women and white women as polar opposites. Racial difference is marked in profound ways through the construction of gendered

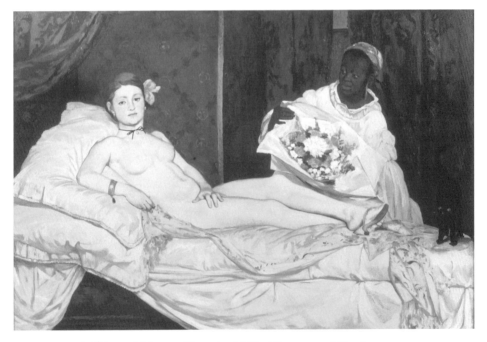

Fig. 1. Édouard Manet, *Olympia,* 1863. (Courtesy of Musée d'Orsay, Paris.)

differences between Black and white womanhood, especially with respect to their sexuality.

Equally compelling but less well known (and largely ignored by art critics) is a provocative painting (see fig. 2) by Marie-Guilhelmine Benois, *Portrait d'une négresse* (Portrait of a Negress), which is believed to be the first painting by a European female of a Black woman. It appears on the cover of volume 4 of Hugh Honour's *Image of the Black in Western Art,* in which it is alluded to as "the most beautiful portrait of a black woman ever painted."[5] This image of a presumably African servant woman with her chest partially bare and a breast exposed, though sensitively rendered, is nevertheless suggestive of the connection in the European mind during the nineteenth century between Black womanhood and sexuality. The obligatory headdress and partial nudity mark her as different from civilized white womanhood. The whiteness of the cloth that drapes her contrasts sharply with the blackness of her body and calls attention to her "otherness" in the realm of the physical and social as well. This association of Black womanhood with hypersexuality, which

Fig. 2. Marie-Guilhelmine Benois, *Portrait d'une négresse,* 1800. (Courtesy of Louvre Museum, Paris.)

her partial nudity underscores, was to persist in the Euro-American imagination long after slavery and colonialism had ended.

The work of feminist historian of science Evelynn Hammonds is instructive because she analyzes the history of the discourse on Black female sexuality, which, she argues, has clustered around three themes:

> the construction of the black female as the embodiment of sex and the attendant invisibility of black women as the unvoiced, unseen—everything that is not white . . . the resistance of black women both to negative stereotypes of their sexuality

and to the material effects of those stereotypes on black women's lives . . . [and] finally, the evolution of a "culture of dissemblance" and a "politics of silence" by Black women on the issue of their sexuality.[6]

In order to understand these cultural constructions of Black women's sexuality, it is instructive to revisit the fifteenth and sixteenth centuries, when Europeans entered the vast continent of Africa and encountered a people they saw as radically different from themselves. What were the English explorers' first impressions of Africans? It was historian Winthrop Jordan, in his classic study *White over Black,* who attempted to answer these questions: What happened when one of the fairest-skinned nations suddenly came face to face with one of the darkest-skinned peoples on earth? What attitudes did they form about these Black bodies whom they confronted? Perhaps Africans' most startling characteristics, which Europeans spent inordinate amounts of time trying to explain, were their dark skin and their nudity, which would be laden with intense racial/sexual meanings for hundreds of years. Their most salient attributes were savagery, bestiality, lecherousness, and being uncivilized.[7]

One of the most bizarre chronicles in the annals of European racism, which has received considerable attention by scholars and writers over the past decade, occurred during the occupation of the Dutch-founded Cape Colony in southern Africa by the British. For my purposes here, it is useful to consider the cultural context in which this incredible saga took place. In the early years of the nineteenth century, a succession of Europeans visited and described this region's indigenous inhabitants. Before the arrival of the British, however, little was known about the San, Khoikhoi, and Xhosa, who were erroneously and pejoratively renamed Bushmen, Hottentots, and Kafirs. Travelers' tales revealed their peculiar physical attributes, which were intended to disassociate them from the human species. The males were said to have only one testicle and the females a large vaginal flap called a tablier and a fatty enlargement of the buttocks called steatopygia. Their language, composed mainly of clicks, sounded like animal noises rather than human speech to ethnocentric Europeans. Their consumption of raw meat put them in the category of beasts and savages, as well. They were relegated to the lowest place on the scale of human life in the great chain of being, only one rung above the ape.

During an era (1880 and following) of "scientific" theorizing about hierarchies among human species, differences among the races, and the

17

development of physical anthropology and ethnology, it was necessary for Europeans to "explain" the nature of Africans, whom they saw as racially inferior and profoundly different from themselves—in skin color, hair texture, body type, sexual behavior, religious practices, dress, language, and values.[8] After Cape Colony was lost, people from southern Africa were literally taken back to England to be viewed as living ethnographic specimens.

Saartjie ("little Sarah" in Afrikaans) Baartman, a South African woman born in 1790, was exhibited with an animal trainer in 1810 as the infamous "Hottentot Venus" in and around London and Paris for over five years.[9] (See figures 3–4.) She emerged from a cage on a raised platform, was presented as an animal to the European community, and was touted as having "the kind of shape which is most admired by her countrymen."[10] She was gazed at, heckled, objectified, caricatured, and dehumanized (see figs.). Eventually she was taken to Paris in 1814; had she escaped the curiosity of the "great" comparative anatomist Georges Leopold Cuvier (1769–1832), she may never have become "immortalized." He examined her "scientifically," especially her genitalia and buttocks to prove that "Hottentots" were in fact inherently different from other human beings, a separate species. He also commissioned several artists attached to the Jardin du Roi to portray her, and after her death in 1815 at the age of twenty-five, he dissected her and preserved her genitalia under a bell jar in the Musée de l'Homme in Paris (see fig. 5).

In his detailed report on her, Cuvier asserts that he had "never seen a human head more resembling a monkey's than hers" and that she moved like a monkey as well.[11] Her genitalia, which he presented first to the Academie Royale de Medecine, were later moved to the Musée de l'Homme for the general public to see. Because of his prominence, his writings on Baartman came to be regarded in scientific circles as an authentic description of the African woman more generically. His focus on her genitalia reinforced the European connection between lasciviousness, sexuality, and animal passion among Africans in general, but particularly among African women. In England, on the other hand, it appears that she was remembered primarily as "an intensely ugly figure, distorted beyond all European notions of beauty."[12] This example also underscores a recurring theme in the "body dramas" that Black women experience. Being Black and female is characterized by the private being made public, which subverts conventional notions about the need to hide and render invisible women's sexuality and private parts. There is nothing sacred about Black women's bodies, in other words. They are not off-limits, untouchable, or unseeable. What happened to Baartman

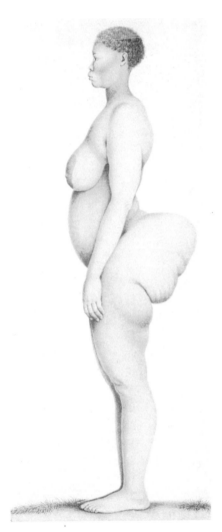

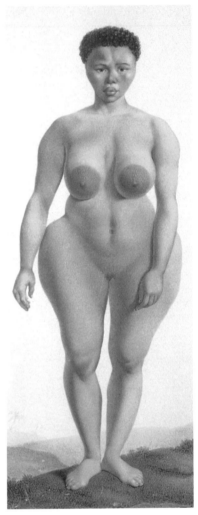

Fig. 3. Nicolas Huet le Jeune,
profile view of Saartjie Baartman, the "Hottentot Venus,"
1815. (Courtesy of Muséum
national d'Histoire naturelle,
Paris.)

Fig. 4. Léon de Wailley,
frontal view of Saartjie Baartman, the "Hottentot Venus,"
1815. (Courtesy of Muséum
national d'Histoire naturelle,
Paris.)

is an extreme example of what a critic of Paul Gauguin's Tahitian women
identifies as a long history of European obsession with the female bodies of the exoticized Other, which the quote that precedes this chapter
captures (see fig. 8). The Black female also came to serve as an icon for

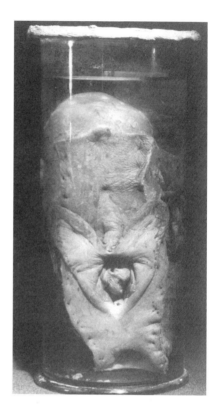

Fig. 5. The preserved genitalia of the "Hottentot Venus," having been dissected by Cuvier. (Courtesy of Musée de l'Homme, Paris.)

Fig. 6. An engraving of a "Hottentot Venus" at the Ball of the Duchess du Barry, 1829. (Courtesy of Olin Library, Cornell University, Ithaca.)

Fig. 7. The "Hottentot Venus," a German caricature from the
beginning of the nineteenth century, from John Grand-Carteret,
1909. (Courtesy of C. W. Stern, Vienna. Private collection,
Ithaca, NY).

Black sexuality in general throughout the nineteenth century, as Sander
Gilman cogently argues in his influential work.[13]

In a European world characterized by racial mythologizing and
rabid racism, the widespread association between Africans and apes
reached absurd proportions in the dehumanization *and* defeminization
of Africans in narratives about the "fact" that apes were in fact copulating with them. By asserting a sexual link between Black women and
apes, moreover, Europeans marked this group of women as lewd, lascivious, and savage—the antithesis of virtuous, European women. In his
study of white attitudes toward Blacks from 1550 to 1812, Winthrop

Fig. 8. Paul Gauguin, *Manoa Tupapau* (Spirit of the Dead Watching), 1892. (Courtesy of Albright-Knox Art Gallery, Buffalo.)

Jordan analyzes this preoccupation with Black female sexuality on the part of white males.

> By calling the Negro woman passionate they were offering the best possible justification for their own passions. Not only did the Negro woman's warmth constitute a logical explanation for the white man's infidelity, but, much more important, it helped shift responsibility from himself to her. If she was *that* lascivious—well, a man could scarcely be blamed for succumbing against overwhelming odds. Further reinforcement for this picture of the Negro woman came from the ancient association of hot climates with sexual activity.[14]

Of course, these arguments also emerged to ease white male guilt about the enslavement and oppression of Africans, but such rationalizations, when aimed specifically at Black women, manifested themselves in two distinct and paradoxical stereotypes—they were disgustingly lustful (Jezebel, according to historian Deborah Gray White) but exceptionally unfeminine.[15] They were alluring but unattractive; they attracted and repelled at the same time.

The profit motive and the insatiable desire for cheap labor during slavery in the New World reinforced the images of African women as beasts of burden, workhorses, and hypersexual. This argument was used to rationalize their involuntary roles as workers and producers of slave children. Their bodies were literally to be used in the fields from sunup to sundown, exploited to fulfill white men's lust and to give birth to slave children who would keep the plantation system afloat.

At the center of the debate about Black women during this period of slavery and its aftermath in the United States, in particular, were arguments about their moral character, which can be seen as an outgrowth of, among other factors, the general preoccupation with women's moral nature on the part of Victorian society.[16] The most persistent theme in the writings of North American white men was the devaluation or defeminization of Black women, which was ironic given the high valuation of American women generally during this time.[17] The notion of woman as saint or virtuous lady in the minds of white men could not have applied to Black women, however, given the need to justify slavery. In fact, the Black woman was devalued not only because of her supposed racial traits but also because she departed from whites' conception of the True Woman—which is indicative of the degree to which prevailing notions about race and gender interacted in the minds of whites (male and female) and resulted in a particular set of attitudes about Black women. Whites felt that notions about the "ideal woman" did not apply to Black women because the circumstances of slavery had prevented them from developing qualities that other women possessed and from devoting their lives to wifehood and motherhood, the proper roles for women. A contemporary historian has commented on this phenomenon:

> Femininity and domesticity were not held sacred by slave owners. Such amenities were outlawed by a system of forced labor, where men, women, and children were considered agricultural machinery, valued primarily for their muscle, endurance, and productive capability. . . . Aside from procreation, black women were assigned few exclusively female roles. Wifely service remained rudimentary. . . . Motherhood might be reduced to giving birth, interrupting work in the

field to nurse the infant, and . . . cooking frugal meals for the young. . . . The slave master felt few compunctions to model the black family after the cult of domesticity.[18]

Additionally, the "devaluation of Black womanhood" is traceable to the sexual exploitation of Black women during slavery. Moreover, the Black woman's allegedly innate racial traits (promiscuity, filthiness, vulgarity, lewdness, indecency, ugliness) tended to cancel out those uniquely feminine traits that white women were assumed to possess (modesty, purity, chastity, beauty).

These constructions of the sexuality of slave women underscore the tenacity of earlier images of African women. With the penetration of Europeans into sub-Saharan Africa during the fifteenth century, memoirs of travelers characterized African women as grotesque, dangerous creatures who engaged in "deviant" sexual behavior.[19] This included incest with fathers. One even reported having seen them deliver more than seven babies at a time. The most persistent attitude, however, was that they were savage and bestial. The violation of the bodies of enslaved African women resulted from such perceptions. They were branded for identification on the shores of West Africa, were raped during the Middle Passage, and were forced to engage in sex and beaten in the fields of slave plantations. Their experiences on slave ships were different than those of African men. They were placed on the quarter deck, not in the hold, where the men were forced and bound. While their incarceration was not as horrible on one level, because they were not packed like sardines or shackled, as was the case with men, they were vulnerable to the sexual exploitation of crew members, who were not discouraged from molesting them.[20] On the auction block, their bodies were exposed, handled, even poked to determine their strength and capacity for childbearing. One auctioneer introduced a slave woman this way: "Show your neck, Betsey. There's a breast for you; good for a round dozen before she's done child-bearing."[21] In order to protect her unborn slave child during beatings, a hole was dug in the ground and the pregnant slave woman was forced to lie prostrate and receive her whipping with her stomach tucked away beyond the reach of the lash.[22]

One of the most despicable experiences to which slave women were subjected occurred in Montgomery, Alabama, between 1845 and 1849, when experimental and gynecological surgery was performed by the "father of American gynecology," J. Marion Sims.[23] The first book to point out the abuse of these slave women was not published until 1976.

With the inception of slavery in North America, African women were conceptualized by whites on the one hand as oversexed and also as something other than woman. Furthermore, their moral stature was said to have deteriorated further during slavery. What made matters worse, the myth continued, was that Black men did not fret about immorality in their women and that other Black women failed to censure them despite their outrageous behavior: "A plantation negress may have sunk to a low point in the scale of sensual indulgence, and yet her position does not seem to be substantially affected even in the estimation of the women of her own race. . . . The truth is that neither the women nor the men . . . look upon lasciviousness as impurity."[24] Black women did not have to live up to a standard of morality because no such values existed in the Black community. Furthermore, Black men never even had to rape their women, because of their constant willingness to engage in sex. In other words, Black women were so thoroughly debased sexually that they willingly gave their bodies to men, making rape a crime with which they were totally unfamiliar. A southern white woman argued that it was ridiculous that a Black woman, "with the brain of a child and the passions of a woman, steeped in centuries of ignorance and savagery, and wrapped about with immemorial vices," should hold the destiny of the Negro race in her hands, as of course other women have the responsibility of doing.[25] The writings of southern white men contain frequent allusions to the Black woman's inherent animalism. The Black-woman-as-animal stereotype, however, is to be distinguished from the more frequently discussed "brute-Negro" stereotype, which was prominent in the minds of Americans, especially southerners, at the turn of the twentieth century but which applied to the Black male. White writers thought that this animal sexuality that Black women possessed did not result in criminal behavior on their part (as was the case with Black men who raped white women) but could be used to justify their sexual exploitation at the hands of white men. In other words, white men could turn to them for the uninhibited sex that was denied them by virtuous, chaste white women. Thomas Bailey, a southern dean at the University of Mississippi, commented on this phenomenon:

> Southerners do not ordinarily have the biological and aesthetic repulsion that is usually felt by Northerners toward the Negro. . . . The memory of ante-bellum concubinage and a tradition of animal satisfaction due to the average negro woman's highly developed animalism are factors still in operation. Not a few "respectable" white men have been heard to express physiological preference for negro women.[26]

Her animality was also manifest in the anger she expressed during quarrels and fights with other women, which were frequent and violent occurrences in the Black community. Savage animal imagery pervades the following description: "Such negroes are raving amazons . . . apparently growing madder each moment, eyes rolling, lips protruding, feet stamping, pawing, gesticulating. . . . This frenzied madness . . . seems beyond control. . . . With the men the manifestations are less violent."[27] Animal imagery is also used in William Dean Howells's *Imperative Duty* (1892), a novella about a white girl who learns that she has Negro ancestry, immediately flees to Boston's Black neighborhoods, and ends up at a Black church so she can "surround herself with the Blackness from which she had sprung."[28] Her descriptions of the women in the church contain animal overtones:

> Rhoda distinguished faces, sad, repulsive visages of a frog-like ugliness added to the repulsive black in all its shades. . . . One old woman . . . opened her mouth like a catfish to emit these pious ejaculations. . . . As the church filled, the musky exhalations of their bodies thickened the air, and made the girl faint; it seemed to her that she began to taste the odor; and these poor people whom their Creator had made so hideous by the standards of all his other creatures, roused a cruel loathing in her. . . . "Yes," she thought, "I should have whipped them, too. They are animals; they are only fit to be slaves."[29]

The Black woman's ugliness, rather than her sexuality, is emphasized in these references to her animal nature. According to Euro-American thinking, the Black woman's promiscuity and physical unattractiveness—overt manifestations of her animal-like traits—cause her to be devalued because she is unable to reach the standard of feminine beauty and behavior required of "ideal" women.

In fact, one of the most persistent themes in the intellectual history of the West has been Negrophobia, the two major components of which are assumptions about the superiority in intellect and physical beauty of whites, especially their women. By contrast the Negro, especially the woman, is ugly, because of her dark complexion, hair texture, and disfigured lips and nose.

It is appropriate in a discussion of cultural constructions of the Black female body to shift to a contemporary example of depictions of Black womanhood that reminds us that the problem is far from resolved, even among white feminists, who, one might assume, would be freer of the historical stereotypes and perceptions that permeated earlier periods. The case of Sojourner Truth, a historical figure from slavery, captures what happened literally to Black women's bodies and also illustrates the way in which Black women continue to be portrayed as the antithesis of white womanhood.

Though Sojourner Truth, nineteenth-century abolitionist and women's rights advocate, is the token Black female among the thirty-nine guests invited to the *Dinner Party*, conceived by artist Judy Chicago, it is not surprising that of the many Black women who might have been selected, Sojourner Truth captured Judy Chicago's imagination and became the lone representative of Black womanhood among the impressive array of women from around the world who are depicted here (see fig. 9). In the words of Judy Chicago, "She was an inspiration to all who heard her and a proud symbol of black women's struggle to transcend the oppression of both their sex and race."[30] Anna J. Cooper, a contemporary of Sojourner Truth and a fellow activist in the struggle for the liberation of Blacks and women, referred to her as "that unique and rugged genius who seemed carved out without hand or chisel from the solid mountain mass."[31]

At this point, a brief summary of the life of Sojourner Truth, second only to Frederick Douglass in terms of her outspoken advocacy of the cause of women's rights among Blacks during the nineteenth century, is in order. Sojourner Truth, whose slave name was Isabella, was born around 1773, having been brought as a child with her parents from Africa and sold as a slave in the state of New York. At age nine, she was sold away from her parents (as were her brothers and sisters before her) to John Nealy for one hundred dollars. Since her former master had been Dutch, she had not learned English, and no one in the family to which she was sold, except for Neely, understood the language she spoke. This led to frequent misunderstandings and punishments, including beatings, for the young Isabella. At one point she was ordered to go to the barn, where her master, who awaited her, stripped her to the waist and gave her the most cruel beating she ever received, without any explanation. She was sold twice more before she was twelve years old. Her last master, John Dumont, raped her and later married her to an older slave, Thomas, for whom she bore five children. Although slavery was ended by law in New York in 1817, her master delayed her emancipation and sold her five-year-old son, Peter, despite his earlier promise to free him. Isabella ran away with her baby and contracted to serve another master for a year. He freed her in 1827. Determined to retrieve her son Peter, who had been sold South, she sued for his freedom in

Fig. 9. Judy Chicago, *The Dinner Party: A Symbol of Our Heritage* (Garden City, NY: Anchor Books, 1979), Sojourner Truth plate, 1979.

Kingston, New York, won the case, and was reunited with her child. For a number of years, she worked in New York City as a domestic, the major source of work and income for Black women in the North during this period. A few years later, she indicates, she was called by God to the ministry and the abolitionist struggle; in June 1843, she left New York City on foot, leaving behind all her possessions to embark upon a new life. It was during this time that she decided to change her name. Though she could neither read nor write, she became well known in the North as an itinerant preacher and was a frequent visitor at antislavery gatherings. She advocated abolition, women's rights, the protection of the poor, and brotherly love. We know of the details of her life because she dictated her autobiography (*Narrative of Sojourner Truth* [1875]), to Frances W. Titus, a friend, and sold her story following her lectures.

She has become immortalized because of the now-controversial reminiscences of Frances D. Gage, who chaired one of the stormiest women's rights conventions of the period, which took place in Akron, Ohio, in 1851, and where Truth is supposed to have uttered the now-disputed speech, "Ar'n't I a Woman."[32] A detailed description of the circumstances surrounding this now-debatable speech, which also appears in Truth's *Narrative,* contains many details about her physicality and her body, a continuing object of the white gaze, male and female:

> The leaders of the movement trembled on seeing a tall, gaunt black woman in a gray dress and white turban . . . march deliberately into the church, walk with the air of a queen up the aisle and take her seat upon the pulpit steps. A buzz of disapprobation was heard all over the house, and such words as these fell upon listening ears: "An abolition affair!" "Woman's rights and niggers!" "Go it, old darkey!" . . . Order was restored and the business of the hour went on. . . . Old Sojourner, quiet and reticent as the "Lybian Statue," sat crouched against the wall on the corner of the pulpit stairs, her sun-bonnet shading her eyes, her elbows on her knees, and her chin resting upon her broad hard palm. . . . ministers came in to hear and discuss the resolutions presented. . . . the atmosphere of the convention betokened a storm. Slowly from her seat in the corner rose Sojourner Truth, who, till now, had scarcely lifted her head. "Don't let her speak," gasped half a dozen in my ear. She moved slowly and solemnly to the front, laid her bonnet at her feet and turned her great, speaking eyes to me. There was a hissing sound of disapprobation above and below. I rose and announced "Sojourner Truth" and begged the audience to keep silent for a few moments. The tumult subsided at once and every eye was fixed on this almost Amazon form, which stood nearly six feet high, head erect, and eyes piercing the upper air, like one in a dream. At her first word, there was a profound hush.[33]

It is at this point that Truth allegedly delivered the now-famous "Ar'n't I a Woman" speech, during which she supposedly exposed her previously covered right arm to the shoulder, showing her tremendous muscle power. It was this image of her that Chicago attempted to capture in a plate from *The Dinner Party.*[34]

Though Sojourner Truth has been immortalized as one of the invited guests to Judy Chicago's dinner party, and though something of the pain and anguish as well as the strength and triumph (symbolized by the clenched fist) of Black womanhood has been captured in the design

29

of the plate, it is curious that the overtly sexual imagery that is dominant in the majority of the other thirty-eight plates, especially in the prevalence of images of the vagina, is conspicuously absent (except for the buttocks) from the Truth plate. It is all the more surprising since Sojourner, like many other nineteenth-century Black women, was a victim of sexual abuse. Slave women were also victims of their reproductive capacity, since they were encouraged and even forced to breed like animals. They were also the South's perpetual wet nurses, providing from their breasts milk for Black and white babies alike. In other words, it was the exploitation of the Black woman's body—her vagina, her uterus, her breasts, and also her muscle—that set her apart from white women and that was the mark of her vulnerability. This exploitation also underscores the ways in which Black and white women experienced their gender differently. The absence of this most essential aspect of what it meant to be a slave woman in the nineteenth century—the inability to control one's own body, which the buttocks on the plate do not capture—is an outstanding flaw in Judy Chicago's conception of Black womanhood. Though she constructs Black womanhood in ways that are profoundly different from her images of white womanhood, it is surprising that the Sojourner Truth plate is void of the appropriate imagery that would have captured essential components of the sexual vulnerability of Black women. Alice Walker called attention to "the problem" of the Sojourner Truth plate in this way:

> [It] is the only one in the collection that shows—instead of a vagina—a face. In fact, three faces. . . . to think of Black women as women is impossible if you cannot imagine them with vaginas. Sojourner Truth certainly had a vagina, as note her lament about her children, born of her body, but sold into slavery.[35]

To conclude, male attitudes toward the female and her body have always been, according to John Updike, paradoxically contradictory: exalt and debase, serve and enslave, injure and comfort, revere and mock.[36] Nowhere is this more apparent than in the case of African American women. Perhaps it is true that no other women have been subjected over time to such stereotypical mythologizing about their bodies and their sexuality. According to Emily Martin's *The Woman in the Body,* poor Black women are still being mistreated by the medical establishment during childbirth. They are treated as purely physical beings, spoken to harshly, strapped down, told they are not in pain, refused comfort, isolated from their husbands.[37]

30

There is an ending to this story that is too extensive to chronicle here. It is a tale of resistance by hordes of Black women, including Linda Brent, whose eloquent slave narrative, *Incidents in the Life of a Slave Girl* (1861), is just one example of the ways in which Black women subverted a patriarchal racial structure that attempted to deprive them of autonomy, especially control of their bodies. It includes the moving story of Fannie Lou Hamer, the legendary civil rights activist whose body and soul were subjected to unimaginable indignities during her woefully painful, yet triumphant, life in the Deep South. Their struggles for liberation from racism, sexism, and physical terrorism, which the story of Sojourner Truth recalls, are beginning to be spoken about in louder voices. A significant aspect of these resistance narratives portrays their courageous quest for the integrity of their bodies, which have historically been displayed, beaten, stripped, bruised, penetrated, overworked, raped, and even lynched.[38]

It is only when we know more about what Black women have endured—at the hands of whites and even within their own communities—how they have fought back, and the ideologies they have had to deconstruct that we can fully appreciate these new songs.

NOTES

1. Barbara Omolade, "Hearts of Darkness," in Ann Snitow, Christine Stansell, and Sharon Thompson, eds., *Powers of Desire: The Politics of Sexuality* (New York: Monthly Review Press, 1983), 350. See also Sander L. Gilman's important work on European representations of Black female sexuality in seventeenth-century art and science in *Sexuality: An Illustrated History* (New York: John Wiley and Sons, 1989).

2. Hortense Spillers, "Interstices: A Small Drama of Words," in Carole S. Vance, ed., *Pleasure and Danger: Exploring Female Sexuality* (Boston: Routledge and Kegan Paul, 1984), 73–100, quoted in Beverly Guy-Sheftall, ed., *Words of Fire: An Anthology of African American Feminist Thought* (New York: New Press, 1995), 359.

3. These essays represent some of the most important scholarly work by Black women scholars to date employing feminist approaches to analyses of Black female sexuality. See also Hortense Spillers, "Mama's Baby, Papa's Maybe: An American Grammar Book," *Diacritics* 17 (summer 1987): 65–81; Lorraine O'Grady, "Olympia's Maid: Reclaiming Black Female Subjectivity," *Afterimage* (summer 1992): 14; Evelynn M. Hammonds, "Black (W)holes and the Geometry of Black Female Sexuality," *differences: A Journal of Feminist Cultural Studies* 6 nos. 2 and 3, 1994, 127–45, and "Toward a Genealogy of Black Female Sexuality: The Problematic of Silence," in Jacqui Alexander and Chandra Talpade Mohanty, eds., *Feminist Genealogies, Colonial Legacies, Democratic Futures* (New

York: Routledge, 1997); Hazel Carby, "'On the Threshold of Woman's Era': Lynching, Empire, and Sexuality in Black Feminist Theory," in Henry Louis Gates Jr., ed., *"Race," Writing and Difference* (Chicago: University of Chicago Press, 1986), 301–15, and "'It Jus Be's Dat Way Sometime': The Sexual Politics of Black Women's Blues," *Radical America* 20 (February 1987), 9–22; and Patricia Hill Collins, "The Sexual Politics of Black Womanhood," in *Black Feminist Thought: Knowledge, Consciousness and the Politics of Empowerment* (New York: Routledge, 1990).

4. O'Grady, "Olympia's Maid," 14.

5. Hugh Honour, *The Image of the Black in Western Art,* vol. 4, *From the American Revolution to World War I,* pt. 2 (Cambridge: Harvard University Press, 1989), 7.

6. Hammonds, "Toward a Genealogy of Black Female Sexuality," 171. Hammonds's article is an important review essay with excellent bibliographic sources. The quote alludes to Spillers's work, cited previously. See also Darlene Clark Hine's pioneering essay, "Rape and the Inner Lives of Black Women in the Middle West: Preliminary Thoughts on the Culture of Dissemblance," *Signs* 14, no. 4 (1989): 915–20; and Evelyn Brooks Higginbotham's groundbreaking theoretical essay, "African American Women's History and the Metalanguage of Race," *Signs* 17, no. 2 (1992): 251–74.

7. See Jordan's chapter titled "First Impressions: Initial English Confrontation with Africans," in *White over Black: American Attitudes toward the Negro, 1550–1812* (Baltimore: Penguin Books, 1968), 3–43. See also Jan Nederveen Pieterse, *White on Black: Images of Africa and Blacks in Western Popular Culture* (New Haven: Yale University Press, 1992), especially the chapter "Libido in Colour," 172–87.

8. Within this context, the Victorian myth of the "dark continent" was constructed and an imperialist discourse of domination developed, which Foucault and others later argued has been a major form of power for colonizers. See Patrick Brantlinger, "Victorians and Africans: The Genealogy of the Myth of the Dark Continent," *Critical Inquiry* 12 (autumn 1985): 166–203. See also Michel Foucault, *The History of Sexuality,* vols. 1–3 (New York: Vintage Books, 1978).

9. See Elizabeth Alexander's book of poetry *The Venus Hottentot* (Charlottesville: University Press of Virginia, 1990), which reintroduces to Western readers the story of Saartjie Baartman. This imaginary rendering of the psyche of Baartman gives her a voice for the first time.

10. See Honour, *The Image of the Black in Western Art,* vol. 4, pt. 2, 52–53, for a discussion of the "Venus Hottentot" and illustrations of her. For detailed discussions of this phenomenon, see Richard D. Altick, *The Shows of London* (Cambridge and London: Harvard University Press, 1978); Bernth Lindfors, "Courting the Hottentot Venus," *Africa: Revista Trimestrale di Studi e Documentazione dell Istituto Italo-Africano* 40, no. 1 (1985): 133–48, and "The Bottom Line: African Caricature in Georgian England," *World Literature Written in English* 24, no. 1 (1984): 43–51; Anna H. Smith, "Still More about the Hottentot Venus," *Africana Notes and News* 26, no. 3 (1984): 95–98; Percival R. Kirby, "The Hottentot Venus," *Africana Notes and News* 6, no. 3 (1949): 55–62, "More About the Hottentot Venus," *Africana Notes and News* 10, no. 4 (1953): 124–34, and "The 'Hottentot Venus' of Musee de l'Homme, Paris," *South African Journal of Science*

50, no. 12 (1954): 319–21; Sander L. Gilman, "Black Bodies, White Bodies: Toward an Iconography of Female Sexuality in Late Nineteenth-Century Art, Medicine, and Literature," *Critical Inquiry* 12, (autumn 1985): 213–19, and *Sexuality: An Illustrated History: Representing the Sexual in Medicine and Culture from the Middle Ages to the Age of AIDS* (New York: John Wiley and Sons, 1989); Anne Fausto-Sterling, "Gender, Race, and Nation: The Comparative Anatomy of 'Hottentot' Women in Europe, 1815–1817," in Jennifer Terry and Jacqueline Urla, eds., *Deviant Bodies and Critical Perspectives of Difference in Science and Popular Culture* (Bloomington: Indiana University Press, 1995).

11. Quoted in Honour, *The Image of the Black in Western Art,* vol. 4, pt. 2, 54.

12. Quoted in Honour, *The Image of the Black in Western Art,* vol. 4, pt. 2, 54.

13. Gilman, "Black Bodies," 287–97.

14. Jordan, *White over Black,* 151.

15. Deborah Gray White, *Ar'n't I a Woman: Female Slaves in the Plantation South* (New York: W. W. Norton, 1985), 27–35.

16. This portion of the chapter is a synthesis of a section of my doctoral dissertation, which was published in the Carlson series *Black Women in the Nineteenth Century,* edited by Darlene Clark Hine (Brooklyn, New York: Carlson Publishing Inc., 1990). See *Daughters of Sorrow: Attitudes toward Black Women, 1880–1920,* vol. 11.

17. See bell hooks' chapter "Continued Devaluation of Black Womanhood," *Ain't I a Woman: Black Women and Feminism* (Boston: South End Press, 1981), 51–86.

18. Mary Ryan, "The Empire of the Mother: American Writing about Domesticity, 1839–1869," *Women and History* (summer–fall 1982): 142–43.

19. For an excellent discussion of early English travel literature and its depiction of Black women, see Jennifer L. Morgan, "'Some Could Suckle over Their Shoulder': Male Travelers, Female Bodies, and the Gendering of Racial Ideology, 1500–1700," *The William and Mary Quarterly* 54 (January 1997): 167–92. See also Linda E. Boose, "'The Getting of a Lawful Race': Racial Discourse in Early Modern England and the Unrepresentable Black Woman," in Margo Hendricks and Patricia Parker, eds., *Women, "Race," and Writing in the Early Modern Period* (New York: Routledge, 1994); Kim F. Hall, *Things of Darkness : Economies of Race and Gender in Early Modern England* (Ithaca: Cornell University Press, 1995); and Anne McClintock, *Imperial Leather: Race, Gender and Sexuality in the Colonial Contest* (New York: Routledge, 1995).

20. See Jennifer Lyle Morgan's "Women in Slavery and the Transatlantic Slave Trade," in Anthony Tibbles, ed., *Transatlantic Slavery: Against Human Dignity* (London: HMSO, 1994), 60–69, for a discussion of the differential treatment of African men and women during the Middle Passage. See also Barbara Bush, *Slave Women in Caribbean Society, 1650–1838* (Bloomington: Indiana University Press, 1990), especially chapter 2. The most extensive analysis of gender issues and the trans-Atlantic slave trade can be found in David Barry Gaspar and Darlene Clark Hine, eds., *More Than Chattel: Black Women and Slavery in the Americas* (Bloomington: Indiana University Press, 1996).

21. White, *Ar'n't I a Woman,* 32.

22. Paula Giddings, *When and Where I Enter: The Impact of Race and Sex on Black Women in America* (New York: William Morrow, 1984).

23. The details of this abuse appeared in Diana E. Axelsen, "Women as Victims of Medical Experimentation: J. Marion Sims' Surgery on Slave Women, 1845–1850," *SAGE: A Scholarly Journal on Black Women* 2, no. 2 (1985): 10–14. The first book to point out the abuse was by British historian Graham Barker-Benfield, *The Horrors of the Half-Known Life: Male Attitudes toward Women and Sexuality* (New York: HarperCollins, 1975); Deborah K. McGregor, *Sexual Surgery and the Origins of Gynecology: J. Marion Sims, His Hospital, and His Patients* (New York: Garland Publishing, 1989); Todd L. Savitt, "The Use of Blacks for Medical Experimentation and Demonstration in the Old South," *Journal of Southern History* 48, no. 3 (August 1982), 332.

24. Phillip A. Bruce, *The Plantation Negro as a Freeman* (New York and London: G. P. Putnam's Sons, 1889), 20.

25. Eleanor Tayleur, "The Negro Woman: Social and Moral Decadence," *The Outlook* 76 (30 Jan. 1904): 270.

26. Thomas P. Bailey, *Race Orthodoxy in the South and Other Aspects of the Negro Question* (New York: Neale Publishing Company, 1914), 43.

27. Howard Odum, *Social and Mental Traits of the Negro: Research into the Conditions of the Negro Race in Southern Towns* (New York: Columbia University Press, 1910), 243–44.

28. William Dean Howells, *The Shadow of a Dream and An Imperative Duty* (1892; reprint, New Haven: College and University Press, 1962), 196.

29. Howells, *Imperative Duty,* 197.

30. Judy Chicago, *The Dinner Party: A Symbol of Our Heritage* (Garden City, N.Y.: Anchor Books/Doubleday, 1979), 88.

31. Anna Julia Cooper, *A Voice from the South by a Black Woman of the South* (Xenia, Ohio: Aldine Publishing, 1892). Reprinted in Henry Louis Gates Jr., ed., *The Schomburg Library of Nineteenth-Century Black Women Writers* series (New York: Oxford University Press, 1988), 141.

32. See Nell Painter's biography of Sojourner Truth, *Sojourner Truth: A Life, a Symbol* (New York: W. W. Norton, 1996), for a detailed discussion of her assessment of the authenticity of the historical narratives surrounding Truth's legendary speech. See also Carleton Mabee, *Sojourner Truth* (New York: New York University Press, 1993) for a detailed discussion of Truth's speech, 67–82.

33. Frances D. Gage's report of the 1851 Akron, Ohio Convention appears in *History of Woman Suffrage*, 3 vols., 1881–1887, edited by Elizabeth Cody Stanton, Susan B. Anthony, and Matilda Joslyn Gage, 115–17. Reprinted by New York: Source Book, 1970. A description of the Akron gathering also appears in *Narrative of Sojourner Truth* (Battle Creek, Michigan, 1878), 131–37. Reprinted by Ayer Company Publishers, Salem, New Hampshire, 1988. I am quoting from this version, pp. 131–33.

34. See Hortense Spillers's critique of Chicago's *The Dinner Party* in "Interstices," 77–78, where Spillers alludes to Alice Walker's insightful and extensive critique as well; Gloria T. Hull, Patricia Bell Scott, and Barbara Smith, eds., "One Child of One's Own: A Meaningful Digression Within the Work(s)—An Excerpt," in *All the Women Are White, All the Blacks Are Men, but Some of Us Are Brave* (Old Westbury, NY: Feminist Press, 1981), 42–43; see also Jennifer DeVere Brody, "Effaced into Flesh: Black Women's Subjectivity," in Ann Kibbey, Thomas Foster, and Carol Siegel, eds., *On Your Left: Historical Materialism in the*

1990s (New York: New York University Press, 1996), 184–205, for a discussion of Chicago's treatment of Sojourner Truth and what Brody argues is a "difficult gendering of black female flesh" (198). Brody also makes an analogy between the "spectacle" of Truth baring her breasts and the Venus Hottentot. There is a growing body of work by Black feminist critics on the problematic "use" of Sojourner Truth by various white feminist scholars. See also Deborah McDowell, "Transferences: Black Feminist Discourse: The Practice of Theory," in Diane Elam and Robyn Wiegman, eds., *Feminism beside Itself* (New York: Routledge, 1995), 93–118.

35. Alice Walker, "One Child of One's Own" (cited in note 34), 43.

36. John Updike, "Venus and Others," *Michigan Quarterly Review* (fall 1990), 495. See also the subsequent special issue on the female body, part 2, *Michigan Quarterly Review* (winter 1991).

37. Emily Martin, *The Woman in the Body* (Boston: Beacon Press, 1987), 139–55.

38. One of the most outrageous lynching incidents in the South occurred in a rural Georgia county in 1919, when a pregnant Black woman's unborn child was cut from her stomach and stomped to death while she watched. This incident is described in John Hope Franklin's *From Slavery to Freedom: A History of Negro Americans* (New York: Alfred A. Knopf, 1947).

Jennifer L. Morgan

"Some Could Suckle over Their Shoulder"

Male Travelers, Female Bodies, and the Gendering of Racial Ideology, 1500–1770

In June 1647, the Englishman Richard Ligon left London on the ship *Achilles* to establish himself as a planter in the newly settled colony of Barbados. En route, Ligon's ship stopped in the Cape Verde Islands for provisions and trade. There Ligon saw a Black woman for the first time; as he recorded the encounter in his *True and Exact History of . . . Barbadoes,* she was a "Negro of the greatest beauty and majesty together: that ever I saw in one woman. Her stature large, and excellently shap'd, well favour'd, full eye'd, and admirably grac'd. . . . [I] awaited her coming out, which was with far greater Majesty and gracefulness, than I have seen Queen Anne, descend from the Chaire of State."[1] Ligon's rhetoric may have surprised his English readers, for seventeenth-century images of Black women did not usually evoke the ultimate marker of civility— the monarchy—as the referent.

Early modern English writers conventionally set the Black female figure against one that was white—and thus beautiful. In *Pseudodoxia Epidemica* (1646), Sir Thomas Browne argued that blackness and beauty were mutually dependent, each relying on the other as antithetical proof of each one's existence.[2] Recently, depictions of Black women in early modern England have attracted scholarly attention. Peter Erickson calls the image of the Black woman a trope for disrupted harmony. Lynda Boose sees Black women in early modern English writing as symbolically

37

"unrepresentable," embodying a deep threat to patriarchy. Kim Hall finds early modern English literature and material culture fully involved with a gendered racial discourse committed to constructing stable categories of whiteness and blackness.[3] As these and other scholars have shown, male travelers to Africa and the Americas contributed to a European discourse on Black womanhood. Femaleness evoked a certain element of desire, but travelers depicted Black women as simultaneously unwomanly and marked by a reproductive value dependent on their sex. Writers' recognition of Black femaleness and their inability to allow Black women to embody "proper" female space composed a focus for representations of racial difference. During the course of his journey, Ligon came to another view of Black women. As he saw it, their breasts "hang down below their Navels, so that when they stoop at their common work of weeding, they hang almost to the ground, that at a distance you would think they had six legs." For Ligon, their monstrous bodies symbolized their sole utility—their ability to produce both crops and other laborers.[4]

Ligon's narrative is a microcosm of a much larger ideological maneuver that juxtaposed the familiar with the unfamiliar—the beautiful woman who is also the monstrous laboring beast. As the tenacious and historically deep roots of racialist ideology become more evident, it becomes clear also that, through the rubric of monstrously "raced" Amerindian and African women, Europeans found a means to articulate shifting perceptions of themselves as religiously, culturally, and phenotypically superior to those Black or brown persons they sought to define. In the discourse used to justify the slave trade, Ligon's beautiful Negro woman was as important as her six-legged counterpart. Both imaginary women marked a gendered whiteness that accompanied European expansionism.[5] Well before the publication of Ligon's work, New World and African narratives that relied on gender to convey an emergent notion of racialized difference had been published in England and Europe. Although this chapter is primarily concerned with England and its imperial expansion, by the time English colonists arrived in the Americas they already possessed the trans-European ethnohistoriographical tradition of depicting the imagined native in which Ligon's account is firmly situated.[6]

Ligon's attitude toward the enslaved has been characterized by modern historians as "more liberal and humane than [that] of the generality of planters."[7] Nevertheless, his text indicates the kind of negative symbolic work required of Black women in early modern English discourse. As Ligon penned his manuscript while in debtors' prison in 1653, he constructed a layered narrative in which the discovery of

African women's monstrosity helped to assure the work's success. Taking the female body as a symbol of the deceptive beauty and ultimate savagery of blackness, Ligon allowed his readers to dally with him among beautiful Black women, only seductively to disclose their monstrosity over the course of the narrative. Travel accounts, which had proved their popularity by the time Ligon's *History . . . of Barbadoes* appeared, relied on gendered notions of European social order to project African cultural disorder. I do not argue here that gender operated as a more profound category of difference than race. Rather, this chapter focuses on the way in which racialist discourse was deeply imbued with ideas about gender and sexual difference that, indeed, became manifest only in contact with each other. White men who laid the discursive groundwork on which the "theft of bodies" could be justified relied on mutually constitutive ideologies of race and gender to affirm Europe's legitimate access to African labor.[8]

Travel accounts produced in Europe and available in England provided a corpus from which subsequent writers borrowed freely, reproducing images of Native American and African women that resonated with readers. These travelers learned to dismiss the idea that women in the Americas and Africa might be innocuous, unremarkable, or even beautiful. Rather, indigenous women bore an enormous symbolic burden as writers from Walter Ralegh to Edward Long employed them to mark metaphorically the symbiotic boundaries of European national identities and white supremacy. The struggle with perceptions of beauty and assertions of monstrosity such as Ligon's exemplified a much larger process through which the familiar became unfamiliar as beauty became beastliness and mothers became monstrous, all ultimately in the service of racial distinctions. Writers who articulated religious and moral justifications for the slave trade simultaneously grappled with the character of the female African body—a body both desirable and repulsive, available and untouchable, productive and reproductive, beautiful and Black. This chapter argues that these meanings were inscribed well before the establishment of England's colonial American plantations and that the intellectual work necessary to naturalize African enslavement—that is, the development of racialist discourse—was deeply implicated by gendered notions of difference and human hierarchy.

Europe had a long tradition of identifying Others through the monstrous physiognomy or sexual behavior of women. Pliny the Elder's ancient collection of monstrous races, *Historia Naturalis*, catalogued the long-breasted wild woman alongside the oddity of Indian and Ethiopian

tribal women who bore only one child in their lifetime.[9] Medieval images of female devils included sagging breasts as part of the iconography
of danger and monstrosity. The medieval wild woman, whose breasts
dragged on the ground when she walked and could be thrown over her
shoulder, was believed to disguise herself with youth and beauty in
order to enact seductions that would satisfy her "obsessed . . . craving
for the love of mortal men."[10] The shape of her body marked her deviant
sexuality; both shape and sexuality evidenced her savagery.

Thus, writers commonly looked to sociosexual deviance to indicate
savagery in Africa and the Americas and to mark difference from Europe. According to *The Travels of Sir John Mandeville,* "in Ethiopia and
in many other countries [in Africa] the folk lie all naked . . . and the
women have no shame of the men." Further, "they wed there no wives,
for all the women there be common . . . and when [women] have children they may give them to what man they will that hath companied
with them."[11] Deviant sexual behavior reflected the breakdown of natural laws—the absence of shame, the inability to identify lines of hered-
ity and descent. This concern with deviant sexuality, articulated almost
always through descriptions of women, is a constant theme in the travel
writings of early modern Europe. Explorers and travelers to the New
World and Africa brought expectations of distended breasts and dangerous sexuality with them. Indeed, Columbus exemplified his reliance
on the female body to articulate the colonial venture at the very outset
of his voyage when he wrote that the earth was shaped like a breast with
the Indies composing the nipple.[12]

Richard Eden's 1553 English translation of Sebastian Münster's *A
Treatyse of the Newe India* presented Amerigo Vespucci's voyage to English readers for the first time. Vespucci did not mobilize color to mark
the difference of the people he encountered; rather, he described them
in terms of their lack of social institutions ("they fight not for the en-
largeing of theyr dominion for asmuch as they have no Magistrates")
and social niceties ("at theyr meate they use rude and barberous fashions, lying on the ground without any table clothe or coverlet").
Nonetheless, his descriptions are not without positive attributes, and
when he turned his attention to women, his language bristles with illuminating contradiction:

> Theyr bodies are verye smothe and clene by reason of theyr
> often washinge. They are in other thinges fylthy and withoute
> shame. Thei use no lawful coniunccion of mariage, and but
> every one hath as many women as him liketh, and leaveth

them agayn at his pleasure. The women are very fruiteful, and refuse no laboure al the whyle they are with childe. They travayle in maner withoute payne, so that the nexte day they are cherefull and able to walke. Neyther have they theyr bellies wimpeled or loose, and hanginge pappes, by reason of bearinge manye chyldren.[13]

The passage conveys admiration for indigenous women's strength in pregnancy and their ability to maintain aesthetically pleasing bodies, and it also represents the conflict at the heart of European discourse on gender and difference. Vespucci's familiarity with icons of difference led him to expect American women with hanging breasts; thus he registers surprise that women's breasts and bodies were neither "wimpeled" nor "hanginge." That surprise is inextricable from his description of childbearing. His admiration hinges on both a veiled critique of European female weakness and a dismissal of Amerindian women's pain. The question of pain in childbirth became a central component of descriptions of Africa and Africans. Vespucci presented a preliminary, still ambiguously laudatory account of Amerindian women. Nonetheless, he mobilized the place of women in society as a cultural referent that evoked the "fylth" and shamelessness of all indigenous people. Thus the passage exposes early modern English readers' sometimes ambivalent encounters with narratives that utilized women's behavior and physiognomy to mark European national identities and inscribe racial hierarchy.[14]

In the narration of Columbus's voyage that appears in *A Treatyse,* Münster situated women both as intermediaries between the intrusive and indigenous peoples and as animal-like reproductive units.[15] On arriving at Hispaniola, Columbus's men "pursewinge [the women and men who had come down to the shore] toke a womanne whom they brought to theyr shyppe . . . fyllinge her with delicate meates and wyne, and clothing her in fayre apparel, & so let her depart . . . to her companie."[16] As Stephen Greenblatt has illustrated, the female "go-between" was crucial in encounter narratives. This woman figured as a pliable emissary who could be returned to her people as a sign of Spanish generosity (in the form of food and wine) and civility (in the form of clothes). She could be improved by the experience. Indeed, her ability to receive European goods—to be made familiar through European intervention—served as evidence of her own people's savagery, disorder, and distance from civility.[17]

In a passage that closely follows, Münster considered another role for indigenous women and children, a role whose proximate contradiction evokes the complicated nature of European assessment of women and their bodies. Describing the behavior of so-called cannibals, Münster avowed that "such children as they take, they geld to make them fat as we doo cocke chikyns and younge hogges. . . . Such younge women as they take, they keepe for increase, as we doo hennes to laye egges."[18] The metaphor of domesticated livestock introduced a notion that became an ideé fixe concerning indigenous and enslaved women's twofold value to the European project of expansion and extraction.[19] This metaphor, however, did not fully encompass the complexity of dangers indigenous women presented for Europe. Despite his respect for female reproductive hardiness, at the end of the volume Vespucci fixed the indigenous woman as a dangerous cannibal:

> There came sodeynly a woman downe from a mountayne, bringing with her secretly a great stake with which she [killed a Spaniard.] The other wommene foorthwith toke him by the legges, and drewe him to the mountayne. . . . The women also which had slayne the yong man, cut him in pieces even in the sight of the Spaniardes, shewinge them the pieces, and rosting them at a greate fyre.[20]

Vespucci made manifest the latent sexualized danger embedded by the man-slaying woman in a letter in which he wrote of women biting off the penises of their sexual partners, thus linking cannibalism—an absolute indicator of savagery and distance from European norms—to female sexual insatiability.[21]

The label *savage* was not uniformly applied to Amerindian people. Indeed, in the context of European national rivalries, the indigenous woman became somewhat less savage. In the mid- to late sixteenth century, the bodies of women figured at the borders of national identities more often than at the edges of a larger European identity. The Italian traveler Girolamo Benzoni, in his *History of the New World* (a 1572 narrative that appeared in multiple translations), utilized sexualized indigenous women both as markers of difference and as indicators of Spanish immorality. His first description of a person in the Americas (in Venezuela in 1541) occurs at the very beginning of his story:

> Then came an Indian woman . . . such a woman as I have never before nor since seen the like of; so that my eyes could not be satisfied with looking at her for wonder. . . . She was

quite naked, except where modisty forbids, such being the custom throughout all this country; she was old, and painted black, with long hair down to her waist, and her ear-rings had so weighed her ears down, as to make them reach her shoulders, a thing wonderful to see. . . . her teeth were black, her mouth large, and she had a ring in her nostrils . . . so that she appeared like a monster to us, rather than a human being.[22]

Benzoni's description invokes a sizable catalogue of cultural distance packed with meaning made visible by early modern conventions of gendered difference. His inability to satisfy his gaze speaks to an obfuscation that Ligon enacted one hundred years later and that Greenblatt argues is the defining metaphor of the colonial encounter. His "wonder" situates her distance.[23] In the context of a society concerned with the dissemblance of cosmetics, as Hall argues, her black-faced body was both cause for alarm and evidence of a dangerous inversion of norms. Her nakedness, her ears, and her nose—all oddities accentuated by willful adornment—irrevocably placed her outside the realm of the familiar. Her blackened teeth and large mouth evoked a sexualized danger that, as Benzoni himself explicitly states, linked her and, by implication, her people to an inhuman monstrosity.[24]

In evoking this singular woman—the like of whom he had never seen—Benzoni departed from his contemporaries. He used his description of her to open his narrative and, through her, placed his reader in the realm of the exotic. This "wonderful" woman alerted readers to the distance Benzoni traveled, but he deployed another, more familiar set of female images to level a sustained critique of Spanish colonial expansion and thereby to insist on the indigenous woman's connection, or nearness, to a familiar European femininity.

Capt. Pedro de Calize arrived with upwards of 4000 slaves. . . .
It was really a most distressing thing to see the way in which these wretched creatures naked, tired, and lame were treated [by the Spaniards]; exhausted with hunger, sick, and despairing. The *unfortunate mothers,* with two or three children on their shoulders or clinging round their necks, overwhelmed with tears and grief, all tied with cords or with iron chains. . . . Nor was there a girl but had been violated by the depredators; wherefore, from too much indulgence, many Spaniards entirely lost their health.[25]

Benzoni utilized the pathetic figure of the fecund mother and the sexually violated young girl against the Spaniards. Such a move was common in the aftermath of Las Casas's *In Defense of the Indians* (circa 1550) and amid the intensified resentment over access to the Americas directed toward Spain by other European nations. In "Discoverie of the . . . Empire of Guiana" (1598), Ralegh stated that he "suffered not any man to . . . touch any of [the natives'] wives or daughters: which course so contrary to the Spaniards (who tyrannize over them in all things) drewe them to admire her [English] majestie."[26] While permitting himself and his men to gaze upon naked Indian women, Ralegh accentuated their restraint. In doing so, he used the untouched bodies of Native American women to mark national boundaries and signal the civility and superiority of English colonizers—in contrast to the sexually violent Spaniards. Moreover, in linking the eroticism of indigenous women to the sexual attention of Spanish men, Ralegh signaled the Spaniards' "lapse into savagery."[27] Benzoni, too, inscribed the negative consequences of too-close associations with indigenous women. For him, sexual proximity to local women depleted Spanish strength. As he prepared to abandon the topic of Indian slavery for a lengthy discussion of Columbus's travels, he again invoked motherhood to prove Spanish depravity: "All the slaves that the Spaniards catch in these provinces are sent [to the Caribbean] . . . and even when *some of the Indian women are pregnant by these same Spaniards,* they sell them without any consciences."[28]

This rhetorical flourish, through female bodies, highlighted the contradictions of the familiar and unfamiliar in the Americas. The woman who opened Benzoni's narrative, in her nakedness and her monstrous adornments, could not be familiar to conquistadors and colonizers, yet in her role as mother, sexual victim, or even sexually arousing female, she evoked the familiar. Benzoni sidestepped the tension inherent in the savage-violated-mother by mobilizing her in the service of publicizing Spanish atrocity. In effect, the Black Legend created (among other things) this confusing figure of pathos—the savage mother whose nurturing quality is both recorded and praised. In order to facilitate the ultimate roles of extractors and extracted, the indigenous woman's familiarity had to be neutralized. Thus the pathos of raped mothers ultimately reverberated back onto Europe, signifying disdain for the Spanish and disregard for monstrous women.[29]

The monstrosity of the native mother had an important visual corollary. A mid-sixteenth-century Portuguese artist, for example, depicted the Devil wearing a Brazilian headdress and rendered his demonic female companions with long, sagging breasts.[30] Toward the end of the century, a multivolume collection of travel accounts, published in Latin and German, augmented the evolving discourse of European civility with visual images of overseas encounters.[31] As Bernadette Bucher has shown, the early volumes of Theodor de Bry's *Grand Voyages* (1590) depicted the Algonkians of Virginia and the Timucuas of Florida as classical Europeans: Amerindian bodies mirrored ancient Greek and Roman statuary, modest virgins covered their breasts, and infants suckled at the high, small breasts of young attractive women (see figs. 10 and 11). These images were always in flux. In the third de Bry volume, *Voyages to Brazil*, published in 1592, the Indian was portrayed as aggressive and savage, and the representation of women's bodies changed. The new woman was a cannibal with breasts that fell below her waist. She licks the juices of grilled human flesh from her fingers and adorns the frontispiece of the map of Tierra del Fuego (see figs. 12 and 13). Bucher argues that absence of a suckling child in these depictions is essential to the image's symbolic weight.[32] Their childlessness signified their cannibalism—consumption rather than production. Although cannibalism was not exemplified by women only, women with long breasts marked such savagery among Native Americans for English readers. Other images of monstrous races—such as the headless Euaipanonoma; the one-footed Sciopods; and the Astomi, who lived on the aroma of apples—slowly vanished from Europe's imagined America and Africa. Once in Africa, however, the place of motherhood in the complex of savagery and race became central to the figure of the Black woman. Unlike other monstrosities, the long-breasted woman—who, when depicted with her child, carried the full weight of productive savagery—maintained her place in the lexicon of conquest and exploration.

American narratives contributed to a discursive triangulation among Europe, America, and Africa. English travelers to West Africa drew on American narrative traditions. Richard Hakluyt's collection of travel narratives, *Principall Navigations* (1589), brought Africa into the purview of English readers. *Principall Navigations* portrayed Africa and Africans in positive and negative terms. The authors' shifting assessments of Africa and Africans "produc[ed] an Africa which is familiar and unfamiliar, civil and savage, full of promise and full of threat." Sixteenth-century ambivalence concerning England's role in overseas expansion required a forceful antidote. In response, Hakluyt presented texts that, through an often conflicted depiction of African peoples, ultimately differentiated Africa and England and erected a boundary that made English expan-

Fig. 10. Young virgin covering her breast, from Thomas Hariot, *A brief and True Report of the New Found Land of Virginia,* in Theodor de Bry, *Grand Voyages,* vol. 1 (Frankfurt am Main, 1590), plate 6. (Courtesy of the John Work Garrett Library of the Sheridan Libraries, Johns Hopkins University.)

sion in the face of confused and uncivilized peoples reasonable, profitable, and moral.[33]

On the West African coast, women's bodies, like those of their New World counterparts, symbolized the shifting parameters of the colonizing venture. English writers regularly directed readers' attention to the sexually titillating topic of African women's physiognomy and reproductive experience. In doing so, they drew attention to the complex interstices of desire and repulsion that marked European men's gaze on Amerindian and African women. Sixteenth- and seventeenth-century writers conveyed a sexual grotesquerie that ultimately made African women indispensable, in that it showed gendered ways of putting African savagery to productive use. Although titillation was certainly a component of these accounts, to write of sex was also to define and expand the boundaries of profit through productive and reproductive labor.

The symbolic weight of indigenous women's sexual, childbearing, and child-rearing practices continued to be brought to bear on England's literary imagination. John Lok, in his account of his 1554 voyage to

Fig. 11. Woman suckling child, from *Eorum Quae in Florida . . .* , in Theodor de Bry, *Grand Voyages,* vol. 2 (Frankfurt am Main, 1591), plate 20. (Courtesy of the John Work Garrett Library of the Sheridan Libraries, Johns Hopkins University.)

Guinea, published forty years later in Hakluyt's collection, reinscribed Africans' place in the human hierarchy. Borrowing verbatim from Richard Eden's 1555 translation of Peter Martyr, Lok described all Africans as "people of beastly living." He located the proof of this in *women's* behavior: among the Garamantes, women "are common: for they contract no matrimonie, neither have respect to chastitie."[34] Eden's Martyr has a long descriptive passage on African oddities; in it the reference to Garamante women is followed by one to a tribe who "have no speeche, but rather a grynnynge and chatterynge. There are also people without heades cauled Blemines, havyinge their eyes and mouth in theyr breast."[35] By not reproducing the entire paragraph, Lok's abbreviation suggests that, by the end of the sixteenth century, the oddities of Africa could be consolidated into the particular symbol of women's sexual availability.

William Towrson's narrative of his 1555 voyage to Guinea, also

Fig. 12. Woman (*left*) holding leg, from *Memorabile Provinciae Brasilae . . .* , in Theodor de Bry, *Grand Voyages,* vol. 3 (Frankfurt am Main, 1592), 179. (Courtesy of the John Work Garrett Library of the Sheridan Libraries, Johns Hopkins University.)

published by Hakluyt, further exhibits this kind of distillation. Towrson depicted women and men as largely indistinguishable. They "goe so alike, that one cannot know a man from a woman but by their breastes, which in the most part be very foule and long, hanging downe low like the udder of a goate."[36] This was, perhaps, the first time an Englishman in Africa explicitly used breasts as an identifying trait of beastliness and difference. He goes on to maintain that "diverse of the women have such exceeding long breasts, that some of them will lay the same upon the ground and lie downe by them."[37] Lok and Towrson represented African women's bodies and sexual behavior so as to distinguish Africa from Europe. Towrson in particular gave readers only two analogies through which to view and understand African women—beasts and monsters.

Some thirty years after the original Hakluyt collections were published, other writers continued to mobilize African women to do complex symbolic work. In 1622, Richard Jobson's *The Golden Trade* ap-

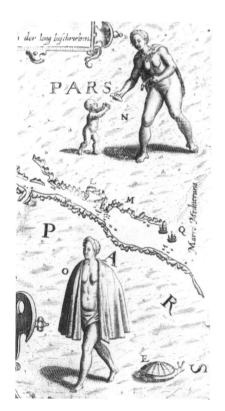

Fig. 13. Women on the map of Tierra del Fuego, from *Vera et Accurate Descriptio eorum omnius Quae Acciderunt Quinque navibus, Anno 1598*, in Theodor de Bry, *Grand Voyages*, vol. 9 (Frankfurt am Main, 1602), 56. (Courtesy of the John Work Garrett Library of the Sheridan Libraries, Johns Hopkins University.)

peared in London, chronicling his 1620–21 trading ventures up the Gambia River.[38] Jobson described strong and noble people on the one hand and barbarous and bestial people on the other, and African women personified his nation's struggle with the familiar and unfamiliar African—a struggle that can also be located along the axis of desire and repulsion. Jobson's association with the "Fulbie" and "Maudingo" people furnishes evidence of this struggle. He described Fulbie men as beastlike, "seemingly more senseless, then our Country beasts," a state he attributed to their close association with the livestock they raised.[39] Unlike many of his contemporaries, Jobson regarded African women with admiration. In contrast to Fulbie men, the women were "excellently well bodied, having very good features, with a long blacke haire."[40] He maintained that the discovery of a "mote or haire" in milk would cause these dairywomen to "blush, in defence of her cleanely meaning."[41] This experience of shame encapsulated a morality and civility to which only women had access. Among the Maudingos of Cassan, newly married women "observ[e] herein a shamefast modestie, not to be looked for, *among such a kinde of blacke or barbarous people.*"[42] Despite his well-meaning description of African women, Jobson recorded their behaviors associated with English civility only inasmuch as they deviated from that which he, and his readers, expected. His appreciation of Fulbie women and Maudingo people was predicated on their ability to exceed his expectations. To Jobson, African women proved the precarious nature of African civility. His narrative, even at its most laudatory, always returned to inferiority. While describing the history of kingship and the great importance of ancestral honor among the Maudingos, Jobson still contended that "from the King to the slave, they are all perpetuall beggers from us." His "wonder" at women's modesty alerted his readers to the culture's abnormality and, implicitly, to its larger absence of civility. Even as he depicted them positively, women became part of the demonstration that, despite kings and history, these Africans were barbarous and ripe for exploitation.[43]

Other English publications continued to locate evidence of savagery and legitimated exploitation in women. After Hakluyt died, Samuel Purchas took up the mantle of editor and published an additional twenty volumes in Hakluyt's series in 1624.[44] In his translation of a fourteenth-century narrative by Leo Africanus, Purchas presented a West Africa sharply delineated from the civilized. Discussion of "the Land of Negros," for example, is preceded by, and thus set apart from, a long section of North Africa. "Negros," unlike their northern neighbors, lived "a brutish and savage life, without any King, Governour, Common-wealth, or knowledge of Husbandry." To confirm this savagery, Leo Africanus asserted that they were "clad . . . in skinnes of beasts, neither had they any peculiar wives . . . and when night came they resorted . . . both men and women into one Cottage together . . . and each man choosing his [woman] which hee had most fanciee unto."[45] This indictment opened the descriptive passages on "Ghinea," thereby making women's sexual availability the defining metaphor of colonial accessibility and Black African savagery.

In the following volume, Purchas published Andrew Battell's "Strange Adventures."[46] Battell spent seventeen years in Angola, from 1590 to 1607, some as captive, some as escapee, and some in service to King James. For sixteen months, Battell stayed near "Dongo" with the "Gaga" people, "the greatest Canibals and man-eaters that bee in the World."[47] Like sixteenth-century observers in Brazil, he highlighted women's unnatural reproductive behavior. This "tribe" of fighters and cannibals rejected motherhood. According to Battell, "the women are very fruitfull, but they enjoy none of their children: for as soon as the woman is delivered of her Childe, it is presently buried quicke [alive]; So that there is not one Childe brought up."[48] Battell positioned his discussion of this unnatural behavior in such a way as to close the debate on African savagery. Gaga savagery began, in his account, with cannibalism and ended with mothers who consented to the killing of the children they bore.

Purchas also provided a translation of Pieter de Marees's "A description and historicall declaration of the golden Kingdome of Guinea." This narrative was first published in Dutch in 1602, was translated into German and Latin for the de Bry volumes (1603–34), and appeared in French in 1605. Plagiarism by seventeenth- and eighteenth-century writers gave it still wider circulation.[49] Here, too, Black women embody African savagery. De Marees began by describing the people at Sierra Leone as "very greedie eaters, and no lesse drinkers, and very lecherous, and theevish, and much addicted to uncleanenesse; one man hath as many wives as hee is able to keepe and maintaine. The women also are much addicted to leacherie, specially, with strange Countrey people . . . [and] are also great Lyers, and not to be credited."[50] As did most of his contemporaries, de Marees invoked women's sexuality to castigate the incivility of both men and women: all Africans were savage. The passage displays African males' savagery alongside their multiple access to women. Similarly, de Marees located evidence of African women's savagery in their unrestricted sexual desire. Given the association of unrestricted sexuality with native savagery, Black female sexuality alone might have been enough to implicate the entire continent. But de Marees further castigated West African women: they delivered children surrounded by men, women, and youngsters "in [a] most shamelesse manner . . . before them all."[51] This absence of shame (evoked explicitly, as here, or implicitly in the constant references to nakedness in other narratives) worked to establish distance. Readers, titillated by the topics discussed and thus tacitly shamed, found themselves further distanced from the shameless subject of the narrative. De Marees dwelt on the brute nature of shameless African women. He marveled that "when the child is borne [the mother] goes to the water to wash & make cleane her selfe, not once dreaming of a moneths lying in . . . as women here with us use to doe; they use no Nurses to helpe them when they lie in child-bed, neither seeke to lie dainty and soft. . . . The next day after, they goe abroad in the streets, to doe their businesse."[52] This testimony to African women's physical strength and emotional indifference is even more emphatic in the original Dutch. In the most recent translation from the Dutch, the passage continues: "This shows that the women here are of a cruder nature and stronger posture than the Females in our Lands in Europe."[53]

De Marees inscribed an image of women's reproductive identity whose influence persisted long after his original publication: "When [the child] is two or three moneths old, the mother ties the childe with a peece of cloth at her backe. . . . When the child crieth to sucke, the mother casteth one of her dugs backeward over her shoulder, and so the child suckes it as it hangs."[54] Frontispieces for the de Marees narrative and the African narratives in de Bry approximate the over-the-shoulder breastfeeding de Marees described, thereby creating an image that could symbolize the continent (see figs. 14, 15, and 16). The image was a compelling one, offering in a single narrative-visual moment evidence that Black women's difference was both cultural (in this strange *habit*) and physical (in this strange *ability*). The word *dug* (which by the early 1660s was used, according to the *Oxford English Dictionary,* to mean both a woman's breasts and an animal's teats) connoted a brute animality that de Marees reinforced through his description of small children "lying downe in their house, like Dogges, [and] rooting in the ground like Hogges" and of "boyes and girles [that] goe starke naked as they were borne, with their privie members all open, without any shame or civilitie."[55]

African women's African-ness seemed contingent on the linkages between sexuality and a savagery that fitted them for both productive and reproductive labor. Women enslaved in the seventeenth and early eighteenth centuries did not give birth to many children, but descriptions of African women in the Americas almost always highlighted their fecundity along with their capacity for manual labor.[56] Seventeenth-century English medical writers, both men and women, equated breastfeeding and tending to children with work.[57] Erroneous observations about African women's propensity for easy birth and breastfeeding reassured colonizers that these women could easily perform hard labor in the Americas while simultaneously erecting a barrier of difference between Africa and England. Sixteenth- and seventeenth-century English women and men anticipated pregnancy and childbirth with extreme uneasiness and fear of death, but at least they knew that the experience of pain in childbirth marked women as members of a Christian community.[58] African women entered the developing discourse of national resources via an emphasis on their mechanical and meaningless childbearing. Early on, metaphors of domestic livestock and sexually located cannibalism relied on notions of reproduction for consumption. By about the turn of the seventeenth century, as England joined in the

Fig. 14. Woman breastfeeding over her shoulder, title page from *Verum et Historicam Descriptionem Avriferi Regni Guineaa,* in Theodor de Bry, *Small Voyages,* vol. 6 (Frankfurt am Main, 1604). Note the contrast between this later depiction and the early representation of a Native American woman in figure 16. (Courtesy of the John Work Garrett Library of the Sheridan Libraries, Johns Hopkins University.)

transatlantic slave trade, assertions of African savagery began to be predicated less on consumption via cannibalism and more on production via reproduction. African women were materialized in the context of England's need for productivity. The image of utilitarian feeding implied a mechanistic approach to both childbirth and reproduction that ultimately became located within the national economy. Whereas English women's reproductive work took place solely in the domestic economy, African women's reproductive work could, indeed, embody the developing discourses of extraction and forced labor at the heart of England's national design for the colonies.[59]

By the eighteenth century, English writers rarely employed Black women's breasts or behavior for anything but concrete evidence of barbarism in Africa. In *A Description of the Coasts of North and South-Guinea . . . ,* begun in the 1680s and completed and published almost forty years later, John Barbot "admired the quietness of the poor babes, so carr'd about at their mother's backs . . . and how freely they suck the

Fig. 15. Women in Africa, from *Verum et Historicam Descriptionem Avriferi Regni Guineaa,* in Theodor de Bry, *Small Voyages,* vol. 6 (Frankfurt am Main, 1604), plate 3. (Courtesy of the John Work Garrett Library of the Sheridan Libraries, Johns Hopkins University.)

breasts, which are always full of milk, over their mother's shoulders, and sleep soundly in that odd posture."[60] William Snelgrave introduced his *New Account of Some Parts of Guinea and the Slave-trade* with an anecdote designed to illustrate the benevolence of the trade. He described himself rescuing an infant from human sacrifice and reuniting the child with its mother, who "had much Milk in her Breasts." He accented the barbarism of those who attempted to sacrifice the child and claimed that the reunion cemented his goodwill in the eyes of the enslaved, who, convinced of the "good notion of White Men," caused no problems during the voyage to Antigua.[61] Having utilized the figure of the breastfeeding woman to legitimize his slaving endeavor, Snelgrave went on to describe the roots of Whydah involvement in the slave trade and its defeat in war at the hands of the Kingdom of Dahomey (both coastal cities in present-day Ghana). "Custom of the Country allows Polygamy to an excessive degree . . . whereby the land was become so

Fig. 16. Native American woman with her child *(two views)*
from Thomas Hariot, *A brief and True Report of the New Found
Land of Virginia*, in Theodor de Bry, *Grand Voyages,* vol. 1
(Frankfurt am Main, 1590), plate 10. (Courtesy of the John
Work Garrett Library of the Sheridan Libraries, Johns Hopkins
University.)

stocked with people" that the slave trade flourished. Moreover, the
wealth generated by the trade made the beneficiaries so "proud, effem-
inate and luxurious" that they were easily conquered by the more dis-
ciplined (read masculine) nation of Dahomey.[62] Thus women's fecundity undermined African society from without and within as they
provided a constant stream of potential slaves.

Abolitionist John Atkins similarly adopted the icon of Black female
bodies in his writings on Guinea: "Childing, and their Breasts always
pendulous, stretches them to so unseemly a length and Bigness that
some . . . could suckle over their shoulder."[63] Atkins then considered the
idea of African women copulating with apes. He noted that "at some
places the Negroes have been suspected to Bestiality" and, while maintaining the ruse of scholarly distance, suggested that evidence "would

tempt one to suspect the Fact." The evidence lay mostly in apes' resemblance to humans but was bolstered by "the Ignorance and Stupidity [of Black women unable] to guide or controll lust."[64] Abolitionists and antiabolitionists alike accepted the connections between race, animality, the legitimacy of slavery, and Black women's monstrous and fecund bodies. By the 1770s, Edward Long's *History of Jamaica* presented readers with African women whose savagery was total, for whom enslavement was the only means of civility. Long maintained that "an oran-outang husband would [not] be any dishonour to an Hottentot female; for what are these Hottentots?"[65] He asserted as fact that sexual liaisons occurred between African women and apes. Nowhere did he make reference to any sort of African female shame or beauty. Rather, Long used women's bodies and behavior to justify and promote the mass enslavement of Africans. By the time he wrote, the association of Black people with beasts—via African women—had been cemented: "Their women are delivered with little or no labour; they have therefore no more occasion for midwifes than the female oran-outang, or any other wild animall. . . . Thus they seem exempted from the course inflicted upon Eve and *her daughters*."[66]

If African women gave birth without pain, they somehow sidestepped God's curse upon Eve. If they were not her descendants, they were not related to Europeans and could therefore be forced to labor on England's overseas plantations with impunity. Elaine Scarry has persuasively argued that the experience of pain—and thus the materiality of the body—lends a sense of reality and certainty to a society at times of crisis.[67] Early modern European women were so defined by their experience of pain in childbirth that an inability to feel pain was evidence of witchcraft.[68] In the case of England's contact with Africa and the Americas, the crisis in European identity was mediated by constructing an image of pain-free reproduction that diminished Africa's access to certainty and civilization, thus allowing for the mass appropriation that was the transatlantic slave trade.

After Richard Ligon saw the Black woman at Cape Verde, he pursued her around a dance hall, anxious to hear her voice, though she ultimately put him off with only "the loveliest smile that I have ever seen." The following morning he came upon two "prettie young Negro Virgins." Their clothing was arranged such that Ligon viewed "their breasts round, firm, and beautifully shaped." He demurred that he was unable "to expresse all the perfections of Nature, and Parts, these Virgins were owners of." Aware of the image of African womanhood already circulating in England, he assured his readers that these women should not be

confused with the women of "high Africa . . . that dwell nere the River
of Gambia, who are thick lipt, short nos'd, and commonly [have] low
forheads."[69] As though their breasts did not adequately set these women
apart, Ligon used these qualifiers to highlight the exception of their
beauty. As were many of his contemporaries, Ligon was quite willing to
find beauty and allure in women who were exceptional—not "of high
Africa"—but whose physiognomy and "education" marked them as improved by contact with Europe.[70]

In the face of Ligon's pursuit, these women, like the beautiful
woman he met the evening before, remained silent. Ligon tried, unsuc-
cessfully, to test the truth of their beauty through the sound of their
speech. Language had been a mark of monstrosity for centuries: Pliny
identified five of his monstrous races as such simply because they lacked
human speech.[71] It appears that decent language, like shame, denoted
civility for Ligon in the face of this inexplicable specter of female African
beauty. Finally, Ligon begged pardon for his dalliances and remarked
that he "had little else to say" about the otherwise desolate island.[72] To
speak of African beauty in this context, then, was justified.

When Ligon arrived in Barbados and settled on a five-hundred-
acre sugar plantation with one hundred slaves, African beauty—if it
ever really existed—dissolved in the face of racial slavery. He saw
African men and women carrying bunches of plantains: "'Tis a lovely
sight to see a hundred handsom Negroes, men and women, with every
one a grasse-green bunch of these fruits on their heads . . . the black
and green so well becoming one another." African people became comparable to vegetation and only passively and abstractly beautiful as
blocks of color. Ligon attested to their passivity with their servitude:
they made "very good servants, if they be not spoyled by the English."[73]
But if Ligon found interest in beauty, as Jobson did in shame, he ultimately equated Black people with animals. He declared that planters
bought slaves so that the "sexes may be equall . . . [because] they cannot live without Wives," although the enslaved choose their partners
much "as Cows do . . . for, the most of them are as near beasts as may
be."[74] When Ligon reinforced African women's animality with descriptions of breasts "hang[ing] down below their Navels," he tethered his
narrative to familiar images of Black women that—for readers nour-
ished on Hakluyt and de Bry—effectively naturalized the enslavement
of Africans. Like his predecessors, Ligon offered further proof of
Africans' capacity for physical labor—their aptitude for slavery—
through ease of childbearing: "In a fortnight [after giving birth] this
woman is at worke with her Pickaninny at her back, as merry a soule

as any is there."[75] In the Americas, African women's pain-free child-bearing thus continued to be central in the gendering of racism.

By the time the English made their way to the West Indies, decades of ideas and information about brown and Black women predated the actual encounter. In many ways, the encounter had already taken place in parlors and reading rooms on English soil, assuring that colonists would arrive with a battery of assumptions and predispositions about race, femininity, sexuality, and civilization.[76] Confronted with an Africa they needed to exploit, European writers turned to Black women as evidence of a cultural inferiority that ultimately became encoded as racial difference. Monstrous bodies became enmeshed with savage behavior as the icon of women's breasts became evidence of tangible barbarism. African women's "unwomanly" behavior evoked an immutable distance between Europe and Africa on which the development of racial slavery depended. By the mid-seventeenth century, that which had initially marked African women as unfamiliar—their sexually and reproductively bound savagery—had become familiar. To invoke it was to conjure up a gendered and racialized figure who marked the boundaries of English civility even as she naturalized the subjugation of Africans and their descendants in the Americas.

NOTES

1. Richard Ligon, *A True and Exact History of the Island of Barbadoes* (London, 1657), 12–13.

2. Thomas Browne, *Pseudodoxia Epidemica: or Enquiries into very many received tenents and commonly presumed truths* (1646), cited in Kim F. Hall, *Things of Darkness: Economies of Race and Gender in Early Modern England* (Williamsburg, Va.: William and Mary College, 1995), 12.

3. Peter Erickson, "Representations of Blacks and Blackness in the Renaissance," *Criticism,* 35 (1993): 514–15; Lynda Boose, "'The Getting of a Lawful Race': Racial Discourse in Early Modern England and the Unrepresentable Black Woman," in Margo Hendricks and Patricia Parker, eds., *Women, "Race," and Writing in the Early Modern Period* (London; New York: Routledge, 1994), 49; Hall, *Things of Darkness,* 4, 6–7.

4. Ligon, *True and Exact History . . . of Barbadoes,* 51.

5. In regard to "whiteness" as defined by "blackness," Toni Morrison asserts that "the fabrication of an Africanist persona is reflexive; an extraordinary meditation on the [white] self; a powerful exploration of the fears and desires that reside in the writerly conscious. It is an astonishing revelation of longing, of terror, of perplexity, of shame, of magnanimity. It requires hard work not to see this." See *Playing in the Dark: Whiteness and the Literary Imagination* (Cambridge: Harvard University Press, 1992), 17.

6. Peter Hulme, *Colonial Encounters: Europe and the Native Caribbean, 1492–1797* (London: Methuen, 1986), 11, 18.

7. P. F. Campbell, "Richard Ligon," *Journal of the Barbados Museum and Historical Society* 37 (1985): 259. For more on Ligon see Campbell, "Two Generations of Walronds," *Journal of the Barbados Museum and Historical Society* 38 (1989): 253–85.

8. Arguments about the primacy of race or gender regarding the original construction of difference constitute an enormous theoretical literature. See, for example, Henry Louis Gates Jr., "Writing, 'Race,' and the Difference It Makes," in Henry Louis Gates Jr., ed., *"Race," Writing and Difference* (Chicago: University of Chicago Press, 1985), 5, who asserts that "race has become a trope of ultimate, irreducible difference." Hortense J. Spillers similarly argues that slavery—the theft of the body—severed the captive from all that had been "gender-related [or] gender-specific" and thus was an "ungendering" process, in "Mama's Baby, Papa's Maybe: An American Grammar Book," *Diacritics* 17 (summer 1987): 65–81. I would posit that, rather than creating a hierarchy of difference, simultaneous categories of analysis illuminate the complexity of racialist discourse in the early modern period. See, for example, Anne McClintock, *Imperial Leather: Race, Gender and Sexuality in the Colonial Conquest* (New York: Routledge, 1995), 61, on the connections between categories of difference; Elsa Barkley Brown, "Polyrhythms and Improvisation: Lessons for Women's History," *History Workshop Journal* 31 (spring 1991): 85–90, on simultaneous categories of analysis; and Ania Loomba, "The Color of Patriarchy: Critical Difference, Cultural Difference, and Renaissance Drama," in Hendricks and Parker, *Women, "Race," and Writing,* 17–34, for cautions on the dangers of erecting hierarchies of difference.

9. Pliny, *Natural History in Ten Volumes,* vol. 2, trans. H. Rockham (Cambridge, Mass.: Harvard University Press, 1969), 509–27; Herodotus, *The History,* trans. David Grene (Chicago: University of Chicago Press, 1987) 4, 180, 191.

10. Richard Bernheimer, *Wild Men in the Middle Ages: A Study in Art, Sentiment, and Demonology* (Cambridge, Mass.: Harvard University Press, 1952), 33–41, quotation on 34. See also Peter Mason, *Deconstructing America: Representations of the Other* (New York: Routledge, 1990), 47–56.

11. *The Travels of Sir John Mandeville: The Version of the Cotton Manuscript in Modern Spelling,* ed. A. W. Pollard (London: 1915), 109, 119.

12. See McClintock, *Imperial Leather,* 22–23, for more on what she labels the "pornotropic" tradition of European eroticized writing on Africa and the Americas.

13. *A Treatyse of the Newe India by Sebastian Münster* (1553), trans. Richard Eden (microprint), (Ann Arbor, Mich.: 1966), [57]. See also Mason, *Deconstructing America,* 55, who links Vespucci's surprise at Indian women's firm breasts with expectations grounded in medieval imagery of wild women with sagging breasts. The language of "fylth" and shame also evoked sodomy and treachery for English readers. See Alan Bray, "Homosexuality and the Signs of Male Friendship in Elizabethan England," in Jonathan Goldberg, ed., *Queering the Renaissance* (Durham, N.C.: Duke University Press, 1994), 48. The wording of Münster's passage materializes many axes of difference.

14. It is significant that this association with sagging breasts, unusual childbearing, and monstrosity emerged so early. Not until the sixteenth century, for

example, did elite European women begin to use corsets to impose an elevated shape on their bodies, and only then did the elevated breasts of corseted women become a marker of refinement, courtliness, and status; Georges Vigarello, "The Upwards Training of the Body from the Age of Chivalry to Courtly Civility," in Michel Feher, Ramona Naddaff, and Nadia Tazi, eds., *Fragments for a History of the Human Body, Part Two* (Cambridge, Mass.: MIT Press, 1989), 154–55. Very soon thereafter, the "unused" breast, preserved among the elite by employing wet nurses for their children, embodied the "classic aesthetic ideal," according to Londa Schiebinger, "Why Mammals Are Called Mammals: Gender Politics in Eighteenth-Century Natural History," *American Historical Review* 98 (1993): 401.

15. Two years after the publication of Münster's *Treatyse*, Richard Eden translated and published Peter Martyr, *The Decades of the New Worlde of West India* (1533), (London, 1555), another description of the Columbus encounters.

16. Münster, *Treatyse*, [4]; Martyr, *Decades of the New Worlde*, 2.

17. Greenblatt discusses the role of the "go-between" through his analysis of Bernal Díaz's conquest narrative. He argues that Doña Marina, a native woman who becomes connected to the Spaniards, is the "object of exchange, agent of communication, model of conversion, the only figure who appears to understand the two cultures, the only person in whom they meet. . . . The site of the strategic symbolic oscillation between self and Other is the body of this woman." See Stephen Greenblatt, *Marvelous Possessions: The Wonder of the New World* (Chicago: University of Chicago, 1991), 143.

18. Münster, *Treatyse*, [5]; Martyr, *Decades of the New Worlde*, 3.

19. Indeed, the language of "increase" permeated seventeenth- and eighteenth-century slaveowners' probate records as planters in the West Indies and the southern colonies laid claim to enslaved women's productive and reproductive value; Jennifer Lyle Morgan, "Laboring Women: Enslaved Women, Reproduction, and Slavery in Barbados and South Carolina, 1650–1750" (Ph.D. diss., Duke University, 1995).

20. Münster, *Treatyse*, quoted in Louis Montrose, "The Work of Gender in the Discourse of Discovery," *Representations*, no. 33 (1991):4.

21. Montrose, "Work of Gender," 5. For more on gender and cannibalism see Carla Freccero, "Cannibalism, Homophobia, Women: Montaigne's 'Des cannibales' and 'De l'amitié,'" in Hendricks and Parker, *Women, "Race," and Writing,* 73–83; for the etymological relationship between Caribs and cannibalism see Hulme, *Colonial Encounters,* 13–42.

22. Girolamo Benzoni, *History of the New World* (1572), trans. W. H. Smyth (London, 1857), 3–4. Printed for the Hakluyt Society.

23. Greenblatt argues that "wonder is . . . the central figure in the initial European response to the New World, the decisive emotional and intellectual experience in the presence of radical difference," in *Marvelous Possessions,* 14.

24. Hall argues that "the painted woman often represents concerns over female unruliness, [and] the power of whiteness. . . . Male writers continually accuse women of hiding their 'blackness' under the fair disguise of cosmetics," in *Things of Darkness,* 89–90. See also Paul-Gabriel Bouce for an early eighteenth-century reference to popular English beliefs correlating the size of a woman's mouth to that of her vagina, in "Some Sexual Beliefs and Myths in Eighteenth-

Century Britain," in Paul-Gabriel Bouce, ed., *Sexuality in Eighteenth-Century Britain* (Totowa, N.J.: Manchester University Press, 1982), 29–46, esp. 31–32.

25. Benzoni, *History of the New World*, 8. For an example of the consequences of the Black Legend for English settlers in the Americas see Karen Ordahl Kupperman, *Providence Island, 1630–1641: The Other Puritan Colony* (Cambridge: Cambridge University Press, 1993), 92–96.

26. Walter Ralegh, "The discoverie of the large, rich, and beautifull Empire of Guiana," in Richard Hakluyt, *The Principal Navigations Voyages Traffiques and Discoveries of the English Nation* (1598–1600), 12 vols. (Glasgow: 1903–5), 10:391, cited in Montrose, "Work of Gender," 20.

27. Karen Robertson, "Pocahontas at the Masque," *Signs* 21, no. 3 (1996): 561, argues that "representation of an Indian woman does involve a dilemma for a male colonist, as expression of the erotic may signal his own lapse into savagery." See also Montrose, "Work of Gender," 21.

28. Benzoni, *History of the New World*, 11 (emphasis added).

29. In eighteenth-century England, writers intent on displaying the *natural* role of motherhood for English women idealized the "savage mother" and in doing so created tension as the dichotomy of civilized-English and savage-Other slipped; Felicity A. Nussbaum, *Torrid Zones: Maternity, Sexuality, and Empire in Eighteenth-Century English Narratives* (Baltimore: Johns Hopkins University Press, 1995), 48–53.

30. Hugh Honour, *The New Golden Land: European Images of America from the Discoveries to the Present Time* (New York: Pantheon Books, 1975), 54–55.

31. Theodor de Bry, ed., *Grand Voyages*, 13 vols. (Frankfurt am Main, 1590–1627). De Bry also published the series *Small Voyages*, 12 vols. (Frankfurt am Main, 1598–1628), chronicling voyages to Africa and the East Indies. Language training among the elite, particularly in Latin, meant that those with access to de Bry's volumes would possess the capacity to understand them. See Lawrence Stone, *The Crisis of the Aristocracy, 1558–1641* (Oxford: Clarendon Press, 1965), 672–702. For a discussion of the availability of books on reproduction and physiognomy see Patricia Crawford, "Sexual Knowledge in England, 1500–1750," in Roy Porter and Mikulas Teich, eds., *Sexual Knowledge, Sexual Science: The History of Attitudes to Sexuality* (Cambridge: Cambridge University Press, 1994), 86.

32. Bernadette Bucher, *Icon and Conquest: A Structural Analysis of the Illustrations of de Bry's Great Voyages,* trans. Basia Miller Gulati (Chicago: University of Chicago Press, 1981), 135, 145. Bucher's analysis includes a complex discussion of the morphology of consumption and an explanation that locates the reversal at the heart of anthropophagy in the icon of the sagging breasts. See Bucher, "Savage Women with Sagging Breasts," in *Icon and Conquest*, 73–120. For the formulation of the long-breasted woman in the Americas see also Mason, *Deconstructing America*, 47–60.

33. Emily C. Bartels, "Imperialist Beginnings: Richard Hakluyt and the Construction of Africa," *Criticism* 34 (1992): 519. See Winthrop D. Jordan, *White over Black: American Attitudes toward the Negro, 1550–1812* (Baltimore: Penguin Books, 1968), 3–43, for further discussion of the fluidity of images of Africa in the early modern European imagination. See also David Armitage, "The New

61

World and British Historical Thought: From Richard Hakluyt to William Robertson," in Karen Ordahl Kupperman, ed., *America in European Consciousness, 1493–1750* (Chapel Hill: University of North Carolina Press, 1995), 52–75. The Hakluyt collection served as "a mythico-historical amalgam intended to introduce . . . conquest and colonization to Europeans"; Bucher, *Icon and Conquest,* 22.

34. "The second voyage [of Master John Lok] to Guinea . . . 1554," in Hakluyt, *Principal Navigations* (1598–1600), 6:167, 168; see also Martyr, *Decades of the New Worlde,* 356. "Garamantes" originally occur in Pliny, who describes them as an Ethiopian race that did not practice marriage. See John Block Friedman, *The Monstrous Races in Medieval Art and Thought* (Cambridge: Harvard University Press, 1981), 15.

35. Martyr, *Decades of the New Worlde,* 356. In this paragraph, Martyr clearly borrows from Herodotus and Pliny.

36. William Towrson, "The first voyage made by Master William Towrson Marchant of London, to the coast of Guinea . . . in the yeere 1555," in Hakluyt, *Principal Navigations* (1598–1600), 6:184. Jordan notes that "many chroniclers [of Africa] made a point of discussing the Negro women's long breasts and ease of childbearing," in *White over Black,* 39–40. Schiebinger places the equation of African women's breasts with the udders of goats in a continuum of European imagery of, and relationship to, the breast. She notes that nineteenth-century ethnologists compared and classified breast size and shape much as they did skulls. Not surprisingly, they used African breasts, like African heads, to prove the linkage between Africans and animals. See Schiebinger, "Why Mammals Are Called Mammals," 402–3, 394. Philip D. Morgan asserts that "[Beginning with Richard Ligon,] Barbadians were the first coherent group within the Anglo-American world to portray blacks as beasts or as beastlike," in "British Encounters with Africans and African-Americans, circa 1600–1780," in Bernard Bailyn and Philip D. Morgan, eds., *Strangers within the Realm: Cultural Margins of the First British Empire* (Chapel Hill: University of North Carolina Press, 1991), 174.

37. Towrson, "The first voyage made by Master William Towrson," 187. Once he categorized them, Towrson relegated women to a passive role in the background of his interactions with Africans, despite the fact that they "worke as well as the men"; Towrson, "The first voyage made by Master William Towrson," 185.

38. Richard Jobson, *The Golden Trade, or a Discovery of the River Gambra . . . by Richard Jobson* (1628), London: Dawsons and Pall Mall, 1968).

39. Jobson, *Golden Trade,* 35.

40. Jobson, *Golden Trade,* 33.

41. Jobson, *Golden Trade,* 36.

42. Jobson, *Golden Trade,* 56 (emphasis added).

43. Unlike many of his contemporaries, Jobson leveled his open-eyed gaze primarily at male African sexuality. In a unique twist on the consequences of the curse of Ham, Jobson maintained that African men carried the mark of the curse in the size of their sexual organs: "[They] are furnisht with such members as are after a sort burthensome unto them, whereby their women being once conceived with child . . . accompanies the man no longer, because he

shall not destroy what is conceived." Jobson's interpretation of the penis corresponded to others' ideas about women's breasts. Both sexual organs are seen as pendulous and distended, somehow disembodied from their owner, and physically burdensome. Subsequently he returned to the subject of women only in terms of their subjugation to men, certain that "there is no other woman [that] can be under more servitude"; Jobson, *Golden Trade*, 58, 52, 54; and Greenblatt, *Marvelous Possessions*, 14.

44. Samuel Purchas, *Hakluytus Posthumus, or Purchas His Pilgrimes* (1624), 20 vols. (Glasgow: J. Maclehose and Sons, 1905).

45. "Observations of Africa, taken out of John Leo his nine Bookes, translated by Master Pory . . . ," in Purchas, *Hakluytus Posthumus*, 5:517.

46. "The Strange Adventures of Andrew Battell . . ." (1625), ed. E. G. Ravenstein, in Purchas, *Hakluytus Posthumus*, 6:367–517.

47. "Strange Adventures of Andrew Battell," 377–78.

48. "Strange Adventures of Andrew Battell," 32.

49. Pieter de Marees, *Description and Historical Account of the Gold Kingdom of Guinea* (1602), trans. and ed. Albert van Dantzig and Adam Jones (Oxford: 1987), xvii.

50. Pieter de Marees, "Description and historicall declaration of the golden Kingdome of Guinea," in Purchas, *Hakluytus Posthumus*, 6:251. Published for British Academy by Oxford University Press. I cite the Purchas edition rather than the modern edition so as to draw on the narrative that early modern English readers encountered.

51. De Marees, "Description and historicall declaration of the golden Kingdome of Guinea," 258–59.

52. De Marees, "Description and historicall declaration of the golden Kingdome of Guinea," 259.

53. De Marees, *Description and Historical Account of the Gold Kingdom of Guinea*, 23.

54. De Marees, "Description and historicall declaration of the golden Kingdome of Guinea," 259.

55. De Marees, "Description and historicall declaration of the golden Kingdome of Guinea," 261.

56. Jordan, *White over Black*, 39.

57. Marylynn Salmon, "The Cultural Significance of Breastfeeding and Infant Care in Early Modern England and America," *Journal of Social History*, 28 (1994): 247–70.

58. Linda Pollock, "Embarking on a Rough Passage: The Experience of Pregnancy in Early Modern Society," in Valerie Fildes, ed., *Women as Mothers in Pre-Industrial England* (New York: Random House, 1990), 45.

59. Ruth Perry argues that the valuation of "Motherhood" developed in England alongside empire so that not until the nineteenth-century did "the production of children for the nation and for the empire constitute childbearing women as a national resource," in "Colonizing the Breast: Sexuality and Maternity in Eighteenth-Century England," *Journal of the History of Sexuality* 2 (1991): 204, 205; see also Greenblatt, *Marvelous Possessions*, 7. Miranda Chaytor maintains that in seventeenth-century England only poor women had "laboring bodies," for as elite women withdrew from household production, their

"entire mental and physical lives" became sexualized and thus defined as non-productive, in "Husband(ry): Narratives of Rape in the Seventeenth-Century," *Gender and History* 7 (1995): 378–407, esp. 396–98.

60. John Barbot, *A Description of the Coasts of North and South-Guinea . . .* , in A. Churchill, ed., *A Collection of Voyages* (London, 1732), 36. See also J. D. Fage, " 'Good Red Herring': The Definitive Barbot," *Journal of African History* 34 (1993): 315–20.

61. William Snelgrave, introduction to *A New Account of Some Parts of Guinea and the Slave-trade* (1734), (London: F. Cass, 1971).

62. Ibid., 3–4.

63. John Atkins, *A Voyage to Guinea, Brazil, and the West-Indies* (1735), (London: F. Cass, 1970), 50.

64. Atkins, *A Voyage to Guinea, Brazil, and the West-Indies,* 108.

65. Edward Long, "History of Jamaica, 2, with notes and corrections by the Author" (1774), Add. Ms. 12405, p364/f295, British Library, London. Long was not alone in his delight at suggesting interspecies copulation. Londa Schiebinger details seventeenth- and eighteenth-century naturalists' investigations of apes. She notes that naturalists "ascribed to [simian] females the modesty they were hoping to find in their own wives and daughters, and to males the wildest fantasies of violent interspecies rape," in *Nature's Body: Gender in the Making of Modern Science* (Boston: Beacon, 1993), 75–114, quotation on 78.

66. Long, "History of Jamaica," p380/f304 (emphasis added).

67. Elaine Scarry, *The Body in Pain: The Making and Unmaking of the World* (New York: Oxford University Press, 1985), 15, 185–91; see also Spillers, "Mama's Baby, Papa's Maybe," 67–68, on the role of inflicted pain as a process of ungendering "female flesh" in slavery.

68. Lyndal Roper, *Oedipus and the Devil: Witchcraft, Sexuality and Religion in Early Modern Europe* (London and New York: Routledge, 1994), 203–4. See also Mary Poovey, *Uneven Developments: The Ideological Work of Gender in Mid-Victorian England* (Chicago: University of Chicago Press, 1988), 24–50, who shows that, during mid-nineteenth-century debates over anesthesia for women in childbirth, members of the medical and religious professions argued that to relieve women of pain would interfere with God and deprive women of the pain that ultimately civilized them. See also Diane Purkiss, "Women's Stories of Witchcraft in Early Modern England: The House, the Body, the Child," *Gender and History* 7 (1995): 408–32, for the connection between pain-free childbirth and accusations of witchcraft. On the connection between midwifery and accusations of witchcraft, Carol F. Karlsen notes that "the procreative nurturing and nursing roles of women were *perverted* by witches," in *The Devil in the Shape of a Woman: Witchcraft in Colonial New England* (New York: Routledge, 1989), 144.

69. Ligon, *True and Exact History . . . of Barbadoes,* 13, 15–16.

70. Another example can be found in John Gabriel Stedman's relationship to the mulatto woman Johanna in his *Narrative of a Five Years Expedition Against the Revolted Negroes of Surinam: Transcribed . . . from the Original 1790 Manuscript,* ed. Richard Price and Sally Price (Baltimore: Johns Hopkins University Press, 1988). His attempts to persuade this almost-English woman to return to Britain with him failed in part because she understood what he did not—that her status as "exceptional" was contingent on her location in Surinam. Had she

gone to England, she would have become, in effect, a "high African" woman. See Homi Bhabha, "Of Mimicry and Man: The Ambivalence of Colonial Discourse," *October* 28 (spring 1984): 108, for a discussion of the symbolic importance of those who occupy the borders of colonial spaces.

71. Friedman, *Monstrous Races in Medieval Art and Thought,* 29.

72. Ligon, *True and Exact History . . . of Barbadoes,* 17. Henry Louis Gates Jr. argues that the primary theme in African American literature is the quest for literacy, a response to white assertions that Blacks lacked "reason." Just as Phillis Wheatley's literacy had to be authenticated by thirteen white male signatories, so all African American writing was an oppositional demonstration of authentic intellect that "was a political act." Ligon's need to hear the voices of the Black women who excited his lust and curiosity suggests a precursor to the Black literary link between reading and reason. "The *spoken* language of black people had become an object of parody at least since 1769," says Gates, in *Figures in Black: Words, Signs, and the "Racial" Self* (New York and Oxford: Oxford University Press, 1987), 5–6 (emphasis added). Ligon wrote out of a period that predated that tradition of parody and instead located reason and civility in spoken language.

73. Ligon, *True and Exact History . . . of Barbadoes,* 44.

74. Ligon, *True and Exact History . . . of Barbadoes,* 47.

75. Ligon, *True and Exact History . . . of Barbadoes,* 51.

76. Greenblatt, *Marvelous Possessions,* 55.

Anne Fausto-Sterling

Gender, Race, and Nation

The Comparative Anatomy of "Hottentot" Women in Europe, 1815–17

A note about language use: Writing about nineteenth-century studies of race presents the modern writer with a problem: how to be faithful to the language usage of earlier periods without offending contemporary sensibilities. In this chapter I have chosen to capitalize words designating a race or a people. At the same time, I will use the appellations of the period about which I write. Hence I will render the French word *Negre* as Negro. Some nineteenth-century words, especially *Hottentot, primitive,* and *savage,* contain meanings that we know today as deeply racist. I will use these words without quotation marks when it seems obvious that they refer to nineteenth- rather than twentieth-century usage.

Introduction

In 1816 Saartjie Baartman, a South African woman whose original name is unknown and whose Dutch name had been anglicized to Sarah Bartmann, died in Paris. Depending upon the account, her death was caused by smallpox, pleurisy, or alcohol poisoning (Cuvier 1817; Lindfors 1983; Gray 1979). Georges Cuvier (1769–1832), one of the "fathers" of modern biology, claimed her body in the interests of science, offering a detailed account of its examination to the members of the French Museum of Natural History. Although now removed, as recently as the early 1980s a cast of her body along with her actual skeleton could be found on display in case #33 in the Musée de l'Homme in Paris; her preserved brain and a wax mold of her genitalia are stored in one of the museum's back rooms (Lindfors 1983; Gould 1985; Kirby 1953).[1]

During the last several years Bartmann's story has been retold by a number of writers (Altick 1978; Edwards and Walvin 1983; Gilman 1985).[2] These new accounts are significant. Just as during the nineteenth century she became a vehicle for the redefinition of our concepts of race, gender, and sexuality, her present recasting occurs in an era in which the bonds of empire have broken apart and the fabric of the cultural systems of the nations of the North Atlantic has come under critical scrutiny. In this chapter I once again tell the tale, focusing not on Bartmann but on the scientists who so relentlessly probed her body. During the period 1814–70 there were at least seven scientific descriptions of the bodies of women of color done in the tradition of classical comparative anatomy. What was the importance of these dissections to the scientists who did them and the society that supported them? What social, cultural, and personal work did these scientific forays accomplish, and how did they accomplish it? Why did the anatomical descriptions of women of color seem to be of such importance to biologists of the nineteenth century?

The colonial expansions of the eighteenth and nineteenth centuries shaped European science; Cuvier's dissection of Bartmann was a natural extension of that shaping. (By "natural" I mean that it seemed unexceptional to the scientists of that era; it appeared to be not merely *good* science; it was forward-looking.) But a close reading of the original scientific publications reveals the insecurity and angst about race and gender experienced by individual researchers and the European culture at large. These articles show how the French scientific elite of the early nineteenth century tried to lay their own fears to rest. That they did so at the expense of so many others is no small matter.

Constructing the Hottentot before 1800

Several of the African women who ended up on the comparative anatomists' dissecting tables were called Hottentots or, sometimes, Bushwomen. Yet the peoples whom the early Dutch explorers named Hottentot had been extinct as a coherent cultural group since the late 1600s (Elphick 1977). Initially I thought written and visual descriptions would help me figure out these women's "true" race; I quickly discovered, however, that even the depictions of something so seemingly objective as skin

67

color varied so widely that I now believe that questions of racial origin are like will-o'-the-wisps. Human racial difference, while in some sense obvious and therefore "real," is in another sense pure fabrication, a story written about the social relations of a particular historical time and then mapped onto available bodies.

As early as the sixteenth century, European travelers circling the world reported on the peoples they encountered. The earliest European engravings of nonwhites presented idyllic scenes. A depiction by Theodor de Bry from 1590, for example, shows Adam and Eve in the garden, with Native Americans farming peacefully in the background. The de Bry family images of the New World, however, transformed with time into savage and monstrous ones containing scenes of cannibalism and other horrors (Bucher 1981). Similarly, a representation of the Hottentots from 1595 (Raven-Hart 1967) shows two classically Greek-looking men standing in the foreground, with animals and a pastoral scene behind. A representation from 1627, however, tells a different story. A man and woman with yellow-brown skin stand in the foreground. The man's hair is tied in little topknots; his stature is stocky and less Adonis-like than before, and he looks angry. The woman, naked except for a loincloth, holds the entrails of an animal in her hand. One of her breasts is slung backward over her shoulder, and from it a child, clinging to her back, suckles. As we shall see, the drawings of explorers discussed here in turn became the working background (the cited literature) of the racial studies of the early nineteenth century, which are presented in a format designed to connote scientific certainty.

The Adamic visions of newly discovered lands brought with them a darker side. Amerigo Vespucci, whose feminized first name became that of the New World, wrote that the women went about "naked and libidinous; yet they have bodies which are tolerably beautiful" (Tiffany and Adams 1985, 64). Vespucci's innocents lived to be 150 years old, and giving birth caused them no inconvenience. Despite their being so at one with nature, Vespucci found Native American women immoral. They had special knowledge of how to enlarge their lovers' sex organs, induce miscarriages, and control their own fertility (Tiffany and Adams 1985). The early explorers linked the metaphor of the innocent virgin (both the women and the virgin land) with that of the wildly libidinous female. As one commentator puts it:

> Colonial discourse oscillates between these two master tropes, alternately positing the colonized "other" as blissfully ignorant, pure and welcoming as well as an uncontrollable, savage, wild

native whose chaotic, hysterical presence requires the imposition of the law, i.e., suppression of resistance. (Shohat 1991, 55)

From the start of the scientific revolution, scientists viewed the
earth or nature as female, a territory to be explored, exploited, and controlled (Merchant 1980). Newly discovered lands were personified as female, and it seems unsurprising that the women of these nations became
the locus of scientific inquiry. Identifying foreign lands as female helped
to naturalize their rape and exploitation, but the appearance on the
scene of "wild women" raised troubling questions about the status of
European women. Hence, it also became important to differentiate the
"savage" land/woman from the civilized female of Europe. The Hottentot in particular fascinated and preoccupied the nineteenth-century sci-
entist/explorer—the comparative anatomist who explored the body as
well as the earth. But just who were the Hottentots?

In 1652 the Dutch established a refreshment station at the Cape of
Good Hope, which not long after became a colonial settlement. The
people whom they first and most frequently encountered there were
pastoral nomads, short of stature, with light brown skin, and speaking a
language with unusual clicks. The Dutch called these people Hottentots,
although in the indigenous language they were called Khoikhoi, which
means "men of men." Within sixty years after the Dutch settlement, the
Khoikhoi, as an organized, independent culture, were extinct, ravaged
by smallpox and the encroachment of the Dutch. Individual descendants of the Khoikhoi continued to exist, and European references to
Hottentots may have referred to such people. Nevertheless, nineteenth-
century European scientists wrote about Hottentots, even though the
racial/cultural group that late-twentieth-century anthropologists believe
to merit that name had been extinct for at least three-quarters of a century. Furthermore, in the eighteenth and nineteenth centuries Europeans often used the word *Hottentot* interchangeably with the word
Bushman.[3] The Bushmen, or Khoisan, or hunter-gatherer Khoi, were
(and are) a physically similar but culturally distinct people who lived
contiguously with the Khoikhoi (Elphick 1977; Guenther 1980). They
speak a linguistically related language and have been the object/subject
of a long tradition of cultural readings by Euro-Americans (Haraway
1989; Lewin 1988; Lee 1992). In this chapter I look at studies with both
the word *Bushman/Bushwoman* and the word *Hottentot* in the titles. Cuvier, for example, argued vehemently that Sarah Bartmann was a Bushwoman and not a Hottentot. The importance of the distinction in his
mind will become apparent as the story unfolds.

69

Constructing the Hottentot in the
French Museum of Natural History

The encounters between women from southern Africa and the great men of European science began in the second decade of the nineteenth century when Henri de Blainville (1777–1850) and Georges Cuvier met Bartmann and described her for scientific circles, both when she was alive and after her death (Cuvier 1817; de Blainville 1816). We know a lot about these men who were so needful of exploring non-European bodies. Cuvier, a French Protestant, weathered the French Revolution in the countryside. He came to Paris in 1795 and quickly became the chair of anatomy of animals at the Museum of Natural History (Appel 1987; Flourens 1845). Cuvier's meteoric rise gave him considerable control over the future of French zoology. In short order he became secretary of the Académie des Sciences, an organization whose weekly meetings attracted the best scientists of the city; professor at the museum and the Collège de France; and member of the council of the university. Henri de Blainville started out under Cuvier's patronage. He completed medical school in 1808 and became an adjunct professor at the Faculté des Sciences, while also teaching some of Cuvier's courses at the museum. But by 1816, the year his publication on Sarah Bartmann appeared, he had broken with Cuvier. After obtaining a new patron, he managed, in 1825, to enter the Académie and eventually succeeded Cuvier, in 1832, as chair of comparative anatomy.

Cuvier and de Blainville worked at the Musée d'Histoire Naturelle, founded in 1793 by the Revolutionary Convention. It contained ever-growing collections and with its "magnificent facilities for research became the world center for the study of the life sciences" (Appel 1987, 11). Work done in France from 1793 to 1830 established the study of comparative anatomy, paleontology, morphology, and what many see as the structure of modern zoological taxonomy. Cuvier and de Blainville used the museum's extraordinary collections to write their key works. Here we see one of the direct links to the earlier periods of exploration. During prior centuries private collectors of great wealth amassed large cabinets filled with curiosities—cultural artifacts and strange animals and plants. It was these collections that enabled the eighteenth-century classifiers to begin their work.

Bruno Latour identifies this process of collection as a move that simultaneously established the power of Western science and domesticated the "savage" by making "the wilderness known in advance, predictable" (Latour 1987, 218). He connects scientific knowledge to a process of accumulation, a recurring cycle of voyages to distant places in which the ships returned laden with new maps, native plants, and sometimes even the native themselves. Explorers deposited these mobile information bits at centers, such as museums or the private collections that preceded them. Scientists possessed unique knowledge merely by working at these locations, which enabled them literally to place the world before their eyes without ever leaving their place of employ. Latour writes: "Thus the history of science is in large part the history of the mobilization of anything that can be made to move and shipped back home for this universal census" (Latour 1987, 225). Cuvier literally lived, "for nearly forty years, surrounded by the objects which engrossed so great a portion of his thoughts" (James 1830, 9). His house on the museum grounds connected directly to the anatomy museum and contained a suite of rooms, each of which held material on a particular subject. As he worked, he moved (along with his stove) from one room to the next, gathering his comparative information, transported from around the world to the comfort of his own home (Coleman 1964).

As centers of science acquired collections, however, they faced the prospect of becoming overwhelmed by the sheer volume of things collected. In order to manage the flood of information, scientists had to distill or summarize it. Cuvier, de Blainville, and others approached the inundation by developing coherent systems of animal classification. Thus the project of classification comprised one aspect of domesticating distant lands. The project extended from the most primitive and strange of animals and plants to the most complex and familiar. The history of classification must be read in this fashion; the attention paid by famous scientists to human anatomy cannot be painted on a separate canvas as if it were an odd or aberrant happening within the otherwise pure and noble history of biology.

During the French Revolution the cabinets of the wealthy who fled the conflict, as well as those from territories that France invaded, became part of the museum's collections. The cabinet of the Stadholder of Holland, for example, provided material for several of Cuvier's early papers. Appel describes the wealth of collected material:

> In 1822, the Cabinet contained 1500 mammals belonging to over 500 species, 1800 reptiles belonging to over 700 species, 5000 fishes from over 2000 species, 25,000 arthropods . . . and an unspecified number of molluscs. (Appel 1987, 35–36)

Cuvier's own comparative anatomy cabinet contained still more. He championed the idea that, in order to classify the animals, one must move beyond their mere surface similarities. Instead, one must gather facts and measurements from all of the internal parts. Without such comparative information, he believed, accurate classification of the animals became impossible. By 1822, among the 11,486 preparations in Cuvier's possession were a large number of human skeletons and skulls of different ages and races.

The human material did not innocently fall his way. In fact he had complained unbelievingly "that there is not yet, in any work, a detailed comparison of the skeletons of a Negro and a white" (Stocking 1982, 29). Wishing to bring the science of anatomy out of the realm of travelers' descriptions, Cuvier offered explicit instructions on how to procure human skeletons. He believed skulls to be the most important evidence, and he urged travelers to nab bodies whenever they observed a battle involving "savages." They must then "boil the bones in a solution of soda or caustic potash and rid them of their flesh in a matter of several hours" (Stocking 1982, 30). He also suggested methods of preserving skulls with flesh still intact, so that one could examine their facial forms.

As we shall see, Egyptian mummies—both animal and human—supplied another significant source that Cuvier used to develop and defend his theories of animal classification. These he obtained from the travels of his mentor-turned-colleague, and eventual archenemy, Étienne Geoffroy Saint-Hilaire. Geoffroy Saint-Hilaire spent several years in Egypt as part of the young general Napoléon Bonaparte's expedition. Cuvier declined the opportunity, writing that the real science could be done most efficiently by staying at home in the museum, where he had a worldwide collection of research objects at his fingertips (Outram 1984).[4] In 1798 Bonaparte took with him the Commission of Science and the Arts, which included many famous French intellectuals. During his years in Egypt, Geoffroy Saint-Hilaire collected large numbers of animals and, of particular importance to this story, several human and animal mummies. By 1800, British armies had defeated the French in Egypt; the capitulation agreement stipulated that the British were to receive all of the notes and collections obtained by the French savants while in Egypt. But in a heroic moment, Geoffroy Saint-Hilaire refused. In the end he kept everything but the Rosetta stone, which now resides in the British Museum (Appel 1987). Once again we see how the fortunes of modern European science intertwined with the vicissitudes of colonial expansion.

Cuvier and de Blainville used the technologies of dissection and comparative anatomy to create classifications. These reflected both their scientific and their religious accounts of the world, and it is from and through these that their views on race, gender, and nation emerge. In the eighteenth century the idea of biologically differing races remained undeveloped. When Linnaeus listed varieties of men in his *Systema Naturae* (1758), he emphasized that the differences between them appeared because of environment. There were, of course, crosscurrents. Proponents of the Great Chain of Being placed Hottentots and Negroes on a continuum linking orangutans and humans. Nevertheless, "eighteenth-century writers did not conceptualize human diversity in rigidly hereditarian or strictly physical terms" (Stocking 1991, 18).

Cuvier divided the animal world into four branches: the vertebrates, the articulates, the molluscs, and the radiates. He used the structure of the nervous system to assign animals to one of these four categories. As one of his successors and hagiographers wrote: "The nervous system is in effect the entire animal, and all the other systems are only there to serve and maintain it. It is the unity and the multiplicity of forms of the nervous system which defines the unity and multiplicity of the animal kingdom" (Flourens 1845, 98).[5] Cuvier expected to find similarities in structure within each branch of the animal world. He insisted, however, that the four branches themselves existed independently of one another. Despite similarities between animals within each of his branches, he believed that God had created each individual species (which he defined as animals that could have fertile matings). As tempting as the interrelatedness was to many of his contemporaries, Cuvier did not believe that one organism evolved into another. There were no missing links, only gaps put there purposely by the Creator. "What law is there," he asked, "which would force the Creator to form unnecessarily useless organisms simply in order to fill gaps in a scale?" (Appel 1987, 137)[6]

Cuvier's emphasis on the nervous system makes it obvious why he would consider the skull, which houses the brain, to be of utmost importance in assigning animals to particular categories. It takes on additional significance if one remembers that, unlike present-day taxonomists, Cuvier did not believe in evolution. At least in theory, he did not build the complex from the primitive, although his treatment of the human races turns out to be more than a little ambiguous in this regard. Instead he took the most complex as the model from which he derived all other structures. Because humans have the most intricate nervous system, they became the model to which all other systems compared. In each of his *Leçons d'anatomie comparée*, he began with human structures and developed those of other animals by comparison (Coleman 1964). In this sense, his entire zoological system was homocentric.

73

Cuvier's beliefs about human difference mirror the transition from an eighteenth-century emphasis on differences in levels of "civilization" to the nineteenth-century construction of race. His work on Sarah Bartmann embodies the contradictions such a transition inevitably brings. In 1790, for example, he scolded a friend for believing that Negroes and orangutans could have fertile matings and for thinking that Negroes' mental abilities could be explained by some alleged peculiarity in brain structure (Stocking 1982). By 1817, however, in his work on Sarah Bartmann, he brandished the skull of an Egyptian mummy, exclaiming that its structure proved that Egyptian civilization had been created by whites from whom present-day Europeans had descended (Cuvier 1817).[7]

Cuvier believed in theory that all humans came from a single creation, a view we today call monogeny. He delineated three races: Caucasians, Ethiopians (Negroes), and Mongolians. Despite uniting the three races under the banner of humanity (because they could interbreed), he found them to contain distinct physical differences, especially in the overall structure and shape of the head. One could not miss the invisible capabilities he read from the facial structures:

> It is not for nothing that the Caucasian race had gained dominion over the world and made the most rapid progress in the sciences while the Negroes are still sunken in slavery and the pleasures of the senses and the Chinese [lost] in the [obscurities] of a monosyllabic and hieroglyphic language. The shape of their head relates them somewhat more than us to the animals. (Coleman 1964, 166)

Cuvier, it is worth noting, was opposed to slavery. His was "a beneficent but haughty paternalism" (Coleman 1964, 167). In practice, however, his brother Frédéric, writing "under the authority of the administration of the Museum" (i.e., brother Georges), would include Georges Cuvier's description of Sarah Bartmann as the only example of the human species listed in his *Natural History of the Mammals* (Geoffroy Saint-Hilaire and Cuvier 1824, title page). Accompanying the article were two dramatic illustrations similar in size, style, and presentation to those offered for each of the forty-one species of monkeys and numerous other animals described in detail. The Hottentots' inclusion as the only humans in a book otherwise devoted to mammalian diversity suggests quite clearly Cuvier's ambivalence about monogeny and the separate creation of each species. Clearly, his religious belief system conflicted with his role in supporting European domination of more distant lands. Perhaps this internal conflict generated some of the urgency he felt about performing human dissections.

Other scientists of this period also linked human females with apes. While they differentiated white males from higher primates, using characteristics such as language, reason, and high culture, scholars used various forms of sexual anatomy—breasts, the presence of a hymen, the structure of the vaginal canal, and the placement of the urethral opening—to distinguish females from animals. Naturalists wrote that the breasts of female apes were flabby and pendulous—like those in the travelers' accounts of Hottentots (Schiebinger 1993). Cuvier's description of Sarah Bartmann repeats such "observations." The Hottentot worked as a double trope. As a woman of color, she served as a primitive primitive: she was both a female and a racial link to nature—two for the price of one.

Although Cuvier believed that the human races had probably developed separately for several thousand years, there were others, who we today call polygenists, who argued that the races were actually separate species (Stepan 1982). Presentations such as those in the *Natural History of the Mammals* provided fuel for the fire of polygeny. Cuvier's system of zoological classification, his focus on the nervous system, and his idea that species were created separately laid the foundations for the nineteenth-century concepts of race (Stocking 1982, 1990; Stepan 1982).

In Search of Sarah Bartmann

In contrast to what we know about her examiners, little about Bartmann is certain. What we do know comes from reading beneath the surface of newspaper reports, court proceedings, and scientific articles. We have nothing directly from her own hand. A historical record that has preserved a wealth of traces of the history of European men of science has left us only glimpses of the subjects they described. Hence, from the very outset, our knowledge of Sarah Bartmann is a construction, an effort to read between the lines of historical markings written from the viewpoint of a dominant culture. Even the most elementary information seems difficult to obtain. Cuvier wrote that she was twenty-six when they met and twenty-eight when she died, yet the inscription in the museum case that holds her body says that she was thirty-eight (Kirby 1949). She is said to have had two children by an African man, but de Blainville (1816) says that she had one child. One source says that the single child was dead by the time Bartmann arrived in Europe. According to some accounts, she was the daughter of a drover who had been killed by Bushmen. According to others, she was herself a Bushwoman (Altick 1978; Cuvier 1817). One London newspaper referred to her as "a Hottentot of a mixed race," while a twentieth-century writer wrote that he was "inclined to the view that she was a Bushwoman who possessed a certain proportion of alien blood" (Kirby 1949, 61).

Some sources state that Bartmann was taken in as a servant girl by a Boer family named Cezar. In 1810 Peter Cezar arranged to bring her to London, where he put her on exhibition in the Egyptian Hall of Piccadilly Circus.[8] She appeared on a platform raised two feet off the ground. A "keeper" ordered her to walk, sit, and stand, and when she sometimes refused to obey him, he threatened her. The whole "performance" so horrified some that abolitionists brought Cezar to court, charging that he held her in involuntary servitude. During the court hearing on 24 November 1810, the following claims emerged: The abolitionists charged that she was "clandestinely inveigled" from the Cape of Good Hope without the permission of the British governor, who was understood to be the guardian of the Hottentot nation "by reason of their general imbecile state" (Kirby 1953, 61). In his defense, her exhibitor presented a contractual agreement written in Dutch, possibly after the start of the court proceedings. In it Bartmann "agreed" (no mention is made of a signature, and I have not examined the original), in exchange for twelve guineas per year, to perform domestic duties for her master and to be viewed in public in England and Ireland "just as she was." The court did not issue a writ of habeas corpus because—according to secondhand accounts—Bartmann testified in Dutch that she was not sexually abused, that she came to London of her own free will in order to earn money, that she liked London and even had two "black boys" to serve her, but that she would like some warmer clothes. Her exhibition continued, and a year later, on 7 December 1811, she was baptized in Manchester, "Sarah Bartmann a female Hottentot of the Cape of Good Hope born on the Borders of Caffraria" (Kirby 1953, 61). At some point prior to 1814, she ended up in Paris, and in March 1815 a panal of zoologists and physiologists examined her for three days in the Jardin du Roi. During this time an artist painted the nude that appears in Geoffroy Saint-Hilaire and Cuvier's tome (1824). In December 1815 she died in Paris, apparently of smallpox, but helped along by a misdiagnosis of pleurisy and, according to Cuvier, by her own indulgence in strong drink.

Why was Bartmann's exhibition so popular? Prior to the nineteenth century there was a small population of people of color living in Great Britain. They included slaves, escaped slaves, and the children of freedmen sent to England for an education. Strinkingly, the vast majority of the nonwhite population in England was male. Thus, even though people of color lived in England in 1800, a nonwhite female was an unusual sight (Walvin 1973). This, however, is an insufficient explanation. We must also place Bartmann's experiences in at least two other contexts: the London entertainment scene and the evolving belief systems about sex, gender, and sexuality.

The shows of London and those that traveled about the countryside were popular forms of amusement. They displayed talking pigs, animal monsters, and human oddities—the Fattest Man on Earth, the Living Skeleton, fire-eaters, midgets, and giants. Bartmann's exhibition exemplifies an early version of ethnographic displays that became more complex during the nineteenth century. After her show closed, "the Venus of South America" appeared next. Tono Maria, a Botocudo Indian from Brazil, publicly displayed the scars (104 to be exact) she bore as punishment for adulterous acts. In time, the shows became more and more elaborate. In 1822 an entire grouping of Laplanders shown in the Egyptian Hall drew fifty-eight thousand visitors over a period of a few months. Then followed Eskimos and, subsequently, a "family grouping" of Zulus, all supposedly providing live demonstrations of their "native" behaviors. Such displays may be seen as a living, nineteenth-century version of the early-twentieth-century museum diorama, the sort that riveted my attention in the American Museum of Natural History when I was a child.[9] The dioramas, while supposedly providing scientifically accurate presentations of peoples of the world, instead offer a Euro-American vision of gender arrangements and the primitive that serves to set the supposedly "civilized" viewer apart, while at the same time offering the reassurance that women have always cooked and served and men have always hunted (Haraway 1989).

Sometimes the shows of exotic people of color involved complete fabrication. A Zulu warrior might really be a Black citizen of London, hired to play the part. One of the best documented examples of such "creativity" was the performer "Zip the What-is-it," hired and shown by P. T. Barnum. In one handbill, Zip was described as having been "captured by a party of adventurers while they were in search of the Gorilla. While exploring the river Gambia . . . they fell in with a race of beings never before discovered . . . in a PERFECTLY NUDE STATE, roving among the trees . . . in a manner common to the Monkey and the Orang Outang" (Lindfors 1983, 96). As it turns out, Zip was really William Henry Johnson, an African American from Bridgeport, Connecticut. He made what he found to be good money and in exchange kept mum about his identity. Interviewed in 1926, at the age of eighty-four, while still employed at Coney Island, he is reported to have said, "Well, we fooled 'em a long time, didn't we?" (Lindfors 1983, 98)

The London (and in fact European) show scene during the nineteenth century became a vehicle for creating visions of the nonwhite world.[10] As the century progressed, these visions "grew less representative of the African peoples they . . . were meant to portray. . . . Black Africa was presented as an exotic realm beyond the looking glass, a fantasy world populated by grotesque monsters—fat-arsed females, bloodthirsty warriors, pre-verbal pinheads, midgets and geeks" (Lindfors 1983, 100). From this vision Britain's "civilizing colonial mission" drew great strength. And it is also from this vision, this reflection of the other, that Europe's self-image derived; the presentation of the exotic requires a definition of the normal. It is this borderline between normal and abnormal that Bartmann's presentation helped to define for the Euro-American woman.

Bartmann's display linked the notion of the wild or savage female with one of dangerous or uncontrollable sexuality. At the "performance's" opening, she appeared caged, rocking back and forth to emphasize her supposedly wild and potentially dangerous nature. The London Times reported: "She is dressed in a colour as nearly resembling her skin as possible. The dress is contrived to exhibit the entire frame of her body, and spectators are even invited to examine the peculiarities of her form" (Kirby 1949, 58). One eyewitness recounted with horror the poking and pushing Bartmann endured, as people tried to see for themselves whether her buttocks were the real thing. Prurient interest in Bartmann became explicit in the rude street ballads and equally prurient cartoons that focused on her steatopygous backside.[11]

According to the Oxford English Dictionary, the term steatopygia (from the roots for fat and buttocks) was used as early as 1822 in a traveler's account of South Africa, but the observer said the "condition" was not characteristic of all Hottentots nor, for that matter, characteristic of any particular people. Later in the century, what had been essentially a curiosity found its way into medical textbooks as an abnormality. According to Gilman, by the middle of the nineteenth century the buttocks had become a clear symbol of female sexuality, and the intense interest in the backside a displacement for fascination with the genitalia. Gilman concludes, "Female sexuality is linked to the image of the buttocks, and the quintessential buttocks are those of the hottentot" (Gilman 1985, 210).[12] Female sexuality may not have been the only thing at stake in all of the focus on Bartmann's backside. In this same historical period, a new sexual discourse on sodomy also developed. Male prostitutes, often dressed as women, walked the streets of London (Trumbach 1991), and certainly at a later date the enlarged buttocks became associated with female prostitution (Gilman 1985). Until more historical work is done, possible relationships between cultural constructions of the sodomitical body and those of the steatopygous African woman will remain a matter of speculation.

Bartmann's story does not end in England. Her presentation in Paris evoked a great stir as well. There was a lively market in prints showing her in full profile; crowds went to see her perform. And she became the subject of satirical cartoons filled with not particularly subtle sexual innuendo. The French male's sexual interest in the exotic even became part of a one-act vaudeville play in which the male protagonist declares that he will love only an exotic woman. His good, white, middle-class cousin, in love with him, but unable to attract his attention, disguises herself as the Hottentot Venus, with whom he falls in love, making the appropriate mating, even after the fraud is revealed. (The full story has many more twists and turns, but this is the "Cliffs Notes plot"[Lindfors 1983, 100].)

Of all the retellings of Bartmann's story, only Gould's attempts to give some insight into Bartmann's own feelings. We can never see her except through the eyes of the white men who described her. From them we can glean the following. First, for all her "savageness," she spoke English, Dutch, and a little French. Cuvier found her to have a lively, intelligent mind; an excellent memory; and a good ear for music. The question of her own complicity in and resistance to her exploitation is a very modern one. The evidence is scant. During her "performances" "she frequently heaved deep sighs; seemed anxious and uneasy; grew sullen, when she was ordered to play on some rude instrument of music" (Altick 1978, 270). Writing in the third person, de Blainville, who examined her in the Jardin du Roi, reported the following:

> Sarah appears good, sweet and timid, very easy to manage when one pleases her, cantankerous and stubborn in the contrary case. She appears to have a sense of modesty or at least we had a very difficult time convincing her to allow herself to be seen nude, and she scarcely wished to remove for even a moment the handkerchief with which she hid her organs of generation. . . . [H]er moods were very changeable; when one believed her to be tranquil and well-occupied with something, suddenly a desire to do something else would be born in her. Without being

angry, she would easily strike someone. . . . [S]he took a dislike to M. de Blainville, probably because he came too near to her, and pestered her in order to obtain material for his description; although she loved money, she refused what he offered her in an effort to make her more docile. . . . She appeared to love to sleep; she preferred meat, especially chicken and rabbit, loved (alcoholic) spirits even more and didn't smoke, but chewed tobacco. (de Blainville 1816, 189)

In this passage, de Blainville expressed the same conflicts evinced two centuries earlier by Vespucci. He found Bartmann to be modest, good, sweet, and timid (like any modern, "civilized" Frenchwoman), but he could not reconcile this observation with what seemed to him to be the remnants of some irrational wildness (including habits such as chewing tobacco), which were out of line for any female he would wish to call civilized.

It is also worth comparing de Blainville's language to that used by Geoffroy Saint-Hilaire and F. Cuvier in the *Natural History of the Mammals*. In the section describing *Cynocephalus* monkeys (which follows immediately on the heels of Sarah Bartmann's description), they write that "one can see them pass in an instant from affection to hostility, from anger to love, from indifference to rage, without any apparent cause for their sudden changes" (Geoffroy Saint-Hilaire and Cuvier 1824, 2). They write further that the monkeys are "very lascivious, always disposed to couple, and very different from other animals, the females receive the males even after conception" (Geoffroy Saint-Hilaire and Cuvier 1824, 3). Clearly, de Blainville's language echoes through this passage, framing the scientists' concerns about human animality and sexuality.

Constructing the (Nonwhite) Female

Although Bartmann was a theater attraction and the object of a legal dispute about slavery in England, it was in Paris, before and after her death, that she entered into the scientific accounting of race and gender. This part of the story takes us from Sarah's meeting with scientists in the Jardin du Roi to her death, preservation, and dissection by Georges Cuvier—and to other scientific and medical dissections of nonwhites in the period from 1815 to, at least, the 1870s.[13]

The printed version of de Blainville's report to the Société Philomatique de Paris (given orally in December 1815 and appearing in the so-ciety's proceedings in 1816) offers two purposes for the publication. The first is "a detailed comparison of this woman [Sarah Bartmann] with the lowest race of humans, the Negro race, and with the highest race of monkeys, the orangutan," and the second is to provide "the most complete account possible of the anomaly of her reproductive organs" (de Blainville 1816, 183). De Blainville accomplished his first purpose more completely than his second. On more than four occasions in this short paper he differentiates Bartmann from "Negroes" and throughout the article suggests the similarity of various body structures to those of the orangutan.

De Blainville began with an overall description of Sarah Bartmann's body shape and head. He then systematically described her cranium (one paragraph), her ears (two long, detailed paragraphs), her eyes (one paragraph), and other aspects of her face (five paragraphs, including one each devoted to her nose, teeth, and lips). In terms of printed space, her facial structure was the most important aspect. The final segment of his paper includes brief accounts (one paragraph each) of her neck, trunk, and breasts. In addition, he briefly described her legs, arms, and joints, devoting a full paragraph, complete with measurements, to her steatopygous buttocks.

De Blainville's attempts to get a good look at her pudendum, espe-cially at the "hottentot apron," which Cuvier finally succeeded in de-scribing only after her death, were foiled by her modesty (see earlier discussion). Despite this, de Blainville offers three full paragraphs of description. He verbally sketches the pubis, mentioning its sparse hair covering and lamenting that, from a frontal view, one could not see the vaginal labia majora but stating that, when she leaned over or when one watched from behind as she walked, one could see hanging appendages that were probably the sought-after elongated labia minora.

De Blainville's ambivalences emerge clearly in the written text. He placed Bartmann among other females by reporting that she menstru-ated regularly, "like other women," but noted that she wasn't really like white women because her periodic flow "appear[ed] less abundant" (de Blainville 1816, 183). (Debates about menstruation from the turn of the eighteenth century considered menstruation a measure of full human-ity; the heavier the flow, the higher one's place in nature [Schiebinger 1993].) Although the person who showed her in Paris claimed that she had a highly aggressive sexual appetite—one day even throwing herself on top of a man she desired—de Blainville doubted the truth of the spe-cific incident. Not to have her too closely linked to European women,

however, he also suggests that the modesty he observed might have resulted from her presence for some years among Europeans, conceding
that, even after so many years, "it is possible that there still remained
something of the original" (de Blainville 1816, 183). Finally, de Blainville suggests "that the extraordinary organization which this woman offers" (de Blainville 1816, 189) is probably natural to her race, rather
than being pathological. In support of his contention, he cites travelers
who found the same peculiarities—of jaws, buttocks, and labia—among
"natives" living in their home environments. Hence, he finishes with the
assertion of natural racial difference.

In de Blainville's text different parts of the body carry specific meanings. To compare the Negro and the orangutan, he spends paragraphs on
detailed descriptions of the head, face, jaws, and lips. He uses these to
link Hottentots to orangs, writing that the general form of the head and
the details of its various parts, taken together, make clear that Hottentots
more closely resemble orangs than they do Negroes. He repeatedly invokes Pieter Camper's facial angle (Gould 1981; Russett 1989), the shape
and placement of the jaws, and—in somewhat excruciating detail—the
arrangement and structure of the ears. These passages evoke the tradition
of physiognomy elaborated by Lavater (1775–78), whose work, widely
translated into French and other languages, offered a basis for Gall's
phrenology and a method of using the face to read the internal workings
of animals. Of humans Lavater wrote:

> The intellectual life . . . would reside in the head and have the
> eye for its center . . . the forehead, to the eyebrows, [will] be a
> mirror . . . of the understandings; the nose and cheeks the
> image of the moral and sensitive life; the mouth and chin the
> image of the animal life. (Graham 1979, 48)

When de Blainville and then Cuvier offered detailed comparisons between Sarah Bartmann's cheeks and nose and those of Caucasians, they
set forth more than a set of dry descriptions. Her "moral and sensitive
life" lay evident upon the surface of her face.[14]

It is to the description of the genitalia that de Blainville turns to
place Bartmann among women. Here he balances his belief in the civilizing effects of Europe against a scarcely hidden savage libido. The gender norms of white women appear as a backdrop for the consideration
of "savage" sexuality. Although he gave detailed descriptions of most of
her exterior, de Blainville did not succeed in fully examining Bartmann's
genitalia. Where he failed on the living woman, Cuvier succeeded after

her death. Clearly a full account of this "primitive woman's" genitalia was essential to putting her finally in her appropriate place. By exposing them to what passed for scientific scrutiny, Cuvier provided the means to control the previously uncontrollable. Triumphantly, he opened his presentation to the French Academy with the following: "There is nothing more celebrated in natural history than the Hottentot apron, and at the same time there is nothing which has been the object of such great argumentation" (Cuvier 1817, 259). Cuvier set the stage to settle the arguments once and for all.

Twentieth-century scientific reports open with an introduction that uses previously published journal articles to provide background and justification for the report to follow. In Cuvier's piece we see the transition to this modern format from an older, more anecdotal style. Rather than relying on official scientific publications, however, Cuvier relied on travelers' accounts of the apron and the steatopygia. In later works, although these anecdotal, eyewitness testimonials fade from sight, they remain the source for knowledge incorporated into a more "objective" scientific literature. (Sexologists William Masters and Virginia E. Johnson, for example, in their scientifically dispassionate work *Human Sexual Response* include a claim that African women elongate their vaginal labia by physical manipulation; their cited source is a decidedly unscientific [by modern standards] compendium of female physical oddities that dates from the 1930s but draws on nineteenth-century literature of the sort discussed here [Masters and Johnson 1966, 58].)

To set the stage for his revelations about the Hottentot apron, Cuvier first needed to provide a racial identity for his cadaver (which he referred to throughout the article as "my Bushwoman"). Travelers' accounts indicated that Bushmen were a people who lived much deeper in "the interior of lands" than did Hottentots. The apron and enlarged buttocks were peculiarly theirs, disappearing when they interbred with true Hottentots. Cuvier believed that the confusion between Bushmen and Hottentots explained the inconsistent nature of travelers' reports, since some voyagers to the Cape of Good Hope claimed sightings of the Hottentot apron, while others did not. Nevertheless, he had to admit that many people did not believe in the existence of a Bushman nation. Cuvier threw his weight behind what he believed to be the accumulation of evidence: that there existed "beings almost entirely savage who infested certain parts of the Cape colony . . . who built a sort of nest in the tufts of the brush; they originated from a race from the interior of Africa and were equally distinct from the Kaffir and the Hottentot" (Cuvier 1817, 261). Cuvier believed that the Bushman social structure had degenerated, so that eventually "they knew neither government nor proprieties; they scarcely organized themselves into families and then only when passion excited them. . . . They subsisted only by robbery and hunting, lived only in caves and covered their bodies with the skins of animals they had killed" (Cuvier 1817, 261). By naming Bartmann as a Bushwoman, Cuvier created her as the most primitive of all humans—a female exemplar of a degenerate, barely human race. Despite his lack of belief in evolution, he constructed her as the missing link between humans and apes.

To the modern reader, several noteworthy aspects emerge from these introductory passages. First, Cuvier melds the vision of an interior or hidden Africa with the hidden or interior genitalia of the Hottentot Venus. This becomes even clearer in subsequent passages in which, like de Blainville, he complains that when he examined her as a living nude in the Jardin du Roi in 1815 she "carefully hid her apron either between her thighs or more deeply" (Cuvier 1817, 265). Second, he connects a hidden (and hypothetical) people from the deep African interior with an animal-like primitiveness. The passage about making nests from brush tufts evokes monkey and ape behaviors (chimps sleep each night in nests they weave from tree branches). Cuvier's goal in this paper was to render visible the hidden African nations and the hidden genitalia. By exposing them he hoped to disempower, to use observation to bring these unknown elements under scientific control. In the remainder of the account, Cuvier devoted himself simultaneously to the tasks of racial and sexual localization. Where among humans did these interior people belong, and what did their women conceal in their body cavities?

In his presentation to the members of the Museum of Natural History, Cuvier moved from a description of the exterior, living, and never quite controllable Bartmann (for he needed her permission to examine her hidden parts) to the compliant cadaver laid out before him, now unable at last to resist his deepest probings. In both life and death Sarah Bartmann was a vessel of contradictions. He found that her "sudden and capricious" movements resembled those of a monkey, while her lips protruded like those of an orangutan. Yet he noted that she spoke several languages, had a good ear for music, and possessed a good memory. Nevertheless, Cuvier's vision of the savage emerged: belts and necklaces of glass beads "and other savage attires" pleased her, but more than anything she had developed an insatiable taste for "l'eau-de-vie" (Cuvier 1817, 263).

For fully one-fifth of the paper we read of her exterior. Cuvier paints what he clearly found to be a picture gruesome in its contradictory aspects. Only four and a half feet tall, she had enormous hips and buttocks but otherwise normal body parts. Her shoulders and back were graceful, the protrusion of her chest not excessive, her arms slender and well made, her hands charming, and her feet pretty. But her physiognomy—her face—repelled him. In the jutting of the jaw, the oblique angle of her incisors, and the shortness of her chin, she looked like a Negro. In the enormity of her cheeks, the flatness of the base of her nose, and her narrow eye slits, she resembled a Mongol. Her ears, he felt, resembled those of several different kinds of monkeys. When finally, in the spring of 1815, she agreed to pose nude for a painting, Cuvier reported the truth of the stories about the enormity of her protruding buttocks and breasts—enormous hanging masses—and her barely pilous pubis.[15]

When she died, on 29 December 1815, the police prefect gave Cuvier permission to take the body to the museum, where his first task became to find and describe her hidden vaginal appendages. For a page and a half the reader learns of the appearance, folded and unfolded, of the vaginal lips, of their angle of joining, the measurements of their length (more than four inches—although Blumenbach reportedly had drawings of others whose apron extended for up to eight inches) and thickness, and the manner in which they cover the vulval opening. These he compared to analogous parts in European women, pointing out the considerable variation and stating that in general the inner vaginal lips are more developed in women from warmer climates. The variation in vaginal development had, indeed, been recognized by French anatomists, but a mere ten years earlier, medical writers had failed to connect differences in vaginal structures to either southern races or nonwhite women. In a straightforward account of "over-development" of vaginal lips, Dr. M. Baillie, a British physician and member of the Royal Society of Medicine of London (whose book was translated into French in 1807), wrote matter-of-factly of this variation, listing it among a number of genital anomalies but not connecting it to non-European women (Baillie 1807). As Gilman (1985) points out, however, by the middle of the nineteenth century elongated labia had taken their place in medical textbooks alongside accounts of enlarged clitorises, both described as genital abnormalities, rather than as part of a wide range of "normal" human variation.

Cuvier acknowledged the great variation in length of the inner vaginal lips found even among European women. But nothing, he felt, compared to those of "negresses" and "abyssynians," whose lips grew so large that they became uncomfortable, obliging their destruction by an operation carried out on young girls at about the same age that Abyssinian boys were circumcised. As an aside that served to establish a norm for vaginal structure and a warning to those whose bodies did not conform, we learn that the Portuguese Jesuits tried in the sixteenth century to outlaw this practice, believing that it was a holdover from ancient Judaism. But the now-Catholic girls could no longer find husbands because the men wouldn't put up with such "a disgusting deformity" (Cuvier 1817, 267); finally, with the authorization of the Pope, permission was made possible by a surgeon's verification that the elongated lips were natural rather than the result of manipulation, and the ancient custom resumed.

Cuvier contrasts the vaginal lips of Bushwomen with those of monkeys, the near invisibility of which provided no evidence to link them to these primitive humans. But the steatopygia was another matter. Bartmann's buttocks, Cuvier believed, bore a striking resemblance to the genital swellings of female mandrills and baboons, which grow to "monstrous proportions" at certain times in their lives. Cuvier wanted to know whether the pelvic bone had developed any peculiar structures as a result of carting around such a heavy load. To answer the question, he made use of his well-established method of comparative anatomy, placing side by side the pelvis of "his bushwoman," those of "negresses," and those of different white women. In considering Bartmann's small overall size, Cuvier found her pelvis to be proportionally smaller and less flared, the anterior ridge of one of the bones thicker and more curved in back, and the ischial symphysis thicker: "All these characters, in an almost unnoticeable fashion, resemble one another in Negro women, and female Bushwomen and monkeys" (Cuvier 1817, 269). Just as the differences themselves were practically imperceptible, amidst a welter of measurement and description, Cuvier imperceptibly separated the tamed and manageable European woman from the wild and previously unknown African.

But something worried Cuvier. In his collection he had also a skeleton of a woman from the Canary Islands. She came from a group called the Guanche (extinct since shortly after the Spanish settlement), a people who inhabited the islands before the Spanish and who, by all accounts, were Caucasians. An astonished Cuvier reported to his colleagues that he found the most marked of Bartmann's characteristics not in the skeleton of Negro women but in that of the Canary Islander. Since he had too few complete skeletons to assess the reliability of these similarities, he turned finally to more abundant material. In the last part of his account, he compares the head and skull (which "one has always used to classify nations" [Cuvier 1817, 270]) of "our Bushwoman" with those of others in his collection.

Bartmann's skull, he wrote, mixed together the features of the Negro and the Mongol, but, chiefly, Cuvier declared that he "had never seen a human head more similar to those of monkeys" (Cuvier 1817, 271). After offering more detailed comparisons of various bones in the skull, Cuvier returned in the last few pages of his paper to the problem that concerned him at the outset—did the Bushmen really exist as a legitimate people, and just how far into the interior of Africa did they extend? Here he relied once more on travelers' reports. Although modern voyagers did not report such people in northern Africa, Herodotus and others described a group that seemed in stature and skin color to resemble the Bushmen. According to some sources, these people invaded Abyssinia, although the evidence in Cuvier's view was too prescientific to rely on. But he could be sure of one thing. Neither the

> Bushmen, nor any race of Negros, gave birth to the celebrated people who established civilization in ancient Egypt and from whom one could say that the entire world had inherited the principles of law, science and perhaps even religion. (Cuvier 1817, 273)

At least one modern author had suggested that the ancient Egyptians were Negroes with wooly hair, but Cuvier could be sure that this, too, was in error. All he needed to do was compare the skulls of ancient Egyptians with those of the pretender races. One can picture him, as he spoke, dramatically producing from beneath his dissecting table the skulls of Egyptian mummies, those very same ones brought back by Geoffroy Saint-Hilaire from the Napoleonic incursion into Egypt.

Cuvier studied the skulls of more than fifty mummies. These, he pointed out, had the same skin color and large cranial capacity as modern Europeans. They provided further evidence for "that cruel law that seems to have condemned to eternal inferiority those races with depressed and compressed crania" (Cuvier 1817, 273). And finally, he presented to his museum colleagues that skull of the Canary Islander whose skeleton had so troublingly resembled Bartmann's. This too "announced a Caucasian origin" (Cuvier 1817, 274), which is the phrase that concludes his report. In this last section of his paper we watch him struggle with his data. First, he realized that he had a Caucasian skeleton that looked identical to Bartmann's. If he could not explain this away (what modern scientists call eliminating outliers—data points that don't neatly fit an expected graph line), his thesis that Bushmen represented a primitive form of humanity was in trouble. But that wasn't all that worried him: if his thesis was in trouble, so too was the claim of European superiority on which European and American colonization, enslavement, and disenfranchisement so depended. Thus, he went to considerable trouble to explain away the Guanche skeleton; ultimately he succeeded by using the scientific spoils of colonial expansion—the Egyptian mummies captured during Napoleon's Egyptian campaign.

Conclusion

This chapter places the scientific study of nonwhite women in several contexts. The investigations were, to be sure, part of the history of biology and, especially, a component of the movement to catalog and classify all the living creatures of the earth. But this movement was in turn embedded in the process of European capitalist expansion. Not only did traders and conquerers, by collecting from around the world, create the need for a classification project, but they also required the project to justify continued expansion, colonialism, and slavery. Further entangling the matter, the vast capital used to build the museums and house the collections came from the economic exploitation of non-European goods—both human and otherwise. This entire chapter is an argument against a narrowly constructed historiography of science; instead, I more broadly socialize the history of Euro-American biology in the first quarter of the nineteenth century by exposing its intersections with gender, race, and nation.

If one looks at the process less globally, one sees Cuvier and de Blainville as significant actors in a period of scientific change. From the perspective of the history of Euro-American biology, parochially extracted from its role in world expansion, one can say that the biologists of this period, and Cuvier in particular, made enormous scientific progress with the "discovery of the great information content of the internal anatomy of the invertebrates" (Mayr 1982, 183). According to this view, Cuvier "discovered" the importance of the nervous system as a way to organize animals. But "Cuvier's vision of the animal world was deeply coloured by that of the human society in which he was forced to make his way" (Outram 1984, 65). Far from reflecting some underlying natural system, Cuvier's use of the nervous system in his classification schemes had a homocentric starting point. The ideas formed a meshwork. Cuvier gave the focus on the nervous system and brain (obtained from his conviction that classification should proceed from the most complex—in this case human—structure to the simplest) the status of scientific fact by developing a reasonably coherent story about how the structure of the nervous system enabled him to classify all animals. Once scientists agreed on the validity of Cuvier's animal classification scheme, this agreement fed back on the question of human classification. It seemed only "natural" to focus on the structure of the brain (as reflected in cranial and facial characteristics) to obtain evidence about the relative standing of the human races.

Sarah Bartmann's story is shocking to modern sensibilities. The racism of the period seems obvious—even laughable. But in the rush to create distance between nineteenth-century racist science and our modern, putatively less racist selves, even highly sophisticated scholars often lose sight of an important point. The loss becomes evident when I am asked (as I frequently am) what the *real* truth about Bartmann was. Just how big were those forbidden parts? The question reflects an ongoing belief in the possibility of an objective science. It suggests that, now that we have escaped all that silly racism of the nineteenth century, we ought to be able to get out our measuring tapes and find the real truth about other people's bodies. In this chapter I argue that Bartmann's bodily differences were constructed using the social and scientific paradigms available at the time. The historical record tells us nothing about her agency; we can only know how Europeans framed and read her. Were she somehow magically alive today, contemporary biologists or anthropologists might frame and read her differently, but it would be a framing and reading, nevertheless. One contemporary difference might be that the varying worldwide liberation movements could offer her a context in which to contest the constructions of Euro-American science. In fact we see such contestations regularly in debates over such questions as brain size, race, and IQ (Maddock 1992; Schluter and Lynn 1992; Becker, Rushton, and Ankney 1992); brain shape and gender; and genetics and homosexuality (Fausto-Sterling 1992).

In *Playing in the Dark,* Toni Morrison (1992) makes her intellectual project "an effort to avert the critical gaze from the racial object to the racial subject; from the described and imagined to the describers and imaginers" (Morrison 1992, 90). By analogy I look at the fears and anxieties of the scientists, rather than worrying about the (in)accuracies of their descriptions of Sarah Bartmann and other people of color. To quote further from Morrison:

The fabrication of an Africanist persona is reflexive; an extraordinary meditation on the self; a powerful exploration of the fears and desires that reside in the writerly conscious. It is an astonishing revelation of longing, of terror, of perplexity, of shame, of magnaminity. It requires hard work *not* to see this. (Morrison 1992, 17)

For our purposes we need only substitute the word "scientific" for the word "writerly." What can we glean of the fears, desires, longings, and terrors that perfuse the works we've just considered? And how are race, gender, and nationality woven into the story? In the following list I include some of the paired contradictions that emerge from my reading of Cuvier and de Blainville.

conquest	resistance
human	animal
surface	interior
tame	wild
sexually modest	libidinous
civilized	savage
compliant	angry
ruler	subject
powerlessness	hidden power
male	female
white	nonwhite
colonizer	colonized

The simultaneous anxiety about European women and the savage Other is especially clear in de Blainville's account. He identified Bartmann as a woman because she menstruated. But she also drank, smoked, and was alleged to be sexually aggressive—all masculine characteristics. And if Bartmann, a woman, could behave thus, why not French women? Furthermore, the soap-opera dramas about Bartmann that played in contemporary Paris suggested that French men, despite their "civilization," actually desired such women; civilization kept the European woman under control, decreasing the danger of rebellion but thwarting male desire. Minute scientific observation converted the desire into a form of voyeurism, while at the same time confining it to a socially acceptable location.

Cuvier most clearly concerned himself with establishing the priority of European nationhood; he wished to control the hidden secrets of

Africa and the woman by exposing them to scientific daylight. The French Revolution had frightened him, and certainly the prospect of resistance from other peoples must have seemed terrifying (Outram 1984; Appel 1987). Hence, he delved beneath the surface, bringing the interior to light; he extracted the hidden genitalia and defined the hidden Hottentot. Lying on his dissection table, the wild Bartmann became tame, the savage civilized. By exposing the clandestine power, the ruler prevailed. But one need only look at the list of anxieties glossed from the scientific literature to know how uneasy lay the head that wore a crown.[16]

NOTES

Acknowledgments: This paper was written with the financial support of the National Science Foundation, Fellowship #DIR-9112556 from the Program in History and Philosophy of Science. I would like to thank Evelynn Hammonds, Joan Richards, Gregg Mitman, and Londa Schiebinger, for reading and commenting on recent drafts of this paper. Londa Schiebinger also kindly shared with me drafts of chapters of her book *Nature's Body: Gender in the Making of Modern Science* (Boston: Beacon Press, 1993).

1. In 1992 the Musée de l'Homme had removed the remnants of the Bartmann exhibit. In its place was a modern one entitled "All Relatives, All Different," celebrating human genetic diversity. Discussion of Bartmann could still be found in a part of the exhibit devoted to the history of scientific racism.

2. There is also a book of poetry featuring the Venus Hottentot in the title poem; see Elizabeth Alexander, *The Venus Hottentot* (Charlottesville: University Press of Virginia, 1990).

3. The Dutch word for Bushman is *bosjeman,* which translates as "little man of the forest." This is also the translated meaning of the Malay word *orangutan.*

4. This is in perfect accord with Latour's account of how scientific knowledge is constructed.

5. All translations from works cited in the original are mine.

6. In fact, de Blainville's break with Cuvier came over just this question. He devised a different classificatory system based on external rather than internal characters, but he linked his divisions by creating intermediate groupings.

7. The question of the racial origins of European thought has been raised in our own era by the work of Martin Bernal (1987).

8. The detailed ins and outs of her sale and repurchase may be found in the references in note 11.

9. In contrast to the family groupings of Lapps, Eskimos, and Zulus, the displays of Bartmann, Tono Maria, and Zip made no attempt to present a working culture.

10. Nonwhites were not the only "others" constructed. I plan to address the use of "freaks" in the construction of the Other in a book-length account of the construction of race and gender by biologists, anthropologists, and sociologists.

11. All the details cited here may be found in Altick 1978; Edwards and Walvin 1983; Gould 1985; Kirby 1949, 1953; and Lindfors 1983. Remarkably, prurient interest in the figure of the Hottentot continues to this day. Gould (1985) discusses a 1982 cover of the French magazine *Photo* that features a naked woman named "Carolina, La Vénus hottentote de Saint-Domingue." In the copy of the Geoffroy Saint-Hilaire and Cuvier held by the Brown Library, the frontal drawing of Bartmann (which exhibited her breasts in full form) has been razored out. The mutilation was first noticed by librarians in 1968. This is not the first time I have encountered such mutilation of material of this sort.

12. Although the bustle was not invented until 1869, various fashions in the eighteenth and nineteenth centuries accentuated the backside of middle- and upper-class white women (Batterberry and Batterberry 1977). The relationship between these fashions and scientific accounts of the body has yet to be detailed.

13. There were at least seven articles, falling into three chronological group-ings, published in scientific journals in England, France, and Germany. The first two, by Henri de Blainville and Georges Cuvier, exclusively on Sarah Bartmann, were published in 1816 and 1817, respectively. The second group, containing two by German biologists, appeared in the 1830s. The first of these was written by Johannes Müller (1801–58) (Müller 1834), a physiologist and comparative embryologist, while the second, written by Frederick Tiedemann (1781–1861) (Tiedemann 1836), professor of anatomy and physiology at the University of Heidelberg and Foreign Member of the Royal Society of London, appeared in 1836. Müller's article is about a Hottentot woman who died in Germany and is in the same scientific style as the French papers. Tiedemann's work, on the other hand, represents a scientific departure. Although Bartmann's is among a wide variety of brains obtained from museum collections, it is not the focus of the article. From a scientific point of view, Tiedemann's study represents a tran-sition from a period in which scientists offered detailed examinations of the out-side of the body, while focusing on a single individual and describing all body parts. Tiedemann awarded priority to one organ—the brain. A comparison of the brains of Europeans, Negroes, and orangutans convinced him that there was no difference among the humans. He used his results to condemn the practice of slavery. His method, though, is primitive compared to the approach of the scientists working in the 1860s (Marshall 1864; Flower and Murie 1867), whose work provides a useful contrast to the changing scientific and political times. In this chapter I will consider the first two exemplars, reserving detailed examination of the other works for a future occasion.

14. Outram (1984) documents Cuvier's dispute with Franz Joseph Gall over the scientific nature of phrenology. But Cuvier clearly believed in the principle that the face could be read for deeper meaning.

15. In the seventeenth century, breasts—as natural and social objects—had undergone a transformation, as male social commentators launched a success-ful campaign to do away with wet-nursing and reestablish the breast as an ob-ject that connected women to nature through the act of nursing. For middle- and upper-class white women, doing the right thing with the right kind of breasts hooked them into a growing cult of domesticity, which exploded as the nineteenth-century ideal for gender relationships for the middle and upper classes in Europe and America. This naturalization of motherhood worked hand

in glove with the desexualization of white women (Schiebinger 1993; Perry 1991). Perry cites Thomas Laqueur (1986) as explaining "this cultural reconsideration of the nature of women's sexuality as part of a process . . . committed to sweeping clean all *socially* determined differences among people [emphasis added]" (Perry 1991, 212), instead relocalizing difference in the biological body. No part of the body escaped unscathed from this process.

16. In one of the lovely ironies of history, Cuvier himself was dissected when he died (in 1832), and his brain and head measurements were taken. In a ranking of 115 men of note, Cuvier's brain weight came in third (Turgenev's was first). The French as a group ranked behind Americans and the British. The author of this 1908 paper concluded that "the brains of men devoted to the higher intellectual occupations, such as the mathematical sciences . . . [or] those of men who have devised original lines of research [Cuvier] and those of forceful characters, like Ben Butler and Daniel Webster, are generally heavier still. The results are fully in accord with biological truths" (Spitzka 1908, 215). In a second, larger sample, Spitzka included four women—mathematician Sonya Kovaleskaya, physician Caroline Winslow, actress Marie Bittner, and educator and orator Madame Leblais—who ranked 134th–137th in brain weight.

REFERENCES

Altick, Richard D. 1978. *The Shows of London.* Cambridge: The Belknap Press of Harvard University.

Appel, Toby A. 1987. *The Cuvier-Geoffroy Debate: French Biology in the Decades before Darwin.* Oxford: Oxford University Press.

Baillie, Mathieu. 1807. *Anatomie pathologique des organes les plus importans du corps humain.* Paris: Crochard.

Batterberry, Michael, and Ariane Batterberry. 1977. *Mirror Mirror: A Social History of Fashion.* New York: Holt, Rinehart and Winston.

Becker, Brent A., J. Philippe Rushton, and C. Davison Ankney. 1992. "Differences in Brain Size." *Nature* 358:532.

Bernal, Martin. 1987–91. *Black Athena: The Afroasiatic Roots of Classical Civilization,* vols. 1 and 2. New Brunswick, N.J.: Rutgers University.

Bucher, Bernadette. 1981. *Icon and Conquest: A Structural Analysis of the Illustrations of de Bry's Great Voyages.* Trans. Basia Miller Gulati. Chicago: University of Chicago Press.

Coleman, William. 1964. *Georges Cuvier, Zoologist: A Study in the History of Evolution Theory.* Cambridge: Harvard University Press.

Cuvier, Georges. 1817. "Faites sur le cadavre d'une femme connue à Paris et à Londres sous le nom de Vénus Hottentotte." *Mémoires du Musée nationale d'histoire naturelle* 3:259–74.

de Blainville, Henri. 1816. "Sur une femme de la race hottentote." *Bulletin du Société philomatique de Paris,* 183–90.

Edwards, Paul, and James Walvin. 1983. *Black Personalities in the Era of the Slave Trade.* Baton Rouge: Louisiana State University Press.

Elphick, Richard. 1977. *Kraal and Castle: Khoikhoi and the Founding of White South Africa.* New Haven: Yale University Press.

Fausto-Sterling, Anne. 1992. *Myths of Gender: Biological Theories about Women and Men.* 2d ed. New York: Basic Books.

Flourens, P. 1845. *Cuvier: Histoire de ses travaux.* 2d ed. rev. and corr. Paris: Paulin.

Flower, W. H., and James Murie. 1867. "Account of the Dissection of a Bushwoman." *Journal of Anatomy and Physiology* 1:189–208.

Geoffroy Saint-Hilaire, Etienne, and Frédéric Cuvier. 1824. *Histoire Naturelle des Mammifères,* vols. 1 and 2. Paris: A. Belin.

Gilman, Sander L. 1985. "Black Bodies, White Bodies: Toward an Iconography of Female Sexuality in Late Nineteenth-Century Art, Medicine and Literature." *Critical Inquiry* 12 (autumn): 204–42.

Gould, Stephen Jay. 1981. *The Mismeasure of Man.* New York: Norton.

———. 1985. "The Hottentot Venus." In *The Flamingo's Smile: Reflections in Natural History,* 291–305. New York: Norton.

Graham, John. 1979. *Lavater's Essays on Physiognomy: A Study in the History of Ideas.* Berne: Peter Lang.

Gray, Stephen. 1979. *Southern African Literature: An Introduction.* New York: Barnes and Noble.

Guenther, Mathias Georg. 1980. "From 'Brutal Savage' to 'Harmless People': Notes on the Changing Western Image of the Bushmen." *Paideuma* 26:124–40.

Haraway, Donna. 1989. *Primate Visions: Gender, Race, and Nature in the World of Modern Science.* New York: Routledge.

James, John Angell. 1830. *Memoir of Clementine Cuvier, Daughter of Baron Cuvier.* New York: American Tract Society.

Kirby, Percival R. 1949. "The Hottentot Venus." *Africana News and Notes* 6:55–62.

———. 1953. "More about the Hottentot Venus." *Africana News and Notes* 10: 124–34.

Laqueur, Thomas. 1986. "Orgasm, Generation, and the Politics of Reproductive Biology." *Representations* 14:1–41.

Latour, Bruno. 1987. *Science in Action: How to Follow Scientists and Engineers through Society.* Milton Keynes: Open University Press.

Lavater, J. C. 1775–78. *Physiognomische Fragmente zur Beförderung der Menschenkenntnis und Menschenliebe.* Leipzig: Weidmanns Erben und Reiche, H. Steiner und Companie.

Lee, Richard B. 1992. "Art, Science, or Politics? The Crisis in Hunter-Gatherer Studies." *American Anthropologist* 94, no. 1:31–54.

Lewin, Roger. 1988. "New Views Emerge on Hunters and Gatherers." *Science* 240:1146–48.

Lindfors, Bernth. 1983. "The Hottentot Venus and Other African Attractions in Nineteenth-Century England." *Australasian Drama Studies* 1:83–104.

Linnaeus [Carl von Linne]. 1758. *Caroli Linnaei Systema Naturae: Regnum Animale.* 10th ed. Stockholm.

Maddock, John. 1992. "How to Publish the Unpalatable?" *Nature* 358:187.

Marshall, John. 1864. "On the Brain of a Bushwoman; and on the Brains of Two Idiots of European Descent." *Philosophical Transactions of the Royal Society of London,* 501–58.

Masters, William H., and Virginia E. Johnson. 1966. *Human Sexual Response.* Boston: Little, Brown.

Mayr, Ernst. 1982. *The Growth of Biological Thought: Diversity, Evolution, and Inheritance.* Cambridge: Belknap Press of Harvard University.

Merchant, Carolyn. 1980. *The Death of Nature: Women, Ecology, and the Scientific Revolution.* San Francisco: Harper and Row.

Morrison, Toni. 1992. *Playing in the Dark: Whiteness and the Literary Imagination.* Cambridge: Harvard University Press.

Müller, Johannes. 1834. "Ueber die äusseren Geslechtstheile der Buschmänninnen." *Archiv für Anatomie, Physiologie und Wissenschaftliche Medicin,* 319–45.

Outram, Dorinda. 1984. *Georges Cuvier: Vocation, Science, and Authority in Postrevolutionary France.* Manchester: Manchester University Press.

Perry, Ruth. 1991. "Colonizing the Breast: Sexuality and Maternity in Eighteenth-Century England." *Journal of the History of Sexuality* 2:204–34.

Raven-Hart, Rowland. 1967. *Before Van Riebeeck: Callers at South Africa from 1488 to 1652.* Cape Town: C. Struik.

Russett, Cynthia Eagle. 1989. *Sexual Science: The Victorian Construction of Womanhood.* Cambridge: Harvard University Press.

Schiebinger, Londa. 1993. *Nature's Body: Gender in the Making of Modern Science.* Boston: Beacon Press.

Schluter, Dolph, and Richard Lynn. 1992. "Brain Size Differences." *Nature* 359: 181.

Shohat, Ella. 1991. "Imaging Terra Incognita: The Disciplinary Gaze of the Empire." *Public Culture* 3, no. 2:41–70.

Spitzka, Edward Anthony. 1908. "A Study of the Brains of Six Eminent Scientists and Scholars Belonging to the American Anthropometric Society, together with a Description of the Skull of Professor E. D. Cope." *American Philosophical Society Transactions* 21:175–308.

Stepan, Nancy. 1982. *The Idea of Race in Science: Great Britain, 1800–1960.* Hamden, Conn.: Archon.

Stocking, George W., Jr. 1982. *Race, Culture, and Evolution: Essays in the History of Anthropology.* Chicago: University of Chicago Press.

———. 1987. *Victorian Anthropology.* New York: Free Press.

———, ed. 1991. *Colonial Situations: Essays on the Contexualization of Ethnographic Knowledge.* Madison: University of Wisconsin Press.

Tiedemann, Frederick. 1836. "On the Brain of a Negro, Compared with That of the European and the Orang-outang." *Philosophical Transactions of the Royal Society of London,* 497–558.

Tiffany, Sharon W., and Kathleen J. Adams. 1985. *The Wild Woman: An Inquiry into the Anthropology of an Idea.* Cambridge, Mass.: Schenkman.

Trumbach, Randolf. 1991. "Sex, Gender and Sexual Identity in Modern Culture: Male Sodomy and Female Prostitution in Enlightenment London." *Journal of the History of Sexuality* 2:187–203.

Walvin, James. 1973. *Black and White: The Negro and English Society, 1555–1945.* London: Allen Lane and Penguin.

PART

Lisa Collins

Economies of the Flesh

Representing the Black Female Body in Art

During my first quarter of graduate school a professor asked me and a friend of mine, a white male student, to stand in front of our class on representations of race and gender in popular culture. Somewhat alarmed but also having no reason to doubt her judgment, I got up and stood in front of the blackboard. After an anxious glance to my friend, I looked out. Sixty eyes—and I remember all of them as being attached to white bodies—were scurrying nervously between Nathan and me. The professor then asked the students to call out what they saw. They chose to focus on Nathan. "Tall," "thin," and "smart looking" were the comments that I heard. Next the professor asked about me. At this, I tasted my own dread and began to detest the professor and all of the eyes on me. Horror came from my belated realization that what would come out of the students' mouths would be the product of history, particularly the history of conquest, enslavement, lynching, and rape. Although I knew that my Black female body signified both triumph and terror, I now recognized that both of these referents were enmeshed in systems of visual exposure and bodily violence. Aware that my body was bound in these systems and that the comments would be informed by this history, I fled my body, for I was unsure if the students would be able to observe and remark without doing violence once again. Away in my thoughts, I dreamt of protection from such visibility.

In this chapter I explore the source of this contemporary visual predicament, the brutal history of enforced overexposure of Black women's bodies, as well as visual responses to it in the context of Western art history. Specifically, I am interested in images of the unclothed Black female body (and lack of such images), for it is this figure that until recently has been most stridently denied in museum art by African American artists, precisely because it is overburdened by historical tensions of race, gender, and sexuality. In the early 1990s, art historian Judith Wilson set out to investigate the avoidance of the Black female nude in African American art history. Her initial exploration was suggestive; she discovered no adult Black female nudes created by African American artists during the entire nineteenth century.[1] Only during the twentieth century, she offers, did the Black female body become a "permissible subject" for Black American artists.[2]

Portrayals of the Black female nude, however, are also rare in comparison to the numerous examples of white female nudes in the larger categories of American and European art history. The Image of the Black in Western Art Research Project, a vast archive of over twenty-five thousand images of Black people, contains only one full nude of an African American woman from the nineteenth century, and it was created by a visiting Swiss artist.[3] The other nineteenth-century and early twentieth-century nudes of Black women are few.[4] The use of the unclothed Black female body within the important artistic category of the nude is scrutinized in the first part of this chapter, where I examine historical and aesthetic factors that have so charged the representation of the Black female figure in visual culture. Taking nineteenth-century and early twentieth-century museum and popular art as my subjects, I explore how economies of the flesh—that is, various markets for Black female bodies— have affected the creation and reception of images of Black women in Western Europe and the United States. In the second part of the chapter, I reveal strategies adopted by contemporary visual artists to confront this burdened history by analyzing recent representations of the unclothed Black female body.

The Nude

Avoidance of the Black female nude is striking because the nude has been a central subject in Western art since it was constructed as a subject in ancient Greece. Early nudes, however, typically depicted the male body. During the Italian Renaissance, when artists revisited the art of ancient Greece, the unclothed male body was used to symbolize what were considered to be universal ideals. Heroic action, pathos, triumph, and perfectibility were thought to be communicated by the male nude. Yet since the seventeenth century, the male nude has retreated from view, and portrayals of the female nude have predominated. Evidence of the completeness of this shift is that the very phrase "the nude" now conjures up the images of Venus and Aphrodite that line museum galleries.

The female nude has been the subject of much aesthetic and academic contemplation. Formalist art historians such as Kenneth Clark, author of the most widely read book on the topic, tout the unclothed female figure in art as the sophisticated transference of physical desire into beautiful images. For Clark, the successful (male) artist can transform the female body from its "vulgar" naked state to a "celestial" ideal through the means of "symmetry" and "measurement."[5] In other words, the female body is profane yet capable of conversion. Feminist art historians frequently understand the female nude—as well as formalist criticism of it—as an attempt to control women's bodies through various strategies of containment. For example, Gill Saunders argues that "since nudity is the prime signifier of sexuality," male fears of women's sexuality surface in and play out on images of the nude.[6] Drawing attention to the long history of the male artist/female model relationship, Saunders critiques the products of this history for continually portraying the unclothed female body as an "anonymous available object," one that is perpetually accessible to male intrusion.[7]

Missing from most formalist and feminist scholarship on the nude is a discussion of the unclothed Black body in art. White artists and white models, as well as white viewers, are too often assumed. Although recent revisionist scholarship has begun to explore images of Black people in Western art, few nudes have been discovered by this research, and most of those found have been male. For example, in his survey of Black subjects in visual culture from the American Revolution to World War I, Hugh Honour reveals the repeated use of the seminude Black male figure among abolitionists beginning in the 1780s (fig. 17). In chains, kneeling, and accompanied by the rhetorical question "Am I Not a Man and a Brother?" this abolitionist emblem portrays the Black man as grateful for being "'doubly freed' from paganism and human bondage."[8] This compromised symbol of antislavery thought both relies upon the association of the male body with heroism and triumph and denies its power, for here the potential power of the male body is curtailed by the figure's bent legs and outstretched hands, a familiar position of humility and submission. Although Honour does not find many examples of the unclothed Black female body in Western art, he points to a reason for her absence. In terms of abolitionist politicking, he suggests that the representation of the Black female body would have been

101

Fig. 17. Wedgwood cameo, *Am I Not a Man and a Brother?*, nineteenth century. Jasperware. Smithsonian Institution, National Numismatic Collection, Washington, D.C. Courtesy of Douglas Mudd.

Fig. 18. Token, *Am I Not a Woman and a Sister?*, 1838. Copper. Smithsonian Institution, National Numismatic Collection, Washington, D.C. Courtesy of Douglas Mudd.

even more problematic than the representation of the Black male body because her body could not be positioned to promote solely "philanthropic" thoughts, for it was too closely associated with "libidinal" actions.[9] Thus, for Honour, the Black female body could not unequivocally signify the promise of freedom, for she was already too entangled in her abused flesh.

It was precisely this entanglement that made the image of the enslaved Black female body an important one in abolitionist appeals to women. Forty years after the appearance of her counterpart, abolitionists in the United States adopted an image of a partially clad female supplicant framed by the words "Am I Not a Woman and a Sister?" (fig. 18). Strategically targeted at women, this image appeared in the women's sections of newspapers, as well as on popular art forms such as tokens, dishware, and textiles sold by antislavery women at fundraising events.[10] Shown on her knees, bare-breasted, and in chains, this icon explicitly linked nudity with vulnerability and slavery with sexual violence in order to outrage women and press them to agitate for abolition.

Visual Legacies of the Nineteenth Century

This tension surrounding the Black female body—the fact that the body evokes a racialized, sexualized, and exploitative history—is evident in the few nineteenth-century artistic depictions of the Black female nude. These portrayals are also highly formulaic; the Black female body connotes exotica and erotica and serves as an allegory for freedom and its necessary inverse, enslavement. Most of the extant works are Western European in origin, frequently French, and although the individual works might not have been widely viewed in the United States, they are indicative of a larger cultural climate that surrounded and constructed the Black female body in the West. Underlying the three categories of representation—exotica, erotica, and allegory—is a link between the body and various markets for Black female labor. Literary scholar Hortense Spillers has noted that the enslavement of Black women "relegated them to the marketplace of the flesh."[11] This inhumane economic history has deeply affected art history, for nineteenth-century visual culture consistently linked the Black female figure with slave, sexual, and service economies.

Nowhere is this entanglement of market and visual economies more evident than in the various drawings and paintings of Saartjie Baartman created for French scientific texts and natural history museums. Saartjie Baartman was deceived into being exhibited in Europe in the early nineteenth century. Europeans paid to see the "Hottentot Venus" because they wanted to witness a woman thought to be their opposite on the chain of being.[12] By paying money to view Baartman, viewers revealed their faith in the visual: they were eager to link the idea of African inferiority—which implicitly allowed for the subordination of Black people—with a visible representation of this difference. This trade in money for a stare or a peek at a woman taken from Africa and positioned as a curio in Europe has become the paradigmatic example of the Western exoticization of the Black female body.

Exoticism frequently meshes with eroticism. Thus the second and related visual model for viewing the Black female body was as an emblem of sensuality and an object of lust. During the nineteenth century a few European artists—unlike their colleagues in the United States—attempted to depict what they saw as the sensuality, availability, and desirability of Black women. Jules-Robert Auguste, a French artist active during the first half of the century, created erotic images of frolicking women, Black and white. These charged and sensuous pictures of unclothed women enjoying each other's bodies served as a form of private

Fig. 19. Jules-Robert Auguste, *Les amies,* ca. 1820–30.
Watercolor heightened with gouache on parchment. Musée
national du Louvre, Paris. Réunion des Musées Nationaux/Art
Resource, New York City.

titillation for the artist. A wealthy man, Auguste neither exhibited nor
sold his work; instead, his images were created solely to satisfy his own
visual appetite.[13] *Les amies,* a watercolor thought to have been completed in the 1820s, shows a naked Black woman playfully poised on the
lap of a partially dressed white woman (fig. 19). Contrasts between the
brown and pink skin of the women, as well as the "oriental" textiles on
which they lie, heighten the lushness of this private and voyeuristic
glimpse of interracial play and affection between women.

Édouard Manet's *Olympia,* however, demonstrated to the French
Salon of 1865 that the Black female body need not be undressed to
evoke the erotic (see fig. 1 on page 15). Drawing from an established visual legacy of the Black figure as servant in the shadows, laboring for
white people and often attending to white women, Manet employed a
fully dressed West Indian maid to imbue his painting with illicit sexual-

ity. Laura, the barely visible Black woman, serves, and serves as contrast to, the stark white female beauty of the wealthy prostitute. Artist and critic Lorraine O'Grady draws attention to the Black domestic's double value in this famous painting. She is, O'Grady suggests, a "two-in-one": both Jezebel and Mammy, the embodiment of both sexuality and servitude.[14] Laura's presence in *Olympia* draws from and continues the visual economy of Black erotic servitude at the same time that it hints at the market economy that most likely pressed her to leave the Caribbean and work in France. Art historian Albert Boime points to the connection between the maid's labor, her body, and her value in a racialized and sexualized economy: "The West Indian maid (identified by her headdress) has been induced to come to Paris for work, and she has been impressed into the service of a high-class prostitute whose very existence depends upon the signs of status that go right to the heart of imperial darkness."[15] Manet's painting signals that the Black woman no longer needs to be undressed in mid-nineteenth-century visual culture for her presence to signify the imperialist-inflected sex trade.

Olympia was unveiled to the French public in 1865, the same year that the Thirteenth Amendment was ratified and slavery was officially abolished in the United States. The end of slavery was frequently commemorated in the visual arts, often in sculpture. Serving as symbols for freedom and liberation, Black figures were frequently depicted in these monuments. Yet not unlike the entanglement between the exotic and the erotic, these allegorical works, particularly those depicting Black women, were also subject to eroticizing in the nineteenth century. Hugh Honour's crucial observation of the link between "philanthropic" thoughts and "libidinal" actions is clearly demonstrated in the Italian artist Giacomo Ginotti's tribute to emancipation. Created in 1877, *Abolition of Slavery* is a life-size marble sculpture that portrays a recently freed young woman whose hands are still bound together with irons but whose ankle chains have just been broken (fig. 20). Importantly, however, the woman's bound hands are strategically positioned to emphasize her maturing breasts, and her eyes are conveniently downcast. These factors serve to create an opportune moment for the viewer to stare unabashedly at the former slave's nubile body, which is covered only by jewels and a dangling Christian cross. In this work, the sexual availability of the young woman is offered as the prize of emancipation. Thus the freedom from bondage that the sculpture's title evokes is trivialized by the artist's eroticization of the newly freed Black female body.

A similar eroticizing of the recently freed female body takes place in the only known nineteenth-century representation of an unclothed

Fig. 20. Giacomo Ginotti, *Abolition of Slavery,* 1877. Marble. Museo Nazionale di Capodimonte, Naples.

African American woman created in the United States. During an extended visit in the United States, the Swiss artist Frank Buchser spent time in the Upper South, where he used members of the newly freed Black population as well as his Black mistress, a southern-born, Washington, D.C.–based clerk, as subjects for his art.[16] *Black Girl in a Stream* was most likely created during a summer visit of 1867 (fig. 21). The painting depicts a young woman, possibly his mistress, poised in a secluded West Virginia glade with the sun streaming down on her brown skin and on the creek in which she stands.[17] Like that of Giacomo Ginotti's model, the woman's gaze is conveniently directed away—in this work she is looking sideways at the lush foliage—yet her body is turned toward the viewer to reveal her firm belly and full breasts. The young woman clearly positioned as an object of beauty and desire,

Fig. 21. Frank Buchser, *Black Girl in a Stream,* ca. 1867–70.
Oil on canvas. Kunstmuseum Solothurn, Solothurn. Photograph: Swiss Institute for Art Research, Zurich.

Buchser's painting was exhibited in New York but not sold.[18] Thus, in
an era when private collectors were the primary purchasers of art in the
United States, Buchser's painting of an idyllic scene, replete with a sensual and available Black woman, was evidently not deemed an acceptable purchase. At the time, American art collectors were beginning to
drop their previous objections to depictions of the nude in art. Thus
perhaps partially fueling the painting's lack of acceptance was the continuing resistance on the part of the powerful—which had begun during slavery to hide their sexual aggressions—to publicly acknowledging
the Black female body as a locus of beauty or yearning.

Fig. 22. Edmonia Lewis, *Forever Free*, 1867. Marble. Howard University Gallery of Art, Washington, D.C.

The same year that Frank Buchser completed what may have been the first painting of a fully nude Black woman in the United States, Mary Edmonia Lewis, the first documented U.S.-born woman sculptor of African American and Native American descent, completed her own monument to emancipation. *Forever Free,* the earliest tribute to the abolition of slavery by an artist of color, directly responds to the visual legacy of the nineteenth century (fig. 22). Completed in Rome four years after the Emancipation Proclamation, this 1867 marble group shows a partially dressed man standing triumphantly, with his arm, which has just recently been freed from chains, raised toward the sky. Kneeling in prayer next to him is a dressed young woman looking gratefully upward. Unlike either Giacomo Ginotti's tribute to the Emancipation Proclamation, and the sexual availability of the newly freed, or Frank Buchser's eroticization of the former Washington, D.C., clerk,

Lewis's female figure is categorically removed from the realm of the sexual. Highly aware of the nineteenth-century visual repertoire for Black female figures, which portrayed them as exotic and erotic even within allegorical works, Lewis created a young woman who is neither unclothed nor available to humans. Instead, her childlike female figure is belted and bent over into a position that implies gratitude and devotion to a spiritual power.

Another angle on the American sculptor's strategy of displacement is offered by art historian Kirsten Buick. She suggests that Lewis's use of white marble, as well as her handling of the material to imbue the female figure with long straight hair and "keen European figures," was the result of a conscious decision on the part of the artist to eliminate the subject's ethnicity and, in this way, to remove the female figure from an already eroticized visual economy.[19] Of Lewis's figurative approach, Buick writes: "While their appearance conforms to Neoclassical standards of beauty, the subject matter belies those standards. She erased, even as she called forth, a dangerous ethnicity."[20] Given this, the female figure in *Forever Free* can be seen as embodying two strategies of displacement: the shift from the sexual to the spiritual realm, as well as the shift from a "dangerous ethnicity" (blackness) to a safer one (whiteness). Edmonia Lewis's attempt to remove the Black female figure from a racialized and sexualized economy through the suppression of evidence of her race and her sex can be viewed as part of a larger pattern of resistance by Black women to sexual danger.

Culture of Dissemblance

According to historian Darlene Clark Hine, Black women in the United States created a "culture of dissemblance"—a politics of silence, evasiveness, and displacement—in an attempt to protect themselves from sexual violation.[21] Drawing attention to nineteenth-century narratives by Black women, Hine notes that every female slave narrative contains a reference to rape.[22] Combined with the disclosure of this form of terror, however, is another recurrence. Each narrative charts various strategies of resistance to sexual assault, as well as methods to protect women's bodily integrity and private selves. One of the strategies developed from this history is the creation of a "self-imposed invisibility," which can afford Black women a space where they are temporarily shrouded in secrets and silence and thus not overly visible or exposed. Edmonia Lewis's *Forever Free* can be understood as participating in this culture of dissemblance, for the freed woman in the sculpture is made somewhat invisible; her blackness is removed from view, and visible markers of her gender are largely hidden. Perhaps wary of the relationship between visibility and assault, Lewis attempted to "veil" her freed woman and, in this manner, protect her from harm.

Darlene Clark Hine argues that Black women's desires to protect their bodies, escape sexual and economic exploitation, and secure reasonable employment are central to understanding protest and movement in African American history. Likewise, she reveals a learned set of behaviors, attitudes, and strategies that Black women have adopted to counter their sexual vulnerability and protect their inner selves. As evidence of the institutionalization of this culture of dissemblance, Hine points to the creation and growth of Black women's clubs at the turn of the twentieth century. Concerned with challenging derogatory images of Black women's sexuality, clubwomen often attempted to accomplish their goals by suppressing their own sexuality.[23] By shunning outward expressions of sexuality, they hoped to build a space where Black women could wield more control over their bodies and gain dignity and respect within the dominant culture.

Josephine Baker

While the Black women's club movement was gaining strength and influence in the United States, however, the culture of dissemblance was exploded by a young woman from St. Louis. In 1925, Josephine Baker left the chorus lines of New York, where she was limited to performing as a comic, for Paris. There she captured, and was captured by, the city's mood and became the premier example of exotica and erotica. Crossing her eyes, swinging her hips, and wearing her infamous banana skirt, she was catapulted into her role as icon of hot sexuality.[24] One European writer of the period remarked that Baker lent "a whiff of jungle air and an elemental strength and beauty to the tired showplace of Western civilization."[25] Challenging all conventions of prudity and propriety, Josephine Baker was a visual predicament. When the clubwomen were advocating discretion in the United States, she appeared nude in France. While they were downplaying their sexuality, she was flouting hers. When the clubwomen were seeking venues for "dignified" work, she became rich and powerful as a "scandalous" dancer. And, most important, while they encouraged imposed invisibility, she craved visible exposure. And she got it. After her success as a performer in Paris, Baker was con-

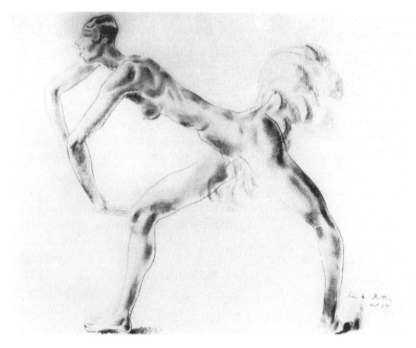

Fig. 23. Jean Isy de Botton, *Portrait of Josephine Baker,* 1929.
Charcoal on paper. Artists Rights Society (ARS), 2002
NY/ADAGP, Paris.

stantly the subject of art and by the mid-1920s had been "drawn, painted, sketched, caricatured, photographed, [and] filmed."[26]

It is no wonder that some of these works were saved and now can be viewed in the Image of the Black in Western Art archive. In fact, Frank Buchser's painting of the young woman in the southern glade and two works that portray Josephine Baker are the only images in the entire collection that depict completely nude Black American women. One of these images, a 1929 drawing by French artist Jean Isy de Botton, shows a dancing Baker wearing only the skimpiest of costumes, a plume of tail feathers (fig. 23). Although her body was famous for its double-jointedness, it is highly contorted in this work. Her super-long arms are turned impossibly, and her legs are of more stature than her torso. However, the real focus of the drawing is Baker's rear end. With it decorated only by feathers, the picture visually represents a comment made by Baker regarding the wide appeal of her backside. As a young woman in Paris, she exclaimed, "My face and rump were famous!"[27] Josephine Baker's face, though, is not the center of this work; instead, as was the ase with her predecessor Saartjie Baartman, the focal point is her exposed black buttocks.

Eerily, Baartman and Baker are the two Black women who appear most frequently unclothed in the archive of Black images in Western art. Thus the "Hottentot Venus" and the "Black Venus" are linked by virtue of being the two most visually fetishized Black female bodies in Europe. And although a century passed between Baartman's death and Baker's Paris debut, there are parallels in how they were viewed in Europe. Both were thought to embody exotica and erotica. And both were paid to reveal this difference. Yet there are also crucial distinctions between the two, particularly concerning agency and influence. For example, while Baartman was pressed into being exhibited as a spectacle, Baker wielded control over her performances. After her success in Paris, she largely defined the conditions of her work. In addition, Baker was highly rewarded for her nude and seminude performances and for a time was considered the world's wealthiest Black woman. Finally, whereas Baartman died an early death and was then subjected to a cruel dissection, Baker died triumphantly after a tribute to her fifty-year career and was given a lavish and honorable French funeral.

Baker's legacy, her willingness to market her unclothed body for viewers who were eager to witness what one called "savage grace" and "eroticism personified," creates a visual predicament for artists who admire her brilliance as a performer but who are also contemporary heirs to the culture of dissemblance.[28] Painter Emma Amos reveals this tension. In a 1985 print titled *Creatures of the Night,* Amos works to counter Baker's image of sexual availability by taking her off the stage and situating her within the context of the jungle (fig. 24). Since Baker owned various jungle animals, Amos fittingly represents the performer with her preferred pet, a leopard. Although this reconstruction serves to remove Baker from the spotlight and the surface desires of her viewers, it also continues her association with the "whiff of jungle air," an imperialist fantasy of conquest and romance that the performer herself encouraged. Pairing a seminude Baker with a black leopard also works to evoke the grace, beauty, and strength of both, as well as their vulnerabilities in a hostile world. In this print, Amos attempts a revisionist use of the nude; she resituates Baker's body in order to tell an overlooked piece of her story. Here Baker's nudity is used to suggest not exotic sexuality but vulnerability. Emma Amos reveals this concern: "I was asked if I ever did nudes and I said I'd never do nudes of black women, forgetting I'd done her [Billie Holiday] and Josephine. It's meant to pull you in and show how vulnerable they are."[29] In her portrait of Baker, Amos uses nudity

Fig. 24. Emma Amos, *Creatures of the Night*, 1985. Four silk collagraphs. Courtesy of the artist. Photograph by Becket Logan. (Billie Holiday is depicted on the top left. Josephine Baker is pictured on the bottom right.)

to focus on the underside of female sexuality, to emphasize the danger component of the "pleasure and danger" dyad.

The history of the traffic in the Black female body causes a crisis of representation, particularly for artists who have inherited the culture of dissemblance. Although Emma Amos has produced nudes of Josephine Baker and Billie Holiday, she works comfortably neither with nor from the nude. The sight of the Black model's body haunts her, for it conjures up various economies of the flesh. Concerning this visual predicament Amos remarked, "Their figures unclothed reminded me too painfully of the slave market."[30] Likewise in 1995, when asked about her attempts to work with the unclothed Black female body, she responded, "I did not want to see black women with no clothes on. It means something else when a black woman has no clothes on. . . . It means that you are for sale."[31] Clearly, visibility for Amos—as well as for other heirs to dissemblance—is directly linked to vulnerability, lack of power, and the potential for sexual exploitation. This appears to be the logic behind much of the avoidance of the Black female body.

Recent Representations of the Black Female Nude

The absence of the Black female nude in African American art is telling. At closer look, the avoidance, as well as the rare depiction, of the nude reveal histories of anguish and pride that continue to surround the Black female body. Highly aware of these histories, as well as of their visual portrayals, artists Emma Amos, Alison Saar, and Renée Stout create work that tries to reposition the Black female body within these already established visual economies. They try also to expand the range of visual possibilities by taking the body elsewhere. For example, in order to recuperate the Black female body, both Saar and Stout fuse Western and non-Western histories, concepts, and artistic practices in their endeavors to expand a limited and limiting history.

Influences on Alison Saar's works are multiple and diverse. Her mother's (artist Betye Saar) interests in mysticism, rituals, and the occult, as well as black diasporic, African, and Asian artistic practices are some. In addition, her father's work as a conservator brought her into contact with art and artifacts from all over the globe, including Chinese frescoes, mummies, and pre-Columbian and African art. It was her apprenticeship with her father that led to her sculpting; she learned to carve in order to restore art.[32] At Scripps College, Saar studied African, Haitian, and Afro-Cuban art with art historian Samella Lewis and wrote her thesis on African-American folk art. As her interest in African influences on the art of the Black Diaspora parallels the work of art historian Robert Farris Thompson, she also acknowledges his work as a major source of inspiration.[33]

Since the creation of her first sculpture in 1981, Saar has grappled with the crisis surrounding the representation of the Black female body. Her first sculpture, *Si j'étais blanc* (If I Were White), takes as its theme a Josephine Baker song about inequality (fig. 25). Thus, like Emma Amos, Saar was compelled to approach the legacy of this highly visible performer. As this initial piece represents a significant break with her previous work—a shift from abstract paperwork to carved figurative sculpture—it seems fitting that this initial piece confronts Josephine Baker, an attempt to battle the problem of visibility up front. However, although the work evokes the "overseen" performer, her bodily presence

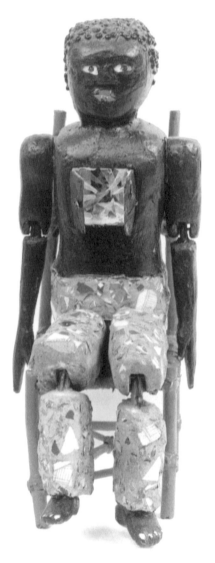

Fig. 25. Alison Saar, *Si j'étais blanc*, 1981. Mixed media. Courtesy of the artist.

is denied; instead, the sculpture depicts a young Black boy seated in a bright red chair. Saar has discussed her choice of figures, and, like Emma Amos, she refrains from working with live models. Similarly, because she is uncomfortable with the easy collapse between the subject of art and its creator, Saar consciously works to avoid this conflation through her frequent use of male figures.[34]

Although this piece avoids the female form, it makes way for its later depiction by turning toward Black Diasporic artistic practices. To expose the horror of Baker's song, Saar portrays the boy with an open chest filled with shards of glass. This filled cavity in the center of the body recalls figurative Kongo *minkisi,* traditional sacred objects from the Congo-Angola region used to effect change. Similarly, the boy's legs are made of cement and embedded with fragments of blue and white tile. Both the glass and tile are found objects, typical of materials used by the Black folk artists Saar admires. Robert Farris Thompson has discovered both white tile and glass at Kongo-inspired gravesites and yards in the United States.[35] Glass bottles, he suggests, are often used to "arrest the spirit"; guide it to another world; and, in this way, prevent it from haunting survivors.[36] Given this, perhaps the glass shards reveal not only the fallout of a debilitating desire to be white but also the possibility of another more equitable world.

Space between the material and spiritual worlds is a recurring theme in Alison Saar's work. In 1989, she created an installation entitled "Crossroads," which included three nearly life-size figures and piles of stones positioned around a central cross, representing the road between the two worlds (fig. 26). One of the figures is of a nude female spirit who guards the crossroads. The traditional Yoruba concept of the crossroads as a place of potentiality as well as its embodiment, Eshu-Elegba, not only survived the Middle Passage, but was rearticulated throughout the New World.[37] Drawing from her interest in these rearticulations, Saar aptly chose the crossroads as the site to represent the Black female body.

As this charged intersection represents a place where different paths converge and where both danger and possibility lie, it befits the presentation of the Black female body. Knowledgeable of Black women's history and representation in the West, Saar works to wrest the body from visual economies that define it solely as exotica and erotica by situating it within the West African and Black Diasporic notion of the crossroads. Here the body that is often viewed as deviant and exotic in the West is typically, and sometimes stereotypically, seen as natural and life-giving. Saar's figure stands at the crossroads of both traditions, at the intersection of peril and potential.

Simultaneously entangled within, yet desiring to transcend, the doctrine and dogma that label Black female sexuality as exotic and erotic, Saar's tin-covered wood sculpture depicts a sensual, albeit guarded, woman. Her guardedness is evident in her posture. While one arm is positioned behind the figure's head, making her breasts available and enticing, the other arm cradles her stomach, protecting her from harm. This dual gesture of exposure and protection characterizes the figure. How-

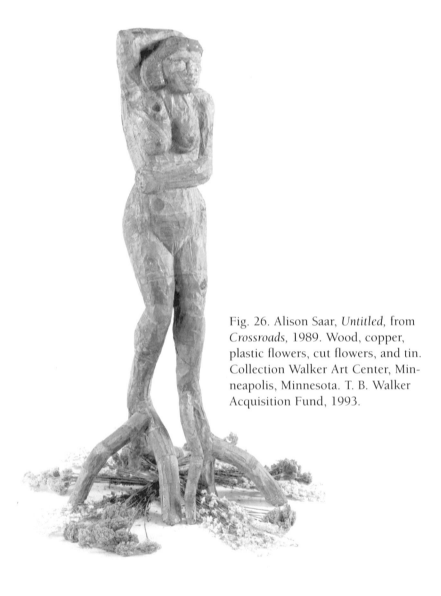

Fig. 26. Alison Saar, *Untitled*, from *Crossroads*, 1989. Wood, copper, plastic flowers, cut flowers, and tin. Collection Walker Art Center, Minneapolis, Minnesota. T. B. Walker Acquisition Fund, 1993.

ever, the poetry behind the figure, "Grass Fingers," by Angelina Weld Grimké, a romantic Black writer, bathes her in overt sensuality.[38]

> Touch me, touch me,
> Little cool grass fingers,
> Elusive, delicate grass fingers.
> With your shy brushings,

Touch my face—
My naked arms—
My thighs—
My feet.[39]

The tenor of Grimké's poem exposes Saar's intent. She works to construct an environment where Black female sexuality can begin to escape the sexual and economic marketplace and, for a moment, revel in itself. This is no small feat given that Black female sexuality has been subject to centuries of dehumanizing controls. During slavery, for example, Black women's bodies were viewed as capable of both economic and reproductive labor. Black women were often forced to bear children— the more children, the more labor the slave economy had access to.

Today, however, in this "advanced" capitalist economy, Black female reproduction—particularly of poor women—is seen as a threat to the country's health. In short, Black women's reproductive capacities have shifted from being viewed as a benefit to being viewed as a burden on the national economy. However different plantation and capitalist economies may be, what they have in common is an economic imperative to control Black female sexuality. Alison Saar confronts the legacy of this history, and although she cannot escape it, she attempts to reclaim the Black female body and bring it into view to both remind us of this history and offer us possibilities. The figure's sexuality is evident; Saar endows her with full breasts and a slightly protruding belly. Yet the woman spirit also has inhuman features for her legs turn to roots: she is literally grounded to the earth.

Further symbolizing the potentiality of the crossroads and the woman who guards it is the fact that Saar produced this figure while three months pregnant with her first child. She suggests that the experience of pregnancy increased her interest in spirituality, particularly ideas about "where life came from and where life went after we were done living it on this level."[40] In this way, Saar's female spirit symbolizes multiple convergences: pregnancy—the conflation of two lives in one body; the site where Western notions and histories of the Black female body meet West African ideas; and most evidently, the place where the spiritual and material worlds connect. In situating the Black female figure at the nexus of multiple histories and traditions, Saar does not remove the body from either visual or market economies—for indeed, the crossroads is yet another economy, a site of bartering and trade—but rather expands the scope of visual potential.

A similar strategy for expanding the representational potential of the Black female body is developed by multimedia artist Renée Stout. Alison Saar and Renée Stout share many interests and concerns. Both explore the spiritual world, ritual, magic, mystery, and healing in their work. Both, for instance, were drawn to the grave of Marie Laveau, the legendary nineteenth-century Voudou priestess of New Orleans. Likewise, both have created work that explores the notion of the crossroads. Inspiration from the work of Black Atlantic scholar Robert Farris Thompson is acknowledged by both artists. Their approach to materials is also parallel. Both use found objects for their evocative power and energy. Discussing her interest in these materials, Saar explains: "I really liked the fact that found metals and found pieces of wood have a kind of history. . . . I liked that these materials had had another function at one time and that that ghost is still hanging around."[41] Stout also collects found objects for their history and memory. Underlying their shared interests in the crossroads and their fascination with discarded objects is a traditional West and Central African belief: "the belief that physical places and material objects contain spirits who can harm or cure, and the belief that deliberate human action can draw on these spirits to influence what happens in the world."[42]

Renée Stout's path to studying African principles and retentions was not direct. She began her training in painting and worked in a realist mode. However, in the mid-1980s, when she moved from painting to working with found objects and carving from wood, her work transformed. Accompanying this transformation was an increased sense of artistic freedom that enabled Stout to follow her visions and feel protected on her search. Of this profound shift, she states:

> This total creative freedom led to another level of awareness, and it almost seemed that my life started getting really harmonious once I started working in this way. I started feeling like there were ancestors watching or saying, "You know what? You're finally on the right path."[43]

One place where her sense of newfound freedom took her was back to the mysterious *nkisi nkondi* figure that had first enthralled her as a ten-year-old at the Carnegie Museum in Pittsburgh. Over the years this figure has repeatedly pulled her back to the museum to contemplate its secrets. The *nkisi nkondi* figure that Stout revisits in Pittsburgh is part of a larger category of Kongo *minkisi* (plural form of *nkisi*). It is not difficult to see how these objects captured the attention of an artist attuned to mystery.

Minkisi are sacred medicines and charms thought to enclose spirits that are prepared in Kongo territory (part of present-day Congo and Angola) for both healing and aggressive purposes.[44] Typically containing things such as leaves, earth, ashes, seeds, stones, herbs, and sticks, *minkisi* can take figurative and nonfigurative forms. When combined with singing, drumming, dancing, and vows, they take on life and can effect change for their owner.[45] They can influence a wide range of change: from honing business skills to bringing someone back to health to resisting colonization. The *nkisi nkondi* figure, in particular, is a powerful, traditional oath-taking object. Covered with nails and other pointed objects, the figure symbolizes the tyings or nailings of various arguments, lawsuits, vows, and other dealings.[46]

In 1988, Renée Stout activated her fascination with and knowledge of *minkisi* to re-present the Black female body. In so doing, she boldly confronted the entrenched crisis of representation surrounding the body. Like Alison Saar, Stout drew from non-Western artistic practices and blended them with Western ones to confront the quagmire. Named after a burdened Western concept, *Fetish #2* stands five feet and three inches tall (fig. 27). This mixed-media sculpture represents a fusion: the mystery and power of *minkisi* with the figure of Stout's own U.S.-based body. To create the work, Stout cast herself in plaster and then painted the mold with layers of black paint. By casting herself, she avoided the charged and troubled relationship between artist and model and embraced working with and finding inspiration in her own body. In presenting herself as a power figure, Stout resituates the Black female body. The body is rescued from being "overseen" as exotica and erotica because now it is both empowered and protected, for dangling around the woman's neck is a generous supply of *minkisi*-like charms.[47]

In addition, the figure's abdomen contains objects protected by glass. Mirrors and glass are frequently a part of *minkisi*. Often attached to the exterior, as they are in *Fetish #2*, they signify power, what Robert Farris Thompson has called "the flash and arrest of the spirit."[48] Stout was taken with this aspect of *minkisi*. "I was always impressed with the mystery of what lay behind the mirror. I knew that what was behind the mirror was positive," she says.[49] Stout has placed a turn-of-the-century photograph of a baby, dried flowers, and a stamp from Niger behind the glass. In this way the woman's belly, the site of her reproductive labor, is positively reclaimed.[50] And the woman's body is no longer overly available, as it is gently veiled in mystery and grace.

Renée Stout is interested in the presence, meaning, and purpose of Kongo *minkisi*. In *Fetish #2*, she draws upon their use as agents of heal-

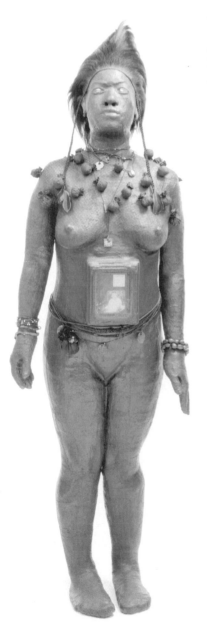

Fig. 27. Renée Stout, *Fetish #2*, 1988. Mixed media. Dallas Museum of Art, Dallas, Texas. Metroplitan Life Foundation Purchase Grant.

ing in multiple ways. Not only is her female figure laden with protective bundles and embedded with the power of glass and objects, but the entire process of creating the sculpture, she tells us, became a vehicle for personal protection. "I felt like in creating that piece, if I never created another one, I had created all that I needed to protect me for the rest of my life," she explains.[51] Like Alison Saar, Renée Stout positions the Black female figure at the crossroads of histories and traditions to confront the visual legacies of the past and to expand the realm of the imaginable.

The history of various markets for Black female bodies, or economies of the flesh, troubles representations of the Black female body. Since this body has been overseen, viewed as perpetually available, a curio, erotica, and exotica, it is not surprising that its representation has either upheld these confines or been avoided altogether. Since the Black female body has been overly visible—and dangerously so—for so long, it makes sense for heirs of the culture of dissemblance to remove the body, cover it, and protect it from harm. Yet this absence is really not an absence, for it draws attention to itself by attempting to hide. Artists and cultural historians such as Emma Amos, Alison Saar, and Renée Stout are unearthing this entrenched absence by retelling the history of the Black female body and re-presenting it. In so doing, they create space for reflection and change. They enable viewers to reflect upon the economies of the flesh, and, just as importantly, they provide a visual language that continues to address the legacies of the past while encouraging the possibility of a self-determined Black female presence. These artists boldly confront visual predicaments and offer us visual possibilities.

NOTES

1. Judith Wilson, "Getting Down to Get Over: Romare Bearden's Use of Pornography and the Problem of the Black Female Body in Afro-U.S. Art," Gina Dent, ed., in *Black Popular Culture* (Seattle: Bay Press, 1992), 121. In her article, Wilson notes that inspiration for her exploration of the Black nude came from the late art historian Sylvia Ardyn Boone.

2. Wilson, "Getting Down to Get Over," 114.

3. Personal correspondence with Karen C. C. Dalton, Director and Curator, Image of the Black in Western Art Research Project and Photo Archive, Harvard University, 7 Oct. 1996.

4. These nudes largely depict African women and women of African descent not living in the United States.

5. Kenneth Clark, *The Nude: A Study in Ideal Form* (Washington D.C.: National Gallery of Art, 1956; reprint, Princeton: Princeton University Press, 1990), 71.

6. Gill Saunders, *The Nude: A New Perspective* (New York: Harper and Row, 1980), 73.

7. Saunders, *The Nude,* 74. For another feminist analysis of the nude, see Lynda Nead, *The Female Nude: Art, Obscenity and Sexuality* (London: Routledge, 1992).

8. Hugh Honour, *The Image of the Black in Western Art*, vol. 4, *From the American Revolution to WWI*, pt. 1 (Cambridge: Harvard University Press, 1989), 64.

9. Honour, *Image of the Black in Western Art*, vol. 4, pt. 1, 166.

10. Phillip Lapsansky, "Graphic Discord: Abolitionist and Antiabolitionist Images," in Jean Fagan Yellin and John Van Horne, eds., *The Abolitionist Sisterhood: Women's Political Culture in Antebellum America* (Ithaca: Cornell University Press, 1994), 206. For more on abolitionist imagery, see Jean Fagan Yellin, "The Abolitionist Emblem," in *Women and Sisters: The Antislavery Feminists in American Culture* (New Haven: Yale University Press, 1989), 3–26.

11. Hortense Spillers, "Interstices: A Small Drama of Words," in Carole S. Vance, ed., *Pleasure and Danger; Exploring Female Sexuality* (Boston: Routledge and Kegan Paul, 1984; reprint, London: Pandora Press, 1989), 76.

12. Sander L. Gilman, "Black Bodies, White Bodies: Toward an Iconography of Female Sexuality in Late Nineteenth-Century Art, Medicine, and Literature," *Critical Inquiry* 12 (autumn 1985): 212.

13. Hugh Honour, *The Image of the Black in Western Art,* vol. 4, *From the American Revolution to WW I,* pt. 2 (Cambridge: Harvard University Press, 1989), 153.

14. Lorraine O'Grady, "Olympia's Maid: Reclaiming Black Female Sexuality," *Afterimage* 20 (summer 1992): 14.

15. Albert Boime, *The Art of Exclusion: Representing Blacks in the Nineteenth Century* (Washington, D.C.: Smithsonian Institution, 1990), 4.

16. Hugh Honour, *The New Golden Land: European Images of America from the Discoveries to the Present Time* (New York: Pantheon, 1975), 209.

17. It's likely that the model was his mistress, a woman he called "Phryne" in his diary. For more on this relationship, see David B. Dickens, "Frank Buchser in Virginia: A Swiss Artist's Impressions," *Virginia Cavalcade* 38 (1988): 6–7. Also see Rudolph P. Byrd, "American Images for Circulation: The Black Portraiture of Frank Buchser," in William U. Eiland and Laura Mullins, eds., *Frank Buchser: A Swiss Artist in America, 1866–1871* (Athens: Georgia Museum of Art, 1996), 46.

18. Honour, *Image of the Black,* vol. 4, pt. 2, 166.

19. Kirsten Buick, "The Ideal Works of Edmonia Lewis: Invoking and Inverting Autobiography," *American Art* 9 (summer 1995): 14.

20. Kirsten Buick, "Edmonia Lewis in Art History: The Paradox of the Exotic Subject," in Leslie King-Hammond and Tritobia Hayes Benjamin, eds., *Three Generations of African American Women Sculptors: A Study in Paradox* (Philadelphia: Afro-American Historical and Cultural Museum, 1996), 14.

21. Darlene Clark Hine, "Rape and the Inner Lives of Black Women: Thoughts on the Culture of Dissemblance," in *Hine Sight: Black Women and The Re-Construction of American History* (Brooklyn: Carlson Publishing, 1994), 37–38.

22. Hine, "Rape and the Inner Lives of Black Women," 38.

23. Hine, "Rape and the Inner Lives of Black Women," 44–45.

24. Donald Bogle, *Brown Sugar: Eighty Years of America's Black Female Superstars* (New York: Da Capo Press, 1980), 48.

25. Bogle, *Brown Sugar,* 48.

26. Josephine Baker and Jo Bouillon, *Josephine,* trans. Mariana Fitzpatrick

(New York: Harper and Row, 1977; reprint, New York: Marlow and Company, 1988), 66.

27. Baker and Bouillon, *Josephine,* 71.

28. Baker and Bouillon, *Josephine,* 51.

29. Lucy Lippard, "Floating Falling Landing: An Interview with Emma Amos," *Art Papers* 15 (Nov.–Dec. 1991): 15.

30. Mildred Thompson, "Interview: Emma Amos," *Art Papers* 19 (Mar.–Apr. 1995): 23.

31. bell hooks, "Interview with Emma Amos," *Artist and Influence* 14 (1995): 34.

32. Judith Wilson, "Hexes, Totems and Necessary Saints: A Conversation with Alison Saar," *Real Life* 19 (winter 1988–89): 36.

33. bell hooks, "Talking Art with Alison Saar," in *Art on My Mind: Visual Politics* (New York: New Press, 1995), 30.

34. hooks, "Talking Art with Alison Saar," 30.

35. Robert Farris Thompson, *Flash of the Spirit: African and Afro-American Art and Philosophy* (New York: Random House, 1983; reprint, New York, Vintage, 1984), 135–42.

36. Robert Farris Thompson, *Flash of the Spirit,* 132.

37. Robert Farris Thompson, *Flash of the Spirit,* 18–33.

38. Born in 1880 in Boston and raised in a family of both Black and white activists, Angelina Weld Grimké was named after her great-aunt, the noted white abolitionist and suffragist Angelina Grimké Weld. Literary scholar Gloria Hull has posited that the Black poet held romantic, albeit "thwarted," feelings for women. See Gloria T. Hull, *Color, Sex, and Poetry: Three Women Writers of the Harlem Renaissance* (Bloomington: Indiana University Press, 1987), 138–41.

39. Angelina Weld Grimké, "Grass Fingers," in Countee Cullen, ed., *Caroling Dusk: Anthology of Verse by Negro Poets* (New York: Harper and Brothers, 1927), 38.

40. Text accompanying the piece at the Walker Art Center, Minneapolis.

41. Wilson, "Hexes, Totems and Necessary Saints," 38.

42. George Lipsitz, "Diasporic Intimacy in the Art of Renée Stout," in Marla C. Berns, ed., *"Dear Robert, I'll See You at the Crossroads": A Project by Renée Stout* (Santa Barbara: University Art Museum, 1995), 9. Lipsitz cites Theophus Smith's work as informing his own. See Theophus H. Smith, *Conjuring Culture: Biblical Formations of Black America* (New York: Oxford, 1994).

43. Curtia James, "Interview: Renée Stout," *Art Papers* 18 (July–Aug. 1994): 3.

44. Anthropologist Wyatt MacGaffey writes that *minkisi* were first seen in West Central Africa by westerners in the fifteenth century and were almost immediately recognized as a threat to Christian authority. In addition, these objects took on increased importance as the crisis of the shaping of colonial structures gained force in the 1880s, when Portuguese, French, and Belgian authorities all attempted to create colonial systems in the region. See Wyatt MacGaffey, "The Eyes of Understanding: Kongo Minkisi," in Wyatt MacGaffey and Michael D. Harris, *Astonishment and Power: Kongo Minkisi and the Art of Renée Stout* (Washington, D.C.: National Museum of African Art, 1993), 30, 33.

45. Robert Farris Thompson, "Kongo Civilization and Kongo Art," in Robert

Farris Thompson and Joseph Cornet, *The Four Moments of the Sun: Kongo Art in Two Worlds* (Washington, D.C.: National Gallery of Art, 1981), 37.

46. Robert Farris Thompson, "Kongo Civilization and Kongo Art," 38.

47. Michael D. Harris discusses how Stout's figure "straddles the tradition of the female nude, the self-portrait, and that of ritual fetish objects" in his article "Ritual Bodies—Sexual Bodies: The Role and Presentation of the Body in African-American Art," *Third Text* 12 (autumn 1990): 87. Also see his essay "Resonance, Transformation, and Rhyme: The Art of Renée Stout," in Mac-Gaffey and Harris, *Astonishment and Power.*

48. Thompson, *Flash of the Spirit,* 118.

49. Renée Stout, quoted in Robert Farris Thompson, "The Song That Named the Land: The Visionary Presence of African-American Art," in Robert Rozelle, Alvia Wardlaw, and Maureen McKenna, eds., *Black Art—Ancestral Legacy: The African Impulse in African-American Art* (Dallas: Dallas Museum of Art, 1989), 132.

50. In her discussion of *Fetish #2,* Africanist art historian Marla C. Berns notes that Stout's work shifts the focus of the *nkisi* from a "source of communal strength and agency" to one of "self-empowerment." Likewise she points out that Stout adapts "the aggressive, menacing and explicitly male aspects of the *nkisi nkondi* figure for her own (female) purposes." See Marla C. Berns, "On Love and Longing: Renée Stout Does the Blues," in *"Dear Robert, I'll See You at the Crossroads,"* 27.

51. Renée Stout, *Kindred Spirits: Contemporary African-American Artists,* prod. Clayton Corrie, dir. Christine McConnell (Dallas: KERA-TV, 1992), videocassette.

REFERENCES

Baker, Josephine, and Jo Bouillon. *Josephine.* Trans. Mariana Fitzpatrick. New York: Harper and Row, 1977. Reprint, New York: Marlowe and Company, 1988.

Berns, Marla C., ed. *"Dear Robert, I'll See You at the Crossroads": A Project by Renée Stout.* Santa Barbara: University Art Museum, 1995.

Bogle, Donald. *Brown Sugar: Eighty Years of America's Black Female Superstars.* New York: Da Capo Press, 1980.

Boime, Albert. *The Art of Exclusion: Representing Blacks in the Nineteenth Century.* Washington, D.C.: Smithsonian Institution Press, 1990.

Buick, Kirsten. "Edmonia Lewis in Art History: The Paradox of the Exotic Subject." In Leslie King-Hammond and Tritobia Hayes Benjamin, eds., *Three Generations of African American Women Sculptors: A Study in Paradox,* 12–15. Philadelphia: Afro-American Historical and Cultural Museum, 1996.

———. "The Ideal Works of Edmonia Lewis: Invoking and Inverting Autobiography." *American Art* 9 (summer 1995): 5–19.

Byrd, Rudolph P. "American Images for Circulation: The Black Portraiture of Frank Buchser." In William U. Eiland and Laura Mullins, eds., *Frank Buchser: A Swiss Artist in America, 1866–1871,* 43–49. Athens: Georgia Museum of Art, University of Georgia, 1996.

Clark, Kenneth. *The Nude: A Study in Ideal Form.* Washington, D.C.: National Gallery of Art, 1956. Reprint, Princeton: Princeton University Press, 1990.

Dickens, David B. "Frank Buchser in Virginia: A Swiss Artist's Impressions." *Virginia Cavalcade* 38 (1988): 4–13.

Gilman, Sander L. "Black Bodies, White Bodies: Toward an Iconography of Female Sexuality in Late Nineteenth-Century Art, Medicine, and Literature." *Critical Inquiry* 12 (autumn 1985): 204–42.

Grimké, Angelina Weld. "Grass Fingers." In Countee Cullen, ed., *Caroling Dusk: Anthology of Verse by Negro Poets,* 38. New York: Harper and Brothers, 1927.

Harris, Michael D. "Ritual Bodies—Sexual Bodies: The Role and Presentation of the Body in African-American Art." *Third Text* 12 (autumn 1990): 81–95.

Hine, Darlene Clark. "Rape and the Inner Lives of Black Women: Thoughts on the Culture of Dissemblance." In *Hine Sight: Black Women and the Re-Construction of American History.* Brooklyn: Carlson Publishing, 1994.

Honour, Hugh. *The Image of the Black in Western Art.* Vol. 4, *From the American Revolution to WWI.* Cambridge: Harvard University Press, 1989.

———. *The New Golden Land: European Images of America from the Discoveries to the Present Time.* New York: Pantheon, 1975.

hooks, bell. *Art on My Mind: Visual Politics.* New York: New Press, 1995.

———. "Interview with Emma Amos." *Artist and Influence* 14 (1995): 33–46.

Hull, Gloria T. *Color, Sex, and Poetry: Three Women Writers of the Harlem Renaissance.* Bloomington: Indiana University Press, 1987.

James, Curtia. "Interview: Renée Stout." *Art Papers* 18 (July–August 1994): 2–5.

Lapsansky, Phillip. "Graphic Discord: Abolitionist and Antiabolitionist Images." In Jean Fagan Yellin and John C. Van Horne, eds., *The Abolitionist Sisterhood: Women's Political Culture in Antebellum America,* 201–30. Ithaca: Cornell University Press, 1994.

Lippard, Lucy. "Floating Falling Landing: An Interview with Emma Amos." *Art Papers* 15 (November–December 1991): 13–16.

MacGaffey, Wyatt, and Michael D. Harris. *Astonishment and Power: Kongo Minkisi and the Art of Renée Stout.* Washington, D.C.: National Museum of African Art, 1993.

Nead, Lynda. *The Female Nude: Art, Obscenity and Sexuality.* London: Routledge, 1992.

O'Grady, Lorraine. "Olympia's Maid: Reclaiming Black Female Subjectivity." *Afterimage* 20 (summer 1992): 14–15, 23.

Rozelle, Robert, Alvia Wardlaw, and Maureen McKenna, eds. *Black Art—Ancestral Legacy: The African Impulse in African-American Art.* Dallas: Dallas Museum of Art, 1989.

Saunders, Gill. *The Nude: A New Perspective.* New York: Harper and Row, 1989.

Smith, Theophus H. *Conuring Culture: Biblical Formations of Black America.* New York: Oxford, 1994.

Spillers, Hortense. "Interstices: A Small Drama of Words." In Carole S. Vance, ed., *Pleasure and Danger: Exploring Female Sexuality,* 73–100. Boston: Routledge and Kegan Paul, 1984. Reprint, London: Pandora Press, 1989.

Stout, Renée. *Kindred Spirits: Contemporary African-American Artists.* Produced by Clayton Corrie and directed by Christine McConnell. Dallas: KERA-TV, 1992. Videocassette.

Thompson, Mildred. "Interview: Emma Amos." *Art Papers* 19 (March–April 1995): 21–23.

Thompson, Robert Farris. *Flash of the Spirit: African and Afro-American Art and Philosophy.* New York: Random House, 1983. Reprint, New York: Vintage, 1984.

Thompson, Robert Farris, and Joseph Cornet. *The Four Moments of the Sun: Kongo Art in Two Worlds.* Washington, D.C.: National Gallery of Art, 1981.

Wilson, Judith. "Getting Down to Get Over: Romare Bearden's Use of Pornography and the Problem of the Black Female Body in Afro-U.S. Art." In Gina Dent, ed., *Black Popular Culture,* 112–22. Seattle: Bay Press, 1992.

———. "Hexes, Totems and Necessary Saints: A Conversation with Alison Saar." *Real Life* 19 (winter 1988–89): 36–41.

Yellin, Jean Fagan. *Women and Sisters: The Antislavery Feminists in American Culture.* New Haven: Yale University Press, 1989.

Lisa E. Farrington

Faith Ringgold's *Slave Rape* Series

Thirty years ago, Faith Ringgold's painting *The Flag Is Bleeding* (fig. 28) was exhibited for the first time. The American flag dripping blood etched itself into the memories of those who viewed it at New York's Spectrum Gallery. Over the next several decades, Ringgold became a formidable artist and personality. She is one of very few women of color who helped to spearhead both the Black and Feminist Art Movements in New York in the early 1970s. A political and creative powerhouse, Ringgold has been credited with raising the tradition of quilt-making from the realm of craft to that of fine art. She has also pierced the near-impenetrable armor of the art world—no small accomplishment for an African American woman. Now, her "story quilts" (narrative paintings bordered with quilted fabric) hold honored places in the collections of many great repositories of art.[1]

At a recent conference on African American culture, renowned art historian Robert Farris Thompson spoke enthusiastically about Ringgold's paintings of the 1960s. Due to their stark political imagery, these works have received a great deal of art-historical attention, as have Ringgold's "story quilts" of the 1980s and 1990s, well known for their unique format and engaging narratives.[2] There are, however, works from the intervening period of the 1970s that have been examined only superficially. They consist of a group of *thangka* paintings known as the *Slave Rape* series.

A *thangka* (pronounced "ton-kah") is a sacred Tibetan painting bordered in quilted fabric. In the summer of 1972, Ringgold saw her first *thangkas* at the Rijksmuseum in Amsterdam and was immediately inspired to "unstretch" her own canvases and replace their standard wooden stretchers with soft fabric borders. Ringgold found the portability of the *thangkas* irresistible. For years, the artist had been compelled to carry her large-scale paintings up and down the fourteen

Fig. 28. Faith Ringgold, *The Flag Is Bleeding,* 1967. Oil on canvas, 72 x 96 inches. (Courtesy of the artist's collection.) © Faith Ringgold.

flights of stairs that led to her Harlem apartment because, as she recalls, "the elevator, damn it, was too small."[3] In the *thangkas,* Ringgold discovered a solution to the problem: "I could do this. I could get rid of my frames, the glass, the cumbersome heavy stretchers and frame my paintings in cloth. That way I could roll up my paintings and put them in a trunk and ship them in the same way I used to ship my daughter's clothes to camp."[4] The *thangkas* prompted Ringgold (both a mother and an artist) to associate their fabric borders with her children's clothing—items that could be easily folded for shipping. Experimenting as she did throughout her career with the form and content of her art made it possible for Ringgold to reject the time-honored tradition of painting on canvas for a method that creatively and practically suited her needs.

Ringgold was, in fact, one of several women artists who were experimenting with fabric at the time. Artists such as Miriam Schapiro, Betye Saar, Judy Chicago, and Joyce Kozloff were engaged in deconstructing the modernist, minimalist tradition that had effectively marginalized decorative and fabric art. In the art of these women form became content; their work granted so-called woman's art long-overdue precedence.[5] Within a decade, Ringgold would be utilizing the fabric format as the basis for her story quilts.

The importance of the *thangkas* lies in the fact that they form a vital link between the artist's earlier works on canvas and her later quilted paintings. Yet Ringgold's *thangkas* remain her least-known works. The *Slave Rape thangkas*, like their Tibetan predecessors, have no stretchers. This feature makes them intimate and inviting, especially since the fabric must be handled as each *thangka* is unfolded for viewing. The colors are incandescent and intense; the paintings depict playful images with an uncommon theme—nude Black women who frolic in lush foliage. Indeed, Ringgold's figures constitute one of the rare instances in Western art wherein the Black female nude is portrayed.

Unlike most of the traditional nudes that have proliferated since antiquity, the women in the *Slave Rape* paintings are active and armed. They provide a stark contrast to classic Western female nude images, in which women are usually presented as passive and defenseless. Furthermore, Ringgold's enigmatic figures are rendered in a flat, two-dimensional fashion, and their facial expressions, disturbingly, allude to caricature. This chapter will examine the artist's highly idiosyncratic configuration, in the *Slave Rape* series, of the female nude and the complex motivations that inspired Ringgold (and a number of her contemporaries) to appropriate images that, for decades, had been construed as negative—and even stereotypical (see fig. 29).

The nude figures in many of the *Slave Rape* paintings are nonheroic in appearance. They seem vulnerable within the context of the narrative. Their faces stare out at us in surprise, and their lips form little "O" shapes, as if mouthing silent cries for help. The distressed expressions, however, do not communicate to the viewer a bona fide sense of the women's predicament. On the contrary, one finds little tension in these lyrical renderings. Ringgold's works seem almost playful—a fact that unmistakably contradicts their theme. The figures, like the landscapes that surround them, are lush and fecund. The sumptuous corporeality of these full-breasted women seems to mock the dire subject of the series, as does the artist's deliberately unsophisticated portrayal. Yet, as we will see, Ringgold's seemingly lighthearted rendering of the tragic subject of slave rape serves a critical purpose for both the artist and the viewer.

The *Slave Rape* paintings constitute a visual and metaphorical reification of the history of the enslaved African. The desire to comprehend this past was the chief motivating factor in Ringgold's decision to paint the series. "*Slave Rape* was . . . like going back and trying to understand

Fig. 29. Faith Ringgold, *Help:* Slave Rape *Series #15*, 1973. Acrylic on canvas, 45 x 23 inches. (Courtesy of the artist's collection.) © Faith Ringgold.

some of the roots of black women coming here," explains Ringgold. "What were we doing here? What is the history of us coming to this country, and what were we like before we got here? I wanted to be in touch with that."[6] Beyond this inquiry into Ringgold's African past is the artist's expression of a need to understand her women ancestors, who managed, against the odds, to survive their enslavement. Ringgold brings to *Slave Rape* a knowledge of the facts of slavery and a deliberate refiguring of those facts. She empowers these women and transforms them from victims into victors within the context of a narrative. In doing so, Ringgold deconstructs a number of Black female stereotypes.

Most striking in this series is the ability of the figures to allude to and also subvert Black stereotypes. Derisive characters such as Mammy, Jezebel, Sambo, and the like were popularized at the turn of the twentieth century concurrently with the passing of "Jim Crow" legislation, which served to institutionalize segregation. Both phenomena functioned to recapture a lost social order—that of the master and the slave—wherein Blacks were subjected by law to white control. At the same time that Blacks were being legally isolated, they were being socially denigrated. African Americans were portrayed as shiftless, stupid, lazy, irresponsible, and dangerous. These false constructs quickly became part of the American consciousness and worked their dreadful magic by representing Blacks in subservient and powerless roles, often with grossly exaggerated features. In these negative portrayals, the complex American social dynamic between the majority and the minority was reinforced and perpetuated. Furthermore, Black women suffered an added burden—they had to deal with a second set of stereotypes that were grounded not in race but in gender.[7]

The abundant and elaborate mythology that has been assigned to African American women has been characterized by author and activist Frances Beale as "malicious." Black women, Beale explains, have been molested and abused; they have suffered economic exploitation; they have been forced to serve as maid and wet nurse to white families, and as a result, their own children often have been neglected. These women have been socially manipulated, physically raped, and used to undermine their own households. Finally, Beale concludes, Black women have been powerless to reverse this syndrome.[8] Yet are Black women truly powerless in this regard? Certainly in the case of the visual arts, the answer is no. Although for African American women racism and sexism have worked together to create "a hell of a history to live down," the false paradigms that portray Black women as both physically unattractive and sexually promiscuous, passive and aggressive, good caregivers to white children and bad mothers to their own children, have all been challenged by Black artists.[9] The efforts of women artists of color, in conjunction with those of Black male artists, have resulted in a partial dismantling of these myths. Black feminist author bell hooks and historian

Patricia Morton have argued that Black artists actively have appropriated and exploited their own negative stereotypes in order to assert control over them.[10]

The three most popular of these stereotypes have been identified by Morton as the passive, domestic worker, or "Mammy"; the emasculating "Matriarch," or Superwoman; and the chronically promiscuous "Jezebel." These myths, Morton explains, serve to justify white fears and alleviate status anxieties by projecting what is feared onto others—a practice that both rationalizes and perpetuates oppression. The devastating consequences of these stereotypes have necessitated the creation of new images that counteract existing ones. Concerted efforts to accomplish this occurred first during the Harlem Renaissance and again at the time of the Civil Rights Movement. During these periods, Black artists were inspired to use visual imagery as a countermeasure to weaken the impact of negative Black stereotypes. In the 1950s and 1960s, Blacks offered alternative sets of cultural definitions and images that resulted in major structural changes—changes reflected in the decline of the acceptance of stereotypes in popular culture.[11] One of the most ubiquitous and tenacious of these stereotypes was that of Aunt Jemima.

Jeff Donaldson and Joe Overstreet, two artists of the Black Art Movement, took advantage of the likeness of Aunt Jemima, using it in their own art to transform the docile "Mammy" into an image of power. Jeff Donaldson's *Aunt Jemima (and the Pillsbury Dough Boy) '64* (1963–64) (fig. 30) presents viewers with a physically commanding woman who is locked in violent conflict with a pot-bellied, club-wielding policeman. The pair are set against the background of an American flag whose stripes have been distorted to form chevron patterns reminiscent of African textiles (which perhaps serves as a metaphor for a reordered American state). Donaldson redefines Aunt Jemima as a "Superwoman"—someone who is quite capable of protecting herself against police brutality by direct, one-on-one confrontation with her uniformed attacker.

In Joe Overstreet's *The New Jemima* (1964) (fig. 31), a "pop rendition of the pancake maker-turned-warrior" smiles cheerfully out at the viewer.[12] Yet Jemima's smile takes on an alternate meaning when seen in conjunction with the machine gun that she fires from her hip. Pancake-like wafers fly through the air like clay targets in a skeet shoot, and their fluttering forms lead the viewer's eye to the words stenciled across the top of the canvas: "Made in the USA." The message alludes both to the stereotype of Aunt Jemima and to the violent and dangerous reaction to the stereotype that she embodies.

Fig. 30. Jeff Donaldson, *Aunt Jemima (and the Pillsbury Dough-boy) '64*, 1963–64. Oil on raw linen, 51 5/8 x 52 inches. (Courtesy of the artist's collection.)

Perhaps the most arresting of the attacks on the Mammy stereotype is Betye Saar's 1972 construction *The Liberation of Aunt Jemima* (fig. 32). Saar challenges the convention of the Black domestic in a manner similar to that of both Donaldson and Overstreet, utilizing literally—and metaphorically—layered symbolism. In this work, Saar incorporates the silk-screened face of Aunt Jemima, taken directly from the pancake box, and repeats it in a patterned backdrop. Saar then places in front of this pop-art screen a grotesque rendition of the same icon with bulging eyes; thick, intensely red lips; and a smile that is more grimace than grin. Jemima, who is of course rotund, wears her traditional bandana and shapeless dress. Imbedded in the front of her skirt is another variation on the theme—a third "Mammy," who also smiles as she holds a white infant in her left arm.

Upon careful examination, the viewer realizes that the dress worn

Fig. 31. Joe Overstreet, *The New Jemima*, 1964. Construction, 102 3/8 x 60 3/4 x 17 inches. (Courtesy of the Menil Collection, Houston.)

Fig. 32. Betye Saar, *The Liberation of Aunt Jemima*, 1972. Mixed media, 11 3/4 x 8 x 2 3/4 inches. (Courtesy of the collection of the University of California, Berkeley.)

by this figure is in actuality a magnified black fist—the sign of "Black Power"—and that the infant she holds is resting on the apex of that fist. The baby cries, its face is smudged with dirt, and its brows are deeply furrowed with anxiety. This is hardly a conventional rendition of the subject, which would typically portray the Mammy as a helpful caregiver to her white charges. Instead, Saar offers the viewer an unpleasant alternative—that of a neglected, sullen infant for whom the smiling nanny has little empathy.

As the viewer's attention is turned away from this disturbing scene to reenter the larger framework of the composition, he or she is made to acknowledge the broom that the stout, grimacing figure holds in her right hand. Almost as an afterthought, the viewer notes the small pistol held in the same hand and the larger rifle, potent with lethal energy, that is positioned at the left side of the figure and that balances the broom compositionally. Yolanda Lopez and Moira Roth describe this assemblage as psychologically and politically explosive. Saar's powerful Aunt Jemima, they argue, is reconfigured from an obsequious servant into a woman participating in her own liberation.[13] Saar, like Overstreet, accomplishes this feat of empowerment by arming her figure and, consequently, negating her subservient and passive status.

Each of these three works is meant to portray a "benign matron turned urban guerrilla" who has awakened from her smiling passivity with a vengeance.[14] Yet, by eradicating all evidence of passivity and complacency, these artists have, in fact, replaced Aunt Jemima with a new archetype—that of the black "Superwoman." Gone is the benevolent matron. In her place stands an angry and violent fighting machine, ready to do battle with guns or fists, posing malevolent danger to man and child. Although empowering, the Superwoman is not necessarily more realistic than the Mammy. In this regard, Ringgold's *Slave Rape* series differs from the works of her contemporaries in ways that at first may not be apparent.

Paralleling the works of Donaldson, Overstreet, and Saar, the *Slave Rape* paintings serve to reconfigure the Black stereotype and undermine its negative impact. Ringgold has armed her protagonists and likened them, visually, to Black caricatures through the subtle use of rounded eyes, widely opened mouths, brightly painted lips, animated postures, and cartoon-like expressions of surprise (see fig. 33). However, Ringgold's appropriation of the stereotype differs from those mentioned earlier in several important ways. For instance, the feature of Ringgold's figures are moderately, rather than grossly, exaggerated. In addition, while Ringgold's women are armed to do battle, they also exhibit fear and surprise and are thus more sympathetic as characters than the invulnerable Superwoman, whose self-sufficiency garners her neither compassion nor support. By utilizing a subtler approach to the theme of the Black female stereotype, Ringgold is able to acknowledge the vulnerability of these African women while simultaneously asserting their active resistance to victimization.

Fig. 33. Faith Ringgold, *Fight:* Slave Rape *Series #13*, 1973. Acrylic on canvas, 45 x 28 inches. (Courtesy of the artist's collection.) © Faith Ringgold.

Several details further confound a straightforward reading of the *Slave Rape* paintings. First, the theme of women being chased by slave catchers is deadly serious. The figures are completely preoccupied with their predicament. They cry out, run in panic, and fight their attackers. Yet the viewer does not sense any genuine distress on their parts. The scene is distinctly humorous, even satirical, due to the stiff, awkward, and even weak gestures of the figures and their animated expressions. The artist purposely has fused a grim theme with a facetious rendering, and the use of humor is the key to the symbolism of the *Slave Rape* series.

Ringgold's humor diminishes the horrors of the past. The artist, through exaggerated gestures and expressions, undermines the gravity of the drama by enhancing its comic nature. She mitigates the horror of slave rape by depicting it as somewhat less than horrible. In this way, the viewer can absorb the image—and the lesson—without becoming unnerved by the subject matter. If the artist did not temper the theme in this manner, the paintings might well be deemed unpalatable by the viewer and, in effect, become useless as communicative vehicles. Ringgold's intention is first to draw the viewer into the image before revealing the true nature of the subject. Moira Roth explains that Ringgold's formal techniques, while seemingly naive, are both deliberate and sophisticated. "If we read Ringgold carefully," Roth asserts, "we are forced to face that hidden and ugly part of our history. Here again, however, the narrative often sweetens the message by its beguiling tone." In the case of the *Slave Rape* portrayals, the beguiling tone is achieved through the clear blue skies and the colorful flowers that crowd the landscape, as well as through the seemingly playful body language of the women.[15]

Ringgold's method of using humor to veil a more profound political or social statement serves not only to instruct her audiences but also to give the artist an outlet for the inevitable frustrations that come with living in an oppressive society. In a broader context, many who find themselves living in difficult situations use humor as a coping mechanism. For example, beyond the scope of the visual arts one can find a similar use of humor in African American folktales and fiction. Subjects such as lynching, unemployment, and poverty are routinely addressed with irony and satire. These jokes are often directed inward, upon Blacks themselves, and can be harsh to the point of cruelty. Yet making light of oppression helps African Americans to adjust to the intolerable aspects of their lives and history that cannot be altered. Joking serves as a safety valve, channeling off tensions and mitigating rage and frustration.[16] In an insightful essay entitled "The Meaning of Laughter," Philip Sterling notes that there has been no anguish in the lives of African Americans that could not be met with both laughter and tears. Tears are surrender. Laughter is consolation and, ultimately, triumph.[17]

Reforming both an oral and a written tradition into a pictorial language, Ringgold uses satire as a weapon of defense and exorcism. She has coined the phrase "wild art" to describe art by Black women that is designed to purge the painful emotions that are associated with living under oppression. For Ringgold, "wild art" is about rage; it is about the things that we are powerless to change. In the artist's own words, "It is an obsession we cannot escape. So we isolate it, picture it, and then we are free to let it go."[18] The routine and systematic rape of enslaved African women has haunted American history, distorting in myriad ways the true identity of Black women. This disturbing historical fact is what Ringgold "pictures" and what she ultimately "lets go." Through the painting process, the artist worked to reinterpret Black womanhood and counteract the many stereotypes that were a consequence of the ordeal of slavery.

One such stereotype was that of the "Jezebel." Mistaken beliefs that African women were sexually promiscuous and, like animals, fit only for breeding formed the foundation for the "Jezebel" myth. This fiction began the moment African women were taken as prisoners—the very moment Ringgold has chosen to capture on canvas. The torment of rape was reserved primarily for enslaved women, who, during the Middle Passage, were nightly brought above decks for this ordeal. Refusal to submit often meant death, thus posing a terrible moral dilemma for the African women. Submission to the European sailors, however abhorrent, meant possible survival and even some measure of protection from the worst horrors of the voyage. Thus, after examples had been made of the first few uncooperative women (usually by way of beatings), many others chose to capitulate without resistance. Hence, before even arriving in the New World, African women were labelled promiscuous and lacking in morals by the very Europeans who had repeatedly raped them.[19]

Once the African woman was in the New World, her sexuality quickly became a commodity. She was seen as a breeder—an animal whose monetary value could be calculated precisely in terms of her ability to reproduce. Thus, her experience of motherhood was shaped, through the slave system, by capitalist efforts to harness her fertility for its dollar value. By closely associating the Black woman's sexuality with money, the system of slavery presented her as a prostitute. Who else would "sell" her own body? Furthermore, slavery created a situation wherein the enslaved woman was sexually abused by her white master and simultaneously despised by her white mistress, who blamed the slave woman for her husband's infidelities. The mistress often reacted to her own predicament by further mistreating the slave woman, and the latter found herself trapped in a relentless cycle of abuse.[20]

The consequences of this painful history are eloquently addressed by Alice Walker in her book *In Search of Our Mothers' Gardens,* where the author refers to Black women of the past as "crazed Saints" who "stared out at the world wildly, like lunatics—or quietly, like suicides" and who

Fig. 34. Faith Ringgold, *Fight: To Save Your Life*, 1972. Oil on canvas *thangka* by Willi Posey, 87 × 48 inches. (Courtesy of the artist's collection.) © Faith Ringgold.

"without a doubt, were our mothers and grandmothers."[21] It is difficult to look at Ringgold's painting *Fight: To Save Your Life* (fig. 34) without imagining the crazed saints to whom Walker refers. Ringgold's monumental nude does indeed peer out at us "wildly." She stands frozen and timeless, and the viewer is left either to stare at the figure's improbable image or to turn away from the blank emptiness of her gaze, which is, to use Walker's words, as "mute as a great stone."[22]

Identified by the artist as self-reflexive, the woman in *Fight* signifies both a universal and a personal experience. By 1972, when Ringgold painted this work, she had survived the deaths, from heroin abuse, of her first husband and of her older brother. For many years, the artist strove to overcome these tragedies, to raise her daughters alone, to support her family on a public school teacher's salary, and, simultaneously, to become a successful artist. Often coping alone with the burdens of motherhood, with her losses as a wife and sister, and with the racial and gender-based discrimination of the art world, Ringgold incorporated these experiences into the "selfless abstraction"—again to use Walker's phrase—of the stark, lone figure in *Fight*.[23]

Ringgold's woman gently and carefully holds her rounded stomach, perhaps intending to draw our attention to the abdomen as the locus of the uterus and of life. We are thus reminded, as Walker suggests, that this woman is more than an objectified victim; she is presented as a shrine of motherhood and future generations. Yet, despite this association, Ringgold's figure remains tragic. Unclothed except for the overlapping leaves that brush her shoulders, unprotected except for the carefully carved axe that she holds at her side, Ringgold's slave-to-be is frozen with surprise. Her gaze is locked with ours, and the artist's desperate cry echoing back through time, "Fight, to save your life," seems to fall on deaf ears. This woman, like Eve, has been expelled abruptly from the Garden, and she is stunned by the sudden and permanent change in her circumstances.

In the *Slave Rape* series, Ringgold consciously places herself in the time of her ancestors, those brave African women who survived the horror of being uprooted and carried off to slavery in America. By locating herself in the past, Ringgold is able to stand with her ancestors, put weapons in their hands, and aid them in avoiding capture. Symbolically, she has traveled back in time in order to alter the future. This technique of exploring the African past in order to alter or to reveal some aspect of the present has been utilized successfully by a number of African Americans in the visual arts as well as in literature.[24]

Walker, in another excerpt from *In Search of Our Mothers' Gardens*, describes her similar motivation, as a Black poet, to examine her own history:

> Guided by my heritage of a love of beauty and a respect for strength—in search of my mother's garden, I found my own. And perhaps in Africa over two hundred years ago, there was just such a mother; perhaps she painted vivid and daring decorations in oranges and yellows and greens on the walls of her hut . . . perhaps she wove the most stunning mats or told the most ingenious stories of all the village story tellers.[25]

Both Ringgold and Walker have found comfort and courage in an examination of the past. Ringgold's paintings, like Walker's poetry, recreate the vivid colors, woven patterns, and stories of past generations.

The *Slave Rape* series documents a great tragedy—a circumstance of enslavement and degradation that these women nonetheless survived, leaving a legacy of endurance to their artist-daughters. Significantly, the *Slave Rape* series represents Ringgold's first joint project with

her own mother, Willi Posey. Posey, a well-known Harlem clothing de-
signer, fashioned the fabric borders for *Slave Rape* and continued until
her death in 1981 to work with her daughter on much of her fabric art
throughout the 1970s.[26] Ringgold considers herself a "living link between generations of strong, secure women," and this, she says, gives
her the confidence to survive in today's chaotic world. Ringgold's
method of metaphoric time travel constitutes a form of creative exploration that can be both enlightening and empowering, as it is in the
Slave Rape series. However, it must be noted that life in Africa, as some
have argued, has never been quite the idyll imagined by many African
Americans.[27]

How then do Ringgold's nudes of the past specifically function to
alter negative perceptions of Black women in the present? Before this
question can be answered, it is essential to understand how the nude itself functions in art-historical terms. The "nude" has been defined by
writer-historian Kenneth Clark as an unclothed body that is comfortably
"clothed in art," whereas the "naked" body is one that is "deprived of
clothes, huddled, and defenseless." Art historian John Berger believes
that rather than implying a state of discomfort or embarrassment,
nakedness refers to a "real" woman whose prosaic form has been exalted
by the artist. Both definitions, however, imply the objectification of the
female body. Berger merely shifts the identity of the figure being objectified from an anonymous nude woman to one who embodies "the
painter's personal vision of a particular woman."[28]

According to historians Carol Duncan and Gill Saunders, male
artists "reenact, in hundreds of particular variations, a remarkably limited set of fantasies" that place the female nude in the role of victim. She
must be passive, receptive, and available, and she must be controlled
through assimilation to male desire, objectification, or degradation. In
this way, the male artist/viewer is able to place himself in the role of con-
queror, dominator, or savior. The nude female body is commonly presented as sexual spectacle—an invitation to voyeurism. Thus, female
sexual experience is equated with surrender and victimization.[29]

The question remains, then; where do Ringgold's figures fit within
the context of these paradigms? The female figures in the *Slave Rape* series are unclothed but are not deprived of clothing. Ringgold portrays
them as "nudes"—in a state of dress to which they are accustomed (or
that is "comfortable" for them); still, they experience discomfort similar to that associated by Clark with the "naked" figure. This discomfort,
however, is not derived from their state of undress but rather from the
physical threat to their bodies posed by the slave catcher.

Ringgold's women are neither huddled nor defenseless; their fertile bodies and lush surroundings suggest their prosperity; the weapons they hold in their hands indicate their ability to defend themselves. The figures are neither anonymous (since they are portraits of the artist and her daughters) nor particularized (since they simultaneously symbolize all enslaved African women). Traits such as passivity and submission are eschewed in favor of the more traditionally masculine attributes of energy and cognition. In fact, these women cannot be defined as either nude or naked; they do not completely accommodate traditional definitions of the female nude. It is precisely this obfuscation of artistic conventions that gives the *Slave Rape* series its authority. In a feat of inversion, the *Slave Rape* paintings take the subject of the abduction of African women—a subject that suggests the domination and victimization of women by men—and effectively rewrites the history.[30]

When women artists like Ringgold paint the female nude, they become the objects of their own self-reflexive desires as well as active surveyors of their own bodies. If Duncan's assessment—that male representations of the female nude are in large part about the assertion of the artist's sexual domination—is correct, it would follow that when women paint themselves, they are asserting dominion over their own bodies.[31] As feminist art critic Maryse Holder notes, many women artists of recent decades have deliberately refrained from imitating male artists in their representations of the nude. Instead, they record an experience that empowers female "sexualism" with mythic qualities (such as the ability of African women to triumph over slave catchers). Such depictions enhance self-discovery and promote a sense of self-worth. In fact, the very nature of women artists painting the female nude implies a contradiction of terms, since the male gaze is replaced by a female one. Although women traditionally have been seen as objects rather than as creators of art, their roles as creators, particularly with the nude image, transform conventions. Within this context we can begin to understand how Ringgold's images work to create new paradigms for the representation of Black women.

Audre Lorde believed that women's fearless and open acceptance of their own bodies and sexuality—what she called the "erotic"—is vital for overcoming sexual oppression. In *Sister Outsider,* Lorde explains that she used the power of the erotic to battle debilitating states of being such as resignation, despair, self-effacement, depression, and self-denial.[32] Within this framework, Ringgold, too, uses the Black nude form as an empowering element. By tapping into Lorde's conceptualization of the erotic as a state of sexual self-awareness, Ringgold is able to reclaim the Black

144

woman's body and image and replace the stereotype of sexual promiscuity (or, in the case of the Mammy, asexual passivity) with one that acknowledges female sexuality. Ringgold's wide-eyed, naked women communicate an acceptance and awareness of their bodies as entities that exist independently of male control. The women do not pose or posture for male delectation; they do not avert their eyes from a male gaze; they do not display inviting smiles. They are aware that they are being watched, but their bodies, configured as they are by a woman artist, do not accommodate the scrutiny of their male attackers or of their male viewers.

The *Slave Rape* portrayals also invert power relations. In traditional Western art, clothed figures, when juxtaposed with unclothed ones, are often associated with protection and domination. The unclothed figures are seen as either victimized or vulnerable. According to Saunders, images featuring clothed men and naked women show rescuer and rescued, hero and victim, as gendered divisions. Hero/victim portrayals, notes Saunders, seem to have been particularly popular during the nineteenth century, when artists such as Ingres, Burne-Jones, Prud'hon, and Millais used the demands of the narrative to excuse and validate the nudity of the female character. Such works "set up a range of opposites: the armored male figure active, hard, invulnerable . . . against the naked female soft, vulnerable, unprotected." These images also reaffirmed the woman's subordinate role in society, much like post-Reconstruction stereotypes reaffirmed the subordinate role of Blacks in America.[33]

By juxtaposing nude women with a clothed man in several of the series's paintings, Ringgold has adhered to the hero/victim formula (see figs. 29 and 35). The man is represented by legs that are clad in white pants and black boots—the only parts of his fleeing figure that are visible at the left edge of the painting. Yet despite this work's affinity with nineteenth-century European paintings, Ringgold alters the conventional reading by introducing several unconventional elements. First, as has been noted, the women are armed. They may be unclothed, but they are not unprotected. Second, the male figure is not the hero; he appears to be as much a victim as the women and is apparently running away from them. Third, the slave catcher has been decapitated metaphorically by the picture's left edge and, as such, has been disempowered. The artist once referred to this cropped male figure as "a fragment of a man." Her comment points to the fact that this fragmentation results in a decentered universe that strips man of his privilege.[34] Traditional roles have been inverted. The nude figures are active and empowered by their weapons; the clothed male figure, while active, acts in a cowardly fashion and is powerless and unarmed.

Fig. 35. Faith Ringgold, *Help: Slave Rape Series #16*, 1973. Acrylic on canvas, 45 x 28 inches. (Courtesy of the artist's collection.) © Faith Ringgold.

There exists a complex relationship between the fact that the women in *Slave Rape* are armed and the fact that they have been armed by the painter, whose very brush can be interpreted as a weapon of sorts. This relationship can be analyzed through an examination of the "penis-as-paintbrush" metaphor and its complement, the "canvas-as-virgin." These two concepts were articulated by the French impressionist Renoir and by the Russian expressionist Kandinsky, respectively. When asked how he painted after his hands had become crippled, the arthritic Renoir replied, "With my prick" (a comment that Renoir's son, who is also his biographer, tellingly describes as a rare testimony "to the miracle of the transformation of matter into spirit"). Kandinsky, in likening the canvas to the virgin, and the act of painting to forcible intercourse (or rape), wrote, "I learned to battle with the canvas . . . to bend it forcibly to [my] wish. At first it stands there like a pure chaste virgin. . . . And then comes the willful brush which first here, then there, gradually conquers it with all the energy peculiar to it, like a European colonist." For Kandinsky, painting becomes an act of force imposed upon the virgin canvas. Ironically, he equates it with the "rape" by European colonizers of lands such as Africa and, by extension, the women of those lands.[35]

In the *Slave Rape* series, a woman (the artist) now holds the "penis/paintbrush." With this metaphorical weapon, Ringgold singularly empowers her female figures. In the narrative, the artist's paintbrush is transformed into a weapon of castration—the axe. Within the Freudian context of downward displacement, if one interprets the slave catcher's missing head as a castration, the rape of these African women becomes virtually impossible. (Of course, downward displacement hardly seems necessary since the male figure has, in fact, been cut off below the genitals.) Ringgold's fragmentation (and, as such, objectification) of the once-empowered slave catcher renders *him* the sexual object. By mutilating the male rather than the female, Ringgold succeeds in conflating victim and victimizer.

Ringgold's rendering of the women in the *Slave Rape* series further deconstructs gender paradigms in that several of these active women appear to be pregnant. Despite the existence of women warriors and hunters in Western iconography, mothers automatically have been exempted from violent activity. The mother's capacity to give life has been viewed as "profoundly incompatible with the act of dealing with death," an idea that precludes her participation in life-taking activities. Warrior and hunter figures, such as Athena and Diana, embody the antithesis of motherhood. As virgins, their chastity is linked to their bravery and military prowess.[36] Ringgold's figures, because they are both pregnant and armed, challenge such manmade social constructs.

The way in which the *Slave Rape* series deals with concepts of beauty with regard to women of color adds a further dimension to the series. Judy Chicago and Miriam Schapiro contend that the woman

147

artist, "seeing herself as loathed, takes that very mark of her otherness and by asserting it as the hallmark of her iconography, establishes a vehicle by which to state the truth and beauty of her identity."[37] Though this statement refers, in fact, to female genitalia, I would argue that the mark of "otherness" that Ringgold foregrounds in the *Slave Rape* series is one of ethnicity. The artist uses African-style jewelry, coiffures, and facial features to accentuate the ethnic appearance of these women—an appearance that, for much of American history, undoubtedly has been "loathed."

Sander Gilman's analysis of the treatment of Black women's bodies in visual culture offers a useful model for understanding Ringgold's approach. Gilman has demonstrated that Black women's bodies have been subjected to excessive pathological distortions and have been perceived both sexually and racially as "other." Their bodies have been reduced to signs of sexual abnormality and difference. Furthermore, Black female sexuality, as conceived by white society, has been the object of profound attraction and fear: "It could be said, therefore, that the political issues involved in the representation of the female body by black women artists are even more complex than those that have faced white women." This being the case, the value of the Black woman artist's endeavor to represent her own body cannot be overstated. The *Slave Rape* figures, within the context of their own environment (that of the painted landscape) and as seen through the eyes of a Black woman (those of the artist), are not portrayed as "other" but as "self." The male European interloper becomes the "other," and Ringgold effectively establishes, to use the words of Schapiro and Chicago, a "vehicle by which to state the truth and beauty of her identity."[38]

Ringgold's series mirrors the efforts of many women artists who in recent decades have attempted to reclaim the nude. Women are searching for ways to reform their own image as free of patriarchal influences. As Saunders explains, "Women artists who wish to challenge the existing stereotypes of the female nude as erotic spectacle are using a variety of techniques: the reworking of myths, the deconstruction of dominant visual codes, parody, [and] role-reversal."[39] Ringgold takes advantage of virtually all of these strategies and depicts for us new women who exist outside of the limiting framework of the conventional, male-produced, white nude. Ringgold's series is the result of a woman artist reclaiming what has always been hers but had been usurped from her—control over her body and a voice with which to speak about it.[40]

NOTES

1. Moira Roth, "Keeping the Feminist Faith," in Michele Wallace, ed., *Faith Ringgold: Twenty Years of Painting, Sculpture and Performance (1963–1983)* (New York: Studio Museum in Harlem, 1984), 13; Judith Brodsky, "Exhibitions, Galleries, and Alternative Spaces," in Norma Broude and Mary Garrard, eds., *The Power of Feminist Art: The American Movement of the 1970s, History and Impact* (New York: Harry N. Abrams, 1994), 106; Maude S. Wahlman, *Signs and Symbols: African Images in African-American Quilts* (New York: Studio Books and the Museum of American Folk Art, 1993), 117; Hilary J. Steinitz, "Faith Ringgold," in *Gumbo Ya Ya: Anthology of Contemporary African-American Women Artists,* compiled by Lyle Saxon (New York: Midmarch Art Press, 1995), 226; Moira Roth, "The Field and the Drawing Room," in *Faith Ringgold Change: Painted Story Quilts* (New York: Bernice Steinbaum Gallery, 1987), 9.

2. "Continuity and Change in African-American Art," symposium, City University of New York Graduate Center, 3 Feb. 1995. *The Flag Is Bleeding* (1967) was reproduced on the cover of Broude and Garrard, *Power of Feminist Art*; several of Ringgold's story quilts have become the basis for a series of children's books, including *Tar Beach* (New York: Crown, 1991), winner of the Caldecott Honor Book Award and the Coretta Scott King Award for Illustration in 1992.

3. Faith Ringgold, "Faith Ringgold: Archives of American Art Oral History," interview by Cynthia Nadelman, transcript, 6 Sept. to 18 Oct. 1989, Archives of American Art, Washington, D.C., and New York, 116–18.

4. Faith Ringgold, *We Flew over the Bridge: The Memoirs of Faith Ringgold* (Boston: Little Brown, 1995), 194.

5. Norma Broude, "The Pattern and Decoration Movement," in Broude and Garrard, *The Power of Feminist Art*, 208–25. Miriam Schapiro and Sherry Brody's construction *Seraglio* was inspired by an Eastern motif—the word *seraglio* refers to the harem of a Turkish sultan. A component of the multimedia construction *Dollhouse* (and part of *Womanhouse*, an installation realized in a house in Hollywood, California, and designed by students and faculty of the Feminist Art Program at the California Institute of the Arts), the *Seraglio* comprised a miniature room decorated with richly patterned fabric curtains, wall coverings, and brocaded bedding.

6. Ringgold, "Faith Ringgold: Archives of American Art Oral History," 234.

7. Steven C. Dubin, "Symbolic Slavery: Black Representations in Popular Culture," *Social Problems* 34, no. 2 (1987): 122, 131; Angela Davis, *Women, Race and Class* (New York: Random House, 1983), chap. 11 *passim;* Patricia Morton, *Disfigured Images: The Historical Assault on Afro-American Women* (Westport, Conn.: Praeger, 1991), chap. 3 *passim.*

8. Frances Beale, "Double Jeopardy: To Be Black and Female," in Toni Cade Bambara, ed., *The Black Woman: An Anthology* (New York: Penguin, 1970), 92.

9. Michelle Wallace, *Black Macho and the Myth of the Superwoman* (New York: Dial, 1979; reprint, New York: Verso, 1991), 133; bell hooks, *Black Looks: Race and Representation* (Boston: South End Press, 1992).

10. hooks, *Black Looks,* 65; Morton, *Disfigured Images,* xiii.

11. Morton, *Disfigured Images,* xv, 10–11. See also Davis, *Women, Race, and*

Class, 182; W. E. B. DuBois, "Criteria of Negro Art," *Crisis* (Oct. 1926): 297; Alain Locke, "The American Negro as Artist," *American Magazine of Art* (Sept. 1931): 211–20, *The New Negro: An Interpretation* (New York: A. and C. Boni, 1925), *Negro Art: Past and Present* (Washington, D.C.: Association of Negro Folk Education, 1936), and *The Negro in Art: A Pictorial Record of the Negro Artist and the Negro Theme in Art* (Washington, D.C.: Associates in Negro Folk Education, 1940); and Dubin, "Symbolic Slavery," 138.

12. Mary Schmidt Campbell, *Tradition and Conflict: Images of a Turbulent Decade, 1963–73* (New York: Studio Museum in Harlem, 1985), 64.

13. Campbell, *Tradition and Conflict*, 65; Yolanda M. Lopez and Moira Roth, "Social Protest: Racism and Sexism," in Broude and Garrard, *Power of Feminist Art*, 146.

14. Campbell, *Tradition and Conflict*, 54.

15. Davis Robertson, *Wonders of the World* (Middlesex, England: Penguin, 1977), 85; Dubin, "Symbolic Slavery," 130; Moira Roth, "A Trojan Horse," In *Faith Ringgold: A Twenty-Five Year Survey*, ed. Eleanor Flomenhatt (Hempstead, N.Y.: Fine Arts Museum of Long Island, 1990), 49.

16. See Philip Sterling, ed., *Laughing on the Outside: The Intelligent White Reader's Guide to Negro Tales and Humor* (New York: Grosset and Dunlap, 1965), *passim*, including W. E. B. DuBois, "Ten Phrases," 226, first published in *Crisis* (July 1922), and Langston Hughes, "Feet Live Their Own Lives," 235–37, featuring the character "Simple," who first appeared in 1943 in a weekly column Hughes was writing for the *Chicago Defender.* Martin Grotjahn notes a similar phenomenon in Jewish humor: "The persecuted Jew who makes himself the butt of the joke deflects his dangerous hostility away from the persecutors onto himself. The result is not defeat or surrender but victory and greatness." See Grotjahn, *Beyond Laughter* (New York: McGraw Hill, 1957), 22, quoted in Mel Watkins, *On the Real Side: Laughing, Lying, and Signifying—The Underground Tradition of African-American Humor that Transformed American Culture, from Slavery to Richard Pryor* (New York: Simon and Schuster, 1994), 10. Also see Dubin, "Symbolic Slavery," 131.

17. Sterling, *Laughing on the Outside*, 23.

18. Faith Ringgold, "Wild Art Show," *Women's Art Journal* (spring–summer 1982): 18.

19. Martin Ros, *Night of Fire: The Black Napoleon and the Battle for Haiti*, (New York: Sarpedan, 1994), 18.

20. Davis, *Women, Race and Class*, 3–29 (esp. 7), 172–201; Patricia Hill Collins, *Black Feminist Thought: Knowledge, Consciousness and the Politics of Empowerment* (New York: Routledge, 1990), 50; Jacqueline Jones, *Labor of Love, Labor of Sorrow: Black Women, Work and the Family, from Slavery to the Present* (New York: Basic Books, 1985), 11–43.

21. Alice Walker, *In Search of Our Mothers' Gardens* (New York: Harcourt, Brace, Jovanovich, 1983), 232.

22. Walker, *In Search of Our Mothers' Gardens*, 232.

23. Ringgold, *We Flew over the Bridge*, 197, 33–34, 44, 53–59, 83, 138–39, 140–42, 191.

24. Ringgold, *We Flew over the Bridge*, 197. In addition to artists as varied as Aaron Douglas, Alison Saar, Malcolm Bailey, Betye Saar, Jeff Donaldson, Lois

Mailou Jones, and Renée Stout, see, for example, the following: Barbara Chase Riboud (also a visual artist), *Sally Hemings* (New York: Avon, 1979); Toni Morrison, *Beloved* (New York: Alfred A. Knopf, 1987); Barbara Hill Rigny, *The Voices of Toni Morrison* (Columbus: Ohio State University Press, 1991), chap. 3; Maya Angelou, *The Collected Poems* (New York: Random House, 1994), 32–33, 84, 108–9; and Nikki Giovanni, *My House* (New York: William Morrow, 1972), 47–50. In another genre, the film *Sankofa* offers an account of a poignant incidence of time travel: the heroine (a twentieth-century African American model named Mona) finds herself trapped in the time of slavery and subject to all the horrors of that age. See Haile Gerima, *Sankofa* (Washington, D.C.: Mypheduh Films, 1995), video recording.

25. Walker, *In Search of Our Mothers' Gardens*, 243.

26. Ringgold, quoted in Kathy Larkin, "Mother, Daughter, Artist," *Daily News* (20 Nov. 1983), 4; Ringgold, *We Flew over the Bridge*, 76–78, 196, 199, 201, 216, 236, 250.

27. Keith R. Richburg, *Out of America: A Black Man Confronts Africa* (New York: HarperCollins, 1997).

28. Kenneth Clark, *The Nude: A Study in Ideal Form* (New York: Pantheon, 1956), 3; John Berger, *Ways of Seeing* (London: Penguin, 1972), 54, 57.

29. Gill Saunders, *The Nude: A New Perspective* (London: Harper and Row, 1989), 23; Carol Duncan, "The Aesthetics of Power in Modern Erotic Art," in Arlene Raven, Cassandra L. Langer, and Joanna Frueh, eds., *Feminist Art Criticism* (New York: HarperCollins, 1991), 60. Traditional images of huntresses such as Diana and warriors such as Athena and the Amazons do not specifically conform to Duncan's characterizations. The same holds true for allegorical figures that embody concepts such as Victory, Justice, Virtue, and Revolution. See Clark, *The Nude*, 184–89, 220–23. Although there are nude female figures that do not conform to Duncan's qualifications, there are a great many more that do.

30. Ringgold, *We Flew over the Bridge*, 96. Ringgold's penchant for rewriting history recurs in a much later series from 1991 entitled *The French Collection*. See Faith Ringgold, *The French Collection: Part I* (New York: Being My Own Woman Press, 1992).

31. Danielle Knafo, "In Her Own Image: Women's Self-Representation in Art" (paper presented at the New School for Social Research, New York, 12 and 26 Mar. 1996); Carol Duncan, "Virility and Domination in Early Twentieth-Century Vanguard Painting," in Norma Broude and Mary Garrard, ed., *Feminism and Art History: Questioning the Litany* (New York: Harper and Row, 1982), 293–314; Maryse Holder, "Another Cuntree: At Last a Mainstream Female Art Movement," in Raven, Langer, and Frueh, *Feminist Art Criticism: An Anthology*, 20; and Linda Nochlin, "Some Women Realists," in *Women, Art, Power and Other Essays* (New York: Harper and Row, 1988), 103.

32. Audre Lorde, *Sister Outsider* (Freedom, Calif.: Crossing Press, 1984), 56, 58.

33. Dubin, "Symbolic Slavery," 131; Saunders, *The Nude*, 7, 95.

34. Ringgold, *We Flew over the Bridge*, 197; Rachel Blau DuPlessis, "For the Etruscans: Sexual Difference and Artistic Reproduction—The Debate over a Female Aesthetic," in Hester Eisenstein and Alice Jardine, eds., *The Future of Difference* (Boston: G. K. Hall, 1980), 139–40.

35. Auguste Renoir, quoted in Janet Hobhouse, *The Bride Stripped Bare: The Artist and the Nude in the Twentieth Century* (London: Jonathan Cape, 1988), 9; Wassily Kandinsky, "Reminiscences," in *Kandinsky: Complete Writings on Art,* vol. 1 (Boston: G. K. Hall, 1982), 372, first published in *Kandinsky: 1901–1913* (Berlin: Verlag Der Sturm, 1913), quoted in Max Kozloff, "The Authoritarian Personality in Modern Art," *Artforum* (May 1974): 46.

36. Nancy Huston, "The Matrix of War: Mothers and Heroes," in Susan Rubin Suleiman, ed., *The Female Body in Western Culture: Contemporary Perspectives* (Cambridge: Harvard University Press, 1986), 129, 128.

37. Miriam Schapiro and Judy Chicago, "Female Imagery," *Womanspace Journal* 1 (summer 1973): 14.

38. Sander Gilman, *Difference and Pathology: Stereotypes of Sexuality, Race, and Madness* (Ithaca: Cornell University Press, 1985), 76–130, quoted in Lynda Nead, *The Female Nude: Art, Obscenity, and Sexuality* (New York: Routledge, 1992), 75; Schapiro and Chicago, "Female Imagery," 73.

39. Saunders, *The Nude,* 117, 129.

40. Susan Rubin Suleiman, "(Re)writing the Body," in Suleiman, *The Female Body in Western Culture,* 7.

Rachel Adams

The Black Look and 'the Spectacle of Whitefolks'

Wildness in Toni Morrison's *Beloved*

"Freaky," said Milkman. "Some freaky shit."
"Freaky world," said Guitar. "A freaky, fucked-up world."
—Toni Morrison, *Song of Solomon*[1]

Few readers of Toni Morrison's *Beloved* (1987) recall that early in the novel Sethe, Denver, and Paul D visit a carnival freak show. The Black customers approach the fairgrounds "breathless with the excitement of seeing whitepeople loose: doing magic, clowning, without heads or with two heads, twenty feet tall or two feet tall, weighing a ton, completely tattooed, eating glass, swallowing fire, spitting ribbons, twisted into knots, forming pyramids, playing with snakes and beating each other up." These loose "whitepeople" are the carnival's main attraction, freaks who boast feats of strength and agility, amazing extremes of shape and size, and bodies that press at the very boundaries of the human.

All too soon, this compelling description is revealed as the fickle promise of a publicity agent. But the carnival's failure to live up to the wonders anticipated by its advertising, and the obvious racism of its employees, are of little consequence for the Black visitors determined to enjoy its pleasures: "the barker called their children names ('Pickaninnies free!') but the food on his vest and the hole in his pants rendered it fairly harmless. In any case it was a small price to pay for the fun they might not ever have again. Two pennies and an insult were well spent if it meant seeing the spectacle of whitefolks making a spectacle of themselves." Enduring the insults of a resentful carnival staff, the Black spectators delight in the unprecedented sight of white performers on display for their entertainment. For once, instead of being the object of surveillance, the Black fairgoer is a member of the audience who has paid to point and stare at the "spectacle of whitefolks making a spectacle of themselves." Despite the performers' hostility—"One-Ton Lady spit at them" and "Arabian Nights Dancer cut her performance to three minutes instead of the usual fifteen she normally did"—or perhaps because of it, the Black audience draws together, a sense of community reinforced through their perceived differences from the freaks onstage.

Paul D takes particular enjoyment in the experience of carnival. An ideal consumer, he buys candy for Sethe and Denver and gawks at the freaks' spectacular bodies.[2] But his credulity reaches its limits when he confronts an ordinary Black man playing the part of a Wild African Savage. Otherwise willing to suspend his disbelief, Paul D vehemently rejects the conventions of spectatorship that should govern his reception of the show: "When Wild African Savage shook his bars and said wa, wa, Paul D told everybody he knew him back in Roanoke."[3] It is not surprising that the only Black person in the troupe is masquerading as a Wild African Savage, the role of dangerous exotic predictably assigned to nonwhite carnies. By claiming familiarity with this man, who is not from savage Africa but Roanoke, Paul D disrupts the fiction of his absolute alterity and the apparently solid boundary between spectator and performer.

This richly evocative confrontation was diffused when *Beloved* was made into a film (Oprah Winfrey, 1999) that faithfully reproduces the dialogue but in so muted a form that its significance is lost. Amid the noise of the crowd, Paul D's words are reduced to a lighthearted aside rather than a powerful intervention in the fairgoers' enjoyment of the spectacle. The carnival scene has been treated with similar neglect in the extensive body of criticism devoted to Morrison's fiction. This chapter will argue that it provides an important key to understanding *Beloved*. As Morrison once remarked, her fiction is intended to provide "the kind of information you can find between the lines of history. . . . It's right there in the intersection where an institution becomes personal, where the historical becomes people with names."[4] In what follows, I read *Beloved* as a novel that gives voice to stories about the freak show that otherwise lurk "between the lines of history." When Paul D locates the Wild African Savage within a familiar context, he translates the institution of human exhibition into something of personal consequence for each member of the community. The freak show's treatment of race—the combination of ex-

154

otic costuming and pseudoscientific ballyhoo—might seem so
that it virtually goes without saying. If the Black man masquerad
Wild African Savage is such a crude and self-evident manifestation of
racial stereotyping that it hardly needs interpretation, the reaction of audiences to such performances is less easily explained.

Paul D's response to the spectacle has numerous counterparts in
memoirs and legends about carnival life. This chapter will consider a
number of historical analogues to the encounter fictionalized in *Beloved*,
in which the Wild Man's act is disrupted by the unruly behavior of audience members. Analysis of these interruptions provides an alternative
perspective on the portrait of freak shows that has emerged in preceding
chapters, for it shifts the focus from an interpretation of their content to
an interpretation of their reception. The interruption draws attention to
the role of spectators, who did not simply absorb the tableaux of bodies
exhibited before them but responded actively to what they were seeing.
Historical evidence about spectatorship reveals that freak shows offered a
particularly unconvincing form of racial performance; that, when it came
to wild men and savage tribes, audiences rarely seem to have believed
what they saw. Indeed, in the age of the confidence man epitomized by
Barnum's maxim, "A sucker is born every minute," it appears that one of
the primary pleasures of viewing a racial exhibit was to disclose its fraudulence.[5] Spectators' desire to unmask the racial freak as a hoax did not
mean that they questioned the exhibit's underlying assumption of white
supremacy, but their reactions betray that, in their eyes, the natives of
Africa or Asia assumed a dubious status akin to that of Martians, mer-
maids, or missing links. Even when the exotics were what they claimed
to be—Igorots from the Philippines, African pygmies, Ubangi women—
they were subject to impudent prodding by customers who had to touch
to believe. For an audience composed of African Americans who bore the
burden of such racial stereotypes, the delight of revelation was magnified,
for it was a moment when, catching white showmen in the act, they could
briefly seize control of representation.

This is the information "between the lines of history" that Morrison summons up in her scene of carnivalesque reversal and unmasking,
which occurs immediately before the mysterious Beloved's appearance
and is of great consequence to the events that follow. The episode, in
which the collective identity of the spectators is broken down and reconfigured, becomes a paradigm for the narrative's broader concern
with the difficulty of forming alliances among persons who have endured intense suffering. As the audience of ex-slaves at the freak show

draws together, it reveals a troubling aspect of communities that have the potential to heal but rely on the exclusion of even more marginalized others in order to identify as a group.

Under Morrison's pen, Paul D's meeting with the Wild African Savage unmasks the pernicious fiction of racist stereotypes but not of race itself. Ultimately, the arsenal for collective healing is stored as a form of racial memory transmitted bodily from one generation to the next. Like freaks, Morrison's characters are defined entirely in corporeal terms; emotions are projected outward onto the contours of their bodies, which are so often scarred, wounded, or disabled. Ancestral traumas pulsate in the blood of their offspring, and memories materialize as rememories so concrete a person can bump into them.[6] Morrison's preoccupation with physicality is distinct from the positions articulated in act 2, where freaks are evidence of a common humanity that transcends superficial differences between spectators and the unfortunate figures onstage. Instead, the body becomes a foundation for the formation of communal bonds and the exclusion of outsiders. If Morrison disputes the false opposition between freak and normal, she insists on other intractable differences: race enables the Black spectator to identify with the Wild African Savage, and race precludes identification with the other freaks. *Beloved* ends by denying that those who bear the legacy of slavery in their bodies could unite with those who do not on the basis of a mutual humanity. The sideshow freak, whose properties are soon transferred onto the freakish Beloved, is a figure for the impossibility of that union.

The Black Look and "the Spectacle of Whitefolks"

Paul D's spirited interruption of the freak show is a fictional rendition of numerous historical accounts in which a wild man's act is stopped short by the antics of an unruly spectator. The episode, as Morrison describes it, draws attention to the contours of the racial freak's performance and reception as they occurred in the past; in turn, a sustained consideration of historical evidence offers insight about the scene's significance to the novel. The wild man was a stock sideshow personality, along with other common types such as fat ladies, tattooed people, giants, and midgets. During the period of their greatest popularity, freak shows consistently trafficked in representations of non-Western races that combined anthropology and entertainment, pseudoscientific jargon, and fantastic hyperbole. In doing so, they offered simplified answers to the pressing concerns about race that would have provoked their predominantly white audiences, already anxious about the consequences of slavery and its aftermath, great waves of seemingly unassimilable immigrants, and imperial expansion.[7] As James W. Cook Jr. writes of Barnum's famous "What Is It?" the "scientific" questions raised by an African American man advertised as a missing link "quickly spilled over into even more controversial questions of racial definition, politics, and property."[8] Freak-show savages equated race with a monstrous deviance made clearly legible on the surfaces of the body. The interior of the tent or dime museum mapped the differences between freak and normal in concrete spatial terms: the physical separation between the onlooker and the living tableaux on the exhibition platform announced itself as a vast, existential divide between spectacularly individuated deviance and the comfortable anonymity of normalcy. As the Black body was transformed into a hyper-visible spectacle, the audience aspired to blend together into a transparent, homogenous whiteness. Those most anxious about their own status as citizens applauded the reassuring vision of nonwhite bodies that absolutely could not be assimilated.[9]

Indeed, whether foolish and docile or wild with rage and bloodlust, the unassimilability of the dark-skinned body was the dominant message conveyed by the racial freak. I use the terms "racial freak" and "wild man" interchangeably to refer to a particular kind of exhibition that linked the spectacle of ferocious wildness to racial and national differences. As W. C. Thompson explained in his 1905 memoir, *On the Road with a Circus*, "the original circus wild man, the denizen of Borneo, was white, but his successors have almost invariably had dark skins."[10] The predictability of such connections between wildness and dark skin was confirmed by journalist Scott Hart, who noted in 1946 that "most Wild men from Borneo are amiable Negro boys from about the circus lot who are trained to growl, flash a set of fake tusks and eat raw meat. . . . The Wild Man is always from Borneo. The Bear Woman is from the darkest wilds of Africa. The Pinheaded Man is from the jungle-ridden regions of Somewhere."[11] The formulaic print "ethnographies" that often accompanied these exhibits associated wildness with remote geographical locales. A pamphlet on Waino and Plutano, the Wild Men of Borneo, for example, informed the reader, "Borneo is an island so large that England, Ireland, and Scotland might be set down in the middle of it. The interior of this vast island is a dense forest, inhabited by a race of humanity very little different from the animal creation."[12] Couched in pedagogical terms, such explanatory narratives perpetuated commonly held assumptions about the physical and cultural otherness of non-Western and nonwhite people.

In contrast to the presentation of physically disabled freaks, who might answer questions, lecture the audience about their unusual bodies, or demonstrate their capacity to perform everyday activities, the wild man was deliberately inarticulate, his snarls and roars a sign of his absolute inability to communicate through language. "I was all stripped 'cept around the middle and wore a claw necklace; had to make out as if I couldn't talk. 'Twas mighty tiresome to howl and grin all day," recalled a former wild man quoted in Thompson's memoir.[13] Sometimes eating raw meat, biting the heads off live animals, or drinking blood, the wild man's voracious and indiscriminate appetites attested to his preference for the raw to the cooked. Often described in terms of popular evolutionary science as a "missing link," the wild man was said to come from a lost species located somewhere on the developmental chain between human and beast. While such acts were a regular part of low-budget traveling carnivals like the one described in *Beloved,* they were equally popular in more reputable venues such as world's fairs and museums. There, they were greeted with interest by scientific professionals and respectable citizens such as the lawyer George Templeton Strong, who noted in his diary in 1860 that he had "stopped at Barnum's on my way downtown to see the much advertised nondescript, the 'What-is-it.'"[14] In short, while the venue and tenor of the performance might vary, the exhibition of nonwhite persons as wild men, cannibals, and missing links was an acceptable source of entertainment and knowledge for spectators across the social spectrum.

Authenticity was always an important part of the freak show's promotional rhetoric, which advertised exhibits as LIVE! TRUE! REAL! GENUINE! Despite such hyperbolic claims of veracity, the exotic act was the most easily and regularly fabricated of all attractions. More often than not, those advertised as Zulu warriors, Wild Men from Borneo, and Dahomeans were actually people of color from local urban centers.[15] As William C. Fitzgerald noted in an 1897 article on sideshows, "Certainly it is far easier and cheaper to engage and 'fit-up' as the 'Cuban Wonder' an astute individual from the New York slums, than to send costly missions to the Pearl of the Antilles in search of human curiosities."[16] The memoirs of former sideshow managers and employees are unapologetic about the fabrication of ethnographic freaks. Indeed, the creation of a wild man is a recurrent chapter in the formulaic genre of the carnival memoir. Hart tells the following story.

On a platform before the tent a tense, narrow-cheeked man related how the unfortunate individual from Borneo knew the whereabouts of neither father, mother, nor home, and that five thousand dollars would be paid anyone providing such information.

Inside the tent, a fat rural woman said, "Oh, ain't that awful!" A child asked, "You reckon he can get out?" But when dinnertime came, the Wild Man was taken to meet a distinguished local circus fan and his wife. In the ensuing pleasantries, he created a very happy social impression.

With professional awareness, however, the Wild Man failed to mention that he came from South Carolina.[17]

Hart's anecdote exploits the discrepancy between the talker's deliberately mystified rhetoric and the mundane, but quite respectable, activities of the Wild Man upon leaving the display platform. Others are less sanguine about the arrangement between performers and their managers. Thompson describes the career of Calvin Bird, "a negro who hailed from Pearson, GA [who] toured most of the country, mystifying all who saw him and sending them away impressed with a conviction that he was all he was represented to be. Not until he appeared at a Syracuse hospital with a request that his horns be removed was the secret of his unnatural appearance disclosed. Under his scalp was found inserted a silver plate, in which stood two standards. In these, when he was on exhibition, Bird screwed two goat horns."[18] In contrast to the comfortable arrangement between Hart's wild man and his promoters, Bird suffered bodily harm for the sake of his act. Far from demonstrating that he was a missing link, this elaborate ruse proved the wild man to be all too human, the victim of abusive surgeons and greedy showmen. Illustrating his remark that "the life of the professional wild man is an unhappy one at best," Thompson adds the story of a Black man from Baltimore who ran out of money while visiting Berlin and "enlisted as an untamed arrival from Africa with a small American circus then playing abroad. He endured the torture he was compelled to undergo for a month and then stole away to a hospital."[19] There he recuperated from the forced diet of raw horse meat and blood and the chill of performing during cold weather dressed only in a loincloth.[20]

Such anecdotal evidence bespeaks the pragmatic, and often cruel, opportunism of sideshow managers, who cared far less about the authenticity promised in their advertising than the lucrative consequences of maintaining a steady supply of unique and varied attractions. Accounts of their fraudulence are numerous and unsurprising: after all, it was the showman's job to create illusions that amused and deceived his customers, and the wild man conformed to prevailing beliefs about racial inferiority. The standard was set by Barnum, who began his career by exhibiting a racial freak, the elderly, disabled slave named Joice Heth who claimed to be the 161-year-old nurse of George Washington. A Black woman whose body was contorted with age and years of hard labor was easily transformed into a sensation through Barnum's skillful publicity campaign. When an autopsy following Heth's death revealed her to be no more than eighty, Barnum deflected controversy by professing himself the victim of a hoax devised by Heth and her former owners.[21] Barnum's autobiographical writings provide different and somewhat contradictory accounts of these events, but they are consistently uninterested in proving that Heth was what she claimed to be. In some versions, Barnum conspires with Heth to deceive the public, while in others he is innocent, but in each version he establishes humbug as the rule rather than the exception in the showman's trade.[22]

These examples attest to the performative gap between Black actor and stage persona, but also to the frequency with which that disjuncture recurred in narratives about the freak show. As I have argued, the freak show's theatrical conventions induct actors and audiences into a carefully orchestrated relationship, albeit one that was frequently violated by misbehavior on both sides of the velvet rope.[23] In *Beloved*, the ex-slaves experience the carnival, with its "spectacle of whitefolks," as a temporary release from their more ordinary interactions with the white citizens of Cincinnati. The freaks, in turn, feel little obligation to behave professionally when they confront an audience that they deem inferior. The performers' crude disdain is met by the customers' rude jeers and laughter. Facing off in a venue where rowdy, indecorous behavior is the norm, spectators and performers apparently feel free to modulate their behavior in response to one another, allowing for the open exchange of hostilities between marginalized groups.

The festive, unrestrained atmosphere of carnival often gave rise to the kind of disruptive misbehavior that Morrison describes. While it is not particularly surprising to find that racial freaks were local people of color tricked out in costume, more striking is the evidence that *audiences* seemed so rarely to believe what they saw. For instance, having viewed the "What Is It?" at Barnum's Museum, Strong opined, "Some say it's an advanced chimpanzee, others that it's a cross between nigger and baboon. But it seems to me clearly an idiotic negro dwarf, raised, perhaps, in Alabama or Virginia. The showman's story of capture (with three other specimens that died) by a party in pursuit of the gorilla on the western coast of Africa is probably bosh."[24] Strong asserts his own capacity to distinguish between "bosh" and authenticity from the speculations of other observers and the showman's fantastic account of peril and adventure. As the episode from *Beloved* suggests, even Paul D—a customer determined to enjoy the pleasures of carnival—questions the implausible spectacle of a Black man performing as an African savage. Such moments of resistance are to be found across diverse groups of patrons, but the most powerful accounts are of the kind Morrison describes, in which a Black spectator looks with suspicion and disbelief at a racist performance, refuses to enter into its fiction, and loudly enjoins the audience into collective incredulity. In his 1913 biography, circus veteran George Middleton offers a neat parallel to Paul D's encounter with the Wild African savage.

> In the side show we have a big negro whom we had fitted up with rings in his nose, a leopard skin, some assagais and a large shield made out of cows' skin. While he was sitting on stage in the side show, along came two negro women and remarked, "See that nigger over there? He ain't no Zulu, that's Bill Jackson. He worked over here at Camden on the dock. I seen that nigger often." Poor old Bill Jackson was as uneasy as if he was sitting on needles, holding the shield between him and the two negro women.[25]

Like Paul D, the women in Middleton's anecdote disrupt the exhibition, shattering the fourth wall by speaking directly to the stage. The interpellative gesture of recognition—"I know you!"—dispels the illusion of the wild man's absolute alterity, relocating him within the community of onlookers. Instead of a Zulu, he is Bill Jackson; rather than hailing from Africa, he is a dockworker from New Jersey. The account derives its humor from the transformation of the shield intended as a sign of tribal savagery into a barrier to protect the guilty man from the female customers he was supposed to terrorize.

Such examples require us to turn from an analysis of the *content* of freak exhibition to questions of *spectatorship*. The racism of wild men and cannibal acts is crude and obvious, but why were audiences so ready to interrupt these performances? Theories of cinematic reception help to explain the shifting and unpredictable relationship between the spectator and the visual image.[26] Eric Lott has productively applied these insights to an analysis of minstrelsy, where he describes the experience of cinema as "a destabilized structure of fascination, a continual confusion of subject and object" in which "we successively identify, across gender lines, with logical screen representatives of ourselves (heroes, victims), then with seeming adversaries (villains, killers), and so on."[27] Like a film narrative, the freak show implicitly situated the viewer in a particular relationship to its content; however, the response of actual spectators did not always conform to structural expectations.[28] The Black fairgoer faced problems of identification akin to those of the Black film viewer: confronted by representations of African Americans ranging from the uninteresting to the degrading, she had to identify across racial boundaries or forgo the visual pleasures of identification altogether.

Film theory is a useful point of entry for understanding the shifting contours of reception, for it provides the most sustained consideration of the random ways in which any given spectator will identify with, repudiate, or otherwise respond to narrative cinema. Yet such theories have only limited ability to account for live performance. In the scenes I have described, the flash of identificatory insight is followed by a cry that utterly disrupts the action taking place onstage and invites the audience to join in a ritual of communal disbelief. It is impossible for the wild man to continue beyond the moment of recognition, for his act depends on the illusion of his absolute inscrutability. Only during a live encounter can the viewer's response register with and alter the course of the dramatic action. In fact, an important ingredient in the audience's enjoyment of freak shows seems to have been precisely this capacity to deconstruct the visual evidence presented to them. Interruption, misidentification, and the possibility of fraudulence contributed considerably to the show's appeal.

The pleasures of unmasking are part of a broader nineteenth-century preoccupation with the figure of the confidence man, whose reliance on trickery and deception was the unsavoury counterpart to the Horatio Alger story of legitimate success gained through hard work and ingenuity. Neil Harris attributes P. T. Barnum's success with hoaxes to a public that appreciated "the sheer exhilaration of debate, the utter fun of the opportunity to learn and evaluate, whether the subject was an ancient slave, an exotic mermaid, or a politician's honor. Barnum's audiences found the encounter with potential frauds exciting. It was a form of intellectual exercise, stimulating even when the truth could not be determined."[29] Ferreting out deception at the freak show doubtless filled audiences with satisfaction in their ability to distinguish between a scam and the real thing. George Templeton Strong takes manifest pride in recognizing the What Is It? as an ordinary African American and not a missing link. But the particular scenes of recognition that concern me deal more specifically with racial boundaries and identifications *among*

African Americans, who were both viewers and performers. An audience of ex-slaves contemplating the spectacle of a Black man performing as an African savage would have a particularly savvy understanding of the slippery nature of theatrical representation. To hail the savage as "one of us" was a dangerous move because it threatened to equate the African Americans with the barbarism of Africa, but to stop the savage in his tracks gave the lie to that equation, demonstrating the power of the Black look.

In the context of *Beloved,* the moment of recognition is significant because it anticipates the novel's attempt to reverse the terms of slavery, shifting attention from the spectacle of the oppressed Black body to a Black viewer whose gaze implicates "whitefolks" as the architects of that peculiar institution. Assuming the interchangeability of one dark-skinned person for another, the freak show represents the Black body as inherently readable in terms of primitive exoticism. At the same time, it undercuts this assumption by acknowledging that the wild man is only readable as "wild" through an elaborate combination of costume and performance. Invoking the same stereotypes that made the Wild African Savage at the freak show possible, Stamp Paid reflects, "Whitepeople believed that whatever the manners, under every dark skin was a jungle. Swift, unnavigable waters, swinging, screaming baboons, sleeping snakes, red gums ready for their sweet white blood" (198). The same logic that associates all Black bodies with the bestiality of the jungle allows a man from Virginia to masquerade as a savage in a performance that just might be convincing to white audiences. When a canny spectator like Paul D reveals it as a feeble ruse, the infrastructure of racism itself, which assumes the inherent savagery of all Black persons, threatens to crumble. Consistently challenged by the behavior of the slaves themselves, this system of belief requires constant vigilance and a ceaseless supply of new evidence to grant it the status of truth.

The scientific method is represented in *Beloved* as the corrupt means by which racial bigotry is maintained and given legitimacy as empirical fact. Showmen and professionals alike used the rhetoric of science to prove the truth of racial difference. Thus Sethe recalls Schoolteacher's instructions to his pupils "to put her human characteristics on the left; her animal ones on the right. And don't forget to line them up" (193).[30] Schoolteacher, a merciless overseer and even more pernicious pedagogue, begins his chilling lesson with the same assumptions that undergirded Barnum's What Is It?—that the Black body combines human and animal attributes—and then proceeds to use scientific reasoning to detect and categorize those features. The scheme of classification devised by Schoolteacher is all the more horrifying because of the neat alignment of columns, a testament to the potential of empirical data to authorize popular racism. Naming this character Schoolteacher emphasizes the educational function of such taxonomies, which do not simply establish the "truth" of racial inferiority, but guarantee the transmission of that truth from one generation of slaveholders to the next. The encounter with Schoolteacher upsets Sethe enough to prompt her to ask her ailing mistress to define "characteristics" for her, to which Mrs. Garner replies, "a thing that's natural to a thing" (195). This statement encapsulates the circular logic of the slave system, which naturalizes the association between blackness and certain mental and psychological attributes that are used, in turn, to legitimate the bondage of Black people.

It is hardly necessary for Morrison, writing in 1987, to prove that the association of slaves with atavistic savagery is profoundly unnatural. Her contribution is to take the dynamic staged at the carnival, in which Black viewers contemplate with delight "the spectacle of whitefolks making a spectacle of themselves," as a starting point for examining the way that slavery makes whiteness itself a visible quality.[31] The condition of human bondage encourages terrible and otherwise inexplicable acts within the slave community (such as the abandonment or murder of one's own children) but is even more damaging to those who create and enforce that system. Thus Stamp Paid thinks about how the jungle associated with blackness "spread, until it invaded the whites who had made it. Touched them every one. Changed and altered them. Made them bloody, silly, worse even than even they wanted to be, so scared were they of the jungle they had made. The screaming baboon lived under their own white skin; the red gums were their own" (198–99). Stamp Paid asserts that there is nothing natural about the jungle made by those who fear the consequences of their own barbarism. From this perspective, Schoolteacher's insistence that the columns of characteristics be neatly aligned is clearly a defense against the realization that the anarchic jungle lurks within himself, a by-product of his cruelty that must be staved off through the imposition of orderly logic. Likewise, Paul D's recognition that the Wild African Savage is an acquaintance from Roanoke does not simply lift the burden of barbarism from the Black body but relocates that savagery as the brainchild of the whitefolks who manage the carnival's attractions.

Paul D's demystification of the Wild African Savage presages the novel's investment in denaturalizing the stereotype of Black animality by tracing its source to the institution of slavery erected by and for "white-folks." The freak-show savage embodies the abject characteristics attributed to Blacks to justify the persistence of inequalities after slavery and secure the purity of whiteness as his obverse. When Paul D disputes the truth of the Wild Man's mysterious demeanor, he also reveals the fragility of the association between blackness and bestiality, for if "African" is a fictive designation for the nationality of the man before them onstage, then surely "wild" and "savage" are equally fictitious identities. But the trauma of slavery cannot be resolved by one light-hearted moment of reversal: some months later, Paul D will betray Sethe when he responds to the story of the infanticide by telling her, "You got two feet, Sethe, not four" (165), an accusation that becomes the ground for their estrangement. Implying that Sethe's behavior is more animal than human, Paul D refuses to comprehend the impossible situation that drove her to murder her own child as a preferable alternative to relinquishing her to the approaching slave catchers. He invokes a form of wildness that has nothing to do with Africa but is nonetheless all too real. This unfeeling remark is also the occasion for Paul D to remember that he and the other young male slaves at Sweet Home plantation regularly had sex with calves, a practice that likewise blurs the distinction between human and beast. "How fast he had moved from his shame to hers," Paul D thinks later, as he recalls the shared experience of suffering that initially drew him to Sethe but subsequently became painfully divisive.

Intended as an insult, the reminder that Sethe has "two feet" must also invoke the journey to freedom she made late in her pregnancy when, unable to use her swollen feet, she crawled on her hands and knees in a desperate effort to save her unborn infant and reach her children. The extreme horrors of slavery make it difficult, if not impossible, to pass definitive moral judgments about what constitutes properly "human" activity. The wildness mimicked by the freak show's African Savage spreads with infectious power through the novel, punctuating scenes of terror like "the *wildness* that shot up into the eye the moment the lips were yanked back" (71; emphasis mine) to accommodate a bit in the mouth; or Schoolteacher's reaction to the scene of carnage resulting from Sethe's effort to save her children, that "now she'd gone *wild*." The wildness exhibited by these slaves cannot be seen as the antithesis of the slave owner's civility but as a mirror that reflects the way that slavery has contaminated everything, threatening to dissolve moral categories and meaning itself.

Freaking Beloved

The freak-show episode in *Beloved* is about more than the spectacle of whitefolks; it also provides a paradigm for reading the group dynamics that are continually being reworked throughout the rest of the novel as the ex-slaves struggle to define the contours of community. The carnival sequence dramatizes the powerful, ongoing process of identity formation that is called into question with particular force during visits to the freak show. The consolidation of that lumpy cluster of affiliations called identity occurs not only through the positive identification of self but by casting off the negative and undesirable elements that constitute the nonself. Nevertheless, the boundaries of identity, whether individual or collective, must be continually affirmed or reconfigured in response to external challenges. As Eve Sedgwick describes it, "to identify *as* must always include multiple processes of identification *with*. It also involves identification *as against;* but even did it not, the relations implicit in *identifying with* are, as psychoanalysis suggests, in themselves quite sufficiently fraught with intensities of incorporation, diminishment, inflation, threat, loss, reparation, and disavowal."[32] At the carnival, two disenfranchised groups confront one another with derisive animosity. The ex-slaves leer and point at the freaks, while the freaks respond with unconcealed disdain. What happens at this freak show is less a confusion about the boundaries of *individual* self and body, often attributed to encounters with prodigies like conjoined twins, hermaphrodites, and persons with extra or missing limbs, than a confusion about the boundaries of *group* identity. *Beloved* acknowledges similarities between these marginalized communities, the shared suffering that their members are unable to recognize from within the context of their particular experiences of degradation: the bodies of freaks and slaves, conceived as the property of others, bar them from the comforts and privileges of a humanity that exceeds the limits of corporeal identity. In other words, the extreme visibility of dark skin or severe disabilities ensures that the slave and the freak will experience the body as a prison that they cannot escape. Unable to perceive their potential affinities, each camp consolidates the boundaries of its own group identity through the rejection of an even more abject collectivity.

The visit to the fair recalls the group dynamics responsible for Sethe's eighteen-year ostracism and establishes the possibility of her eventual reincorporation into the community.[33] Optimistically called a carnival, this traveling amusement park, which is actually "a lot less than mediocre (which is why it agreed to a Colored Thursday)" (48), has little in common with the ebullient grotesqueries that Bakhtin describes as "carnivalesque." Nonetheless, it maintains one of the most important features of Bakhtinian carnival, the ritualistic inversion of hierarchies and unsettling of power relations. And like the festive reversals recounted by Bakhtin, these category confusions are only temporary, serving more as a safety valve to ensure the stability of the dominant order than contributing to its overthrow; however, they anticipate the more enduring transformations that will occur around the freakish appearance and disappearance of Beloved herself.[34]

As I have noted, the carnival and the freaks that are its central attraction are a poor shadow of the wonders promised by its promotional advertisements. Regardless of its rude performers and staff and mediocre entertainment, "it gave the four hundred black people in its audience thrill upon thrill upon thrill" (48). Far from irrelevant, the carnies' insulting behavior actually contributes to consolidating the bonds of community among the Black customers. Denver, long the object of an exclusionary gaze, takes particular pleasure in being "surrounded by a crowd of people who did not find her the main attraction." As she stands with Paul D and Sethe watching the midget dance, the collective experience of looking "made the stares of other Negroes kind, gentle, something Denver did not remember seeing in their faces. Several even nodded and smiled at her mother" (48). Having encountered persons even more marginal than themselves, the group of onlookers invites Sethe and Denver back into its fold.

But this passing gesture of inclusion is hardly a promising step toward the creation of a more functional and supportive community, for it relies on the spectators' cruel sense of superiority to the freaks. The fat white lady who spits at the audience is amusing because "her bulk shortened her aim and they got a big kick out of the helpless meanness in her little eyes." She becomes an object of humorous derision when her enormous body renders her gesture of disrespect inconsequential. But the "helpless meanness" the Black fairgoers detect in her eyes must be understood as the product of earning her livelihood sitting onstage, where she must endure stares, prodding, and impudent questions. The fat lady's weight imprisons her in much the same way as does the slave's Black skin. *Beloved* demonstrates how the extreme rage engendered by prolonged psychological and physical cruelty may erupt in many ways, including violent aggression between one injured party and another. Although the ex-slaves are conditioned to find pleasure in unlikely places, the "big kick" they get from the fat lady's impotent meanness seems less like the deep, liberating belly laugh of Bakhtinian carnival than the barely repressed hostility that Freud attributes to defensive forms of humor.[35] In the same way that laughter in Tod Browning's *Freaks* is more a hysterical response to the freaks' challenge to bodily integrity than a sign of amusement, the audience's reaction to the freaks in *Beloved* must be linked to recollections of the fact that, as slaves, they were once subjected to the denigrating gaze of whitefolks and the abuse that inevitably accompanied it. "People I saw as a child," Sethe remarks later to Paul D, "who'd had the bit always looked wild after that" (71). The Wild African Savage may invite laughter at his absurd performance but may simultaneously stir more unpleasant memories of a wildness born of fury, humiliation, and physical pain.

Likewise, although she too has felt the pain of being "the main attraction," Denver cannot find the grounds to identify with the carnies' unenviable situation. But the connections Denver is unable to imagine are anticipated by Morrison's use of descriptive language. Denver buys sweets from a refreshment concession "manned by a little whitegirl in ladies' high-topped shoes" (48).[36] The apparent paradoxes in this sentence attest to the plight of a child who must work for a living. The table is "manned," implying a form of labor inappropriate for a young girl whose adult's shoes literalize the burden of responsibilities beyond her years. Forced to stand in someone else's shoes, this pathetic figure, at once man, girl, and woman, is a prototype for Denver, who will also have to compensate for her mother's neglect by working for a living. She too will venture into an adult world wearing clothes that don't fit her. These encounters between fairgoers and carnies, overlaid with hostility and misunderstanding, intimate similarities between the two groups that cannot be perceived by their participants. At this point in the narrative, an awareness of these common bonds is unavailable to the insiders themselves, although it is latent within Morrison's densely allusive prose.

Freaks are beings whose fantastic bodies defy categorization, who are found, in the most literal sense, on the platforms of sideshows, dime museums, and the carnival midway. I designate Beloved a freak to foreground the links between slaves and carnies and to describe the profound indeterminacy of her identity (who is she and where does she come from?), which cannot be disassociated from the otherwise inexplicable physical metamorphoses that she undergoes throughout the course of the narrative. Her presence encourages the development of a healing community among the ex-slaves of Cincinnati but also leaves the uncomfortable possibility that the formation of communities always depends on the exclusion of an even more abject group. Although the freaks' fantastic bodies are long gone by the close of the novel, as is Beloved's equally spectacular embodied form, Morrison's text cautions that the solidification of collective bonds may take place at the expense of less visible, but no less haunting, others. The destructive potential of community is an ongoing concern in Morrison's fiction, from the citizens of Lorain, Ohio, in *The Bluest Eye* (1970), who allow Pecola Breedlove's self-hatred to reach tragic proportions, to the Bottom's rejection of Sula Peace in *Sula* (1973), to the deadly confrontation between the men of Ruby, Oklahoma, and the women in the convent in *Paradise* (1998).

Whereas the carnival freaks briefly and grudgingly unsettle racial hierarchies by allowing Black customers to occupy the position of spectators, the appearance of Beloved, a real freak whose bizarre attributes—unlike those of the Wild African Savage—are never explained or diffused, enables the community to begin working through the traumatic events that continue to haunt their relationships to one another. The particular significance of the carnival excursion for Sethe is reinforced by the manifestation of Beloved directly afterward. Although the embodied Beloved first appears in the chapter following the excursion, her emergence from the river coincides temporally with the visit to the carnival itself, as if the freak show, with its temporary reversals, has somehow produced a more enduring and significant oddity outside its gates. The link between Beloved's materialization and the freak show is suggested by Sethe's initial response, an immediate need to urinate so intense and prolonged that she feels like a freak herself: "Just about the time she started wondering if the carnival would accept another freak, it stopped" (51). The amount of liquid Sethe produces is so copious that she relates it to the breaking water of Denver's birth. It is no accident that Sethe's identification with the freaks occurs in a passage that also mentions the newborn Denver, her own absent mother, and the stranger who will turn out to be her murdered older daughter, Beloved, come back to life. This associative chain implies that relations between enslaved mothers and daughters are akin to the alienating relations of the freak show, where some persons are stripped of autonomy and self-determination as their bodies become the property of others.[37] Sethe's body registers the import of the meeting long before she realizes the identity of the mysterious stranger. Her visceral reaction anticipates the intense bond she will develop with Beloved, which renders desires and memories unavailable for verbal expression in the form of corporeal sensations.[38]

The identification between Beloved and the carnival freaks persists as the bizarre circumstances of her appearance and nature confound rational explanation. Beloved's supernatural qualities have led many critics to interpret her as a ghost, and indeed, the notion of ghostly haunting is useful for describing the persistence of the traumatic memories that she invokes, as well as the spectral presence that haunts the house on Blue-stone Road until Paul D arrives.[39] But this infantile phantom is substantially different from the fully embodied woman who appears after the carnival. The terms *ghost* and *freak* are useful for distinguishing between these two distinctive manifestations, separated from one another by the experience of carnival. Calling the materialized Beloved a freak draws attention to her association with the disempowered persons on display at the sideshow, connections that are embedded at the level of figurative language and that push us to acknowledge affinities between oppressed groups. Moreover, Beloved is a freak because of the unavoidable fact of her body. The intangible quality of ghostliness is inadequate to describe the warm, greedy, desiring sentience of the stranger who appears after the freak show. As I will demonstrate, *Beloved* is a novel relatively uninterested in interiority as such, for it projects the emotional states of its characters onto the surfaces of the human form.

The associative links among motherhood, freaks, and community in *Beloved* are prefigured by Pilate, the most powerful female character in Morrison's *Song of Solomon* (1977). Having fought her way out of her dead mother's body, the newborn baby emerges without a navel, her smooth belly a sign of her detachment from the woman who engendered her. Alienated from one community after another, Pilate is dismayed to find that her disability is unmarketable: "Even a traveling show would have rejected her, since her freak quality lacked that important ingredient—the grotesque. There was really nothing to see. Her defect, frightening and exotic as it was, was also a theatrical failure. It needed intimacy, gossip, and the time it took for curiosity to become drama" (148–49). Similarly, Beloved's freak qualities are not shocking or sensational; they manifest slowly as her difference becomes apparent to the members of Sethe's family and the close-knit society that surrounds it.

Like the carnival freaks, Beloved embodies apparently unresolvable contradictions. She is simultaneously childlike and a grown woman, sick and glowing with health, innocent and fully sexualized, strong and feeble. When Sethe worries about Beloved's weakness, Paul D responds suspiciously that she "can't walk, but I seen her pick up the rocker with one hand" (56). The disparity between Sethe's and Paul D's assessments of Beloved indicates how closely their perceptions of her physical body stem from a more profound sense of her significance to each of their lives. She appears frail and childlike to Sethe, who longs to protect the daughter she was forced to murder; she takes the form of a powerful sexual aggressor to Paul D, who fears the disruption of the tentative new life he has made at the house on Bluestone Road.

Beloved's paradoxical embodiment of frailty and inexplicable strength is a prototype for the physical transformations the other women in the novel will undergo. Akin to the carnival freaks, whose oddities are most commonly defined in terms of deviations in shape and size—"twenty feet tall or two feet tall, weighing a ton" or hardly anything at all—the women at 124 shrink and grow in unexpected ways. The rapidity and excess of these corporeal changes suggest that they in fact describe emotional states. In *Beloved* something akin to the unconscious, where unspeakable and unresolved traumas reside, registers in the external contours of the female form. Early in the novel, Sethe is described as a "quiet, queenly woman," whose emotional fortitude, which enabled her to escape slavery, survive prison, and raise a daughter alone, is conveyed by her powerful, statuesque corporeality. The scars that traverse her back, a "sculpture . . . like the decorative work of an ironsmith too passionate for display" (49), recall wounds that have healed but leave permanent traces of violence and injury. Likewise, Denver's fleshy face and "far too womanly breasts" bespeak a body developed beyond its years. Paul D notices Denver's mature breasts precisely at the moment when she tearfully describes the isolation she and her mother have endured, her excessive size reflecting the emotional growth required of the young girl during years of ostracism from the surrounding community. The unmistakable signs that Denver *has a body*—her tears, hunger, thirst, and pouting—demand her mother's affection in a manner almost unbearable to Sethe, who has been conditioned by enslavement to maintain a distance from her own offspring. Referring to the dangerous love for her own children in corporeal terms, she tells Paul D, "I was big . . . and deep and wide" (162). As Beloved insinuates herself into the household she will challenge the monumentality of both Sethe and Denver, whose statuesque bodies bespeak strength of character but also a dangerously isolated individuation.

As Beloved's needs take their toll on Sethe and Denver, the burden is manifest physically in the shrinking and weakening of their bodies. Initially replicating the joyful excess of the carnival outing, Sethe spends her life savings "to feed themselves with fancy food and decorate themselves with ribbon and dress goods" (242), but as the money runs out, Beloved, with her "basket-fat stomach" (243), continues to expand, demanding "sweets although she was getting bigger, plumper by the day" (239). Beloved's untoward appetites are literally devouring Sethe. Even as they starve, Sethe clothes the household in "carnival dresses" made from gaudy materials that connect the reversals within the carnival gates to the reversals occasioned by Beloved's appearance: as Beloved expands, Sethe shrinks; as Beloved fills with vitality, Sethe droops listlessly; the young Beloved "looked the mother, Sethe the teething child" (250). Threatening to overpower the dwindling bodies within them, the brightly colored garments, in their excess, signal the dangers of excessive, self-consuming desire in a house once devoid of color.

As Beloved grows, Sethe, once a "quiet, queenly woman," becomes thin and fragile. Sethe's desire for Beloved is dangerous because it overpowers concern for her living daughter or her own well-being. Denver observes that "the flesh between her mother's forefinger and thumb was thin as china silk and there wasn't a piece of clothing in the house that didn't sag on her" (239). Akin to the ghostly Beloved that Paul D initially perceived as "thin," the formerly monumental Sethe is frail and weak with hunger, her body literally eaten away by the "thickness" of her love. Similarly, Denver, at one time physically mature for her age, also shrinks, growing not only thinner but also shorter and smaller: "the sleeves of her own carnival shirtwaist cover[ed] her fingers; hems that once showed her ankles now swept the floor" (243). While Denver's weight loss is a consequence of starvation, her shrinking cannot be explained except as a literalization of her dwindling importance in her mother's eyes. Finally, in "a dress so loud it embarrassed the needlepoint seat" (247), Denver ventures out into the community to seek help. Her previous attempt to establish relationships outside her family by enrolling in Lady Jones's makeshift school was greeted with the invitation: "Come in the front door, Miss Denver. This is not a side show" (102). Lady Jones makes an important distinction between active participation and staring, which replicates the alienating dynamics of the sideshow. Denver's second attempt at reintegration is more successful because the community is more willing to acknowledge her effort, responding with the contrition and generosity that it was unable to muster in the past.

Ultimately, the efforts of the entire community are required to counteract Sethe's assertion that she doesn't need the world outside. The crowd of women who gather in front of her house on Bluestone Road witnesses Sethe reliving the traumatic event in which she took the life of the infant Beloved to protect her from the approaching slave catchers. This time, however, she turns her rage outward, brandishing an ice pick at the solitary white man who approaches the house on horseback. Sethe's actions banish Beloved in her embodied form. A process that began with the visit to the carnival ends with the integration of the onlookers (the group of women) with the object of their gaze, as Sethe plunges off the porch into the crowd, "running into the faces of the people out there, joining them and leaving Beloved behind" (261). Abandoning Beloved indicates that she is ready to move beyond both the deadly repression of the past, which took shape as the "thin" baby ghost, and the excesses of dwelling on the past, embodied by the grown "basket-fat" freak Beloved. The point is not that the terrible trauma is resolved at this moment but that her burden cannot be shouldered alone. Individuality and self-reliance are not the antidotes to the un-freedom of slavery in *Beloved,* which concludes that its wounds can be salved only through the formation of new kinds of collectivity. Sethe has made the first toward reentry into a group that, in turn, seems ready to acknowledge her crime as their own. In this, the community recog-nizes that Beloved is the embodiment not simply of Sethe's individual acts but of the greed, barbarism, and wildness of slavery itself, a freak child born of their collective suffering.

Like any freak a being who relies as much on the spectator's imagi-native work as the prodigious contours of her body, Beloved is part of a fragmented story that shifts depending on the teller. Finally, it is forgot-ten, for "remembering seemed unwise" (274). But like conjoined twins, the double meaning of the novel's final injunction, "this is not a story to pass on," remains. Countless readers have pondered the meaning of this ambiguous warning. Is Beloved's a story to be shared with others, to "pass on" from one generation to the next? Or is it a story to leave be-hind, to "pass on" as one moves toward something else? This dual process of identification and dissociation is suggested by the image of "the photograph of a close friend or relative" evoked in one of the novel's final paragraphs that "looked at too long—shifts, and something more fa-miliar than the dear face itself moves there" (275). This uncanny experi-ence, in which the image of a loved one momentarily becomes the "more familiar" reflection of the self, is akin to the moment at the freak show when identity is shattered and reconfigured by encounters with persons so strange that they confuse our very sense of self and other. This tenta-tive recognition of the shifting boundaries between self and body, and the way they might merge with others, is a crucial aspect in the development of a collectivity that can embrace, as well as wound and exclude.

Reclaiming Wild

Baby. Grown woman. Ghost. Memory. Forgotten past. Wound. Healer. Beloved, as many have remarked, is a figure for the impossible but

necessary task of working through collective loss.[40] That process involves healing and forgiveness but too often also entails the scapegoating
of another more unfortunate and dispossessed group. Beloved is also a
freak, for freaks are at once living persons and the bodily projection of
our most profound individual and collective traumas. It is impossible to
see a freak unmediated by the desires and anxieties that filter our perception of extreme alterity. Early in the novel, the Black audience at the
carnival is not ready to recognize its own misfortunes mirrored in the unhappy performers onstage. Seeking entertainment and forgetting, they resist finding images that recall their own exploitation and instead simply
reverse the terms by loading derision onto the freaks. Although freaks
and slaves have both suffered the experience of imprisonment within
their own bodies, the characters in Beloved identify only with the racial
freak. Later, as Sethe stands before them in much the same position, they
are able to acknowledge her suffering as a necessary and painful part of
their own past, literally reincorporating her into the group. Recalling
Mrs. Garner's simple definition of a characteristic as "a thing that's natural to a thing," the community affirms race as the grounds for their
identification with one another and their rejection of outsiders, whether
they be well-meaning abolitionists or the bigots responsible for the jungle so vividly described by Stamp Paid. Banishing Beloved, they also banish the specter of the white man on horseback, the abolitionist Mr. Bodwin, whose benevolence must be rejected along with the slave owners'
cruelty.[41] The grotesque Sambo figurine that decorates the Bodwins'
kitchen implicates him in the same representational system that created
the Wild African Savage.

Any reader tempted to resolve these antagonisms by resorting to a
common humanity would do well to heed the words of Guitar in *Song
of Solomon* when he asserts that "white people are unnatural . . . the disease they have is in their blood, in the structure of their chromosomes"
(156–57). Guitar has learned Schoolteacher's lesson that race is a biological fact, which can be measured scientifically because it is lodged,
like a pathogen, in the body's cellular matter. Patently ridiculous freaks
like the Wild African Savage attest to the fraudulence of these lessons;
the cruelty and abuse exchanged between Black spectators and white
performers remind us of the lesson's palpably real effects. Set loose in
the world, they emerge from the mouth of a man like Guitar, who has
no other vocabulary to articulate his rage at unprovoked violence
against Black citizens. When each group views the other's difference as
the product of an intractable nature, there is little possibility for mutual
recognition. The reconsolidation of communal bonds initiated by the

freak show will take place without challenging more profound racial divisions, lodged firmly in place through the crimes of history. Ultimately, while the meaning of the freak show's invocation of racial essences is called into question, the fact that those essences exist is not.

Beloved ends not with a moment of divisive rage but with the possibility of healing as the community turns inward to shelter its own members. In a final reminder of the excursion to the fair, as Paul D sits by Sethe's bedside to comfort her he "examines the quilt patched in carnival colors" (272), an image that knits together many disparate lives and the pain they endured in a commemorative pattern. Unlike the carnival dresses bought with Sethe's life savings, which represented a retreat into the past at the expense of the future, the "carnival colors" signify the acknowledgment of the past as it is woven into something useful to those alive in the present. As they become part of the quilt, the pieces lose their particularity, each making its own significant and colorful contribution to the pattern.

This pattern continues as Beloved returns to haunt the pages of Morrison's next novel, *Jazz,* in the form of a disheveled, speechless woman named Wild. As Morrison described her to an interviewer, "The woman they call Wild . . . could be Sethe's daughter Beloved. When you see Beloved towards the end, you don't know; she's either a ghost who has been exorcised or she's a real person pregnant by Paul D, who runs away, ending up in Virginia, which is right next to Ohio." Morrison's next sentence, "But I don't want to make all these connections," does not undo what went before but insists on the necessary ambiguity of both wild women, whose significance must be conjoined in part through the reader's own imaginings.[42] Like the Wild African Savage of the freak show, who is at once familiar and exotic, Wild is both known and mysterious, a living woman who suffers pain and hunger and the stuff of local fantasy, "a used-to-be-long-ago crazy girl." But unlike the carnival wild man, whose wildness is as fictive as his African nationality, Wild roams freely through the cane fields of Virginia (and perhaps from one text to another), haunting those she encounters with the possibility that the boundary between their civility and her savagery is less than stable. As Michael Taussig suggests, wildness in ethnographic writing is more than the antithesis of Western rationality and order; it represents the threat, at once terrifying and enticing, of the dissolution of signification itself: "[Wildness] is the spirit of the unknown and the disorderly, loose in the forest encircling the city and the sown land, disrupting the conventions upon which meaning and the shaping function of images rest."[43] This chapter has treated wildness largely in terms of its performative dimensions in an age of confidence men and Barnumesque entertainment. Taussig's observations recall a more serious definition of wildness as the place where reason and order come to an end. In Morrison's fiction, this frightening wildness is born of slavery and the legacy of racism and poverty that survives in its wake. This wildness is not to be found in nature, for it is the product of human history and institutions.

By evocatively linking Wild to Beloved, Morrison suggests that her past is connected to the collective trauma of enslavement that haunts U.S. history and endures in the embodied memories of its citizens. Most of *Jazz* takes place among a generation removed from slavery. Set in 1920s Harlem, the novel focuses on Wild's son Joe Trace as he is caught up in a drama of passion, adultery, murder, and forgiveness. An undomesticated, antimaternal figure, Wild is the apparent antithesis to the urban dwellers of Manhattan. At the same time, although they do not know each other, she seems to have transmitted the pain and disorder of her own life to her offspring. Neat categorical oppositions between past and present, madness and sanity, threaten to become unmoored, as wildness bursts forth at the heart of civilization in Joe's murderous desire for Dorcas, Violet's irrational rage at Dorcas's corpse, the incurable eruptions of Dorcas's skin. Beloved, reincarnated, or simply relocated as Wild, thus perpetually returns to remind the community of what remains outside, inhabiting the abject spaces rejected by even the most marginal persons but unwilling, or perhaps unable, to go away.

NOTES

1. Here, of course, the two Black men are not using the term *freak* in reference to the sideshow. They are invoking the tradition of the African American toasts in which freaks are figures of monstrous (often sexual) excess. The world is "freaky" and "fucked-up" because they can find no more precise way to explain a bewildering, and potentially overwhelming, series of events. While the two uses of *freak* may seem unrelated, the following exploration of Morrison's fiction will reveal continuities between the term's different connotations. On freaks in African American toasts see Bruce Jackson, *"Get Your Ass in the Water and Swim Like Me": Narrative Poetry from Black Oral Tradition* (Cambridge: Harvard University Press, 1974).

2. In her reading of this scene, Emily Miller Budick accuses Paul D of macho posturing. While his actions may betray elements of self-aggrandizement, he also displays an infectious generosity toward Sethe and Denver, which invites other members of the Black community to behave similarly. While Paul D alone cannot heal Sethe's wounds, he begins the important process of her reintegra-

tion into the community. See Budick, "Absence, Loss, and the Space of History in Toni Morrison's *Beloved,*" *Arizona Quarterly* 48 (summer 1992): 117–38.

3. Toni Morrison, *Beloved* (New York: Plume, 1987), 47–49. All subsequent references will be cited parenthetically in the text.

4. Elissa Schappell, "Toni Morrison: The Art of Fiction," *Paris Review* 35, no. 128 (1993): 105. Walter Benn Michaels reads *Beloved* as an allegory for contemporary American understandings of history, in which the past endures in the present in the form of ghosts, who are the literary equivalent of "culture." Culture, in Michaels's controversial argument, boils down to an antiracist racial essentialism. This chapter will connect Morrison's commitment to essentialism to her evocation of the freak show. See Michaels, "'You Who Never Was There': Slavery and the New Historicism, Deconstruction and the Holocaust," *Narrative* 4, no. 1 (1996): 1–16.

5. On the confidence man, see Karen Halttunen, *Confidence Men and Painted Women: A Study of Middle Class Culture in America, 1830–1870* (New Haven: Yale University Press, 1982); Neil Harris, *Humbug: The Art of P. T. Barnum* (Chicago: University of Chicago Press, 1973); Gary Lindberg, *The Confidence Man in American Literature* (New York and Oxford: Oxford University Press, 1982); and Miles Orvell, *The Real Thing: Imitation and Authenticity in American Culture, 1880–1940* (Chapel Hill and London: University of North Carolina Press, 1989).

6. On Morrison's concept of rememory, see Ashraf H. A. Rushdy, "'Rememory': Primal Scenes and Constructions in Toni Morrison's Novels," in *Toni Morrison's Fiction: Contemporary Criticism,* ed. David L. Middleton (New York and London: Garland, 1997), 135–64.

7. On Black-white racial anxiety and the emergence of freak shows in the 1840s, see Leonard Cassuto, "The Racial Freak, the Happy Slave, and the Problems of Melville's Universal Man," in *The Inhuman Race: The Racial Grotesque in American Literature and Culture* (New York: Columbia University Press, 1997). Bluford Adams describes the development of an increasingly hierarchical understanding of race in Barnum's exhibits in "'A Stupendous Mirror of Departed Empires': The Barnum Hippodromes and Circuses," in *E Pluribus Barnum: The Great Showman and the Making of U.S. Popular Culture* (Minneapolis: University of Minnesota Press, 1997).

8. James W. Cook Jr., "Of Men, Missing Links, and Nondescripts: The Strange Career of P. T. Barnum's 'What Is It?' Exhibition," in *Freakery: Cultural Spectacles of the Extraordinary Body,* ed. Rosemarie Garland Thomson (New York: New York University Press, 1996), 140.

9. Rosemarie Thomson, *Extraordinary Bodies: Figuring Physical Disability in American Literature and Culture* (New York: Columbia University Press, 1996).

10. W. C. Thompson, *On the Road with a Circus* (New York: Amsterdam Book Co., 1905), 69.

11. Scott Hart, "How Circus Freaks are Made," *Coronet,* May 1946, 49–50.

12. *What We Know About Waino and Plutano the Wild Men of Borneo* (New York: Damon and Peets, Printers, n.d.), Houghton Library Theater Collection, Harvard University.

13. W. C. Thompson, *On the Road,* 70.

14. George Templeton Strong, *The Diaries*, excerpted in *Writing New York*, ed. Philip Lopate (New York: Library of America, 1998), 211.

15. See Robert Bogdan, *Freak Show: Presenting Human Curiosities for Amusement and Profit* (Chicago: University of Chicago Press, 1985); and Robert Rydell, *All the World's a Fair: Visions of Empire at American International Expositions, 1876–1916* (Chicago: University of Chicago Press, 1984) on the fabrication of ethnographic freaks.

16. "Side Shows," *Strand Magazine* 13 (1897): 409.

17. Hart, "How Circus Freaks Are Made," 49.

18. W. C. Thompson, *On the Road*, 70–71.

19. W. C. Thompson, *On the Road*, 70.

20. The cruelty of showmen eager to exploit the racial freak's potential is also the subject of Eudora Welty's short story "Keela, the Outcast Indian Maiden," in which Lee Roy, a diminutive Black man with a club foot, is kidnapped by a traveling carnival and forced to perform as a savage woman. As Steve, the talker, describes the act, "it was supposed to be a Indian woman, see, in this red dress an' stockin's. It didn't have on no shoes, so when it drug its foot ever-body could see. . . . When it come to the chicken's heart, it would eat that too, real fast, and the heart would still be jumpin'" (76). The figure of "Keela" demonstrates how tenuous the freak's claim to authenticity could be, for not only do nonwhite races slip interchangeably into one another, Black easily becoming Indian, but so do genders. See Eudora Welty, "Keela, the Outcast Indian Maiden," in *A Curtain of Green and Other Stories* (New York: Harcourt, Brace, 1941).

21. On Joice Heth, see Bluford Adams, Neil Harris, and Ben Reiss, "P. T. Barnum, Joice Heth, an Antebellum Spectacle of Race," *American Quarterly* 51 (March 1999): 78–107.

22. See Adams, *E Pluribus Barnum*, for an analysis of different versions of Barnum's autobiography.

23. The freak show's embrace of authenticity seems, on the surface, to differentiate it from the equally popular nineteenth-century form of blackface minstrelsy, which exploited the difference between the white performer and the Black character he was playing. Bill Brown describes the relationship between minstrelsy and the freak show in evolutionary terms, as "a transition from performative subjectivity to unperformed abjection," that is, from the parodic theatricalization of blackface to the static essentialism of the ethnographic curiosity. Whereas the explicit intention of blackface minstrelsy is to mimic blackness (generally by those who are not themselves Black), the freak show represents the intractable savagery of Black bodies as an empirical fact. This is a plausible description of the racial exhibit's intended effects; however, such intentions are complicated by examples that attest to the sideshow as a venue just as invested in performance, parody, and dialogue between audience and performer as blackface minstrelsy. See Brown, *The Material Unconscious: American Amusement, Stephen Crane, and the Economies of Play* (Cambridge: Harvard University Press, 1996), 214.

24. Strong, *Diaries*, 211.

25. George C. Middleton, quoted in Bogdan, *Freak Show*, 176.

26. I am referring to the well-known debates among feminist critics that begin with Laura Mulvey's "Visual Pleasure and Narrative Cinema," in *Film*

Theory and Criticism, ed. Gerald Mast, Marshall Cohen, and Leo Braudy (New York and Oxford: Oxford University Press, 1992), 746–57, which assumes that the gender of the spectator dictates her identification with the screen image. Subsequent criticism, too copious to cite in a note, has demonstrated that spectatorship is far more complicated and varied than Mulvey's direct correlation would suggest.

27. Eric Lott, *Love and Theft: Blackface Minstrelsy and the American Working Class* (New York and Oxford: Oxford University Pres, 1995), 124.

28. Manthia Diawara has acknowledged the Black viewer's particular difficulty identifying with the spectatorial positions established by classic cinematic narratives, as well as the elision of questions of race from debates about cinematic spectatorship, in "Black Spectatorship: Problems of Identification and Resistance," *Screen* 29, no. 4 (1988): 66–76. On race and resistant viewing practices, see also Jacqueline Bobo, *Black Women as Cultural Readers* (New York: Columbia University Press, 1995); Petal Felix and Jacqui Roach, "Black Looks," in *The Female Gaze: Women as Viewers of Popular Culture,* ed. Lorraine Gammon and Margaret Marshment (Seattle: Red Comet Press, 1989), 130–42; Ann Freidberg, "A Denial of Difference: Theories of Cinematic Identification," in *Psychoanalysis and Cinema,* ed. E. Ann Kaplan (New York and London: Routledge, 1990), 36–45; bell hooks, *Black Looks: Race and Representation* (Boston: South End Press, 1992); and Kobena Mercer, *Welcome to the Jungle: New Positions in Black Cultural Studies* (New York and London: Routledge, 1994). Ed Guerrero has applied theories of the gaze to Morrison's fiction in "Tracking 'The Look' in the Novels of Toni Morrison," in *Toni Morrison's Fiction: Contemporary Criticism,* ed. David L. Middleton (New York and London: Garland, 1997), 27–44.

29. Harris, *Humbug,* 75.

30. This scene is consistent with Budick's contention that counting and numerical formations are important in *Beloved* for both enslavers and the ex-slaves who need to make a place for themselves in the free world. Elaborating on the dual significance of counting, she writes that "this book pulls us toward the problematics of what (and who) counts as family and as history, indeed, even what counts as human" ("Absence, Loss, and the Space of History" 130).

31. The imperative to make whiteness visible, robbing it of claims to transcendence and universality, is also crucial to Morrison's critical project. Her *Playing in the Dark: Whiteness and the Literary Imagination* (Cambridge: Harvard University Press, 1992) is one of the finest works of literary criticism to take whiteness as a starting point for an analysis of race.

32. Eve Kosofsky Sedgwick, *Epistemology of the Closet* (Berkeley and Los Angeles: University of California Press, 1990), 61.

33. In an analysis of Morrison's earlier fiction, Eliot Butler-Evans proposes that the desires of her Black female protagonists are often in tension with the communities that surround them. He writes of *Tar Baby,* "Morrison brings to the fore . . . the contentiousness between the desires of the mythical community and those of the black woman whose existence is structured by historical and social circumstances different from those of the community." See Butler-Evans, *Race, Gender, and Desire: Narrative Strategies in the Fiction of Toni Cade Bambara, Toni Morrison, and Alice Walker* (Philadelphia: Temple University Press, 1989), 162.

34. There is an ample body of criticism that debates whether Bakhtinian carnival is a source of revolutionary potential or social containment. See Natalie Zemon Davis, *Society and Culture in Early Modern France* (London: Duckworth, 1975); Simon Dentith, *Bakhtinian Thought: An Introductory Reader* (New York and London: Routledge, 1995); Terry Eagleton, *Walter Benjamin: Towards a Revolutionary Criticism* (London: Verso, 1981); and Peter Stallybrass and Allon White, *The Politics and Poetics of Transgression* (Ithaca: Cornell University Press, 1986).

35. Sigmund Freud, *Jokes and Their Relation to the Unconscious,* trans. James Strachey (New York and London: W. W. Norton, 1960).

36. I also read this moment as a revision of the painful scene in *The Bluest Eye* when Pecola buys candy from a white shopkeeper who recoils at the prospect of taking money from her hand.

37. Many critics have emphasized the primacy of the mother-daughter relationship in *Beloved,* but Morrison herself claims that the murdered child could have been male with much the same effect. On the significance of this female bond, see Lorraine Liscio, "*Beloved's* Narrative: Writing Mother's Milk," *Tulsa Studies in Women's Literature* 11, no. 1 (1992): 31–47; Ashraf Rushdy, "Daughters Signifyin(g) History: The Example of Toni Morrison's *Beloved,*" *American Literature* 64 (Sept. 1992): 567–80; and Cynthia Griffin Wolff, "Margaret Garner: A Cincinnati Story," *Massachusetts Review* 32 (fall 1991): 417–41. Undoubtedly, one aspect of Morrison's project is to revalorize female experience and female storytellers, but her emphasis rests more on the difficulties of motherhood than on an essential female bond between mother and daughter. In fact, relations between mothers and sons are at the center of fictional works such as *Song of Solomon* and *Jazz.* See Morrison's discussion of motherhood in the interview by Cecil Brown in the *Massachusetts Review* 36 (fall 1995): 455–73.

38. Jean Wyatt argues that typically metaphorical relations are literalized by the characters in *Beloved,* who experience the materiality of language inscribed upon their bodies. See Wyatt, "Giving Body to the World: The Maternal Symbolic in Toni Morrison's *Beloved,*" *PMLA* 108 (May 1993): 474–88.

39. For the most sustained discussion of Beloved's ghostly status, see Avery Gordon, *Ghostly Matters: Haunting and the Sociological Imagination* (Minneapolis: University of Minnesota Press, 1997), 183.

40. Melancholia does not figure prominently in this analysis but is a useful critical paradigm for understanding the way that *Beloved,* inflicted with realist detail, also describes the fantastic haunting of a group traumatized by a past with which it has not yet been able to come to terms. For psychoanalytic readings of the novel that make this argument, see David Lawrence, "Fleshly Ghosts and Ghostly Flesh: The Word and the Body in *Beloved,*" *Studies in American Fiction* 19 (autumn 1991): 189–202; and Roger Luckhurst, "'Impossible Mourning' in Toni Morrison's *Beloved* and Michele Roberts's *Daughters of the House,*" *Critique* 37 (summer 1996): 243–61. In *Ghostly Matters,* Avery Gordon also discusses Morrison's interweaving of history—the fictionalized story of Margaret Garner—with the magical realism of a ghost story, a strategy that allows her to narrate events that could not be accessed through more conventional historical or sociological methods.

41. Analyzing *Beloved* as a critique of contemporary liberalism, James Berger

argues for Bodwin's complicity in *After the End: Representations of Post-Apocalypse* (Minneapolis: University of Minnesota Press, 1999).

42. Angels Carabi, "Interview with Toni Morrison," *Belles Lettres* 9 (spring 1994): 39.

43. Michael Taussig, *Shamanism, Colonialism, and the Wild Man: A Study in Terror and Healing* (Chicago: University of Chicago Press, 1987), 219.

Carla Williams

Naked, Neutered, or Noble

The Black Female Body in America and the Problem of Photographic History

The larger society, observing the [Black] women's outrageous persistence in holding on, staying alive, thought
it had no choice save to dissolve the perversity of the
Black woman's life into a fabulous fiction of multiple
personalities. They were seen as acquiescent, submissive
Aunt Jemimas who showed grinning faces, plump laps,
fat embracing arms, and brown jaws pouched in laughter. They were described as leering buxom wenches with
round heels, open thighs, and insatiable sexual appetites.
They were accused of being marauding matriarchs of
stern demeanor, battering hands, unforgiving gazes, and
castrating behavior.
—Maya Angelou, "They Came to Stay"

Images of Black women that are in fact "national, racial, and historical
hallucinations" have been ingrained into the collective conscience of the
United States since slavery.[1] Black women have been depicted either
naked, generally in an ethnographic context, or as laborers, usually domestic, their social status playing a crucial role in the development of visual identity. With rare exceptions, representations of the Black woman
in art and photography have followed these prescribed lines. Using primarily published images as a frame of reference, this discussion gives an

overview of photographic history from the 1850s to the present, a history that has attempted to define the Black female body.

Countless photographers, both famous and anonymous, have photographed Black women. Open any monograph publication of an American twentieth-century portrait photographer or any fairly broad history of photography, and you will discover that nearly everybody has such a photograph. The black skin was often a visual challenge, juxtaposed against a white background or a white body for maximum visual contrast and nothing more, or so it was often claimed. In the history of photography only a handful of books are devoted exclusively to the image of the Black female; these include: *Eve Noire,* by Hans Leuenberger; *Black Woman,* by Chester Higgins; *Jungle Fever,* by Jean-Paul Goude; *Black Ladies,* by Uwe Ommer; and *I Dream a World: Portraits of Black Women Who Changed America,* by Brian Lanker.[2] These few books, marginal within the canon of photographic history, are nevertheless essential to understanding the photographic image of the black female body and how certain images are perpetuated. Although the fact of publication is an inherently problematic measure of validation given that Black photographers and subjects are so rarely, if ever, published, it is especially indicative of the kinds of images that are perpetuated to evaluate what has been sanctioned, often repeatedly, to go into print.

Early twentieth-century African American photographers—including James VanDerZee (1886–1983) in Harlem (see fig. 36); Addison Scurlock (1883–1964) in Washington, D.C.; and Prentice Hall Polk (1898–1984) in Tuskeegee, Alabama—photographed Black women frequently, as commercial customers and as artistic subjects, and these images have been reproduced in several monographic publications.[3] Roy DeCarava's 1955 publication *The Sweet Flypaper of Life,* with text by Langston Hughes, was the first best-selling book of images of Black people by Black people that gained widespread recognition.[4] Additionally, a few other Euro-American photographers published lengthy studies that feature a considerable number of images of Black women, including Bruce Davidson's *East 100th Street,* Aaron Siskind's *Harlem Document,* and Irving Penn's *Worlds in a Small Room.*[5]

Early Images

The history of the photographic image of the Black female body in the United States begins in the 1850s, with a model derived from European

Fig. 36. James VanDerZee, *Nude by the Fireplace,* 1923. (Courtesy of Metropolitan Museum of Art, the Studio Museum in Harlem, Mrs. VanDerZee.)

precedents. During this period, a number of significant developments in Western culture coincided with the invention of photography and contributed to the way in which Black females were regarded and ultimately visualized. The births of "popular culture" and modern visual pornography, the development of the natural sciences and the related disciplines of ethnology and anthropology, and the abolition of slavery both in the colonies and at home were practically simultaneous, and each served to compartmentalize, objectify, and categorize any manifestations of difference from the European ideal.

The decades including and following the abolition of slavery in England (1807), France (1848), and the United States (1865) also saw the rapid colonial/imperial expansion of these nations into Africa, Asia, the Caribbean, and South America. These aggressions and the drive to dominate the indigenous populations subsequently fostered the births of anthropology and ethnology and the study of the natural sciences, including physiognomy and phrenology, all of which existed only through the element of comparison to an "Other," which the colonies provided. The Royal Anthropological Institute of Great Britain and Ireland was founded in 1843; the naturalist Charles Darwin's theory of evolution, *The Origin of Species,* was published in 1859; the Société d'Anthropologie de Paris was founded that same year; and the National Geographic Society debuted in the United States in 1888. The decades at the end of the nineteenth century and the beginning of the twentieth century saw a lucrative international market for ethnographic postcards and prints as colonial expansion and exploration increased in Africa, South America, and Asia. In this climate, "scientific" evaluations based on observable distinctions in skin color, facial structure, and particularly genitalia contributed to difference inevitably being assigned a moral rank, and, consequently, to the association of Blacks with moral deficiency, sexual deviance, and overall inferiority. The stereotype of exaggerated sexuality in the female corresponded with the prevailing attitudes toward all women at that time. Thus Black women were aligned with the weaker, more negative human character traits that could be readily assessed through popular phrenological charts.

Around 1850, Dr. Robert W. Gibbes, a nationally recognized paleontologist, hired local daguerreotypist Joseph T. Zealy (1812–93) to make photographic records of first- and second-generation slaves on plantations near Columbia, South Carolina, for Swiss-born Louis Agassiz (1807–73), the natural scientist and zoologist from Harvard University. Agassiz had observed slaves on the Gibbes plantation for a month before he asked Gibbes to arrange for the photographs; he believed that photographic evidence could validate his theories on the racial inferiority of Blacks.[6]

Fifteen Zealy daguerreotypes survive of five men—Alfred, Fassena, Renty, Jem and Jack—and two women—Delia and Drana (see figs. 37 and 38). Utilizing the frontal/profile, "mug-shot" aesthetic that was favored in ethnography photography, the photographer documented

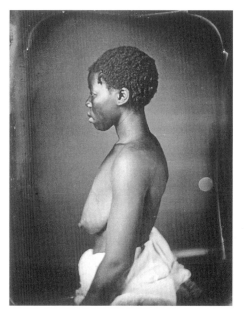

Fig. 37. J. T. Zealy, *Drana* (*profile view*), 1850. (Courtesy of Peabody Museum, Harvard University.)

Fig. 38. J. T. Zealy, *Delia* (*frontal view*), 1850. (Courtesy of Peabody Museum, Harvard University.)

Gibbes's human property in half- and full-length views, stripped to the waist or, for some of the men, totally naked. The men were all African born; Delia and Drana, the daughters of Renty and Jack, respectively, were "country-born" in the United States.[7]

Both Delia and Drana are shown from the waist up in frontal and profile views, showing their right sides. Their printed dresses are not entirely removed for the "scientific" documentation but are pulled down around their waists to expose their breasts, which at most reveal them to be of different ages. The sight of their clothing unceremoniously pulled down to reveal these secondary sexual characteristics is more revealing and ultimately more exploitative of their bodies than their nudity would be. It is an unnatural, forced state emphasized by the lack of clothing rather than nudity. Unlike African tribal women photographed as ethnographic nudes, whose daily wardrobes might consist of little clothing, these American slaves clearly had their clothing removed expressly for the photograph. Consequently the display of flesh is neither sexual nor sensual, yet there is a pornographic element to their inability to determine the display of their bodies. The disavowal of the women's humanity and the refusal to allow them to control the representation of their bodies neutralized their sexuality and sensuality through the photographic act and represented them as naked specimens lacking either identity or power.[8]

The National Geographic Society was founded in Washington, D.C., in 1888, "for the increase and diffusion of geographical knowledge."[9] The first issue of the society's magazine was published in October 1888; however, it was not until the November 1896 issue that the first photograph of a bare-breasted native woman appeared, in an image titled *Zulu Bride and Bridegroom* (fig. 39). Made in the South African Republic, or Transvaal, it showed an African man and woman standing side by side, facing the camera, his right hand crossed in front of him, holding her left hand. They both look directly at the camera, without expression. In the accompanying article, the American author describes all the tribes of the Bantu or Kaffir race, alluding eventually to sexual practice: "These people are of a dark bronze hue, and have good athletic figures. They possess some excellent traits, but are horribly cruel when once they have smelled blood. . . . Nothing but the phenomenal fecundity of the race has kept up its numbers."[10] The language reinforces the assumption that they are no more than the sum of their physical attributes and sexual proclivities.[11] Standards of decency do not apply, especially to the body of the woman, whose partial nudity was potentially more shocking. The couple has been reduced in the text to feral, fecund creatures, no different from wild animals, and the photograph reinforces this characterization.

This photograph established the "National Geographic" aesthetic, which would introduce generations of American males and females to "primitive-style" nudity. Countless examples of bare-breasted or totally nude women of color have appeared in *National Geographic*. Thus, presenting unclothed African bodies to a Victorian audience in the United States could be condoned. As Catherine Lutz and Jane Collins's research indicates:

> The "nude" woman sits, stands, or lounges at the salient center of *National Geographic* photography of the non-Western world. Until the phenomenal growth of mass circulation pornography in the 1960s, the magazine was known as the only mass culture venue where Americans could see women's breasts. Part of the folklore of Euramerican men, stories about secret perusals of the magazine emerged time after time in our conversations with male *National Geographic* readers. . . . When white men tell these stories about covertly viewing

Fig. 39. Anonymous, *Zulu Bride and Bridegroom,* ca. 1896.
(Courtesy of National Geographic Society.)

black women's bodies, they are clearly not recounting a story about a simple encounter with the facts of human anatomy or customs; they are (perhaps unsuspectingly) confessing a highly charged—but socially approved—experience in this dangerous territory of projected, forbidden desire and guilt.[12]

The practice of printing photographs of unclothed native women in *National Geographic* did not occur with any regularity until 1903, when a photograph of two bare-breasted Filipino women was published. Only then, seven years after a Black woman had been depicted, did these images generate a moral debate among the editors.[13]

An Artist's Model

Not all Black women were photographed without their consent; for example, images of Maudelle Bass raise the question of the subjects' participation in the image-making process. Maudelle Bass (later Weston, 1908–89) was a dancer from the 1930s through the 1950s, and a professional artist's model. She was the first Black dancer to study modern dance with choreographer Lester Horton in Los Angeles and danced in 1940 in Agnes DeMille's "Black Ritual," choreographed for Ballet Theatre with an all-Negro cast, for which she was photographed in publicity and performance shots by Carl Van Vechten (1880–1964). She also appeared with dancer and choreographer Pearl Primus (1919–94) in the 1950s. In 1939 Bass posed for painter Diego Rivera (1886–1957) and for photographers including Johann Hagemeyer (1884–1962) and Edward Weston (1886–1958). In August 1939 Rivera began a series of nude paintings of Bass, whom he is said to have considered "the embodiment of ideal beauty and sensuality."[14] In his painting titled *Dancer in Repose,* Bass is depicted seated on a low stool, her broad hips anchoring the composition, with her arms upraised and tucked behind her head, in the standard pose that emphasizes the line of the breast.

In 1931, Weston had written in his journal, "If I had a nude body to work with—a Negress, a black fat Negress, then I could have worked! This desire keeps popping into my mind."[15] Eight years later he found Bass, who did not exactly adhere to his corpulent ideal; yet she was the only Black woman whom Weston would thus photograph. Bass posed for at least eighteen photographs with Weston during July and August 1939, in Carmel, California, where she had gone to perform in a series of African dances.[16] The sittings, which took place at

Weston's father-in-law's home, as well as on the sand dunes at Oceano, were the first nudes that Weston made in this setting, Carmel Highlands, where he had recently settled with his new wife, Charis Wilson. Included were two conventional clothed portraits, one of which was published in *U.S. Camera* in 1941.[17] Bass is shown wearing a polka-dotted dress, seated on the grass against a flowered bush, her legs folded to the side.

Weston used various settings for his nudes of Bass.[18] She was photographed in the same setting described earlier against the flowers, un-clothed, lying with her right arm upraised over her head. Both Bass and the setting are unidealized, her mottled and creased skin looking aged and tired against the tangle of foliage, although she was only thirty-one when the photographs were made. Her heavy breasts sag from their own weight. Bass was also photographed from numerous angles seated on the garden steps. In another view, Bass was photographed kneeling on the grass against a forest of ferns, her arms upraised as if in surrender, look-ing directly at the camera. Her direct engagement is disarming and does not occur with any other models in Weston's nude studies.

"The response to this photograph reveals how sensibilities and taste can change over time. Fifty years ago this image was exhibited without a murmur of protest apparently at the Museum of Modern Art and toured internationally in *World of Weston,* an exhibition sponsored by the State Department," notes Weston scholar Amy Conger. "This photograph of a black woman as if in a jungle with hands raised, sur-rendering, is often found offensive today by people who are sensitive to exploitation."[19] An image of "Maudelle on Dunes" was also exhibited in *World of Weston.* Conger writes: "Weston was primarily interested in the contrast between the background and her black and shiny skin."[20] The dunes images are the only ones that approximate such formal concerns of skin contrasted with sand or even hint at Bass's training as a dancer.

Shortly thereafter, Bass wrote to Weston from her home in San Francisco, stating that she was "wild with delight" when she saw some of the proofs, three of which she planned to use "for advertising."[21] It is not clear which three images she selected, nor if they were ever used, but it is significant to know that she was not only pleased with the re-sults but also planned to use them to represent herself when promoting her dance. What these images also reveal, however, is Weston's discom-fort with Bass's Black body and inability to idealize and "modernize" her as he had so successfully done with Charis Wilson, Tina Modotti, and a number of other white women who had modeled nude for him. Except for the photographs made on the dunes, Bass is not posed to highlight her dancer's form; she is not formalized into angles and curves, nor is she flattered by light and shadow. Interestingly, the nudes of Bass are among the only ones in Weston's oeuvre in which the model's head and face are visible and she engages the camera directly. Weston portrays her as tired and marked, unidealized, and ultimately different from the natural ideal that he promoted in his other work.

Around the same time Johann Hagemeyer, a Carmel-based portrait photographer originally from Amsterdam and a friend of Weston's, also photographed Bass. Hagemeyer, who made his living photographing celebrities and artists who passed through Carmel, produced a sensitive head-and-shoulders portrait study of the dancer. Bass is photographed in close-up, her hand gently touching her cheek while her glassy eyes are fixed with a faraway gaze. Her lined face, furrowed brow, and hands cause her to look older than her years. Photographed from below with strong directional lighting, she is monumentalized, the gravity of her expression matching the serious consideration paid to her as a subject. As an expressive artist in another medium, she is treated as a portrait study; in short, Hagemeyer renders her as a peer.

In 1940 Cedric Gibbons, the Academy Award–winning head of art direction for the Metro-Goldwyn Mayer studio, asked Weston about obtaining prints of the Bass nudes, "having heard that he had photographed 'that black dancer friend of [Miguel] Covarrubias.'"[22] This suggests that the images of Bass were known and collected in artistic circles. Seven years later photographer Manuel Alvarez Bravo (1902–) photographed Bass in Mexico, titling the image he made and published of her *Espejo Negro*, or "Black Mirror."[23] In the photograph, Bass sits on a crumpled cloth against a wall in bright sunlight. "Inspired by the myth of Tezcatlipoca, Lord of the Smoking Mirror," this image of Bass's glistening, almost polished black skin is meant to reflect the world—"the symbol of the *Espejo humeante* (Smoking mirror)"—just as her Black body, like that of the Sable Venus, is meant to symbolize "a Black Eve, mother of humanity."[24]

Bass is exceptional in that she is the only Black female model that appears with some frequency in the work of so many Euro-American artists from this period. Not merely a model, she had a successful artistic career in her own right and so would have surely been sympathetic to— and cognizant of—a fellow artist in another medium. Given her status as an artist and her response to the Weston images it is fair to say that Bass was at least an active contributor to those images that survive of her. Her legacy in photographs provides a glimpse into a period of the twentieth century in which one Black female body came to represent an ideal, a fantasy, a stereotype, and ultimately herself.

Black Is Beautiful

The Kamoinge Workshop, an association of Black photographers, was founded in 1963.[25] Roy DeCarava was the group's mentor and first president.[26] The often-echoed statement "I had never seen any positive images of black people" was the impetus behind their organization—they wanted to picture Black people more fully and positively than they previously had been. In 1965–66, Kamoinge even mounted an exhibition at the Market Place Gallery in Harlem titled "The Negro Woman."[27] During a crucial moment within the Black Art Movement, almost ten years later, Joe Crawford, Beuford Smith, and Joe Walker founded *The Black Photographer's Annual,* which offered African American photographers an opportunity to combat media stereotypes in print.[28] Many of the published works focused on the Black female body, particularly with regard to hairstyle and dress, which during the 1960s had become signifiers of pride and identity. *The Annual's* legacy was its ability to make visible the multiple experiences of Black peoples in the African Diaspora. It also encouraged Black photographers to locate the Black body in an art context.

Published in 1970, Chester Higgins's (1946–) publication *Black Woman,* with text by Harold McDougall, was the first book devoted exclusively to celebrating the Black woman in all of her aspects. Taken as a whole, the book encompasses a range of representations, with an emphasis, but not an exclusive focus, on women wearing Afro hairstyles. Higgins's images range from candid street photography to a more contemplative nude study. "As Chester puts it, these women are of a new breed—a Black Breed," writes McDougall in his introduction. "A breed that has racial pride in being black, and human pride in being a woman. At the same time."[29] McDougall based his text, which accompanies each image as a first-person quotation, on conversations with women in Harlem. In the first section, "Black Sisters into the Black Thing," a portrait of a young Black woman sitting on the beach in a two-piece swimsuit is accompanied by the text: "Black women have to start doing things that are more daring as far as their bodies are concerned. Because we just happen to have much more beautiful bodies."[30] Sporting a short Afro, the woman appears at ease in her mostly exposed, slender body, soaking up the sun. The image and text are empowering, validating not only the Black woman's beauty but, more importantly, her awareness of it.

In the section titled "Old Souls," Higgins presents an older, heavier Black woman as a smiling, warm presence, hand on hip. In the context of the other women in the book, her strength and bearing are at once formidable yet open, the image embracing her corporeality while subverting stereotypes associated with it. While this "paean of praise to the Black Woman," as McDougall describes it, is a triumphant affirmation of Black women as complex human beings, engaged in a myriad of activities and represented in every shape, size, age, and skin tone, it also presents McDougall's and Higgins's "positions as black men" vis-à-vis Black women.[31] Nevertheless, the voice that McDougall attaches to Higgins's subjects has an authenticity that rings true, demanding a reassessment of the Black woman's image in photographs.

Black as Fetish

A permutation of the celebration of Black beauty is the work of French photographer and illustrator Jean-Paul Goude (1940–).[32] His 1980 book *Jungle Fever* is a highly personal, obsessive journal about his feverish love of nonwhite people, from Vietnamese to American Indians, but especially Black American females. However personal, "the 'private' vision emerges via a public preconscious that is heavily invested with the historical accretions of representations," writes Francette Pacteau.[33] Goude fully acknowledges and exploits these referents, concluding his text by stating:

> As a European, let me pause here to say, I have the advantage of being able to describe my romantic conception of blackness from a white point of view. My conception is free of all social connotations because I am European. Americans cannot dissociate themselves from the social implications of their artistic evaluation of black people. . . . So, I really find myself in a strange situation, because on the one hand liberals are embarrassed by my attitude, while racists ironically misinterpret me as one of them. And the blacks? I'm not sure; I think my conception may appeal to some with a sensibility similar to mine. I'm not sure. . . . I am just letting my emotions do the work.[34]

Goude's statement that he relies on emotions to guide his work subverts the standard assumption that Europeans are intellectual while nonwhites are instinctual. Half of Goude's six chapters are dedicated to individual Black women, while two of the other three contain photographs of nude Black women worth displaying yet possibly not quite chapter-worthy. The text guides the reader chronologically through Goude's boyhood and each of his many ethno-romantic fixations.

Along the way there was Radiah, from Mobile, Alabama, whom Goude wanted to improve upon to create a "giant African beauty."[35] For her, Goude invented removable African tribal-scarification marks. His photograph of Radiah in the act of either removing or applying the marks made the newspapers and appeared in the December 1970 issue of the American men's magazine *Esquire*. Goude describes the marks by stating, "They emphasize the savage aesthetics of the face," thus equating the American Radiah with at best an "uncivilized" person and at worst an animal.[36] On the opposite page is a photograph of a nude Radiah lying on the floor of a studio wearing a headwrap made from a dishcloth. Goude conflates the nude, idle Black female body with a symbol, enveloping her head, of domestic labor that is usually associated with the image of the Mammy, thus conjuring up the image of the house servant, of the Black woman in the kitchen.[37] Here, however, she is visualized in the same body as the sexually available Black female capitulating to a fantasy of the Jezebel.[38] The beaded ornamentation added to the dishcloth and the braids of hair barely visible underneath further emphasize her otherwise airbrushed ethnicity.

Next came Toukie Smith, a model whom Goude met through Radiah. He began to photograph her and draw her nude, focusing on her hips and buttocks, cutting up the pictures and reassembling them to exaggerate her already voluptuous features.[39] Literally dehumanizing her and reducing her to body parts, Goude made first a life-size and eventually a twelve-inch cast of her nude body. Of his cast model of Smith he wrote: "I had always admired black women's backsides, the ones who look like racehorses. Toukie's backside was voluptuous enough, but nowhere near a racehorse's ass, so I gave her one. There she was, my dream come true, in living color . . . I saw her as this primitive voluptuous girl-horse."[40] Included are photographs of the artist and model in the studio during the casting, presumably to document the process, but also to suggest her complicity in the spectacle that would transform her, like Radiah, into an animal-like creature. Goude transformed her Black-bodied reality into his white-minded ideal; or, as Pacteau has observed: "Confronted with an excess of difference, the white male subject will excel at defensive ingenuity, making her blackness becoming to his light, brightening up his day with her night."[41] A two-page photograph of a white male hand with a smudge of black literally under its thumb, holding the miniature replica of the nude Black female, who "hated what [Goude] did . . . [and] did not share [his] views," is the most explicit visual representation of Goude's intentions.[42]

Naked, Neutered, or Noble

The Neutralized Woman

Brian Lanker (1947–) was a Pulitzer Prize–winning photojournalist and contract photographer for *Sports Illustrated* magazine when he conceived of the project of photographing Black women who had changed the course of history in the United States. *I Dream a World: Portraits of Black Women Who Changed America* became a best-selling book and calendar and a successful traveling exhibition. Its mission was to uplift, to celebrate women who had accomplished something noteworthy in their lives and to share their stories and images with the masses. The seventy-five portraits range from head shots to full standing shots, from photographs with seamless studio backdrops to those with forest perches. The portraits are of extraordinary women to be sure, each deserving of her own book, but life accomplishments are difficult, if not impossible, to convey photographically.

Among the subjects there are award-winning performers and writers, a choral director, two MacArthur fellows, three Pulitzer Prize winners, an Emmy-winning journalist, politicians, grassroots civil rights activists, educators, an architect, a curator, newspaper publishers, a bishop, sports champions, a child-care provider, a neurosurgeon, heads of non-profit organizations, a chef, a storyteller, and a visual artist. The two least educated or celebrated subjects are midwives, one of whom, depicted in an eyelet sleeping cap and a tweed coat with a fur collar, is revealed to be the childhood mammy of the photographer's white wife, seemingly included as a personal, posthumous tribute.[43]

As Maya Angelou points out in her foreword, the women literally share a "sameness of gaze," which is ultimately problematic.[44] Only ten of the women even smile; the rest are so possessed with the solemnity of their blackness that it is oppressively palpable. Taken as a whole, they are noble savages gone to the extreme, none of them, in the photographic space, possessed of either complexity or corporeality that would identify her as a woman, let alone a sexual being. Indeed, their bodies cease to exist altogether: only eleven of the women either wear short sleeves or go sleeveless, the facts of their flesh carefully and decorously hidden amid the folds and shadows. They are aggressively covered up, their physicality and sexuality sublimated to and exclusive of their achievements, which are articulated in a page of text facing each image. Two fair-skinned women tentatively reveal their décolletage, yet only dancer Katherine Dunham speaks directly about her publicly sexual image, and then refutes it, stating: "I never thought of myself as sexy. I didn't think of what we were doing onstage as sexy, because I could always feel and know that there was something solid, that authentic feeling under it."[45]

The nude Black female body appears only once, as an out-of-focus sculpture in the foreground of artist Elizabeth Catlett's (1915–) portrait, with her bespectacled head emerging from behind it. She states: "I was working always with the black theme. I did a whole series on black women. Nobody was doing black women. I am a black woman. That's what I know most about."[46] Catlett's own images of Black women tend toward the full-bodied and sensuous; her sculptures celebrate the body. Ultimately, her statement highlights the missing element within the images in Lanker's volume. The photographs are inextricably examples of being looked at and interpreted by an outsider, not of picturing one's self. While the women's words are provided to carry the authenticity of narrative, their visual images are still the creation of someone else, a white man determined not to repeat any stereotypes in his depictions and in the process nevertheless reinforcing one of the neutered Black female denied her sexuality. The prima-ballerina-turned-painter Janet Collins states: "When you get to be an exceptional black, you don't belong to the white and you don't belong to the black. You are too good for the black and you will always be black to the white."[47] Likewise, if you are a Black woman noted for her sexuality, you are unworthy of praise.

The images discussed in this essay are among the most accessible images of Black women in photographic history, yet they are repeatedly reproduced without discussion of the subject's desire or role in the image-making process. The simple fact of the matter is that in most cases, that information is simply not known and will forever be left up to conjecture. Contemporary historians and theorists such as Deborah Willis, Coco Fusco, Kellie Jones, Judith Williamson, and Lisa Collins have begun to address the image of the Black female body in all of its complexity. Evaluating the history of the photographic image of Black women is a crucial beginning for intelligent art and analysis. The theoretical discussion that arises from issues of representation is best left to cultural theorists.

Given the legacy of images created of Black women, it is an especially complex task for contemporary Black women to define their own image, one that necessarily both incorporates and subverts the stereotypes, myths, facts, and fantasies that have preceded them. Black female photographic artists including Clarissa Sligh, Renée Cox, Roshini Kempadoo, Carrie Mae Weems, Joy Gregory, Lorna Simpson, Maxine Walker, and Cynthia Wiggins have already begun to do so with a breathtaking range of image making. Some write an autobiography of the body, using their own likenesses and those of other Black women to explore shared experiences and perceptions, including both universal injustices against and celebrations of the Black female body. It is to all of the afore-mentioned artists and writers that the task falls to incorporate visual legacies with contemporary realities in order to present images of real Black women who are no longer acted upon but who possess, in one body, both active voice and visual self-presentation.

NOTES

1. Maya Angelou, "They Came to Stay," in Brian Lanker, *I Dream a World: Portraits of Black Women Who Changed America* (New York: Stewart, Tabori and Chang, 1989), 9.

2. Hans Leuenberger, *Eve Noire* (Munich: Hanns Reich Verlag, 1966); Chester Higgins, *Black Woman,* text by Harold McDougall (New York: The McCall Publishing Company, 1970); Jean-Paul Goude, *Jungle Fever* (New York: Xavier Moreau, 1981); Uwe Ommer, *Black Ladies,* vol. 1, text and foreword by Léopold Sédar Senghor (Paris: Editions du Jaguar, 1986) and vol. 2, text by Cal-ixthe Beyala (New York: Taschen America, 1996); and Lanker, *I Dream a World.* Chester Higgins is African American; all of the other photographers are either European or Euro-American. Also see Deborah Willis and Carla Williams, *The Black Female Body: A Photographic History* (Philadelphia: Temple University Press, 2002), from which portions of this chapter are excerpted; and Kathleen Thompson, Hilary MacAustin, and Darlene Clark Hine, *The Face of Our Past: Images of Black Women from Colonial America to the Present* (Bloomington: Indi-ana University Press, 1999).

3. There are numerous books on VanDerZee's photographs. See, for example, Deborah Willis and Rodger C. Birt, *VanDerZee: Photographer, 1886–1983* (New York: Harry N. Abrams, 1993). Also see *The Historic Photographs of Addison N. Scurlock* (Washington, D.C.: The Corcoran Gallery of Art, 1976); and *P. H. Polk: Through These Eyes: The Photographs of P. H. Polk,* exhibition catalog (Newark, Del.: University Gallery of the University of Delaware, 1998).

4. Roy DeCarava and Langston Hughes, *The Sweet Flypaper of Life* (New York: Simon and Schuster, 1995; reprint, Washington, D.C.: Howard University Press, 1988). "The initial publication . . . [of] three thousand clothbound and twenty-two thousand paperbound copies . . . was soon supplemented by a sec-ond printing of ten thousand copies"; see Peter Galassi, introduction to *Roy De-Carava: A Retrospective* (New York: Museum of Modern Art, 1996), 22.

5. Bruce Davidson (1933–), *East 100th Street* (Cambridge: Harvard University Press, 1970); Aaron Siskind (1903–91), *Harlem Document: Photographs, 1932–1940* (Providence, R.I.: Matrix Publications, 1981); Irving Penn (b. 1917), *Worlds in a Small Room* (New York: The Viking Press, 1974). Davidson's book featured 121 photographs, made over a two-year period, of Blacks and Latinos in an East Harlem neighborhood that was not his own. Thirty-four of the portraits are of Black women or girls; of those, ten are shown on or in bed, three are naked, and another three are in bed with men. Davidson's photographic project

was undertaken more than thirty years after Aaron Siskind made the photographs included in his book, but Davidson's images were published eleven years earlier. Siskind's book includes accompanying text from the Federal Writers Project; oral histories gathered by Ralph Ellison, Frank Byrd, Dorothy West, and Vivian Morris; and a foreword by Black photographer Gordon Parks, who called the book "a mirror of [his] own past" (5). The American Penn's publication included images of African women.

6. For more in-depth discussions of Agassiz and the commission of these images, see Brian Wallis, "Black Bodies, White Science: The Slave Daguerreotypes of Louis Agassiz," *American Art* 9 (summer 1995): 39–60; Elinor Reichlin, "Faces of Slavery," *American Heritage* 28 (1977): 4–5; Melissa Banta and Curtis M. Hinsley, "Biological Anthropology: Evolution from Daguerreotype to Satellite," in *From Site to Sight: Anthropology, Photography, and the Power of Imagery* (Cambridge, Mass.: Peabody Museum Press, 1986), 56–71; and Lisa Gail Collins, "Historic Retrievals: Confronting Visual Evidence and the Documentation of Truth," *Chicago Art Journal* (spring 1998): 4–17.

7. The designation is from the label attached to the daguerreotype.

8. For standard art-historical discussions of *naked* versus *nude,* see John Berger, *Ways of Seeing: A Book* (New York: Penguin, 1977); and Kenneth Clark, *The Nude: A Study in Ideal Form* (Princeton: Princeton University Press, 1956).

9. C. D. B. Bryan, *The National Geographic Society: 100 Years of Adventure and Discovery* (New York: Harry N. Abrams, 1987), 24.

10. George F. Becker, "The Witwatersrand and the Revolt of the Uitlanders," *National Geographic* 7 (Nov. 1896): 349.

11. Whites were not the only audience for the periodical. For some African Americans, the Black female bodies in *National Geographic* served another purpose. As comedian Richard Pryor used to joke, *National Geographic* was the black man's *Playboy,* which makes clear that whites were not the only audience for these images. See Catherine A. Lutz and Jane L. Collins, *Reading National Geographic* (Chicago and London: University of Chicago Press, 1993), 172.

12. Lutz and Collins, *Reading National Geographic,* 172.

13. Lutz and Collins, *Reading National Geographic,* 89, 169.

14. Laurance P. Hurlburt, "Diego Rivera (1886–1957): A Chronology of His Art, Life and Times," in Cynthia Newman Helms, ed., *Diego Rivera: A Retrospective* (New York and London: W. W. Norton, 1986), 96, 98.

15. Edward Weston, *Daybooks,* ed. Nancy Newhall, vol. 2 (New York: Horizon Press, 1966), 206.

16. Theodore E. Stebbins Jr., *Weston's Westons: Portraits and Nudes* (Boston: Museum of Fine Arts, 1989), n.p.

17. *U.S. Camera 1941,* vol. 2, *This Year's Photography,* ed. T. J. Maloney, pictures judged by Edward Steichen (New York: Duell, Sloan and Pierce 1941), 157. Bass is wrongly identified as "Mandelle." No description of the image or comment by the photographer is given in the index.

18. The prints described here are project prints from around 1950. They were part of a mock-up for an unpublished book by Nancy Newhall of Weston's nudes. Along with these, there were to be two other images of Bass in that collection. See Amy Conger, *Edward Weston: Photographs from the Collection of the*

Center for Creative Photography (Tucson: Center for Creative Photography, University of Arizona, 1992), fig. 1480.

19. Conger, *Edward Weston,* fig. 1476.

20. Conger, *Edward Weston,* fig. 1481.

21. Maudelle Bass to Edward Weston, 1 Sept. 1939, Edward Weston Archives, Center for Creative Photography, University of Arizona. My thanks to Amy Rule for bringing the letter to my attention.

22. Covarrubias had designed sets for Josephine Baker's *Le Revue Nègre.* See Bryan Hammond, *Josephine Baker.* Compilation by Bryan Hammond. Biography by Patrick O'Connor. Foreword by Elizabeth Welch (London: Bulfinch Press, 1988), 30; Conger, *Edward Weston,* fig. 1475.

23. The image was also published as *La Negra* (1959).

24. Nissan N. Perez, "Visions of the Imaginary, Dreams of the Intangible," in *Revelaciones: The Art of Manuel Alvarez Bravo* (San Diego, Calif.: Museum of Photographic Arts, 1990), 23.

25. *Kamoinge,* meaning "a group of people working together" in Kikuya (an East African language); translation available at <http://www.culturefront.org/culturefront/magazine/98/winter/article.14.html> [cited 3 July 1998].

26. While there is some dispute among former members regarding this attribution, every published source on Kamoinge credits DeCarava as its director. Shawn Walker remembered how his involvement came about: "It was Lou [Draper] that suggested Roy as a mentor in helping us form the workshop. . . . The workshop adopted the name 'Kamoinge.' . . . Roy DeCarava was the president." See Shawn Walker, "Preserving Our History: The Kamoinge Workshop and Beyond," *Ten.8,* no. 24 (ca. 1984), 24.

27. Walker, "Preserving Our History," 24.

28. The first edition was published in 1973; four volumes were published intermittently until 1980, when publication ceased.

29. Harold McDougall, introduction to Higgins, *Black Woman,* n.p.

30. Higgins, *Black Woman,* n.p.

31. Higgins, *Black Woman,* n.p.

32. Jean-Paul Goude declined to give permission for the use of his photographs.

33. Francette Pacteau, *The Symptom of Beauty* (Cambridge: Harvard University Press, 1994), 143.

34. Goude, *Jungle Fever,* 107.

35. Goude, *Jungle Fever,* 31.

36. Goude, *Jungle Fever,* 32.

37. Jewell, K. Sue, *From Mammy to Miss America and Beyond: Cultural Images and the Shaping of U.S. Social Policy* (London: Routledge, 1993), 39.

38. Jewell, *From Mammy to Miss America,* 46–47.

39. Goude, *Jungle Fever,* 40.

40. Goude, *Jungle Fever,* 41.

41. Pacteau, *Symptom of Beauty,* 126.

42. Goude, *Jungle Fever,* 41.

43. Lanker, *I Dream a World,* 10. Lanker describes subject Priscilla Williams as "a remarkable human being who had helped in my wife's upbringing," an interesting inclusion in light of subject and novelist Toni Morrison's text that

accompanies her photograph: "I hate ideological whiteness. I hate when people come into my presence and become white. I'd just been elected to the American Academy of Arts and Letters and a man whom I used to read in anthologies came up to me and said, 'Hello, welcome to the Academy.' Then his third sentence was about his splendid black housekeeper. This little code saying, 'I like black people or I know one,' is humiliating for me—and should have been for him" (Lanker, *I Dream a World,* 32).

44. Angelou, "They Came to Stay," 9.

45. The only two women with décolletage are former model and newspaper publisher Ophelia DeVore-Mitchell and businesswoman Jewell Jackson McCabe. For the Dunham quote, see Lanker, *I Dream a World,* p. 28.

46. Lanker, *I Dream a World,* p. 122. Catlett was awarded a Julius Rosenwald fellowship in 1946 to create work honoring Black women. The series, "The Black Woman in America," consists of fourteen linoleum cuts. See *The Black Woman in America: Prints by Elizabeth Catlett,* exhibition catalog (Urbana-Champaign: Krannert Art Museum and Kinkead Pavilion, University of Illinois, 1993), n.p.

47. Lanker, *I Dream a World,* 19.

Siobhan B. Somerville

"The Prettiest Specimen of Boyhood"

Cross-Gender and Racial Disguise in Pauline E. Hopkins's *Winona*

The contradictory status of the Black woman's body in American culture may be measured in part by the frequency with which it is the site of impersonation. Motivated by both desire and contempt, the tradition of imitating Black women through drag of blackface is pervasive in American history. It is easy to find examples of such performances, beginning with the practice of "acting the wench" on the minstrel stage, in which white men donned blackface and women's clothing to perform caricatures of African American women.[1] White women have also participated in the blackface tradition on stage and screen: Shirley Temple blacked up in 1935 in *The Littlest Rebel*; Sophie Tucker regularly donned blackface in her vaudeville acts; and more recently, Sandra Bernhard, with perhaps more self-conscious irony toward this history, presented impersonations of Black women performers in her 1990 film, *Without You I'm Nothing*.[2] Likewise, African American men's performances of cross-gender drag have been enormously popular, particularly in recent years, as evidenced by widespread fascination with figures such as RuPaul, Dennis Rodman, and the drag queens in Jennie Livingston's documentary *Paris Is Burning*, to name just a few examples.[3]

Indeed, impersonations *of* Black women historically have held a much more central place in American popular culture than have impersonations *by* Black women. One explanation for the dearth of examples of cross-gender impersonations by African American women is the history of racialized constructions by which they, particularly darker-complexioned women, have been granted limited access to the very category of femininity (from which one would presumably cross to a masculine persona).[4] An extraordinarily stark example of these racialized constructions of gender occurs in Harriet Beecher Stowe's *Palmetto-Leaves* (1874), a collection of travel sketches about Florida. In "The Laborers of the South," the book's final chapter, Stowe recalls a memorable scene from her visit to the Mackintosh Plantation, which had been "in old time, the model plantation of Florida":

> Never shall we forget the impression of weird and almost lu-
> dicrous dreariness which took possession of us as Mrs. F——
> and myself sat down in the wide veranda. . . . The black la-
> borers were coming up from the field; and, as one and another
> passed by, they seemed blacker, stranger, and more dismal,
> than any thing we had ever seen.
>
> The women wore men's hats and boots, and had the gait and
> stride of men; but now and then an old hooped petticoat, or
> some cast-off, thin, bedraggled garment that had once been
> fine, told the tale of sex, and had a woefully funny effect.[5]

Unmistakably informed by nineteenth-century ideologies of gender and race that effectively excluded African American women from the very category of "woman," Stowe can view these African American women only as masculine in relation to herself and her companion, the ellipti-cal Mrs. F——.[6] She carefully remarks upon their clothing ("men's hats and boots"), as well as the particular movement of their bodies ("the gait and stride of men"), in contrast to her own seemingly unquestion-able femininity, further stabilized by her position as an immobile white spectator. Ironically, what jars Stowe is not the laboring women's per-ceived resemblance to men; rather, she fixes on the petticoat as the dis-crepancy in this scene. A seeming marker of femininity, the petticoat is revealed to be a racialized image as well: on the body of a Black woman, the petticoat can be understood by Stowe as a key element in a kind of comic drag performance. She naturalizes the masculinity of these women, only to be startled (albeit somewhat pleasantly) by the re-minder—the detail that "told the tale of sex"—that the bodies under-neath so many conflicting signals are female after all. The bodies of African American women in this scene call up implicitly for Stowe the traditions of the minstrel stage, where white men entertained their au-diences with cartoonish impersonations of Black women.

Another explanation for the relative scarcity of representations of

Black women as agents of cross-gender impersonation is their symbolic position within both gender and racial hierarchies in the United States, available as the imagined "other" against which normative subjectivity is constituted. Crossing down, or taking on the status of a supposed social inferior, has been the very spectacle that generates the comic effect of drag and/or blackface in popular culture. Apparently not so funny, at least to mainstream audiences, is the prospect of African American women crossing "up," as the genre of the passing novel, beginning in the nineteenth century, makes clear.[7] Traditionally seen as tragic, representations of Black women's racial passing have held the more serious possibility of usurping cultural authority in contrast to the playful and temporary abandonment that blackface and drag have historically represented to audiences imagined as white and male.

It is significant that the passing genre rests squarely within the same constructions of gender and race that shaped Stowe's description of Black laborers. Only the light-complexioned African American woman—the tragic mulatta—has been figured in fiction as having access to this movement across the color line. In the nineteenth-century novel of racial passing, the mulatta is typically described according to traditional hierarchies of white beauty. In her study of the mulatto figure in American fiction, Judith Berzon notes that Black women are portrayed as "beautiful (in Caucasian terms), morally upstanding, prim, and wealthy (or at least comfortable)."[8] A certain amount of erotic tension and narrative curiosity surrounds this figure, as Werner Sollors has pointed out: "In nineteenth-century American culture the figure of the Quadroon and the Octoroon was such a taboo: puzzling, strangely attractive, forbidden (and, perhaps, attractive *because* forbidden)."[9] Importantly, in comparison to the male mulatto figure, the female mulatta almost inevitably bears a tragic narrative. Berzon notes how generic conventions were tied to the gender of the protagonist:

> In most novels with mulatto characters, the male mixed-blood characters are brave, honest, intelligent, and rebellious. . . . Few male mixed-blood characters are tragic mulattoes in the traditional sense. . . . There are almost no male suicides, whereas there are quite a few suicides by female mulatto characters. While there are some female characters who are race leaders . . . there are not many such women in mulatto fiction.[10]

Berzon's useful observation about the narrative conventions attached to the gender of the mulatto/a figure has been echoed by other critics. In her study of gender and ethnicity in the American novel, Mary Dearborn adds that "the tragic mulatto, usually a woman . . . is divided between her white and black blood. The tragic mulatto trajectory demands that the mulatto woman desire a white lover and either die (often in white-authored versions) or return to the black community."[11]

When the mulatta figure impersonates white men, combining racial passing with cross-dressing, she does so ostensibly only for purposes of escape. In the fugitive slave narrative *Running a Thousand Miles for Freedom* (1860), for instance, Ellen Craft assumes the identity of a sickly white man while her darker-complexioned husband, William, poses as her slave in order that the two may escape to the north. In boots, top hat, spectacles, and cropped hair, Ellen makes "a most respectable looking gentleman," whom at least two white women find attractive along the course of the journey.[12] Fictional characters, too, have used similar devices, perhaps most notably the young light-complexioned heroine Eliza Harris in Harriet Beecher Stowe's *Uncle Tom's Cabin* (1852). Attempting to evade relentless slave hunters, Eliza cuts her hair and adapts "to her slender and pretty form the articles of man's attire, in which it was deemed safest she should make her escape."[13]

In a very few instances, the light-complexioned African American woman performs a cross-gender impersonation that is combined with blackface, not to cross boundaries of racial identity but rather to stabilize a racial identity that the mulatta's body itself seems to call into question. In *Incidents in the Life of a Slave Girl* (1861), Harriet Jacobs eludes her master through such a disguise.[14] In her initial escape attempt, a family friend provides her with "a suit of sailor's clothes,—jacket, trowsers, and tarpaulin hat," which enables Jacobs to move through public spaces in safe anonymity. Ironically pointing out the arbitrariness of racial signs, Jacobs also darkens her skin, exaggerating the supposedly biological feature that commits her to slavery in the first place. The disguise works: "I wore my sailor's clothes, and had blackened my face with charcoal. I passed several people whom I knew. The father of my children came so near that I brushed against his arm; but he had no idea who it was."[15] In another example of cross-gender impersonation, Mark Twain echoes Jacobs's strategy in his depiction of Roxy in *Pudd'nhead Wilson* (1894). Roxy "to all intents and purposes . . . was as white as anybody, but the one sixteenth of her which was black outvoted the other fifteen parts and made her a negro."[16] In one part of the novel, when she is running from the law, Roxy disguises herself as a man, appearing as "a wreck of shabby old clothes . . . with a black face under an old slouch hat." (180) She explains, "I give a nigger man a dollar for dese clo'es . . . [and] I blacked my face." (187–88)

Importantly, in these examples of African American women donning men's clothing and black make-up, the motivation is to escape from capture. Their cross-dressing and racial disguise function as tools of passing rather than of theatrical performance, such as blackface minstrelsy or a drag show, performances that seek to expose rather than mask the discrepancy between a body and its disguise.[17] The performer creates the possibility for the audience to acknowledge the disjunction between the performance and the "true" identity. In contrast, passing can be understood as a representational strategy that appropriates the "privileges" of invisibility. An attempt to transcend the disenfranchisement imposed through a stigmatized identity, passing can be understood as a movement toward the privileges that accrue to those whose bodies are perceived as culturally *unmarked.*

In this chapter, I discuss a less well-known fictional instance of an African American woman assuming a male persona combined with blackface, performed by the protagonist of Pauline E. Hopkins's *Winona: A Tale of Negro Life in the South and Southwest* (1902).[18] Hopkins was one of the most important African American women writers at the turn of the century. Between 1900 and 1904, she wrote four novels, numerous short stories, and biographical articles for the Boston-based *Colored American Magazine,* where she also exerted considerable editorial influence.[19] As I will discuss, Hopkins's portrayal of an African American woman in double-layered disguise can be read as a figure for her own position as an African American woman writing at the turn of the twentieth century, within a literary and political sphere dominated by male voices. Yet, precisely because of the unstable meanings of constructions of gender and sexuality during this period, Winona's cross-gender and "blackface" impersonation circulates uneasily in Hopkins's text. Unlike the incidental temporary disguise performed by Jacobs or Roxy, Winona's impersonation serves a very different function: clearly it is not a superficial costume but rather an expression of an inner subjectivity.

Winona, first published as a serialized novel in *Colored American Magazine* in 1902, takes place in the 1850s within a number of different geographical and political settings, including the United States/Canada border, a slave-holding plantation in Missouri, and the frontier state of Kansas. The title character, Winona, is the biracial daughter of an unnamed fugitive slave woman and "White Eagle," the chief of a community of Seneca Indians in Canada. Significantly, *Winona* borrows many conventions from the popular genre of the Western: much of the action of this novel takes place outdoors, in contrast to the interior spaces of domestic fiction; and, except for Winona, the novel is populated overwhelmingly by male characters.[20] Winona's mother dies in childbirth, and when her father, White Eagle, is murdered by slave rustlers, Winona and her stepbrother, Judah, are sold into slavery. A new character, the British lawyer Warren Maxwell, enters the text by arriving in North America in search of heirs to the estate of a wealthy English aristocrat, Lord Carlingford. Through a series of complicated plot twists, Maxwell befriends Judah and Winona and eventually helps them escape their slaveholders. Soon all three join forces with the radical abolitionist John Brown on behalf of the Free-Soil movement in Kansas. After a number of close calls and hairbreadth escapes, the novel concludes with a series of revelations about the characters' origins, including Winona's identity as the lawful heir to the Carlingford estate. In the novel's final scenes, Winona and Maxwell plan their marriage and set sail to live permanently in England.

By opening the novel on the Canadian border, Hopkins uses national and geographical boundaries to symbolize the guiding questions of the novel: "Many strange tales of romantic happenings in this mixed community of Anglo-Saxons, Indians and Negroes might be told similar to the one I am about to relate, and the world stand aghast and try in vain to find the dividing line supposed to be a natural barrier between the whites and the dark-skinned race" (287). With this opening, Hopkins clearly states the project of her novel: to show that the color line is not a "natural barrier," as segregationists attempted to construct it, but rather an arbitrary and ultimately unfounded division. The plot pivots on a series of scenes of passing that expose the permeability of these purportedly "natural barriers" between the so-called races.

Hopkins first demonstrates this fluidity of racial boundaries through the character White Eagle. Early in the novel, we learn that White Eagle was formerly a British nobleman, who fled to Canada in order to escape a mistaken murder charge. He has disguised himself and "passed" into Seneca Indian culture. Reversing the familiar conceit of a light-skinned African American passing for white, Hopkins shows that racial passing is also practiced by whites. She notes that White Eagle is one of "many white men" who "sought to conceal their identity in the safe shelter of the wigwam" (288). Further, Hopkins suggests an identification between White Eagle and his wife, a fugitive slave. Just as he finds safety among the Senecan community, she makes her escape from slavery through the Underground Railroad, which lands her in freedom

in the Canadian wilderness. Moreover, once they are married, this passing white man and African American woman bring up two children:
Judah, an adopted escaped slave; and Winona, a biological daughter.
Both children are raised within the Senecan culture, and Hopkins remarks that Judah "might have been mistaken for an Indian at first
glance" because he "handles the paddle [of the canoe] so skillfully"
(289). Through this family, interracial and intercultural, Hopkins privileges a model of cultural mixture in defiance of the prevailing eugenicist
anxieties of the period.

At the same time that Hopkins seeks to dismantle the "natural barrier" of race, she also attempts to refute naturalized constructions of
gender, a project that carries difficulties and risks, given the period in
which Hopkins was writing. As historians of sexuality have argued, this
period saw two important shifts in cultural understandings of sexuality
in the United States, in particular the emergence of categories of homosexuality and heterosexuality. Before the late nineteenth century, homosexual acts had been punishable through legal and religious sanctions,
but they had not defined individuals as a type.[21] In the late nineteenth
century, a new understanding of sexuality emerged, in which homo- and
heterosexuality became the conditions, and therefore identities, of particular individuals. In the much-quoted words of Michel Foucault, "The
sodomite had been a temporary aberration, the homosexual was now a
species."[22] As I will argue, when Hopkins uses cross-gender impersonation to develop her theme of dismantling naturalized constructions of
gender and race, she also introduces into her text difficult questions
about the representation of homoerotic desire and these "new" sexual
subjectivities.

Hopkins renders the instabilities of categories of race, gender, and
sexuality in a key scene at the center of the text, when Warren Maxwell,
the British lawyer, is taken prisoner for assisting John Brown and his
fighters. Maxwell's illness in prison becomes the narrative device for the
introduction of a new character, Allen Pinks, a "young mulatto" nurse
who volunteers to care for Maxwell and calms the cell with a "soft hush
of a tender voice stilling the tumult" (386). The scenes between Pinks
and Maxwell are the most overtly erotic in the entire novel. At one
point, while Maxwell seems to sleep, Pinks gazes upon him with explicit
desire: "He stood for some moments gazing down on the Saxon face so
pitifully thin and delicate. The brow did not frown nor the lips quiver;
no movement of the muscles betrayed the hopeless despair of the
sleeper's heart" (387). If this description did not mark out clearly
enough Pinks's desire for Maxwell, Hopkins provides unambiguous

physical evidence: "There was a light touch on his hair; a tear fell on his cheek; the nurse had kissed the patient!" (387) Hopkins details, as she simultaneously tempers, the eroticism of this scene. Although Maxwell puzzles over this kiss and questions the identity of his nurse, Pinks deflects both Maxwell's and the reader's curiosity. When Maxwell insists on asking questions about his identity, Hopkins writes, "Allen silenced him firmly and gently" (388). This silencing, however, only kindles Maxwell's own attraction to Pinks:

> Maxwell was fascinated by his nurse; he thought him the prettiest specimen of boyhood he had ever met. The delicate brown features were faultless in outline; the closely cropped black hair was like velvet in its smoothness. He could not shake off the idea that somewhere he had known the lad before in his life. At times this familiarity manifested itself in the tones of the voice soft and low as a woman's, then again it was in the carriage of the head or the flash of the beautiful large dark eyes. (389)

Throughout this scene, Hopkins plays with the reader's knowledge and ignorance. Although the reader may gradually recognize that this "prettiest specimen of boyhood" is Winona in disguise, Maxwell himself ostensibly remains ignorant of the other identity of this "lad," despite his rapt attention to the details of Pinks's body. Thus, while the reader may know that their kiss is "really" heterosexual, to Maxwell the kiss is homoerotic. Although the object of Maxwell's desire is "really" a girl, Maxwell ostensibly knows it only as desire for a boy.

Maxwell remains pleasantly blind to his nurse's identity until a scene in which Pinks, along with John Brown and his followers, storm the prison to help Maxwell escape. It takes the malevolent gaze of the white villain Bill Thomson to see through Pinks's disguise. "If it ain't Winona! . . . a gal dressed up in boys clo's!" (392) he exclaims. Hopkins's use of dialect here is significant because it acts as a kind of vocal cross-dressing for Bill Thomson, who is later revealed to have been passing also. He is actually the English valet guilty of murdering Lord Carlingford. Importantly, when he exposes Winona, Thomson stresses her cross-dressing but never mentions that she has also blackened her face. For Maxwell, however, the reverse is true. Winona's cross-dressing is apparently irrelevant to him; instead he fixates on the effectiveness of her blackface disguise. With his new knowledge, his vision is transformed: he "wondered . . . at his own stupidity in not recognizing Winona; be-

neath the stain with which she had darkened her own exquisite complexion, he could now plainly trace the linaments [sic] that had so
charmed him" (396).

In a brief essay on *Winona* and Bakhtin, Elizabeth Ammons writes:

> The text only permits us to see same-sex attraction, a man ten-
> derly caring for and kissing another man. Complicating the
> scene even more, the name Hopkins gives Winona in drag,
> Allen, is the same name she gave herself when she wanted to
> publish anonymously in the *Colored American Magazine*, Sarah
> Allen—her mother's name. How do we read this dense net-
> work of signs? We know so little about Hopkins's biography
> that we can say almost nothing about her sexual orientation.
> At the same time, this scene, so carefully but obviously coded
> (and therefore inviting decoding), forces us to think broadly
> rather than narrowly about Hopkins's sexuality.[23]

While I agree that this scene raises a number of questions about sexuality, it has implications far beyond biographical speculations about Hopkins's own sexual practices or identity. It seems less urgent to attempt to
confirm whether or not Hopkins herself was a lesbian, or whether she
wrote "lesbian" novels, than to ask how she engaged emerging models
of homo- and heterosexuality, particularly when these models held very
different stakes for African American women and men, who historically
had been sexualized in nineteenth-century popular culture. Questions
of sexuality have shaped the work of writers for whom we lack biographical information or who are not easily classifiable in the terms *homosexual, gay, lesbian,* or *queer.* As Deborah McDowell has implicitly
demonstrated in her insightful discussion of Nella Larsen's *Passing,* one
need not rely on biographical evidence to show that questions about
gender, homoeroticism, and homosexuality are not only relevant but
often necessary for understanding cultural representations of race and
racial difference.[24]

Ammons usefully points to the suggestiveness of this passage, but
her comments might be developed further by placing the "Allen Pinks"
scenes in the context of the entire narrative, particularly because "his"
presence is represented as a response to a previous scene of racial and
sexual violence between men. In prison, before the arrival of Allen
Pinks, Maxwell discovers "a hole for the stove-pipe of the under room
to pass through, but the stove had been removed to accommodate a
larger number of prisoners. This left a hole in the floor through which

one might communicate with those below" (384). This hole positions Maxwell as a kind of voyeur gazing into the crowded cell below: it "afforded diversion for the invalid who could observe the full operation of the slave system" (384). Just as Maxwell, a British citizen, has observed the U.S. "slave system" as an outsider looking on (or down), so he is literally placed above and outside of the "heart-rending scenes . . . enacted before his sight in the lower room" (384). This scene, then, inscribes a racialized and asymmetrical structure of looking and power: the white Maxwell is able to gaze upon the African American prisoners below, but not vice versa.

This hole in Maxwell's cell is significant not only because it structures a hierarchy of race, vision, and knowledge but also because it becomes the site of a corresponding gap in Hopkins's narration. Hopkins describes a scene in which Maxwell is "aroused to greater indignation than usual" by the sound of "heart-rending cries from the lower room" (385). Yet, in the course of this description, Hopkins's narration suddenly meets an obstacle: "Hurrying to the stove-hole [Maxwell] gazed one moment and then fell fainting with terror and nausea upon the floor. He had seen a Negro undergoing the shameful outrage, so denounced in the Scriptures, and which must not be described in the interests of decency and humanity" (385). This crisis in Maxwell's experience of the prison coincides with a crisis in representation: what is "the shameful outrage" that "must not be described" here? In the previous chapter of the novel, Hopkins had been daring enough to include violent and graphic physical details in her description of Maxwell's near-lynching. At this moment in the narrative, however, Hopkins, like the repulsed Maxwell, backs away from a direct representation of "the shameful outrage." Abandoning detail, Hopkins resorts instead to a code phrase for sodomy. The content of this "shameful outrage" is left unspecified, a muteness consistent with the history of confusion around the term *sodomy* itself.[25] One cannot be sure what the "outrage" is, but Hopkins's description suggests that a Black male prisoner is being raped by a white male guard.[26] Although Hopkins mentions neither homosexuality nor sodomy explicitly, it is important to distinguish between the two. This rape may technically be a homosexual act, but its unambiguous content is violence, not desire. A categorization of sex acts that refuses to acknowledge the context of those acts and the structures of power under which they are performed is the source of this confusion. Thus the same silence surrounds and can collapse two very different acts: consensual sex between two men and the often homophobic, misogynistic, and brutalizing crime of rape by one man against another.[27]

What is curious about Hopkins's depiction is that Maxwell identifies cross-racially, with the Black victim of this rape, not the white perpetrator. Significantly, his own mental and physical integrity seems threatened by the specter of this sexual violence between men. Maxwell responds to the scene with an embodied sympathy, becoming faint and "delirious." This moment marks a corresponding disorder and disruption in Hopkins's text. As if the very unspeakability of the rape will result in its unbelievability, Hopkins herself steps into the text to address the reader directly: "Unhappily we tell no tale of fiction," she insists (385). On the one hand, Hopkins's appeal to "decency and humanity" as the reason for her elliptical description of the violence establishes the authority of her narrative voice. Clearly asserting her privileged knowledge of "the shameful outrage," she ostensibly "protects" her reader from the explicit facts of what, according to middle-class sexual ideologies of the period, any respectable reader should *not* know. On the other hand, Hopkins follows this crisis with a critique of organized religion: these "unspeakable" horrors would not occur, she writes, "if Christianity, Mohammedanism, or even Buddhism, did exercise the gentle and humanizing influence that is claimed for them" (385). With this gesture Hopkins abdicates responsibility for the presence of the "shameful outrage" in her text. According to her logic, if organized religion cannot prevent this violence, then Hopkins herself, in an effort to report the truth, cannot be held responsible for its eruption in her text. She invokes the demands of realism to justify her reference to sodomy; at the same time, she removes herself as a cause of its presence, since she is telling "no tale of fiction."[28]

If Hopkins simultaneously foregrounds the narrative rupture while avoiding an actual description of male rape in this scene, she also seems intent on making a distinction between male-male sexual violence and male homoeroticism. The physical and mental delirium resulting from Maxwell's exposure to the scene of male rape becomes the narrative catalyst for the invention of Allen Pinks, who seems to answer Hopkins's call for "a religion that will give the people individually and practically an impetus to humane and unselfish dealing with each other" (385). As is discussed earlier, this "humane and unselfish dealing" takes on an undeniably homoerotic cast in subsequent scenes.

While both Pinks and Maxwell actively participate in eroticizing each other, it is important to note that the figure of Pinks, rather than that of Maxwell, resonates with contemporary understandings of nonnormative sexuality and gender. In the context of turn-of-the-twentieth-century notions of masculinity and sexuality, as George Chauncey has shown, although two men might desire each other, only the feminized partner would be considered "abnormal" or "deviant."[29] Thus, especially given Pinks's ostensibly subordinate position within hierarchies of race and age, Maxwell's desire for Pinks could exist well within the range of expected behavior for "normal" men. Pinks/Winona, however, resembles one of the "intermediate types" that Hopkins's contemporaries, such as Edward Carpenter, Havelock Ellis, and others, attempted to classify in studies of inversion. Conceived of as a man's soul trapped in a woman's body (and vice versa), the figure of the invert represented a perceived mismatch between desire and the body. Later, this model saw a shift in emphasis toward a notion of sexual orientation, articulated as one's sexual object of choice rather than one's gender identity. Hopkins's portrayal of Pinks resonates with the earlier model of the "invert," whose gender identity was thought to be somewhere between male and female. Pinks is a figure with both conventionally masculine and feminine characteristics: s/he is "the prettiest specimen of boyhood," with a voice "soft and low as a woman's."

What makes Hopkins's text unusual is that she does not dismiss Winona's impersonation of Allen Pinks as a temporary, superficial flirtation with inversion and homoeroticism, as one might expect in a story of gender or racial disguise, where the exposure of the "true" identity of a character usually signals a return to the established social order of a fictional world. According to these conventions, one would expect the unveiling of Allen Pinks as Winona to resolve the tensions between male/female, Black/white. Yet, for Winona, exposure inaugurates not a resolution and reversion to a previous stable identity but rather a transformation and a source of new disturbance. After securing Maxwell's escape, Winona herself now experiences a sense of imprisonment outside the walls of the prison. She admits that she had rested more comfortably within her blackface and transvestite *disguise* than in the boundaries of her own female and biracial body. Although the rescue party exhales a general sigh of relief over Maxwell's escape, Winona feels a distinct sense of discomfort: "Winona was silent and constrained in manner. For the first time since she had adopted her strange dress she felt a wave of self-consciousness that rendered her ashamed" (396). Neither the cross-dressing nor the blackface itself produces Winona's sense of shame. Rather, her *exposure* deflates her sense of self-worth:

> During her weeks of unselfish devotion when she had played the role of the boy nurse so successfully, she had been purely and proudly glad. Now, little by little, a gulf had opened be-

tween [herself and Maxwell] which to her unsophisticated mind could not be bridged. There lay the misery of the present time—she was nothing to him. . . . Fate had fixed impassable chasms of race and caste between them. (404–5)

In this passage, Hopkins suggests that the persona of Allen Pinks represents a more accurate rendering of Winona's subjectivity. Her embodiment as the dark-skinned "boy nurse" gives her license to take a more active role in her own desire for Maxwell. The double layering of blackface and cross-dressing erases the problematic position of Winona's body; paradoxically, without her disguise, she becomes invisible to Maxwell as a subject or object of desire. She now faces "impassable chasms of race and caste," seemingly unshakable prohibitions against respectable love between a white man and mulatta woman.

Importantly, unlike the other instances of African American women's cross-gender impersonation mentioned at the beginning of this chapter, Winona wears her disguise not in order to escape capture but rather to enter an all-male space. This space is not only that of the literal prison but also that of the Western adventure, a literary genre that conventionally has no position for an active female character, much less the figure of the mulatta.[30] Through her disguise, then, Winona is able to escape from the narrative expectations attached to the figure of the mulatta heroine by entering temporarily into the role of the Western hero, or at least his (often racialized) male sidekick. Here Hopkins's text reveals that interracial homoeroticism is at the center of this male-centered genre of popular fiction. In fact, it seems more desirable and sanctioned than interracial heterosexuality. Whereas erotic intimacy between a white man (Maxwell) and a younger Black "man" (Pinks) is possible within the supposedly all-male space of the prison, sexual desire between a white man and a younger biracial woman remains culturally forbidden, at least within constructions of race and gender in the United States.

In the final scenes of the novel, however, Hopkins constructs a utopian revision of the legal system, which allows her to refuse and defy the conventions that construct interracial sexuality as inevitably tragic. Back in Canada, Winona and Maxwell are presented with documents—her parents' marriage license and a birth certificate—that prove that she is the legitimate daughter of White Eagle and thus the heir to the Carlingford estate. This proof of the legal interracial marriage of her parents in Canada provides Winona with a legitimate claim to both Black and white identity and to the literal inheritance of her father's property, both of which now entitle her by law to her desire for Maxwell. Yet Hopkins seems to be less than enthusiastic about using the marriage of Winona and Maxwell as a resolution to the novel. In fact, with decided indifference, she renders their marriage completely predictable and unproblematic:

> They made no plans for the future. What necessity was there of making plans for the future? They knew what the future would be. They loved each other; they would marry sooner or later, after they reached England, with the sanction of her grandfather, old Lord George; that was certain. American caste prejudice could not touch them in their home beyond the sea. (435)

Hopkins's tone here is remarkable for its lack of urgency, its utter non-chalance after Winona's previous frustrations about "the impassable chasms" that seemed to separate her permanently from Maxwell.

In the two central episodes within the prison in *Winona*—first, the "shameful outrage" against a Black prisoner by a white guard; and second, the homoerotic fascination between Allen Pinks and Maxwell—Hopkins attempts to untangle conflicting contemporary representations of race and sexuality. By staging a scene of the unspeakable "shameful outrage," Hopkins insists on a distinction between male-male rape, depicted as a means of racial and sexual terror, and homoeroticism, depicted as a calming and tender exchange. Winona's retrospective realization that she is more comfortable as Pinks, along with Hopkins's deferral of her marriage to Maxwell, suggest that Hopkins saw the emergence of new sexual subjectivities as a potential site for generating new narrative conventions. As part of her project to disrupt conventional representations of Black womanhood and racialized desire, Hopkins uses Winona's blackface and transvestism to figure new possibilities for movement across lines of race and gender.

NOTES

1. See Eric Lott, *Love and Theft: Blackface Minstrelsy and the American Working Class* (New York: Oxford University Press, 1993), 159–68.

2. On Shirley Temple, see James Snead, *White Screens, Black Images: Hollywood from the Dark Side,* ed. Colin MacCabe and Cornel West (New York: Routledge, 1994), 47–66; and Donald Bogle, *Toms, Coons, Mulattoes, Mammies, and Bucks: An Interpretive History of Blacks in American Films* New Expanded Edition (New York: Continuum, 1994), 45–52.

3. Other examples include Flip Wilson as "Geraldine," Martin Lawrence as "SheNayNay," and Lady Chablis in *Midnight in the Garden of Good and Evil.*

4. In her discussion of female masculinity, Judith Halberstam has noted that "mainstream definitions of male masculinity as nonperformative" account for the relative absence of a tradition of lesbian drag. See Judith Halberstam, *Female Masculinity* (Durham: Duke University Press, 1998), 234–35. Such models of masculinity as nonperformative have also shaped African American women's access to gender-crossing impersonation.

5. Harriet Beecher Stowe, *Palmetto-Leaves* (Boston: James R. Osgood and Company, 1873), 287, 300–301.

6. On racialized constructions of womanhood in the nineteenth century, see Hazel V. Carby, *Reconstructing Womanhood: The Emergence of the Afro-American Woman Novelist* (New York: Oxford University Press, 1987), 20–39. On the ways that definitions of middle-class white womanhood depended on the exclusion of "other women" in a British context, see Anita Levy, *Other Women: The Writing of Class, Race, and Gender, 1832–1898* (Princeton: Princeton University Press, 1991).

7. This tradition continued in the twentieth century, in fiction such as Charles Chesnutt's *House Behind the Cedars,* Nella Larsen's *Passing,* and Fannie Hurst's *Imitation of Life* and in films such as *Pinky* and *Imitation of Life.*

8. Judith Berzon, *Neither White nor Black: The Mulatto Character in American Fiction* (New York: New York University Press, 1978), 62.

9. Werner Sollors, "'Never Was Born': The Mulatto, An American Tragedy?" *Massachusetts Review* 27 (summer 1986): 302.

10. Berzon, *Neither White nor Black,* 74.

11. Mary Dearborn, *Pocahontas's Daughters: Gender and Ethnicity in American Culture* (New York: Oxford University Press, 1986), 139–40. In a discussion of the mulatto figure in American race melodrama, Susan Gillman concurs that in the conventions of the tragic mulatto tale, the protagonist is most often a woman; see Susan Gillman, "The Mulatto, Tragic or Triumphant? The Nineteenth-Century American Race Melodrama," in Shirley Samuels, ed., *The Culture of Sentiment: Race, Gender, and Sentimentality in Nineteenth-Century America* (New York: Oxford University Press, 1992), 221–43.

12. William Craft, *Running a Thousand Miles for Freedom; or, The Escape of William and Ellen Craft from Slavery* (1860; reprint, Miami: Mnemosyne, 1969), 35, 60. For further discussion of this text, see Ellen M. Weinauer, "'A Most Respectable Looking Gentleman': Passing, Possession, and Transgression in *Running a Thousand Miles for Freedom,*" in Elaine K. Ginsberg, ed., *Passing and the Fictions of Identity* (Durham: Duke University Press, 1996), 37–56.

13. Harriet Beecher Stowe, *Uncle Tom's Cabin; or, Life among the Lowly* (1852; reprint, New York: Penguin, 1987), 545.

14. Harriet A. Jacobs, *Incidents in the Life of a Slave Girl, Written by Herself,* ed. Jean Fagan Yellin (1861; reprint, Cambridge: Harvard University Press, 1987), 112–13.

15. Jacobs, *Incidents,* 111, 113.

16. Mark Twain, *Pudd'nhead Wilson* (1894; reprint, New York: Penguin, 1987), 64. All further references to this edition will be made parenthetically within the text.

17. Houston Baker's discussion of "phaneric" and "cryptic" masks is useful for understanding this distinction. "Cryptic" masks are used for self-disguise, concealing the identity of the performer, while "phaneric" masks offer an instrument for self-display, expressing more fully the "true" identity of the performer. See Houston Baker, *Modernism and the Harlem Renaissance* (Chicago: University of Chicago Press, 1987), 51–52.

18. Pauline E. Hopkins, *Winona: A Tale of Negro Life in the South and Southwest,* in *The Magazine Novels of Pauline Hopkins,* intro. Hazel V. Carby (New York: Oxford University Press, 1988), 287–437; first published in *Colored American Magazine* 5 (May–Oct. 1902). Subsequent references to the Oxford edition will be made parenthetically within the text.

19. After 1904, Hopkins continued to publish her writing, but on a much smaller scale, and she eventually returned to her job as a stenographer at the Massachusetts Institute of Technology, where she worked until her death in 1930. For further discussion of the history of the *Colored American Magazine,* see Carby, *Reconstructing Womanhood,* 121–27. On Hopkins, see also Ann Allen Shockley, "Pauline Elizabeth Hopkins: A Biographical Excursion Into Obscurity," *Phylon* 33 (spring 1972): 22–26.

20. For a brief discussion of the gendered implications of the generic shift from the domestic novel to the Western in the nineteenth century, see Jane Tompkins, *West of Everything: The Inner Life of Westerns* (New York: Oxford University Press, 1992), 38–45.

21. See Michel Foucault, *The History of Sexuality,* vol. 1 (New York: Vintage, 1980). On the invention of the classification of heterosexuality, see Jonathan Katz, "The Invention of Heterosexuality," *Socialist Review* 20 (1990): 17–34.

22. Foucault, *History of Sexuality,* 1:43.

23. Elizabeth Ammons, "Afterword: *Winona,* Bakhtin, and Hopkins in the Twenty-first Century" in John Cullen Gruesser, ed., *The Unruly Voice: Rediscovering Pauline Elizabeth Hopkins* (Urbana: University of Illinois Press, 1996), 217–18.

24. Deborah McDowell, introduction to Nella Larsen, *Quicksand and Passing* (New Brunswick, N.J.: Rutgers University Press, 1986), ix–xxxv.

25. As Jonathan Goldberg notes, "sodomy is, as a sexual act, anything that threatens alliance—any sexual act, that is, that does not promote the aim of married procreative sex (anal intercourse, fellatio, masturbation, bestiality—any of these may fall under the label of sodomy in various early legal codifications and learned discourses)." See Jonathan Goldberg, *Sodometries: Renaissance Texts, Modern Sexualities* (Stanford: Stanford University Press, 1992), 19.

26. The use of sodomy as a form of racial and sexual domination figures powerfully in Toni Morrison's novel *Beloved* (New York: New American Library, 1987), in which Paul D remembers white male guards forcing Black prisoners to perform oral sex at gunpoint (107–8). Thanks to Kimberly Wallace-Sanders for reminding me of the ways Morrison's text echoes the scene in *Winona.*

27. Through the assumption that such acts of rape feminize (and therefore degrade) their victims, they participate in a misogynist logic. For further discussion of anal rape and homophobia, see Eve Kosofsky Sedgwick, *Between Men: English Literature and Male Homosocial Desire* (New York: Columbia University Press, 1985), 225, n. 6.

28. Hopkins's strategy is similar to the intricate interweaving of authorial power and knowledge that D. A. Miller discusses in *The Novel and the Police* (Berkeley: University of California Press, 1988), 2–5: "'Poor Dorothea,' 'poor Lydgate,' 'poor Rosamond,' the narrator of *Middlemarch* frequently exclaims, and the lament is credible only in an arrangement that keeps the function of narration separate from the causalities operating in the narrative. The *knowledge* commanded in omniscient narration is thus opposed to the *power* that inheres in the circumstances of the novelistic world" [italics in original].

29. See George Chauncey, *Gay New York: Gender, Urban Culture, and the Making of the Gay Male World* (New York: Basic Books, 1994), 120–21.

30. For a discussion of Hopkins's use of popular-fiction genres in her serialized novels, see Carby, *Reconstructing Womanhood*, 145–62; and Claudia Tate, *Domestic Allegories of Political Desire: The Black Heroine's Text at the Turn of the Century* (New York: Oxford University Press, 1992), 195–96.

Elizabeth Alexander

"Coming Out Blackened and Whole"

Fragmentation and Reintegration in Audre Lorde's *Zami* and *The Cancer Journals*

"As a Black woman," said the late Audre Lorde, "I have to deal with identity or I don't exist at all. I can't depend on the world to name me kindly, because it never will. If the world defines you, it will define you to your disadvantage. So either I'm going to be defined by myself or not at all" ("Interview with Audre Lorde" with Karla Hammond 18). In essays from her *Sister Outsider* and *A Burst of Light,* as well as in the more narratively autobiographical *Zami: A New Spelling of My Name* and *The Cancer Journals,* Lorde names differences among women, African Americans, lesbians, and other groups as empowering rather than divisive forces and as aspects of identity. The political ideal, as she sees it, should not be a melting pot where all difference is subsumed, usually bending to the descriptive and ideological might of the previously dominant group. Instead, Lorde argues, difference within the self is a strength to be called upon rather than a liability to be altered. She exhorts her readers to recognize how each of them is multifarious and need never choose one aspect of identity at the expense of the others. "There's always someone asking you to underline one piece of yourself," she said in a 1981 interview,

> whether it's *Black, woman, mother, dyke, teacher,* etc.—because
> that's the piece that they need to key in to. They want you to

dismiss everything else. But once you do that, then you've lost because then you become acquired or bought by that particular essence of yourself, and you've denied yourself all of the energy that it takes to keep all those others in jail. Only by learning to live in harmony with your contradictions can you keep it all afloat. . . . That's what our work comes down to. No matter where we key into it, it's the same work, just different pieces of ourselves doing it. ("Audre" 15)

Each of us, says Lorde, needs each of those myriad pieces to make us who we are and whole. Lorde works the science and logic of her own hybridity. "I had never been too good at keeping within straight lines, no matter what their width" (25), she writes in *Zami*. She must make a physical space for herself in a hybrid language, a composite, a creation of new language to make space for the "new" of the self-invented body.

The implications of this thinking for questions of identity are broad. For the self to remain simultaneously multiple and integrated, embracing the definitive boundaries of each category—race, gender, class, et cetera—while dissembling their static limitations, assumes a depth and complexity of identity construction that refute a history of limitation. For the self to be fundamentally collaged—overlapping and discernibly dialogic—is to break free from diminishing concepts of identity. Lorde says, "When I say myself, I mean not only the Audre who inhabits my body but all those feisty, incorrigible black women who insist on standing up and saying 'I *am* and you cannot wipe me out, no matter how irritating I am, how much you fear what I might represent'" (Interview, 104). The self is composed of multiple components within the self and evolved from multiple external sources, an African American women's tradition or mythos.

The Cancer Journals is Lorde's memoir of her battle with the disease, but the scope of the meditation, as well as Lorde's formal freedom, makes it much more. For *Zami* she has invented a name for the book's new, collaged genre: *biomythography*. Neither autobiography, biography, nor mythology, biomythography is all of those things and none of them, a collaged space in which useful properties of genres are borrowed and reconfigured according to how well they help tell the story of a particular African American woman's life. *Biomythography* both refers to each of its eponymous genres and defines itself in its present moment.

I will consider how in this biomythographic mode Lorde's vision of collaged self-construction is mirrored in her compositional choices. With *biomythography* Lorde names a new genre, creating a larger space for her myriad selves. "I feel that not to be open about any of the different 'people' within my identity," she said in an interview, "particularly the 'mes' who are challenged by a status quo, is to invite myself and other women, by my example, to live a lie. In other words, I would be giving in to a myth of sameness which I think can destroy us" (Interview 102).

Both *Zami* and *The Cancer Journals* favor nonlinear narration that plays with chronology as it needs to. Both are autobiographies of Lorde's body. Both books are also erotic autobiographies, with *Zami* in particular describing Lorde's sensual life in intricate detail. The African American woman's body in Lorde's work—specifically, her own body—becomes a map of lived experience and a way of printing suffering as well as joy upon the flesh. Because the history of the Black female sexual body is fraught with lies and distortion, the story of those bodies as told by their inhabitors must take place on new, self-charted terrain with the marks of a traumatic history like a palimpsest. Like Carriacou, the Caribbean home of Lorde's antecedents that she as a child could not find on any map at school, the body of flesh or land that does not accurately exist in white American eyes leaves the inhabitant open for self-invention and interpretation. The flesh, the text, remains scarred, marking the trail to self-creation.

Lorde is preoccupied with things bodily: that which is performed upon the body versus what the body performs and asserts. Cancer surgery and subsequent bodily struggles are the focus of *The Cancer Journals,* while the ingestion of X-ray crystals at a factory job and an illegal abortion are signal episodes in *Zami.* Sexual and spiritual womanlove are what the body performs and how it heals as well as the means by which Lorde finds voice and self-expression. She in-corporates the intellectual and physical aspects of her life, reminding the reader that the metaphysical resides in a physical space, the body. Thus rage and oppression are metabolized to cancer, but she will also "write fire until it comes out my ears, my eyes, my noseholes—everywhere. Until it's every breath I breathe" ("Burst" 76–77). In Lorde's work, the body speaks its own history; she chooses corporeal language to articulate what she could not previously put into words.

In *The Cancer Journals,* for instance, Lorde dreams of a different vocabulary for considering this phenomenon. She recounts a dream in which "I had begun training to change my life" and follows a "shadowy teacher":

> Another young woman who was there told me she was taking a course in "language crazure," the opposite of discrazure (the

cracking and wearing away of rock). I thought it would be very exciting to study the formation and crack and composure of words, so I told my teacher I wanted to take that course. My teacher said okay, but it wasn't going to help me any because I had to learn something else, and I wouldn't get anything new from that class. I replied maybe not, but even though I knew all about rocks, for instance, I still liked studying their composition, and giving a name to the different ingredients of which they were made. It's very exciting to think of me being all the people in this dream. (14–15)

The "formation and crack and composure" of words mirror the process of reconstituting the scarred self. Lorde thinks of herself as all of the people in the dream. She is at once the self who wants to learn about language, the self who explores new selves and ideas, and the censorial teacher-self, as well as the self who gives permission for new exploration, albeit grudgingly. The dream allows for the simultaneous existence of different selves coexisting as a single self, and the contemplation of form, crack, and composure mirrors how the self is continually brought back together from disassembled fragments. Perhaps she is playing also, in the way that dreams play tricks with language, with the words *crazure* and *discrazure,* with first being considered "crazy," as Lorde tells us she has been since elementary school, and then coming to see the roots of *craze* as, in fact, whole and sane. In crazure the lines and fissures are visible but the object—like Lorde herself—remains whole.

In *Zami* Lorde describes the process of constructing herself racially and sexually with race and gender both facts of biology and learned characteristics and social operatives. To be "blackened" reveals not only a process of becoming and being acted upon but also a state of being. Lorde restores the visual impact of "coming out" to suggest her assertion and arrival and also, of course, to play on lesbian "coming out." Hers is a process of becoming Black and lesbian on her own terms as much as it is being named and seen as those things by a larger world. "Blackened" is a positive state to "come out" into, but it also implies being burnt and scarred. The statement's ending—"and whole"—suggests no contradiction between being scarred and being whole (*Zami* 5). In Lorde's work, life experience ever marks and takes shape as visible body memory, as a collage whose assembled scraps always allude to their past and beyond to a collective race memory of the violence of rupture in the Middle Passage, as encoded by the African American collage artist Romare Bearden. When Lorde refers to the "*journeywoman pieces of myself* (*Zami* 5), she configures the self as simultaneously fragmented and reassembled.

Zami's first section is an unlabeled preprologue, a dedication of sorts in which Lorde asks questions in italics and then muses upon them in roman typeface. This introduces us to the dialogism of Lorde's work, in which process is always apparent and the self is presented as an unfinished work in transition and progress. Collage, too, is dialogic at its core, insofar as the cut and torn strips encode a dialogue between past and ever-evolving present. That referentiality of using a scrap that on closer scrutiny can be identified both with its former life and as part of the present fiction recalls Bearden's earlier work, in which pieces were readily associated with their origins. Interestingly, Bearden later worked continually with origami-like paper in ways less obviously allusive to a separate past than his earlier newspaper and magazine cutouts.[1] This gesture reflects the assurance of both self and voice in Bearden's mature work. By engaging visibly in the dialogic aspects of collage, *Zami* ruminates on how the self is put together and how the book is the body for Lorde's ideas about self-construction.

Images of Black people's bodies in American culture have been either hypersexualized or desexualized to serve the imaginings and purposes of white American men and women. African American men have been iconographically exploited as either Black buck (in the nineteenth century, renegade slave; in the twentieth, athlete or criminal) or docile, smiling eunuch (in the nineteenth century, men seen as "Uncles"—Remus, or Jim on the river raft, without children of their own and without discernible sexuality; in the twentieth, obsequious entertainers). Black women, similarly, have been iconographically exploited as the hypersexualized Jezebel who entices the supposedly unrapacious master into her pallet or as the desexualized Mammy who has no children or loves her white "babies" as her own. Her body is very much a part of her image: as Mammy she is a comforting void of avoirdupois, while the Jezebel's curvaceous body is prominently displayed like an emblem of her social status or her essence. It is startling how, even today, there is so little iconographic gray space with these images. Historian Gerda Lerner writes that the postslavery mythology of Blacks was created to maintain social control. She specifically addresses the mythicizing of Black women's sexual freedom and abandon so that they were seen as women who,

> therefore, deserved none of the consideration and respect granted to white women. Every black woman was, by defini-

tion, a slut according to this racist mythology; therefore, to assault her and exploit her sexually was not reprehensible and carried with it none of the normal communal sanctions against such behavior. A wide range of practices reinforced this myth: the laws against intermarriage; the denial of the title "Miss" or "Mrs." to any black woman; the taboos against respectable social mixing of the races; the refusal to let black women customers try on clothing in stores before making a purchase; the assigning of single toilet facilities to both sexes of Blacks; the different legal sanctions against rape, abuse of minors and other sex crimes when committed against white or black women. Black women were very much aware of the interrelatedness of these practices and fought constantly—individually and through their organizations—both the practices and the underlying myth. (163–64)

This continual need to prove oneself sexually respectable—as if one ever could—against such a backdrop of accusation and assumption made the frank discussion of one's own sexuality dangerous. The need to name oneself, rather than leave it to a hostile dominant culture, is shown in *Zami* in the way Lorde and her late-teenaged friends call themselves "The Branded": "We became The Branded because we learned how to make a virtue out of it" (82).

Lorde's mapping of her body is all the more powerful against this history, as is her reclaiming and redefining of the erotic in her groundbreaking essay, "Uses of the Erotic: The Erotic as Power":

The erotic has often been misnamed by men and used against women. It has been made into the confused, the trivial, the psychotic, the plasticized sensation. For this reason, we have often turned away from the exploration and consideration of the erotic as a source of power and information, confusing it with its opposite, the pornographic. But pornography is a direct denial of the power of the erotic, for it represents the suppression of true feeling. Pornography emphasizes sensation without feeling. (54)

Lorde carefully separates eroticism from abuse of sexuality, freeing herself and those who would write after her from the idea that Black women's sexuality is to be whispered about and to be ashamed of. She reminds us that "the very word *erotic* comes from the Greek word *eros,* the personification of love in all its aspects—born of Chaos, and personifying creative power and harmony. When I speak of the erotic, then, I speak of it as an assertion of the lifeforce of women; of that creative energy empowered, the knowledge and use of which we are now reclaiming in our language, our history, our dancing, our loving, our work, our lives" (55). Eroticism as she defines it has nothing at all to do with how African American women are conventionally sexualized.

Lorde keeps readers aware of what the body feels, piece by piece, throughout the narratives. We are always aware of what her body is doing and feeling, from abortion cramps to sweat running between her breasts at 3 A.M. (*Zami* 117). This is in contrast to her mother's "euphemisms of body": "bamsy," "lower region," "between your [not 'my'] legs," all "whispered" (*Zami* 32). Further, Lorde talks about the body as a thing put together and taken apart. In both *The Cancer Journals* and *Zami* she isolates the breast and its symbolic meaning for motherhood and heterosexual beauty and then reconceives her own body by talking about what the breast means to her: yes, it gives her pleasure, but not apart from the rest of her body. The female breast can be prosthetically replaced, but Lorde needs to create and articulate her own grammar of physical significance.

Lorde continually refers to her physical self; phrases such as "when I was five years old and still legally blind" (*Zami* 21) give the reader a corporeal landmark in her life's chronology, calling attention again to the conflict Black women frequently experience between public authority and self-authority. She is blind in the eyes of the law, yet she has already given us accounts of what she sees around her. We have before us, then, a legally blind narrative we have nonetheless come to trust. The emphasis on legality in "legally blind" calls up the ironies of legal and extralegal categories in African American life: "chattel personal" defined full human beings, and so on. Lorde points to a distrust of the American common legal system and asks readers instead to trust her authority as she recounts the details she remembers seeing. Young Audre enters a "sight conversation class" but shows us a "blue wooden booth," "white women," "milk," "black mother," and "red and white tops" (*Zami* 21). It turns out that the seven or eight Black children in her class all have "serious deficiencies of sight"; are all these children wrong and legally deficient? Lorde's authority supersedes legal status and public logic.

Lorde yokes the physical and conceptual when she recalls a doctor who "clip[ped] the little membrane under my tongue so I was no longer tongue-tied" (*Zami* 23). To be tongue-tied is to have an encumbered, surgically correctable tongue as well as to be at a loss for words or without language, and Lorde literalizes this metaphorized tongue: she gives a physical home and tangible, corporeal image to the concept of self-expression. The tongue, the physical organ that enables speech, is clipped that she might speak, and Lorde mines that act of surgical violence, of bodily invasion, to talk about speaking, expression, recreation, and acting. Similarly, when struggling for money, Lorde sells her blood for plasma. Blood is a synecdoche for the surviving body and its sale a metaphor for the idea of "living off of her body," and Lorde refigures "selling one's body" as a tawdry sexual act (though most prostitutes do so to survive as well). That is, she sells a regenerative part so the whole can live.

Moreover, blood "belongs" inside of the body, but Lorde externalizes it, as she constantly turns her body inside out, showing us the hidden insides that amplify how the outside has been maligned and distorted; the metaphysical inside is never known unless she chooses to reveal it. Conversely, the X-ray crystals that Lorde counts in the factory are brought inside the body in another inversion of nature. She buries them deeper and deeper in her body, first secreting them in her thick socks, then taking them into her mouth, chewing them up and imbibing some part of them even as they are spit out in the bathroom.

Lorde's photograph makes up the full front cover of the first edition of *The Cancer Journals*. Here she makes herself, her body, empirical, the best evidence of her arguments and self-definitions. She illustrates that she is all she proclaims herself to be—fat and Black and beautiful—but that cover is also a strange testament to her very physical existence: she is a survivor and alive. She shows us the inside of her body to gain a kind of documentary, empirical, self-referencing authority as an expert on her own life and as the maker of a life on paper. For neither that life, her own, nor that of any Black woman, has ever existed in representation as its possessor experienced it. Consider the case of the Hottentot Venus, a southern African woman named Saartjie Baartman (tribal name unknown) brought to Europe in the early nineteenth century under the impression that she was to earn money performing that she could take back to her family (see Gilman 232–35). Instead, she was exhibited nude in circuses and private balls in London and Paris: eager Europeans paid to see her steatopygia. A French scientist, Georges Cuvier, made a name for himself by performing experiments of an unspecified nature upon her body and by dissecting her buttocks and genitalia after her death at the age of twenty-five. Baartman came to signify sexual and racial difference represented in extremis, as well as the attitude that Black women's bodies were easily commodified and utterly dispensable. Baartman's case

225

represents as well another side of the exploitation of Black women: the burning desire to see further and further inside, to have access to every crack and crevice of a Black woman's body and to that which she has tried to keep sacred. This underlines the power of Lorde showing us her insides, that sanctified, veiled territory that looks so different because she is showing it herself.

Zami's subtitle, "a new spelling of my name," hints that the alphabet—shapes that when put together make discernible meanings—will be rearranged. The "me" or "my" that name represents remains constant: Audre Lorde, as we her readers know her. But the moniker is what is new and what will unfold in the book: what the self is called and what it calls itself are not necessarily identical things. The theme of naming and renaming oneself is familiar within African American culture, of course. Instead of the example of Malcolm X, whose *X* stands as a sign of empty space, negation, and refutation of the white patriarch's legacy, Lorde respells her name altogether. She empties language, even letters, of previous signifiers as she plays with these received symbols. Lorde makes use of all that is available to her, just as African American experience incorporates the joy of transported and reassembled culture as it remembers the ugly rupture of the Middle Passage. Lorde works with that same alphabet to make a newly named and new self altogether. *Spelling* works both as a noun (how the word is spelled) as well as an active verb form (the process of spelling). So Lorde engages in spelling and reinventing, a work in progress who has not necessarily settled at a fixed meaning or identity. "A" new spelling (as opposed to "the") means there are probably more to come.

The way Lorde sees before she gets glasses and the validity of that vision challenge conventional ways of seeing and knowing. The first story she writes as a child, Lorde tells us, is a collage as well as a rebus: "I like White Rose Salada tea" (*Zami* 29), with the rose represented by a picture clipped from the *New York Times Magazine* and by letters spelling her story. "How I Became a Poet" (*Zami* 31–34) challenges the concept of chapters. Unattributed quotations challenge the notion of authorship and attribution.

"Growing up Fat Black Female and almost blind in america requires so much surviving that you have to learn from it or die," Lorde writes in *The Cancer Journals* (40). She spells America with a lowercase *a*, again exercising her prerogative as maker of the body of the book and letting her spelled language bear her perspective on the world. She chooses not to capitalize the name of a country that she sees as "cold and raucous" (*Zami* 11). Carriacou is her ancestral home, but the body of the country, the physical spot, while not locatable in any official text (the map), is utterly integral to her sense of self and ancestry. "Once *home* was a far way off, a place I had never been to but knew well out of my mother's mouth" (*Zami* 13), she continues. If a body of land does not even appear on a paper map but incontrovertibly exists, emitting from her mother's actual body, she must trust her own authority and be utterly free to experience and know it according to an internal family barometer. Invisibility, rather than distorted visibility, ironically provides a higher degree of self-inventive freedom.

Harlem is capitalized while *america* is not; Lorde gives herself that authority of capitalization. For upper- and lowercase letters imply caste or class, both suggested and contained within *case*. Lorde plays with the spelling of her name from the beginning of the biomythography, describing her decision to drop the *y* on her birth name, Audrey, for love of the solidity and visual symmetry of Audre Lorde:

> I did not like the tail of the Y hanging down below the line in Audrey, and would always forget to put it on, which used to disturb my mother greatly. I used to love the evenness of AUDRELORDE at four years of age, but I remembered to put on the Y because it pleased my mother, and because, as she always insisted to me, that was the way it had to be because that was the way it was. No deviation was allowed from her interpretations of correct. (*Zami* 24)

Lorde echoes this theme in *The Cancer Journals*. Discussing the politics of prostheses, she talks about carving one's physical self to someone else's idea of correctness rather than to one's own sense of symmetry. That dangling Y is in a way like a prosthetic limb or breast: once the new and natural shape of the body is to have one breast, just as the new and natural shape of the name is the indeed wonderfully even AUDRELORDE, addenda are prosthetic, unnecessary, and in their way de-forming.

Later, young Audre writes her name at school in what she thinks is her most glorious penmanship, moving slantwise down the page in another kind of symmetry. She works hard at this display, "half-showing off, half-eager to please" (*Zami* 25). She wants to write with pencil, which is how she has learned and the way she thinks is proper, but is given a crayon instead. Crayon, we are to think, is much coarser and less exact than the sharp pencil, for children and not for adults. Lorde makes do, but her teacher says, "I see we have a young lady who does not want to do as she is told" (26). This moment in which the narrator's "right" is presented in opposition to a public "right" is an important trope in Black women's autobiography: without resistance, survival and growth are impossible in an unjust world. Since we have been set up to identify with the narrator, as readers we align ourselves against the tyrannical dominant culture and with the contested genius of the Black girl-child. This is how we learn the lesson that to follow instructions, to play by what you think are the rules, does not always garner the expected perquisites.

In that instance of childhood we see Lorde asserting her own way of *writing*—not yet "spelling" explicitly, as the title would indicate, but spelling in the fundamental way that a child spells when every act of writing is a conscious act of putting together the pieces that make words that then hold meaning. To spell one's name is to create oneself in language, in Lorde's words, to put together "all the journeywoman pieces of myself" into one's most public signifier: the name.

Also present in *Zami* is the signal scene in African American autobiography in which the slave learns to read and to transcend a received legal status, thus entering the domain in which literacy is experienced as freedom. Lorde learns to read and speak simultaneously "because of [her] nearsightedness," distilling from apparent deficiency a new way of learning. Describing this, Lorde establishes a firm link between literacy and self-expression:

> I took the books from Mrs. Baker's hands after she was finished reading, and traced the large black letters with my fingers, while I peered again at the beautiful bright colors of the pictures. Right then I decided I was going to find out how to do that myself. I pointed to the black marks which I could now distinguish as separate letters, different from my sisters' more grown-up books, whose smaller print made the pages only one grey blur for me. I said, quite loudly, for whoever was listening to hear, "I want to read." (23)

This scene demonstrates Lorde's understanding that letters and words have physicality, that language has a body, and that the physical place in which communicated language resides is important. This leads the reader, him- or herself engaged in an act of literacy while reading the book, to reexperience that lost sense of the word's physicality. After this scene, Lorde's mother teaches her "to say the alphabet forwards and backwards as it was done in Grenada" (23). Lorde's logic, bodily and intellectual, finds sense in the so-called backwards as well as in the forwards.

Lorde describes her mother as follows: "My mother was a very powerful woman. This was so in a time when that word-combination of *woman* and *powerful* was almost unexpressable in the white american common tongue, except or unless it was accompanied by some aberrant explaining adjective like blind, or hunchback, or crazy, or Black" (*Zami* 15). For her mother to exist in language as she knows her, Lorde must trust her own knowledge and her own developing linguistic cosmos. She must also become attuned to what she knows outside of spoken language. She says that "my mother must have been *other* than woman" (16) because of her authority, because of the way she did not fit what "the white american common tongue" would represent as "Black and foreign and female in New York City in the twenties" (17). Lorde writes of her mother: "It was so often her approach to the world: to change reality. If you can't change reality, change your perceptions of it" (18). Lorde's mother in some regards provided a blueprint for Lorde's ability to change form to suit her needs, to change an outside perception of her body by inserting her own sense of form, both literary and physical. In an interview with Adrienne Rich, Lorde said she learned from her mother "the important value of nonverbal communication, beneath language. My life depended on it . . . [and] eventually I learned how to acquire vital and protective information without words. My mother used to say to me, 'Don't just listen like a ninny to what people say in their mouth'" ("Interview with Audre Lorde" 715). Language makes space for self-articulation and allows the self-invented body to name itself and to exist. Like so many other African American women writers, Lorde must make a physical space for herself in a hybrid and composite language wherein what she knows is frequently at odds with what the world tells her she should see.

On a family trip to Washington, D.C., Lorde describes the agony of what her eyes actually see. The trip marks the hardest smack with direct racism and segregation that the family had experienced and takes place "on the edge of the summer when I was supposed to stop being a child" (*Zami* 68). Great preparation is made in the family for the trip; food is cooked and packed for the train along with suitcases. Lorde sees everything there "through an agonizing corolla of dazzling whiteness" (69) that at the same time dazzles and blinds. The color of Washington's buildings represents who runs them; it is beautiful, what the family members have come to see, but it is also what they are up against and what they are not, for when they stop on the hot summer day for vanilla ice cream (more blinding whiteness) they are not allowed to eat at the counter. Washington is "real" and "official" as a site of power, and Lorde, on the brink of a new maturity, sees what is painful in the white dazzle: "The waitress was white, and the counter was white, and the ice cream I never ate in Washington, D.C. that summer I left childhood was white, and the white heat and the white pavement and the white stone monuments of my first Washington summer made me sick to my stomach for the whole rest of that trip" (71). Here we see a direct example, as well, of how her body absorbs and metabolizes her life's experiences, including painful ones. Her body holds and manifests that which has happened to her psyche. She develops a long-lasting stomachache from the moment she is acted upon via the seeing power of her eyes, as though the white is a tincture of evil.

Lorde writes of the "secret fears which allow cancer to flourish" (*Cancer* 10). In both books taken together, cancer is inescapably a metaphor for the dangers of growing up poor, female, and Black. She metabolizes the fears that others have of her, from teachers to exploitative employers. The episode where she describes her abortion and the episode when she works in Keystone Electronics most vividly illustrate this.

The abortion segment is graphic, necessarily, "Now all I had to do was hurt" (*Zami* 110), she writes, after she has had the catheter inserted into her uterus. This both isolates and delays bodily experience. The rubber eventually works its way out, as does the fetus. She keeps the reader ever aware of exactly how she is feeling: "This action which was tearing my guts apart and from which I could die except I wasn't going to—this action was a kind of shift from safety towards self-preservation. It was a choice of pains. That's what living was all about" (*Zami* 111). The fetus is, of course, a part of her body as it grows inside of her, but it is a part that she wants to be rid of. To get rid of the life burden of an unwanted child she must have this physical symbol of that invasion removed. Like a tumor, a fetus grows unwittingly.

Lorde has worked in two doctor's offices but cannot type and is young, poor, female, and Black, so she ends up working in a factory that processes X-ray crystals used in radio and radar machinery. The place was "offensive to every sense, too cold and too hot, gritty, noisy, ugly, sticky, stinking, and dangerous" (*Zami* 126). She counts X-ray crystals with Black and Puerto Rican women whose fingers are permanently darkened from exposure to the radiation: "Nobody mentioned that carbon tet destroys the liver and causes cancer of the kidneys. Nobody mentioned that the X-ray machines, when used unshielded, delivered doses of constant low radiation far in excess of what was considered safe even in those days" (*Zami* 126).

Workers could earn bonuses for "reading" crystals past a certain amount, but the factory bosses scrutinized them, making sure they did not discard crystals and claim credit for them. Lorde, in need of money, figures out a way to beat the system. She slips crystals into her socks every time she goes to the bathroom, and once inside the stall, "I chewed them up with my strong teeth and flushed the little shards of rock down the commode. I could take care of between fifty and a hundred crystals a day in that manner, taking a handful from each box I signed out" (*Zami* 146). She chews the crystals and spits them out; they are nonfood but nonetheless "metabolized," as she tells us hatred, too, can be metabolized. The body, then, makes visible also what has been metaphorically imbibed. Lorde's cancer turns the body inside out, alluding to the internal lacerations of chewed X-ray crystals, which are themselves a manifestation of what a poor Black female has to do to survive. Lorde earns unprecedented amounts of money—for the factory, of course—and is laid off shortly thereafter. The X-ray crystals have stained her fingertips, leaving her marked with the work of her class status and for the illness she will eventually develop. She says she has a sense of the fingers burning off (*Zami* 146). A reader of *The Cancer Journals* cannot escape the conclusion that this episode contributed largely to her subsequent illness.

By insistently reminding the reader of her bodily reality, Lorde works toward the body's integration through struggle, a synecdoche for the struggle of the self to remain whole. The women she admires are whole in their variegated bodies. One of the first images she presents of a woman outside of her family is of a woman named DeLois who walks on the street, her "big proud stomach" (*Zami* 4) attracting sunlight. She tells of one of her early, significant love affairs, in Mexico, with a woman, Eudora (*Zami* 161–76), who has had breast cancer—eerily presaging the future of Lorde's own healing, whole-ing process, just as it is "the love of women," though not explicitly erotic love, that heals her in *The Cancer Journals*. Making love, how the body acts, is a counterpart or antidote to what has been done to it. Making love (the erotic) as a creative act (as power) is a self-making and self-defining act. Even autoerotic love, masturbation, is written about as a part of the process of healing the body and making it and the resident psyche whole again (*Cancer* 40).

Lorde survives despite "grow[ing] up fat, Black, nearly blind, and ambidextrous in a West Indian household" (*Zami* 24). "Ambidextrous" plays on the fact that she tells us about sleeping with both men and women, but it also deals more seriously with the notion of self-creation and incorporating power. To be ambidextrous, then, is another instance of bodily states, facts of nature, existing as metaphors for aspects of identity. She talks about her mother as being both, other, and says that she, too, wishes for ambidextrous self-culled sexual identity: "*I have always wanted to be both man and woman, to incorporate the strongest and richest parts of my mother and father within/into me. . . . I have felt the age-old triangle of mother father and child, with the "I" at its eternal core, elongate and flatten out into the elegantly strong triad of grandmother mother daughter, with the "I" moving back and forth flowing in either or both directions as needed*" (7). Identity is fluid, as is demonstrated by the elision of punctuation in "*mother father and child*" and "*grandmother mother daughter.*"

The essay "A Burst of Light" serves as a postscript to *The Cancer Journals*, synthesizing and further distilling many of its ideas. Lorde makes explicit connections between becoming an authority on one's own body and cancer and politics, dying and struggling to live and work. Much of the essay is an exhausting chronicle of the work she keeps up with around the globe as she is fighting the disease; a refrain is "I" (or "we," with her lover, Frances) "did good work." She fights experts and decides she does not want the borders of her body to be invaded. She rejects medical advice when it is her life at stake. When she says she wants to have "enough moxie to chew the whole world up and spit it out in bite-sized pieces, useful and warm and wet and delectable because they came out of my mouth" ("Burst" 62), the image recalls and inverts the chewed and spit out X-ray crystals. *To metabolize* means to take in good and bad and then determine what is useful in the shaping of the self. The act that probably poisoned her can be reenacted to her advantage.

Lorde travels to a holistic healing center and finds a philosophy wherein "the treatment of any disease, and cancer in particular, must be all of a piece, body and mind, and I am ready to try anything so long as they don't come at me with a knife" ("Burst" 83). Divisibility and invasion are worse even than cancer.

She rejects a prosthesis in part because the breast does not "perform," as a leg or an arm does. She realizes it is not its own erotic world, not erotic unto itself, but rather part of a schema of eros she controls and that is integral within her body. She explores what the body performs versus what is done to the body: abortion, cancer surgery. Body language is a necessary part of naming herself in her own tongue.

Lorde's work, as it focuses on her physical existence, emphasizes the literal meaning of incorporation, of putting one's self into a body, or in this case, of speaking of one's self in one's own body. The intellect lives and operates in the body. The heart and soul express themselves through the body. The body manifests the ills of an oppressive world that is especially punishing to women and poor people and people of color. The body is a very specific site in Lorde's work, the location where all this takes place. She is constantly reminding us that she is an inhabitant of a body that has given birth to children, has been nearly blind, and has battled cancer and lost pieces of itself but remains whole, incorporated, integrated. It is "*my body, a living representation of other life older longer wiser*" (*Zami* 7). Bodies express what verbal language cannot.

> I am a scar, a report from the frontlines, a talisman, a resurrection.
> —Audre Lorde, "A Burst of Light:
> Living with Cancer"

In James Alan McPherson's "The Story of a Scar," the African American male protagonist sits in a plastic surgeon's waiting room and from the first page is compelled to ask the African American woman next to him, "As a concerned person, and as your brother, I ask you, without meaning to offend, how did you get that scar on the side of your face?" (97) She rebuffs his bold inquiry and his presumption that she will "read" her own body for him: "'I ask *you*,' she said, 'as a nosy person with no connections in your family, how come your nose is all bandaged up?'" (97) His bandaged nose makes his nosiness legible. As the story proceeds from the man's narrative perspective, the woman tells her story, only to be continually interrupted by the man's presumptions about her narrative. He presumes to know her and to know what the mark on her face signifies. He presumes he has access to that signification because, after all, the mark is visible, and if a Black woman's body is visible, it is therefore accessible, not only to white men, historically, but in this instance to Black men as well.

But she will not let him get away with that and will not let her story be usurped. She "reads" him as well: "'You don't have to tell me a thing,' she said. 'I know mens goin' and comin'. There ain't a-one of you I'd trust to take my grandmama to Sunday school'" (98). The male protagonist persists:

> The scar still fascinated me. . . . The scar was thick and black and crisscrossed with a network of old stitch patterns, as if

some meticulous madman had first attempted to carve a perfect half-circle in her flesh, and then decided to embellish his handiwork. It was so grotesque a mark that one had the feeling it was the art of no human hand and could be peeled off like so much soiled putty. But this was a surgeon's office and the scar was real. It was as real as the honey-blond wig she wore, as real as her purple pantsuit. I studied her approvingly. Such women have a natural leaning toward the abstract expression of themselves. Their styles have private meanings, advertise secret distillations of their souls. Their figures, and their disfigurations, make meaningful statements. (98–99)

As it turns out, the woman has been marked by public violence by a man. Her scar is a history of sorts, a mark she is trying to change. The more she tells of her story the more she gives away of herself, leaving both of them on uncertain ground, but she will not simply cut to the chase and tell the *mere* "story of a scar"; she is telling a piece of her life, telling the story her way regardless of how the listener wants to receive it. The man characterizes her story as "tiresome ramblings," and she becomes angry: "This here's *my* story! . . . You dudes cain't stand to hear the whole of anything. You want everything broke down in little pieces. . . . That's how come you got your nose all busted up. There's some things you have to take your time about" (100).

When she finishes her story, her talk is not interrupted narratively for several pages; she takes over the narrative space of the story with her bodily truth. The male narrator then interrupts and gives a condescending and erroneous conclusion to her story (105). She then takes the space of a long pause and a dramatic drag on her cigarette: "'You know everything,' she said in a soft tone, much unlike her own. 'A black mama birthed you, let you suck her titty, cleaned your dirty drawers, and you still look at us through paper and movie plots'" (105–6).

After the story is finished, after he has had to listen to her truth, "a terrifying fog of silence and sickness crept into the small room, and there was no longer the smell of medicine" (111). There are no longer antidotes, only dis-ease, the fact of the scar and the story of a scar hanging in the air in the doctor's waiting room. That is when we learn of other doctors who have been unsuccessful in their attempts to modify her scar. In the very last line the man asks the woman's name, something that he thinks will provide information, when in fact it is beside the point next to the story he has just been given. It is merely something for him to possess. When Audre Lorde says she gives us "a new spelling of my name," she insists that the names mean less than presumed, that you have to listen to a person tell his or her own story before assuming what the story holds. Lorde tells her own "story of a scar" in *Zami* and *The Cancer Journals* because she understands the imperative to both gather her multiple selves into one body and to name that body, rather than leave the (mis)naming to another.

Lorde continually states that she claims the different parts of herself—"I am lesbian, mother, warrior"—speaking through difference. It is her credo, a way of living, that all people, but particularly those said to be marginalized, must refuse to be divisible and schizophrenic. It is in the way that she takes us through the history of her body, in both *Zami* and *The Cancer Journals,* that Lorde maps the new terrain of what over 100 years ago Linda Brent had to whisper and withhold from her readers: all that a corporeal history embodies. The link between Lorde and Brent is crucial: for both, the issue is control over one's own body and the power to see the voice as a literal functioning *member* of the corpus, an organ that works and must be self-tended.

Sexuality is broad and frequently forbidden discursive terrain for many Black women in both writing and other sorts of public lives. When we do write, we write our sexualities into existence against a vast backdrop, a history, of misrepresentation and essentializing and perversion, appropriations of our bodies and stories about our bodies. This precedes our entry into the Euro-American written universe. Lorde claims that terrain for herself, defining what she thinks of as the erotic, inscribing in her books an actual, fleshly Black woman's body. The effect is like that seen in African American visual artist Howardena Pindell's 1988 painting "Autobiography: AIR/CS560." After a near-fatal car crash in 1979 and lengthy rehabilitation, Pindell suffered memory lapses and manifested her process of recovery and remembering in her work. She "used postcards from friends and collected them in her travels to help jar recollections or explain flashes of images. . . . Her automobile accident produced a need for memory" (Rouse 8). She also began lying on her canvases to leave an imprint of her body with which to work (Pindell). In the painting, then, Pindell left an impression of her fragmented and reassembled body as physical evidence both that the body exists and that she can imagistically create it. The narrative history of the body is a way of interpellating difference and claiming wholeness.

In Lorde's work, as in Pindell's, it takes literal invasion for the self to be reconstituted. Why is the self not conceived as an a priori whole? These images literalize what is historically and metaphorically true in African American women's writing: it is the fissure, the slash of the

Middle Passage, the separation from the originary, that which the physical scar shows and alludes to—all that is an intractable part of African American women's history—that makes possible the integrity of the scar, the integrity of the body's history, and a record of what the scar performs.

NOTE

1. For example, Bearden cuts paper in identifiable iconographic shapes such as the arc of a watermelon slice, the ruffle of a rooster comb, curls of steam engine smoke, or the shape of a guitar. Each of these has specific meaning in Bearden's African American cosmology.

REFERENCES

Gilman, Sander L. "Black Bodies, White Bodies: Toward an Iconography of Female Sexuality in Late Nineteenth-Century Art, Medicine, and Literature," In Henry Louis Gates Jr., ed., *"Race," Writing, and Difference,* 223–63. Chicago: University of Chicago Press, 1986.

Lerner, Gerda, ed. *Black Women in White America: A Documentary History.* 1972. Reprint, New York: Vintage-Random, 1973.

Lorde, Audre. "Audre Lorde: An Interview." With Karla Hammond. *Denver Quarterly* 16 (1981): 10–27.

———. "A Burst of Light: Living with Cancer." In *A Burst of Light: Essays,* 49–134. Ithaca: Firebrand, 1988.

———. *The Cancer Journals.* San Francisco: Spinsters, 1980.

———. Interview. With Claudia Tate. In Claudia Tate, ed., *Black Women Writers at Work,* 100–116. New York: Continuum, 1983.

———. "An Interview with Audre Lorde." With Karla Hammond. *American Poetry Review* (March–April 1980): 18–21.

———. "An Interview with Audre Lorde." With Adrienne Rich. *Signs* 6 (1981): 713–36.

———. "Uses of the Erotic: The Erotic as Power." In *Sister Outsider: Essays and Speeches,* 53–59. Trumansburg, N.Y.: Crossing Press Feminist Series, Calif.: Crossing, 1984.

———. *Zami: A New Spelling of My Name.* Freedom, Calif.: Crossing, 1982.

McPherson, James Alan. "The Story of a Scar." In *Elbow Room: Stories,* 97–112. Boston: Little, 1972.

Pindell, Howardena. Lecture. Philadelphia Museum of Art, Philadelphia, 15 April 1991.

Rouse, Terrie S. "Howardena Pindell: Odyssey." In *Howardena Pindell: Odyssey,* 5–12. New York: Studio Museum in Harlem, 1986.

PART

Doris Witt

What (N)ever Happened to
Aunt Jemima

Eating Disorders, Fetal Rights,
and Black Female Appetite in
Contemporary American Culture

> It occurred to me that the black woman is herself a
> symbol of nourishment.
> —Alice Walker, "Giving the Party"

On 27 April 1989, the Chicago-based Quaker Oats Company announced plans to "update" its Aunt Jemima trademark for the 1990s.
The two-page news release begins:

> Aunt Jemima, one of America's oldest packaged food trade-
> marks and a symbol of quality breakfast products for 100
> years, will be given a new look this year. The facial appearance
> is unchanged. Noticeably different, however, is a new, stylish,
> grey-streaked hairdo, and her headband has been removed.
> Other changes include cosmetic touches such as a different
> style of collar and the addition of earrings.
>   "We wanted to present Aunt Jemima in a more contempo-
> rary light, while preserving the important attributes of
> warmth, quality, good taste, heritage and reliability," said Bar-
> bara R. Allen, Vice President of Marketing for Quaker Oats
> Company's Convenience Foods Division, makers of Aunt

Jemima products. "Based on the results of consumer research over a five-month period, we think the new design does that." ("Aunt Jemima" 1)

This preemptive strike was intended to fortify the corporate line on the trademark's symbolic meaning several weeks before the altered image was itself actually "released" into the American marketplace—or into an ideological battleground, to be more precise, where efforts to "preserve" and valorize the iconography of slavery are fiercely contested. Given the context, the public relations staff at Quaker Oats was obviously not about to comment on *why* the company "wanted" to update the trademark image in the first place.[1]

What are we to make of the longevity of the Aunt Jemima trademark and of the ambiguity of the symbolic attributes that Quaker Oats wants to preserve by keeping it? After all, "warmth" is surely a characteristic of Aunt Jemima as cook; "good taste," of Aunt Jemima food products. "Quality," "heritage," and "reliability" could refer to either. One might infer from this symbolic slippage that the trademark is intended to signify both cook and food. Like her precursors, the big-breasted mammies of post–Civil War lore, Aunt Jemima *prepares* and *is* food; she/it is the ever-smiling source of sustenance for infants and adults.[2] Yet one obstacle faced by Quaker Oats in trying to maintain this dual symbolic meaning, while presenting the visual image of Aunt Jemima in a more "contemporary" light, is that the new picture could be said to represent not so much a servant producer as a middle-class consumer. Ex cathedra pronouncements of Barbara Allen notwithstanding, the 1990s' Jemima looks more like a "Mrs." than an "Aunt." And viewed from this perspective, "good taste" should be her attribute as a discriminating shopper, not as a stack of pancakes.[3]

Of course, one assumption I am begging here is that a middle-class Black matron has a "look" that we all readily recognize. This is a problem that Jean-Christophe Agnew neatly skirts. Near the end of a December 1989 *Village Voice* review of Susan Strasser's *Satisfaction Guaranteed: The Making of the American Mass Market*, Agnew pauses momentarily in an attempt to resolve the contradictions posed by the upscale Aunt Jemima:

For instance, what are we now to make of a figure like Aunt Jemima, whose 100-year old kerchief was finally removed from her head during her most recent makeover last July? Now she is said to *look like* Oprah Winfrey. But then again,

Oprah's face and body have themselves been inducted into the
Wiz's vast warehouse of interchangeable cultural signifiers.
(30, emphasis added)[4]

By invoking the instability of Winfrey as a referent, Agnew dismisses the
possibility of making meaning of Aunt Jemima at all ("looks like" ad in-
finitum).[5] In particular he would appear to be alluding to the highly
publicized sixty-seven-pound weight loss in 1988 of the popular talk-
show hostess and television producer and perhaps also to tabloid alle-
gations that an August 1989 *TV Guide* cover picture of the newly slim
Winfrey depicted her face atop Ann-Margret's body.[6]

What, then, ever happened to Aunt Jemima? Nothing and everything. On the one hand, the trademark is where it has been for the last
century, on grocery-store shelves, and the same (conflicted) fears and
desires that gave rise to it in 1889 surely underwrite its retention today.[7]
Yet without going so far as to label Aunt Jemima and Oprah Winfrey interchangeable, one might well conclude, on the other hand, that the updated trademark needs also to be interpreted in new ways. Neither the
cultural work performed by African American women nor the manner
in which they are interpellated as subjects is today precisely what it was
a century ago. For if Aunt Jemima foregrounds one axis of American desire, for Black women to be the ever-smiling *producers* of food, to be nur-
turers who themselves have no appetite and make no demands, then
Oprah Winfrey surely also foregrounds another, complementary axis,
one that has been latent in popular fascination with the Aunt Jemima
trademark from its inception: that is, American fear of what Black
women *consume,* or perhaps more precisely American obsession with
Black female appetites. This concern has played itself out on numerous
levels, from gastronomic to sexual to economic. The (foreclosed) question, What does Aunt Jemima eat?, quickly mutates to encompass other
aspects of Black female consumption, including access to the wealth and
power that can satisfy desire. One surely suspects, after all, that popular
interest in Winfrey's eating habits is in no small part a function of her
enormous wealth. She earned ninety-eight million dollars in 1992 and
1993 alone, making her the top-earning entertainer in America (see
Newcomb and Gubernick 97).

Much fine work has been done on this Mammy/Jezebel dichotomy
by scholars ranging from Angela Davis, Barbara Christian, bell hooks,
and Deborah Gray White to Hortense Spillers, Deborah McDowell, Patricia Hill Collins, K. Sue Jewell, and many others.[8] My own contribution
differs, however, in its literalization of "consumption." I take dietary

practices to be fundamental to the ways we come to understand our-selves as embodied, sexed, gendered, raced, classed, religious, local, re-gional, and national subjects. I take the dietary practices of African American women, moreover, to be fundamental to the making of Amer-ican subjectivities. To appropriate for my working hypothesis one of the more famous dicta of French gastrophile Jean Anthelme Brillat-Savarin, tell me what African American women are said to eat, and I shall tell you what Americans fear they are.[9]

In the remainder of this chapter I attempt to unpack this overarch-ing claim by looking more specifically at the relationship between (1) the construction of Black female appetite in contemporary American culture and (2) debates over the boundaries and ontological status of the "embodied" subject. In particular, I focus on the interlocking do-mains of "eating disorders" and "fetal rights." African American women have, by and large, been perceived as absences both in discourses of eat-ing disorders and in the specularization of the anorexic and bulimic body; African American women have been very much a presence both in the discourses of fetal rights and in the specularization of fetal and neonate bodies—especially the purported epidemics of "fetal alcohol syndrome" and "crack babies" in the 1980s. Each of these topics has generated a tremendous amount of discussion in both popular and aca-demic circles, but for the most part not in the same breath. What fol-lows, then, is a conjectural cross-mapping.

"Fat Is a Black Woman's Issue"

I begin with the former. Anorexia nervosa refers to self-imposed starva-tion; bulimia is also called the binge-purge cycle. Since the late 1960s and early 1970s—the period of Black Power, second-wave feminism, Stonewall, and other liberatory social movements—both have been widely construed in popular and academic discourses as symptoms displayed by young, presumptively heterosexual white women from middle- and upper-class nuclear families. In addition to the multitude of articles on dieting and body image in popular young women's maga-zines, I have in mind here mainly the work of white feminist scholars such as Kim Chernin, Joan Jacobs Brumberg, and, to a lesser extent, Susan Bordo. Less well known among humanists would be the clinical research of psychiatrists and other medical professionals who publish their findings in the *International Journal of Eating Disorders*, founded in 1981. Here, too, with very few exceptions the object of their gaze has been young, bourgeois, female, and white.[10] As readers who are familiar with this subject will realize, there are significant differences in the models proposed for interpreting eating disorders: Chernin and Bordo basically view disorderly eating as normative female behavior, Chernin from a feminist psychoanalytic perspective and Bordo from a feminist Foucauldian perspective. Brumberg sets forth an explanatory model in which biology, psychology, and culture interact, and she is more receptive to biomedical analyses of eating disorders as a "pathology" that can be treated with a combination of drugs and therapy than are Chernin and Bordo.

My initial question in approaching this topic was "Why are African American women absent from these discourses about eating disorders?" Diverse students, friends, and colleagues with whom I discussed the topic concluded that Black women do not "get" eating disorders. Two of my African American women students reached this conclusion even in the context of telling me about their experiences with Slim-Fast and Dexatrim.[11] My early inquiries having thus led me to believe that this was a topic worth pursuing, I reframed the question. Rather than assuming that African American women were absent from discourses about eating disorders, I began asking, "Where are African American women?" "How are they present?" One answer was in the index and footnotes—literally, in Brumberg's otherwise meticulously researched history of anorexia, *Fasting Girls*. The sole entry in her index on African American women reads: "Blacks, as anorectics, 284n14" (361). Needless to say, there is no comparable entry reading "Whites, as anorectics, everything but 284n14."

What intrigued me was why someone who interrogates the cultural construction of white female appetite with such brilliance would relegate women of color to a footnote. There Brumberg repeats the claim of medical researcher George Hsu that "the rarity among blacks of anorexia nervosa and bulimia is the result of cultural differences that protect young black women from the negative self-image and intense pressure for slimness that are part of the white middle-class experience" (see note 10). Brumberg then comments: "These data, if correct, are telling evidence of the separateness of black culture and white culture and their differential strengths" (284). Black women protected from a negative self-image? Is *The Bluest Eye*'s Pecola Breedlove then solely a product of Toni Morrison's vivid imagination, created out of whole cloth? The proviso "if correct" surely indicates that Brumberg recognized the inadequacy of such an analysis, particularly in its conflation of "negative self-image" with "intense pressure for slimness." One reason for her reluctance to pursue this issue, I would speculate, is that to ask about the appetites, dietary practices, and bodies of African American women is tantamount to making the domain of eating disorders—as she and many others have constructed it—collapse. Black women are not just a footnote but a constitutive footnote; they are not just an absence in eating disorders but a constitutive absence, and this is an important distinction.

For whereas the creation of mammy/cook figures such as Aunt Jemima entailed a naturalization and/or biologization of Black female cooking skills, these discourses of eating disorders have also relied upon a naturalization of Black female appetite. This is particularly true of the work of Kim Chernin. In her book *The Obsession: Reflections on the Tyranny of Slenderness,* Chernin argues that "women" have not been allowed to have a "natural" relationship to "our" appetites and bodies.[12] She claims that Western culture fears fully developed womanhood and that the emergence of anorexia nervosa and bulimia in conjunction with the rise of second-wave feminism is a sign of women's conflicted feelings about "our" mothers and about inhabiting adult women's bodies. In effect, the anorectic attempts to resolve these conflicts by retaining the body of a child. Chernin argues that "large size, maturity, voluptuousness, massiveness, strength, and power are not permitted if we wish to conform to our culture's ideal. Our bodies, which have knowledge of life, must undo this fullness of knowing and make themselves look like the body of a precocious child if we wish to win the approval of our culture" (94). For Chernin, "large size, maturity, voluptuousness, massiveness, strength, and power" are valorized terms, ideals to which "we" have not been "permitted" to aspire. But given that traits such as "strength" and "power" have historically been attributed to African American women in the context of an indictment of Black matriarchy—as exemplified most notoriously by Daniel Moynihan's 1965 report *The Negro Family: The Case for National Action*—one might well question what relationship Black women have had to Chernin's "we."[13]

Viewed from this perspective, Chernin's complaint seems to be that the hegemonic subject positions available to bourgeois white women have not been constituted in the same way as the positions available to Black women, particularly those of the lower classes. Yet she never explicitly addresses the fact that her model for the anorectic is an adolescent white female. Indeed, Chernin even includes a chapter in *The Obsession* called "The Matriarch" that invokes a mythic past of female power and has no reference to race.[14] Intriguingly, however, at the very start of the book she quotes from a poem collected in *Passion,* by Black feminist essayist and poet June Jordan. After acknowledging that "nothing fills me up at night," the poem's speaker proceeds to detail her sleep-interrupting desire for food ("cherry pie hot from the oven with Something like Vermont/Cheddar Cheese," et cetera) as a symptom of other emotional needs (Chernin 12). She concludes with a self-admonition to be "writing poems, writing poems" rather than rummaging around in her refrigerator "in the middle of the night" (12). In a subsequent annotation of the poem, Chernin refers to Jordan as a "woman" and never questions her relationship to ideals such as "massiveness, strength, and power." To have acknowledged Jordan's race, class, and historical location would have disrupted the models of female development Chernin was setting up. It would have denaturalized them by forcing her to confront the ways in which her conceptions of the "natural"—"natural bodies" and "natural appetites"—are already inscribed by differences of gender, race, class, sexuality, sexual orientation, and historicity.

Of course, as the subject matter of Jordan's poem would tend to suggest, one is by no means hard-pressed to locate writings by African American women that foreground their own appetites, dietary practices, and bodies. These topics appear repeatedly in the work of Jordan's peers—contemporary African American fiction writers such as Alice Walker, Gloria Naylor, and Carolyn Ferrell.[15] Furthermore, several contributors to *The Black Women's Health Book* incorporate discussion of dietary practices into a more comprehensive agenda to improve the mental and physical health of African American women, as does Black feminist scholar bell hooks in *Sisters of the Yam: Black Women and Self-Recovery*.[16] In these works food is treated in conjunction with drugs and alcohol, as a habit-forming substance that African American women can and do abuse. Similar themes are sounded in popular culture. To cite one of the more intriguing examples, in 1989 *Essence* magazine printed an autobiographical essay entitled "Fat Is a Black Woman's Issue." Author Retha Powers was herself appropriating the title of Susie Orbach's path-breaking book *Fat Is a Feminist Issue*. Orbach had helped to pioneer second-wave feminism's exploration of dieting and food obsession as normative female behaviors, but hers was a polemic that largely ignored women of color.

Taking issue with such exclusions, Powers writes about her obsession with the "dirty, sinful act" of eating and details her struggles to stop the (literally) self-destructive cycle of dieting, binging, purging, and laxative abuse (78). She censures, furthermore, persons who told her over the years that her large size was "acceptable in the Black community" (78). Whereas Chernin and Orbach see pressure on middle-class white women to be thin as a form of cultural gynophobia, Powers views the *lack* of this pressure on her—as an African American woman—as a sign of racism. In some of the essays collected in *Unbearable Weight*, Susan Bordo has begun to develop a systematic assessment of the racial and class inscriptions of the consuming female body. Extrapolating from her subtle and innovative work on bourgeois white women and eating disorders, Bordo suggests that the hegemony of Western culture and upward class mobility has resulted in increased pressure on African American women—such as Powers—to become slender bodies. In other words, they are expected to emulate the controlled bodily boundaries idealized for middle-class white women.[17] While I would not want to downplay the role of the mass media or of class positioning in the demographics of eating disorders, it does, however, seem to me that in the process of linking upward class mobility to compulsory starvation for African American women, Bordo inadvertently naturalizes lower-class Black female appetite.[18]

In this respect, perhaps the most persuasive work being done on African American women and food is that of sociologist Becky Thompson, who has recently been researching what she calls "eating problems" among women of color. Thompson argues that women across the spectrum of race, ethnicity, class, and sexual orientation display symptoms of a troubled relationship to food. Many eat to suppress emotions, particularly the post-traumatic stress of incest and sexual assault, as well as the strain of living in a white-supremacist, heterosexist, capitalist patriarchy. Clearly one might critique all this work, Thompson's included, for its tendency to naturalize *male* appetites, but my aim here is not to engage in the debate over whether eating disorders are normative or pathological or to stake out the most purely constructivist position for myself.[19] Rather, I want to stress several different points.

While for the purposes of this essay I have found it useful to assimilate starving, binging, and binging and purging under one rubric, appetite, it is surely even more important for us to make distinctions among the discourses, practices, and spectacles of anorexia, bulimia, and obesity. One reason I particularly mention Powers's essay is that she not only denaturalizes but also foregrounds the conflation of African American women's bodies and *fat*. For if Black women have been absences in the discourses of eating disorders, they most certainly have been highly visible in the specularization of corpulence in American culture. Donald Bogle recounts in *Toms, Coons, Mulattoes, Mammies and Bucks,* for instance, the gastronomic lengths to which actress Louise Beavers was forced in order to replicate the stereotypical bodily boundaries of "mammy." Perhaps best known currently for her portrayal of

Delilah in John Stahl's film version of *Imitation of Life* (1934), Beavers regularly went on "force-feed diets, compelling herself to eat beyond her normal appetite. Generally, she weighed close to two hundred pounds, but it was a steady battle for her to stay overweight. During filming . . . she often lost weight and then had to be padded to look more like a full-bosomed domestic who was capable of carrying the world on her shoulders" (Bogle 63). Beavers's ordeal would tend to suggest, then, that the widespread conflation of Black female bodies and fat is inseparable from the phantasmatic desires (and cultural representations) of the hegemonic white imaginary.[20]

In *Feminism without Women,* cultural theorist Tania Modleski has explicated these desires by analyzing in detail contemporary culture's "horror of the body" and the "special role played by the woman of color as receptacle" of these fears (130). She argues, for example, that in the film *Crossing Delancey* (1988) the "function of the fat, sexually voracious black woman . . . is to enable the white Jewish subculture, through its heterosexual love story, to represent itself in a highly sentimentalized, romanticized, and sublimated light, while disavowing the desires and discontents underlying the civilization it is promoting" (130). It is imperative, Modleski continues, that we "consider the ways in which ethnic and racial groups are played off against—and play themselves off against—one another" (130). In light of her comments it is surely significant that both Orbach and Chernin explicitly refer to how their identities as Jewish women have shaped their attitudes toward food and body size. "I was a Jewish beatnik," Orbach recalls, "and I would be *zaftig*" (xv).[21]

Even while acknowledging that fat has functioned as a site of (and psychic resolution for) interracial and interethnic conflict, we should not overlook the fact that many African American women have appropriated the spectacle of the large Black female body as a form of political protest. Here one thinks of a tradition stretching from actresses such as Hattie McDaniel to contemporary rappers such as Queen Latifah and Salt 'N' Pepa.[22] In her "Ladies First" video, for example, Queen Latifah flaunts her refusal to conform to American culture's pervasive imagery of female slimness while also positioning herself, according to historian Tricia Rose, "as part of a rich legacy of black women's activism, racial commitment, and cultural pride" (164). The members of Salt 'N' Pepa, by contrast, often foreground butts in their videos; Rose claims that in so doing they appropriate "a complex history of white scrutiny of black female bodies, from the repulsion and fascination with and naked exhibition of Sara Bartmann as 'The Hottentot Venus' in the early 1800s to the perverse and exoticized pleasure many Europeans received from Josephine Baker's aggressively behind-centered dances" (167–68).[23]

In short, African American women have always been "presences" in discussions about eating disorders, particularly in specular form as the naturalized fat body. Consequently, it is important to recognize that what a good many African American women have been appropriating in recent years is not so much the practices of disorderly eating as the discourses themselves. For by appropriating a set of discourses in which the individual has an "unnatural" relationship to her appetite, African American women are contesting normative Black female subject positions and insisting upon their psychological complexity as human beings. They are refusing to be the constitutive absence, the "natural," in the binary through which American appetites have historically been constructed.

To talk about eating disorders as a discourse that can be appropriated as a tactic of resistance is surely problematic, however, since it threatens to trivialize the health hazards for African American women of symptoms such as excess weight, binging and purging, and laxative abuse. As writers in *The Black Women's Health Book* point out, women of color have less access to nutritional food and quality health care than do economically privileged whites, and, consequently, they are more prone to preventable health problems such as hypertension and "sugar" diabetes. Supporting their claims, the *New York Times* reported in January 1994 that "doctors appear to be less likely to tell black women to quit smoking and drinking during pregnancy than they are to tell white women" ("Study" A16). Given such demographic inconsistencies in American medical care, one might well greet with pleasure the news that the health of African American women is both under investigation and of interest to the editors of the newspaper of record. Yet I have an ulterior motive in referring to this particular article from the *Times*. I repeat: "Doctors appear to be less likely to tell black women to quite smoking and drinking *during pregnancy* than they are to tell white women" (emphasis added).

It would, after all, surely be inaccurate to say that there have been no discourses in recent years of Black female appetite. For if the desires of middle-class adolescent white women have been constructed since the late 1960s largely via eating disorders, so the desires of young Black women have been constructed in terms of motherhood and matriarchy. Young white women purportedly want nothing more than to be thin; young Black women, nothing more than to be pregnant.[24] The discussions of "crack babies" and "fetal alcohol syndrome" that proliferated during the 1980s were, moreover, far more concerned with Black female appetites than with Black fetuses. Indeed, while doctors have been careful to warn pregnant white women to quite smoking and drinking, they have reported analogous practices of Black women to the police. In the next section of this chapter, I hope to better understand not just this conflation of the pregnant Black body with the "dangerous" body but also the reasons underlying this discursive slippage between the appetites of Black women and the health of Black fetuses.[25]

"The Most Perilous Environment"

Midway through a 1990 article on the emergence of "fetal rights," *Nation* contributor Katha Pollitt pondered: "How have we come to see women as the major threat to the health of their newborns, and the womb as the most dangerous place a child will ever inhabit?" (410) Pollitt was responding to a trend that has been gaining force in conjunction with the movement to recriminalize abortion, a trend epitomized by Gerald Leach's comment in his 1970 book *The Biocrats:* "Quite simply, the womb has become the most perilous environment in which humans have to live" (137). A quarter of a century later, an evolutionary biologist at Harvard, David Haig, brought Leach's claim to fruition by using Darwinian theory to interpret human pregnancy. Because sexual reproduction results in a child's sharing "only half of its genes with the mother," Haig claims that many "difficulties in pregnancy probably come about because there are genetic conflicts between what is best for the mother's genes and what is best for fetal genes" (qtd. in Lipsitch C3). But since under most circumstances the fetus cannot survive if the woman carrying it dies, Haig concludes that pregnancy is "a conflict of interest within a basically peaceful society" (qtd. in Lipsitch C3). In *The Mother Machine* (1985), Gena Corea stresses that such utero-phobia "is not a modern idea" (251). This contemporary flowering of concerns about fetal endangerment is, she and such others as Pollitt contend, at least in part a backlash against second-wave feminism and the Supreme Court's 1973 decision granting women (limited) rights to abortion.

The fetus has indeed emerged as a miniature "person" in its own right.[26] It is granted a status theoretically equal to and in practice above that of the woman who carries it by doctors who now officially specialize in the field of maternal-fetal medicine rather than ob-gyn. The fetus is even the subject of advertisements by the General Motors Corporation, whose researchers have been developing "the first 'pregnant' crash dummy" because, in their words, "Not all passengers can be seen. But they all need protection" (General Motors A16). "Protection from whom?" one might well ask. In her provocative 1992 essay, "The Abortion Question and the Death of Man," Mary Poovey explains how feminist use of both privacy and equality arguments in advocating for abortion has inadvertently contributed to this sacralization of the fetus as a justification for curtailing women's rights. Certainly feminist arguments for abortion have, she points out, been readily appropriated by persons who oppose that right. Thus the slogan "equal rights for women" becomes the bumper sticker "Equal Rights for Unborn Women." In the rhetoric of antiabortionists, Poovey writes, terms such as "'choice,' 'privacy,' and 'rights' invert effortlessly into their opposites, precisely because, regardless of who uses them, these terms belong to a single set of metaphysical assumptions" (249).

Such appropriations are enabled, in other words, by the fact that the "rights" discourses invoked by many feminists rely on the prior figuration of a body—what Poovey calls a "metaphysics of substance"—that is normatively rational, bourgeois, white, heterosexual, and male (241). In this metaphysics the mark of female difference is the womb, which means that, unlike the male body, the female body is always presumptively pregnable.[27] Poovey's response to this dilemma is to insist that advocates for women's reproductive rights not downplay differences among women, differences such as class, race, sexuality, ethnicity, and nationality that determine any given woman's access to "rights." She insists, moreover, that we need to develop a politics that foregrounds the contingency of the "body" and that recognizes that rights are only constituted in a matrix of relationships. It would be difficult to find fault with Poovey's efforts to formulate an approach to reproductive freedom that is less easily appropriated by opponents of feminism and that does not privilege heterosexual middle-class white women as the norm. Yet her analysis (like that of Pollitt) falls short in one important respect. Neither fully takes into account the fact that fetal rights have not emerged solely as a backlash against white feminists, a backlash that is simply played out on the bodies of lower-class women of color because they are more vulnerable to social control than are wealthy whites. Rather, women of color have been a primary target of fetal-rights activists because fear of the Black womb—and by extension, I would argue, fear of the Black female appetite—has provided a primary model from which contemporary fears of white wombs have been derived.

Such fears often operate in fascistically friendly ways—hence my initially optimistic response to the *New York Times* article about the failure of doctors to warn pregnant African American women about the

dangers of smoking and drinking during pregnancy. Yet the punitive un-
derpinnings of such concern for Black women's health are amply illustrated by another article that the *New York Times* published the following day, coincidentally, under the heading "Hospital Is Accused of Illegal
Experiments." It seems that the Medical University of South Carolina
had instituted a drug-testing program "intended to force drug-addicted
women who are pregnant to stop using drugs by threatening them with
jail if they fail to cooperate with the hospital's regimen of prenatal visits
and to attend a drug-treatment program" (Hilts A12). Virtually all the
women targeted by this program were African Americans. Nationwide,
as legal scholar Dorothy Roberts has demonstrated in "Punishing Drug
Addicts Who Have Babies: Women of Color, Equality, and the Right of
Privacy," virtually all the women jailed for taking drugs while pregnant,
forced to undergo unwanted caesareans, or otherwise subjected to forms
of maternal "prior restraint" have been lower-class women of color.

This obsession with "perilous" Black wombs has precedent in the
late 1960s and 1970s—precisely the period when the discourses of eating disorders began taking on their current configurations. In addition
to the obvious example of the Moynihan Report, much Black Power and
Black Arts rhetoric shared the era's fascination with Black matriarchy,
racial genocide, the pill, and abortion. Such African American political
activists as Nation of Islam leader Elijah Muhammad and comic-turned-
nutritionist Dick Gregory not only developed extended critiques of
Black dietary practices (namely of soul food, which they viewed as
"filthy" and "unhealthy") but also focused their critiques particularly on
pregnant and nursing Black women.

In the second volume of his dietary manual *How to Eat to Live,* for
example, Muhammad advises African American women to

> EAT GOOD FOOD so that you will be able to give your baby good,
> pure milk.
> You can drink cows' milk; your own milk glands will put it
> into the right stage for your child. Be careful as to what kind of
> drugs you take while nursing your baby. And do not take fasts
> while you are breast-feeding an infant or even while you are
> pregnant. If you like, you may eat once a day while pregnant or
> breast-feeding your baby, but you are not forced to do so. You
> should not go for two or three days without eating. (90)

The fact that from a contemporary vantage point these strictures seem
quite mild surely suggests the extent to which we have increasingly

become accustomed to treating the bodies of pregnant women as having value only in relation, and in subordination, to the body of the zygote, embryo, or fetus they carry. Muhammad's directive to "eat good food so that you will be able to give your baby good, pure milk" calls to mind a telling question legal theorist Patricia Williams has posed about a Washington, D.C., case in which a judge imprisoned a pregnant African American woman, "ostensibly in order to *protect* her fetus" (184). "Why," Williams muses, "is there no state interest in not simply providing for but improving the circumstances of the woman, whether pregnant or not?" (184) Why, I ask, did the study cited in the *New York Times* not ask whether doctors advised Black women to stop smoking and drinking, whether pregnant or not?

Indeed, Muhammad's strictures presage the contemporary resurgence of efforts to place the blame for so-called social "pathology" on the behavior of pregnant women—particularly impoverished, unmarried women of color—rather than on structural forces of discrimination such as regressive tax policies, declining wages and benefits, cuts in social spending, and concentration of toxic waste dumps in areas with large minority and poor populations.[28] In the first volume of *How to Eat to Live*, Muhammad begins by chastising Black women for their failure to breast-feed but rapidly escalates his rhetoric:

> The baby eats poisonous animals, fowls and vegetables and drinks milk that is not his milk—it belongs to the cow's baby, goat's baby and horse's baby. Here the child is reared on animals' and cattle's food.
>
> This is why we have such a great percentage of delinquency among minors. The child is not fed from his [sic] mother's breast—she is too proud of her form. . . .
>
> When the baby reaches the age of 10, and if it is a male, most of them begin to indulge in drinking alcoholic beverages and using tobacco in one form or another.
>
> Alcohol and tobacco, with their poisonous effect upon the male, cut his life down, as far as his reproductive organs are concerned. He is unable to produce his own kind. (88–89)

The selfish vanity of the Black woman in refusing to breast-feed her son [sic] leads inexorably to his "delinquency," to his alcohol and drug addiction, and then to his impotence or sterility. Yet if such comments are perhaps to be expected from an avowed advocate of Black patriarchy, I was somewhat surprised to encounter similar sentiments coming from the more progressive, women's rights sympathizer Dick Gregory. In his *Dick Gregory's Political Primer,* for example, the then-fasting fruitarian claims that "more boy babies die at birth or shortly thereafter than girl babies, because they are unable to survive the mucus in the mother's system" (260). In Gregory's dietary schema, mucus is a form of what structural anthropologists refer to as ritual "pollution."[29] Such pollution results, Gregory contends, from the consumption of an "unhealthy" diet of soul food and dairy products.

Roberts insists that efforts to understand the motivating force behind this fixation on fetal contamination absolutely must begin with reference to the class, race, and sexuality of the women most likely to be punished for violating fetal-endangerment laws. The discussions of crack babies that proliferated during the 1980s stemmed, she suggests, far more from a cultural imperative to control impoverished women of color than from one to ensure the health and safety of their children:

> If prosecutors had instead chosen to prosecute affluent women addicted to alcohol or prescription medication, the policy of criminalizing prenatal conduct very likely would have suffered a hasty demise. Society is much more willing to condone the punishment of poor women of color who fail to meet the middle-class ideal of motherhood. (1436)

Roberts claims, moreover, that the "government's choice of a punitive response" to prenatal drug use "perpetuates the historical devaluation of Black women as mothers" (1423). Whereas Hortense Spillers has explained the hegemony of American belief in the myth of Black matriarchy as a legacy of slavery's erasure of the Name and Law of the Black Father, Roberts construes the current fixation on lower-class Black maternity as, in part, a legacy of Black women's abuse as "breeders" during slavery (see Spillers). Thus slave owners would whip pregnant slaves by forcing them "to lie down in a depression in the ground while they were whipped. This procedure allowed the masters to protect the fetus while abusing the mother" (Roberts 1438). Such brutality serves, Roberts observes, "as a powerful metaphor for the evils of a fetal protection policy that denies the humanity of the mother" (1438).

In fact, it seems to me that we are witnessing more than a cultural imperative to control women of color; we are witnessing a cultural imperative to control the *appetites* of women of color so as to control the *ontological status* of America. Hence my appropriation of Brillat-Savarin as the speculative thesis of this essay. Given the current level of fixation on national purity, it is, consequently, surely a risky undertaking for African American women to foreground the individual body and appetite as a strategy of empowerment: as Poovey's analysis of the rhetoric of "rights" would suggest, such discourses can readily be redeployed to legitimate ideologies in which Black women are a source of pollution. I envision here the shift from "Fat Is a Feminist Issue" to "Fat Is a Black Woman's Issue" to "Fat Is a Black Fetal Issue"—and indeed studies on whether a "fatty" maternal diet causes childhood cancer have already been conducted (see Raloff). What I wonder is if in constructing the discourse in this fashion, we reinforce American fears of the Black feminine as what Julia Kristeva terms the "abject"—as that which calls into question the boundaries between food and not-food, self and not-self; as that which, because of its overdetermined historical conflation with food, reminds us that our bodily boundaries are not impermeable.[30]

Many of the contributors to *The Black Women's Health Book* acknowledge this double bind. To remain silent about Black female health problems and appetites is to be complicit in a larger cultural erasure of the lives and needs of women of color. At the same time, it is a tricky business for African American women to appropriate discourses that originated via the inscription of their oppression. Can there exist an "anorexic" or "bulimic" Black woman? Can there exist a Caucasian crack baby? Or is the former inevitably defined as a wanna-be-white and the latter as an honorary Black? In the epilogue to his study of male sexuality and social disease in late nineteenth-century England, *Talk on the Wilde Side*, Ed Cohen writes that we need to "imagine how we can historically problematize the ways the 'oppositional' terms of dominance come to be embedded within the categories of resistance" (213). Cohen is referring here specifically to the widespread use of the term *queer* among activists for lesbian and gay rights, but his general point is surely applicable here as well (5). In order to develop an agenda for bettering Black women's health, scholars and activists must work to develop a vocabulary in which Black women are not already inscribed as (1) natural (and therefore never in need of social benefits, such as medical care) or (2) unnatural (and therefore always in need of social regulation).

In a 1987 address entitled "Sick and Tired of Being Sick and Tired: The Politics of Black Women's Health," Angela Davis negotiated these contradictory obstacles by insisting on the "urgency of contextualizing Black women's health in relation to the prevailing political conditions. While our health is undeniably assaulted by natural forces frequently beyond our control, all too often the enemies of our physical and emotional well-being are social and political" (19). Davis proceeded to discuss De-

partment of Defense spending, CIA operations in Angola, Reagan's nom-
ination of Robert Bork to the Supreme Court, apartheid in South Africa,
and continuing congressional support for the Nicaraguan contras—all of
which she construed as integral to the politics of Black women's health.
"We must," she concluded, "learn consistently to place our battle for universally accessible health care in its larger social and political context"
(25). In her refusal to distinguish between bodily and social boundaries,
in her insistence (along with Audre Lorde) that "battling racism and battling heterosexism and battling apartheid share the same urgency inside
me as battling cancer," Davis offers a template for the sort of political
praxis Mary Poovey has in mind (Davis 26).[31] It is a template for a political praxis that, at the very least, attempts to be less than amenable to
reappropriation by the reactionary right. The efficacy of such "politics
unbound" is yet to be determined, but it seems to me that Davis's lead is,
as ever, a wise one to follow.

NOTES

Portions of this essay are excerpted from my dissertation, "What Ever Happened
to Aunt Jemima? Black Women and Food in American Culture" (University of
Virginia, 1995). I am indebted to Barbara Green, Tania Modleski, Alice Gambrell,
Janet Lyon, and audiences at the Universities of Iowa, Notre Dame, Pittsburgh,
and SUNY–Buffalo for their thoughtful responses to an earlier draft. I also thank
Deborah McDowell, Eric Lott, Susan Fraiman, and Bluford Adams for their ongoing involvement with the project that gave rise to this essay.

1. I received the two-page release ("Aunt Jemima Trademark Design to Be
Updated") from Quaker Oats, along with a publicity pamphlet, *The Quaker Q
and How It Grew,* in response to my (repeated) inquiries for information about
the trademark.

2. For a concise history of the "mammy" stereotype, see Phil Patton's "Mammy:
Her Life and Times."

3. And, of course, "good taste" would be the attribute of the consumer who
chooses to buy Aunt Jemima products. Judith Williamson's discussion of such
semantic shifts in *Decoding Advertisements* has been very helpful to my thinking
about the Aunt Jemima trademark. The title of a 1989 *Newsweek* article by Marcus Mabry, "A Long Way from 'Aunt Jemima'"—which focuses on advertisers'
efforts to reach an expanding Black consumer market in the 1980s—would suggest that the trademark image has been antithetical to the recognition of Black
consumer appetites.

4. Agnew's description is slightly inaccurate. The kerchief was removed during the 1968 makeover and replaced with a headband.

5. My analysis here draws on an early essay by Julia Kristeva. In "From Symbol to Sign"—excerpted from her thesis, *La Révolution du langage poétique*—
Kristeva argues that the "second half of the Middle Ages (thirteenth to fifteenth

centuries) was a period of transition for European culture: thought based on the sign replaced that based on the symbol" (64). The mode of the symbol "is a cosmogonic semiotic practice where the elements (symbols) refer back to one or more unknowable and unrepresentable universal transcendence(s). . . . [W]ithin its vertical function, the sign refers back to entities of lesser dimensions that are more *concretized* than the symbol. . . . Within their horizontal function, the units of the sign's semiotic practice are articulated as a *metonymic chain of deflections* [*écarts*] that signifies a *progressive creation of metaphors*" (64–70). In other words, Agnew begins neither with the Quaker Oats press release telling us that the new image preserves the abstract symbolic meaning of the old one nor in treating it as a sign that has "vertical" reference to "entities of lesser dimensions that are more *concretized* than the symbol" (that is, a middle-class consumer). Instead he interprets the trademark via what Kristeva calls its "horizontal" reference, embarking upon a "*metonymic chain of deflections* [*écarts*] that signifies a *progressive creation of metaphors*" (70).

6. The *TV Guide* scandal was fodder for tabloids, comedians, and others during the fall of 1989. Joshua Gamson discusses briefly the significance of the *TV Guide* misrepresentation in *Claims to Fame: Celebrity in Contemporary America* (100). The vicissitudes of Winfrey's weight and the minutiae of her dietary habits are documented by Nellie Bly in *Oprah! Up Close and Down Home*. Her most recent weight loss has also provided the occasion for "the fastest-selling cookbook in history," Rosie Daley's *In the Kitchen with Rosie: Oprah's Favorite Recipes* (Sanz and Fisher 85). Daley is Winfrey's personal chef.

7. I discuss the history of the trademark in the prologue to my dissertation.

8. See, for example, discussions of the ideology and/or portrayal of Black womanhood in Davis's "The Legacy of Slavery: Standards for a New Womanhood"; Christian's "Images of Black Women in Afro-American Literature: From Stereotype to Character"; hooks's *Ain't I a Woman*; White's *Ar'n't I a Woman?*; Spillers's "Mama's Baby, Papa's Maybe: An American Grammar Book"; McDowell's introduction to Nella Larsen's *Quicksand and Passing*; Collins's *Black Feminist Thought*; and Jewell's *From Mammy to Miss America and Beyond*. Jewell also has a chapter specifically on Aunt Jemima in her dissertation, "An Analysis of the Visual Development of a Stereotype: The Media's Portrayal of Mammy and Aunt Jemima as Symbols of Black Womanhood."

9. This is the fourth aphorism listed in the preamble to *The Physiology of Taste* (3).

10. Two exceptions include James J. Gray, Kathryn Ford, and Lily M. Kelly, "The Prevalence of Bulimia in a Black College Population"; and George L. K. Hsu, "Are the Eating Disorders Becoming More Common in Blacks?"

11. Their comments, I should mention, were unsolicited on my part. The issue arose when each student was explaining excessive class absences and her failure to turn in work on time. Perhaps I was merely adjudged likely to sympathize with such an excuse, but I have no reason to doubt the sincerity of either student.

12. See, for example, the prologue (1–3).

13. The text of what is widely known as the "Moynihan Report" is reprinted in *The Moynihan Report and the Politics of Controversy: A Transaction Social Science and Public Policy Report* (1967).

14. She does so, I stress, just as the neoconservative and new right backlash came to fruition with the ascendancy of Ronald Reagan (and his demonization of "Cadillac-driving welfare queens") to the U.S. presidency.

15. One thinks, for example, of Walker's *Meridian.* Eponymous heroine Meridian Hill displays symptoms of anorexia that might be interpreted using Caroline Bynum's analysis of medieval women saints in *Holy Feast and Holy Fast,* as well as Chernin's psychoanalytic analysis of contemporary anorexia nervosa. In Naylor's *Linden Hills,* aspiring buppie Roxanne Tilson frequently indulges in late-night binges, and one of the Nedeed wives from the book's fictive past has cooked, purged, and starved, until, we are told, she literally "eat[s] herself to death" (190). Honey, the narrator of Ferrell's "Eating Confessions," is by contrast an overweight African American woman who socializes with her friend Rose at the "Monday Night Determination Diet Meeting" (453). Their food-structured relationship is disrupted, however, when Rose meets a man and loses weight and Honey uses food in an unsuccessful attempt to lure her away from him.

16. See, for example, Georgiana Arnold's "Coming Home: One Black Woman's Journey to Health and Fitness."

17. Thus in *Unbearable Weight* Bordo writes:

> Arguably, a case could once be made for a contrast between (middle-class, heterosexual) white women's obsessive relations with food and a more accepting attitude toward women's appetites within African American communities. But in the nineties, features on diet, exercise, and body image problems have grown increasingly prominent in magazines aimed at African American readers, reflecting the cultural reality that for most women today—whatever their racial or ethnic identity, and increasingly across class and sexual-orientation differences as well—free and easy relations with food are at best a relic of the past. (103)

18. As she acknowledges, moreover, there have long been regulatory practices of Black femininity—hair straightening, skin bleaching, et cetera—and any discussion of Black women and eating disorders needs to situate eating practices as part of a whole range of practices through which African American women have, in Judith Butler's term, historically "performed" their identities.

19. I am grateful to Valerie Sayers and Kevin Kopelson for questioning my omission of male appetite, and I hope to offer a more detailed response in the near future.

20. In *Imitation of Life,* the book on which subsequent movies were based, Fannie Hurst describes Delilah as "a buxom negro woman who, with the best intentions in the world, swelled the food budget so considerably" (100). Shortly thereafter Hurst writes that "there was no suppressing the enormity that was Delilah, nor was there desire to suppress it" (103).

Curiously, however, notwithstanding the attention recently paid to *Imitation of Life* in the academy, to my knowledge no one has pointed out that two years after *Imitation of Life* appeared, Hurst published a brief autobiographical narrative entitled *No Food with My Meals.* There she describes her obsession with the slimming craze, which she says began to overcome her around 1931—just as she was writing *Imitation of Life,* "Some women are born frail," Hurst announces, with characteristic aplomb. "Some have frailty thrust upon them. Still others achieve it, and at what price glory!" (2) Hurst concludes *No Food with My Meals* with a list of "acknowledgments" (55), including one "to the books written during this period which abound perhaps unduly in foods coveted by their author" (56). Though Hurst never directly mentions *Imitation of Life,* she might be admitting that her own desire for and fear of food (and fat) resulted in her having projected onto the character Delilah a psychology untouched by the slimming fad. Delilah, in other words, represents a dual mode of novelistic wish fulfillment: she is both the object of Hurst's derision, that which Hurst loathes in herself, and what Hurst wishes she could be—able to experience and satisfy her appetite "naturally."

21. Brumberg points out that she is "not a recovered anorectic nor . . . the mother of an anorexic daughter" but otherwise does not dwell on possible personal investments she might have in her scholarly work on anorexia (1). I would like to thank Gloria-Jean Masciarotte for pointing out to me that one can only talk about anorexic, bulimic, or fat bodies via reference to the ethnicity of the body under consideration. There are, in other words, distinctions to be made among Caucasian, Jewish, Italian, Chinese, Chicana, and other ethnic bodily "norms." I hope to respond in greater detail to Masciarotte's comments in the future.

22. When criticized for playing stereotypical "mammy" characters, McDaniel was known to have responded, "Why should I complain about making seven thousand dollars a week playing a maid? If I didn't, I'd be making seven dollars a week actually being one!" (qtd. in Bogle 82)

23. Roxanne Brown's *Ebony* article, "Full-Figured Women Fight Back," offers a less explicitly politicized example of how African American women have appropriated the large female body as a mode of cultural resistance. My thanks to the audience member at the University of Iowa who questioned my failure to mention "black bottoms" in an earlier draft of this chapter.

24. This despite the fact that from 1970 to 1980, according to Mimi Abramovitz, "the unmarried black birth rate . . . fell by 13 percent, while that of whites rose by 27 percent" (354). In *Regulating the Lives of Women,* Abramovitz further points out that the "dramatic increase in the percentage of births to unmarried black women reflects a drop in the overall fertility and birth rates of *married* black women relative to *unmarried* black women, and not an increase in child bearing by the latter" (354).

25. One reader suggested that I ought perhaps to be explicit in stating that because Black women are, in the Moynihanian view, always pregnant, "the fat body is interchangeable with the pregnant body." In the process of writing an affirmation of this comment, I realized that I am not at all sure that my analysis actually demonstrates it—at least not in sweeping semiotic terms rather than local historicized ones. In addition, one would need to take into account variations in the representation of the fat body: sometimes breasts are emphasized, sometimes stomachs, sometimes butts. Sometimes the boundaries are (as Susan Bordo would doubtless point out) "wiggly" and at other times, controlled (see 191–92).

26. Rosalind Petchesky discusses the significance of technologies enabling fetal visualization in her *Abortion and Woman's Choice* (335–45). See also Robyn Rowland's discussion of fetal personhood in *Living Laboratories* (118–55).

27. In *The Female Body and the Law,* feminist political theorist Zillah Eisen-

stein also explores the ramifications of the legal presumption that the womb is the sign of female difference.

28. I use quotation marks around "pathology" to emphasize my disagreement with the racist, homophobic, patriarchal assumptions embedded in "culture of pathology" arguments about inner cities, for instance the assumption that male-headed nuclear households should be normative.

29. Ritual pollution, according to Mary Douglas, stems from a violation of socially constructed boundaries such as those of gender. See her *Purity and Danger.*

30. Kristeva develops her theory of abjection in *Powers of Horror.*

31. Davis is quoting here from Audre Lorde's *A Burst of Light* (116–17).

REFERENCES

Abramovitz, Mimi. *Regulating the Lives of Women: Social Welfare Policy from Colonial Times to the Present.* Boston: South End Press, 1988.

Agnew, Jean-Christophe. "Shop till You Drop: How the West Was Sold." Review of *Satisfaction Guaranteed: The Making of the American Mass Market,* by Susan Strasser. *Voice Literary Supplement,* December 1989, 29–30.

Arnold, Georgiana. "Coming Home: One Black Woman's Journey to Health and Fitness." In Evelyn C. White, ed., *The Black Women's Health Book: Speaking for Ourselves,* 269–79. Seattle: Seal Press, 1990.

"Aunt Jemima Trademark Design to Be Updated." News release. Chicago: Quaker Oats Co., 27 April 1989.

Bly, Nellie. *Oprah! Up Close and Down Home.* New York: Zebra-Kensington, 1993.

Bogle, Donald. *Toms, Coons, Mulattoes, Mammies, and Bucks: An Interpretive History of Blacks in American Films.* 1973. Viking. Reprint, New York: Continuum, 1991.

Bordo, Susan. *Unbearable Weight: Feminism, Western Culture, and the Body.* Berkeley: University of California Press, 1993.

Brillat-Savarin, Jean Anthelme. *The Physiology of Taste.* 1825. Trans. M. F. K. Fisher. San Francisco: North Point, 1986.

Brown, Roxanne. "Full-Figured Women Fight Back." *Ebony,* March 1990, 27–31.

Brumberg, Joan Jacobs. *Fasting Girls: The History of Anorexia Nervosa.* New York: Plume-Penguin, 1989.

Bynum, Caroline Walker. *Holy Feast and Holy Fast: The Religious Significance of Food to Medieval Women.* Berkeley: University of California Press, 1987.

Chernin, Kim. *The Obsession: Reflections on the Tyranny of Slenderness.* New York: Perennial-Harper, 1981.

Christian, Barbara. "Images of Black Women in Afro-American Literature: From Stereotype to Character." 1975. In *Black Feminist Criticism: Perspectives on Black Women Writers,* 1–30. New York: Pergamon, 1985.

Cohen, Ed. *Talk on the Wilde Side: Toward a Genealogy of a Discourse on Male Sexualities.* New York: Routledge, 1993.

Collins, Patricia Hill. *Black Feminist Thought: Knowledge, Consciousness, and the Politics of Empowerment.* 1990. Boston: Unwin Hyman. Reprint, New York: Routledge, 1991.

Corea, Gena. *The Mother Machine: Reproductive Technologies from Artificial Insemination to Artificial Wombs.* New York: Harper, 1985.

Daley, Rosie. *In the Kitchen with Rosie: Oprah's Favorite Recipes.* New York: Knopf, 1994.

Davis, Angela. "The Legacy of Slavery: Standards for a New Womanhood." In *Women, Race and Class,* 3–29. New York: Vintage-Random, 1981.

———. "Sick and Tired of Being Sick and Tired: The Politics of Black Women's Health." In Evelyn C. White, ed., *The Black Women's Health Book: Speaking for Ourselves,* 18–26. Seattle: Seal Press, 1990.

Douglas, Mary. *Purity and Danger: An Analysis of the Concepts of Pollution and Taboo.* London: Ark-Routledge, 1966.

Eisenstein, Zillah. *The Female Body and the Law.* Berkeley: University of California Press, 1988.

Ferrell, Carolyn. "Eating Confessions." *Callaloo* 12, no. 3 (1989): 453–64.

Gamson, Joshua. *Claims to Fame: Celebrity in Contemporary America.* Berkeley: University of California Press, 1994.

General Motors. Advertisement. *Washington Post,* 16 May 1994, A16.

Gray, James J., Kathryn Ford, and Lily M. Kelly. "The Prevalence of Bulimia in a Black College Population." *International Journal of Eating Disorders* 6, no. 6 (1987): 733–40.

Gregory, Dick. *Dick Gregory's Political Primer.* Ed. James R. McGraw. New York: Perennial-Harper, 1972.

Hilts, Philip J. "Hospital Is Accused of Illegal Experiments." *New York Times,* 21 January 1994, A12.

hooks, bell. *Ain't I a Woman: Black Women and Feminism.* Boston: South End Press, 1981.

———. *Sisters of the Yam: Black Women and Self-Recovery.* Boston: South End Press, 1993.

Hsu, L. K. George. "Are the Eating Disorders Becoming More Common in Blacks?" *International Journal of Eating Disorders* 6, no. 1 (1987): 113–24.

Hurst, Fannie. *Imitation of Life.* 1933. Reprint, New York: Pyramid, 1974.

———. *No Food with My Meals.* New York: Harper, 1935.

Jewell, Karen Sue Warren. "An Analysis of the Visual Development of a Stereotype: The Media's Portrayal of Mammy and Aunt Jemima as Symbols of Black Womanhood." Ph.D. diss., Ohio State University, 1976.

———. *From Mammy to Miss America and Beyond: Cultural Images and the Shaping of U.S. Social Policy.* New York: Routledge, 1993.

Jordan, June. *Passion: New Poems, 1977–1980.* Boston: Beacon Press, 1980.

Key, Janet. "At Age One Hundred, a New Aunt Jemima." *Chicago Tribune,* 28 April 1989, sec. 3, 1,6.

Kristeva, Julia. "From Symbol to Sign." Trans. Seán Hand. 1970. In Toril Moi, ed., *The Kristeva Reader,* 62–73. New York: Columbia University Press, 1986.

———. *Powers of Horror: An Essay on Abjection.* 1980. Trans. Leon S. Roudiez. New York: Columbia University Press, 1982.

Leach, Gerald. *The Biocrats.* New York: McGraw-Hill, 1970.

Lipsitch, Marc. "Genetic Tug-of-War May Explain Many of the Troubles of Pregnancy." *New York Times,* 20 July 1993, C3.

Lorde, Audre. *A Burst of Light.* Ithaca: Firebrand, 1988.

Mabry, Marcus. "A Long Way From 'Aunt Jemima': As Black Consumers' Spending Grows, Marketers Target Them with Hipper and More 'Authentic' Ads." With Rhonda Adams. *Newsweek*, 14 August 1989, 34–35.

McDowell, Deborah. Introduction to Quicksand *and* Passing, by Nella Larsen, ix–xxxvii. New Brunswick, N.J.: Rutgers University Press, 1987.

Modleski, Tania. *Feminism without Women: Culture and Criticism in a "Postfeminist" Age*. New York: Routledge, 1991.

Moynihan, Daniel P. *The Negro Family: The Case for National Action* ["The Moynihan Report"]. Washington, D.C.: U.S. Department of Labor, 1965.

Muhammad, Elijah. *How to Eat to Live*. Chicago: Muhammad Mosque of Islam No. 2, 1967.

———. *How to Eat to Live*. Bk. 2. Chicago: Muhammad Mosque of Islam No. 2, 1972.

Naylor, Gloria. *Linden Hills*. New York: Viking-Penguin, 1985.

Newcomb, Peter, and Lisa Gubernick. "The Top 40." *Forbes*, 27 September 1993, 97–104.

Orbach, Susie. *Fat Is a Feminist Issue: A Self-Help Guide for Compulsive Eaters*. New York: Berkeley-Paddington, 1978.

Patton, Phil. "Mammy: Her Life and Times." *American Heritage* (September 1993): 78–87.

Petchesky, Rosalind Pollack. *Abortion and Woman's Choice: The State, Sexuality, and Reproductive Freedom*. 1984. New York: Longman, 1984. Reprint, Boston: Northeastern University Press, 1990.

Pollitt, Katha. "'Fetal Rights': A New Assault on Feminism." *Nation*, 26 March 1990, 409–18.

Poovey, Mary. "The Abortion Question and the Death of Man." In Judith Butler and Joan Scott, eds., *Feminists Theorize the Political*, 239–56. New York: Routledge, 1992.

Powers, Retha. "Fat Is a Black Woman's Issue." *Essence*, October 1989, 75–78*ff*.

"The Quaker Q and How It Grew." Pamphlet. Chicago: Quaker Oats Co., 1979.

Rainwater, Lee, and William L. Yancey, eds. *The Moynihan Report and the Politics of Controversy: A Trans-action Social Science and Public Policy Report*. Cambridge: MIT Press, 1967.

Raloff, Janet. "Mom's Fatty Diet May Induce Child's Cancer." *Science News*, 6 January 1990, 5.

Roberts, Dorothy. "Punishing Drug Addicts Who Have Babies: Women of Color, Equality, and the Right of Privacy." *Harvard Law Review* 104 (May 1991): 1419–82.

Rose, Tricia. *Black Noise: Rap Music and Black Culture in Contemporary America*. Hanover, N.H.: Wesleyan University Press, 1994.

Rowland, Robyn. *Living Laboratories: Women and Reproductive Technologies*. Bloomington: Indiana University Press, 1992.

Sanz, Cynthia, and Luchina Fisher. "Cookin' for Oprah." *People*, 16 May 1994, 84–88.

Spillers, Hortense J. "Mama's Baby, Papa's Maybe: An American Grammar Book." *Diacritics* 17 (summer, 1987): 65–81.

"Study Finds Racial Disparity in Warnings to the Pregnant." *New York Times*, 20 January 1994, A16.

261

Thompson, Becky Wangsgaard. "'A Way Outa No Way': Eating Problems Among African-American, Latina, and White Women." *Gender and Society* 6, no. 4 (1992): 545–61.

Walker, Alice. "Giving the Party: Aunt Jemima, Mammy, and the Goddess Within." *Ms.,* May–June 1994, 22–25.

———. *Meridian.* New York: Pocket-Simon, 1976.

Weinraub, Judith. "Model with That Something Extra." *Washington Post,* 4 February 1993, C1,4.

White, Deborah Gray. *Ar'n't I a Woman? Female Slaves in the Plantation South.* New York: W. W. Norton, 1985.

White, Evelyn C., ed. *The Black Women's Health Book: Speaking for Ourselves.* Seattle: Seal Press, 1990.

Williams, Patricia. *The Alchemy of Race and Rights: Diary of a Law Professor.* Cambridge: Harvard University Press, 1991.

Williamson, Judith. *Decoding Advertisements.* London: Boyars, 1978.

Terri Kapsalis

Mastering the Female Pelvis

Race and the Tools of Reproduction

> And if in these days a moment can be spared for
> sentimental reverie, look again, I beg, at the curious
> speculum, and gazing through the confused reflections
> from its bright curves, catch a fleeting glimpse of an old
> hut in Alabama and seven negro women who suffered,
> and endured, and had rich reward.
> —J. Chassar Moir, M.D., *The Vesico-Vaginal Fistula*

During the four years between 1845 and 1849, J. Marion Sims, M.D., conducted surgical experiments on slave women in his backyard hospital in Montgomery, Alabama. These women all had vesico-vaginal fistulas, small tears that form between the vagina and urinary tract or bladder that cause urine to leak uncontrollably. Through repeated surgeries, Sims attempted to repair the fistulas. He is now remembered as the Father of American Gynecology, Father of Modern Gynecology, and Architect of the Vagina. Following the eventual success of the surgical reparation, Sims won illustrious titles, awards, and fame worldwide and praising words in most contemporary gynecology and medical history texts.[1] By his own estimation he became "the second wealthiest of all American physicians."[2] As we shall see, Sims's fame and wealth are as indebted to slavery and racism as they are to innovation, insight, and persistence, and he has left behind a frightening legacy of medical attitudes toward and treatments of women, particularly women of color. These four years of surgical experimentation on slave women represent the foundation of gynecology as a distinct specialty.

Through an investigation of Sims's practices, a number of important distinctions regarding the foundation of gynecology become clear. First, the institution of slavery served medicine in providing subjects for experimentation. The gynecological patients' position as slaves defined their status as medical subjects, situating them as institutionally powerless and therefore as fitting props for the experimenting white physician-turned-master-showman, who revealed, probed, and operated on their vaginas. Slavery enabled the foundation of gynecology and in the process helped define the proper objective of medical experimentation.

Second, the use of the speculum in North America was founded on slave women's bodies. This medical precedent prompts questions that will be asked throughout this chapter: What kind of woman is considered to be most appropriate for speculum examination? How does gynecological display structure physician-patient power differentials? The position of Sims's patients as slaves made them more fitting objects for speculum penetration and the physician's gaze while, at the same time, their status as slaves was reiterated by the physician's probing gaze and penetrating speculum as tools of medical discipline. An investigation of this historic medical innovation provides insight into the way gynecology continues to situate patients.

Third, Sims's surgical experimentation set a precedent for the medical institution's involvement in racist, eugenicist practices concerned with the reproductive capacities of poor women of color. His surgical reparation can be viewed as an early reproductive technology aimed at helping to optimize the reproductive capacity of slave capital. In a welfare-state economy, reproductive technologies to foster pregnancy are often marketed at wealthy, predominantly white women, whereas new technologies aimed at limiting reproduction are most often used experimentally on poor women of color and subsequently aimed at them through accessibility and legislated incentives. Norplant, a surgically implanted contraceptive, will be investigated as a technological offspring of Sims's surgical reparation of vesico-vaginal fistulas. This association does not assume or assert that either technology is inherently "bad" but rather points to the ways in which technological innovation and use are generated by and help reinforce ideological structures, including institutionalized racism. Thus an investigation of Sims's practices provides a look at foundational moments in gynecology. Racism, slavery, and the thrill of medical innovation were all joined in the early days of the discipline. Their reverberations are still felt today.

Master Showman

As a historical player, Sims is key to a consideration of the relationship between performance and gynecology. In fact, performance is often enlisted as an explanatory model for Sims's behavior. In his autobiography, eulogies following his death, and a biography published in 1950, Sims is rhetorically positioned as a sensational surgical performer. His patients, however, are situated as passive, proplike objects rather than co-performers. By simply orchestrating the unveiling of the previously mysterious internal landscape of the live female pelvis, Sims gained vast fame and devoted followers, and his dramatic surgeries cemented his reputation as a master showman. Early in his career, he performed to a small audience of eager physicians in his makeshift backyard hospital, but later he played to larger and larger crowds at the Woman's Hospital in New York, as well as in famous operating theaters abroad.

Seale Harris, M.D., Sims's biographer and the son of one of his disciples, notes, "Sims had a great love for the theater and everything dramatic, and he was fascinated by P. T. Barnum's combination of master showmanship (for which he himself had a not inconsiderable gift)." In his autobiography, Sims mentions "spending time with my good friend Mr. P. T. Barnum" in the summer of 1849 in New Orleans.[3] What might link a surgeon–slave master to a showman-ringmaster? Both exercise mastery over bodies, particularly grotesque bodies (in the sense of either open, oozing bodies or freaks). The high drama of surgery, like the daring circus feat, demands courage in order to perform that which seems impossible. And both the ringmaster and the surgeon–slave master perform to large audiences, commanding center stage.[4]

Barnum's shows and exhibits were simultaneously science, art, education, and entertainment. Oftentimes, ambiguities in race and even species served as the titillating freakishness for his exhibits. For instance, the Leopard Child, a young boy with vitiligo, a condition that causes abnormal pigmentation, was a "favorite with spectators at the American Museum."[5] William Henry Johnson, an African American known as "Zip," was exhibited in Barnum's Gallery of Wonders as a missing link, which could be a "lower order of man" or a "higher order of monkey."[6]

Of special interest is Joice Heth, "a blind, decrepit, hymn-singing" slave woman for whom Barnum purchased "the right to exhibit." He claimed Heth was 161 years old and had been nurse to George Washington.[7] Before her death, Barnum promised Dr. David L. Rogers, "an eminent New York surgeon who had examined Joice upon her first arrival in the metropolis, that he would have the opportunity to dissect her should she die while under Barnum's management."[8] When the time came, there gathered "a large crowd of physicians, medical students, clergymen, and (naturally) editors, each of whom was assessed fifty cents for this extraordinary privilege." In the end, the surgeon found that Heth was not even eighty.

What is freakish is not the boy with vitiligo or the slave women with vesico-vaginal fistulas. Rather, the true atrocities are the methods enlisted to display the "freaks" and the atrocious types of intervention used. Both Sims's and Barnum's spectacles were consistently fashioned as simultaneously passive, proplike freaks and uncontrolled bodies in need of taming. Though one commanded center stage in a hospital and the other in a circus, what links Sims and Barnum is a fascination with difference, ambiguity, and pathology, a fascination that is premised on race, power, exhibition, and visibility.

The Fistula

Sims did not plan to found his career on "disorders peculiar to women." In his autobiography, *The Story of My Life,* he admits, "If there was anything I hated, it was investigating the organs of the female pelvis."[9] Yet "women's problems" seemed to court him in his small general practice. He was repeatedly confronted with one particular condition: the vesico-vaginal fistula. Often a result of hard and extended childbirth, fistulas are what Sims referred to as "the sloughing of the soft parts."

Although white women also developed fistulas, when slaves developed them they were often blamed for not having called on white male physicians during difficult labor: "the [slave] women preferred to suffer in seclusion than to call for help at such time."[10] As Elizabeth Fox-Genovese notes in *Within the Plantation Household,* slaves largely distrusted white doctors, preferring Black "root doctors" and herbal remedies, reflecting "African as well as local folk beliefs."[11] Elaborate systems of care were in place in many slave communities, providing slaves with treatments preferable to what they must have viewed as the dangerous practices upheld by the growing white male medical establishment at that time. But lay practitioners, particularly Black ones, were systematically denounced by physicians who relegated them to the realm of malpractice. In a eulogy for Sims, one physician recounted that Sims "was not slow in finding cases of this disgusting disease, particularly among

the slave population, whose management in accouchement was generally confined to the ignorant midwives of their own colour."[12] A favorite
target of white male physicians, Black midwives were held responsible
for the slaves' vesico-vaginal fistulas.

Almost two-thirds of Montgomery's population at that time was
slaves. Sims's participation in the institution of slavery is explained in his
biography: "The Simses themselves owned a number of Negroes. . . . It
was the only way that they knew, and to them it seemed a good one."[13]
Sims even purchased a slave expressly for the purpose of experimentation when her master resisted Sims's solicitations. Certainly the prevailing institution of slavery afforded Sims an opportune scenario in which
to operate. Sims was then construed as their savior, an "evangelist of
healing to women," who could no longer turn his back on these helpless
sufferers.[14] Part of this messianic role included rescuing them from the
"mis-management" of their own midwives.

Sims did not initially accept the challenge of the fistula. A slave
master contacted him to check on a slave named Anarcha who had been
in labor for three days. Sims proceeded to remove the baby with a for-
ceps. All seemed to be fine with the woman, but five days later Sims
found an extensive fistula that caused her to leak both urine and bowel.
He had never before seen this condition and initially considered it a
"surgical curiosity." Later, after reexamining the literature and finding
that the condition had been noted but no physician had ever successfully repaired it, he explained to the woman's master that there was no
hope of mending the fistula. In his autobiography, Sims re-creates his
words to the master: "Anarcha has an affliction that unfits her for the
duties required of a servant. She will not die, but she will never get well,
and all you have to do is to take good care of her so long as she lives."[15]

Here, Sims's first concern is Anarcha's ability to work. How would
the fistula have made the slave unfit for her duties? While the fistula
made this woman smell of bowel and urine, it would not have diminished her strength or ability to work. Sims's comment could be a reference to the fact that slave women were viewed as the "breeding" property of their masters. The slave's "duties" may refer not only to her labor
as a slave in terms of work in the fields or house but also to her sexual
and reproductive duties: "Owners had a financial interest in slaves producing children and openly encouraged 'breeding.' Women known as
breeders brought higher prices on the slave market and might enjoy special privileges, such as a job in the master's house rather than in the
fields."[16] With this "disgusting disease" the slave would no longer be attractive or fit, thereby affecting her reproductive labor as a woman who

would bear future slave labor. As Deborah Gray White asserts, "The perpetuation of the institution of slavery, as nineteenth century Southerners knew it, rested on the slave woman's reproductive capacity."[17] Viewing Black female bodies as capital, slave owners found this bothersome condition troubling indeed. In addition, slave women were frequently approached as receptacles of white male sexual power: white men "expected to exercise sexual freedom with women slaves. Especially within the planter class, relations with black women provided white men with both a sexual outlet and a means of maintaining racial dominance."[18] The smell of urine and bowel would undoubtedly undermine this particular means of maintaining power over slave women.[19]

Masters were not unfamiliar with slave women being unfit for their duties because of their reproductive organs. Slave women sometimes used the knowledge that masters were particularly invested in their reproductive abilities to their advantage. A number of historians of slavery have noted evidence that some slave women feigned illness related to their reproductive organs, "playing the lady," as it was called, in order to temporarily diminish or eliminate their workload.[20] By "playing the lady," slave women were performing white womanhood, enlisting illness as a mode of resistance in order to manipulate their white masters' historically situated fears regarding the delicate and unpredictable female reproductive organs so vital to the masters' profits. In the case of "playing the lady," we find that femininity, performativity, pathology, and the reproductive organs are frequently thought to be interdependent.

Some masters were unsympathetic to slave women's illnesses, feigned or otherwise, and created various performances of their own that discouraged such resistance. As White notes, "Some masters insisted on giving the 'patient' a thorough examination before excusing her from work."[21] A slave who was "playing the lady" could potentially be faced with a master "playing doctor," a power-laden sexual and fact-finding threat. However, illness affecting slave women's reproductive labor was not taken lightly because it seriously threatened a master's earnings. Physicians such as Sims were called on to help when it was found that indeed the slave woman was not simply "playing."

About a month after Anarcha's examination, another slave woman, Betsey, was sent to Sims for inspection because she could not hold urine. She too had a fistula, and Sims sent her back to her master, explaining that he could do nothing. One month following Betsey's visit, Sims was contacted by a master whose slave Lucy had the same symptoms as Betsey. Despite Sims's protest that the master need not bother sending the woman, Lucy was sent and indeed, upon examination, was found to have a fistula. Sims gave her a bed in his homemade backyard hospital for "Negroes," but he informed her she had to leave the following afternoon. In his autobiography he wrote: "She was very much disappointed, for her condition was loathsome, and she was in hope that she could be cured."[22] Thus, in the autobiography, the stage is rhetorically set for the entrance of willing experimentees.

The next morning Sims attended a white woman who had been thrown from a horse and had landed on her pelvis. Remembering an early lesson from a teacher in medical school, Sims believed that he needed to "relocate" the uterus, an idea consistent with nineteenth-century medical beliefs that the uterus could easily dislodge from its proper place, causing untold emotional and physical problems. In order to "relocate" the uterus, he had the woman assume a position on her knees and elbows, covered her with a large sheet, inserted two fingers into her vagina, and found, just as his teacher had promised, that a suction was created that extended the vagina to full capacity.[23] This event caused Sims to reconsider his ability to repair fistulas. If the vagina would "puff up" in this position, then why couldn't he introduce an instrument that would enable him to visualize the fistula and thus repair it?

Conveniently enough, Lucy was still in Sims's backyard hospital. He bought a pewter spoon on his way home. Upon arrival, he hurriedly assembled his two medical-student apprentices and placed Lucy in the knee-chest position for examination: "Introducing the bent handle of the spoon I saw everything, as no man had ever seen before. The fistula was as plain as the nose on a man's face."[24] This historic moment has since achieved mythological status as the first use of a vaginal speculum, commonly known as Sims's speculum, in North America (see fig. 40).

"As plain as the nose on a man's face" is a strange expression to use in conjunction with the initial "discovery" of vaginal visibility. It is as though Sims saw his own image, a self-portrait, reflected back at him in the pewter spoon. I will consider the implications of the speculum as a place for self-reflection later in this chapter. What is significant is the fact that the speculum was "discovered" in a slave woman's body. Visibility, ownership, labor, capital, medical discovery, and slavery all met at the site of the first speculum exam.

The Speculum

Although vaginal speculums in various forms had been noted as early as A.D. 97, they had not found their way into modern American medical

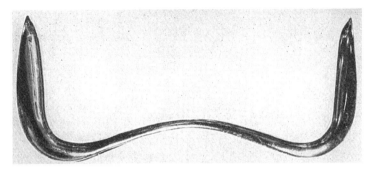

Fig. 40. Sims's speculum. In Emil Novak, M.D., and Edmund R. Novak, M.D., eds., *Textbook of Gynecology*. Baltimore: Williams and Wilkins, 1956.

practice until Sims examined Lucy.[25] There is no question that the speculum is a highly significant technology, and its discovery in part accounts for Sims's title, as the Father of Modern Gynecology. In eulogizing Sims, W. O. Baldwin, M.D., emphasized the instrument's importance:

> The day which made him great was the day the idea of his speculum first dawned upon him—that day when he first conceived the thought of throwing an abundance of light into the vagina and around the womb, and at the same time obtaining ample space to work and ply his instruments. . . . The instrument caused his name to flash over the medical world like a meteor in the night. Gynaecology to-day would not deserve the name of a separate and cultivated science, but for the light which Sims's speculum and the principles involved in it have thrown upon it.[26]

Images of light and enlightenment abound in Baldwin's text. By "throwing an abundance of light" into the dark cavity, Sims made the invisible visible. One cannot help but recall here Freud's notion of woman as "the dark continent" and its "link to the nineteenth-century colonialist imagination."[27] If woman is dark, in this case doubly "dark" due to her mysterious anatomy and African origins, Sims is the source of enlightenment, constructing knowledge about her internal depths. In her discussion of medical stories in women's films of the 1940s, Mary Ann Doane has analyzed the continual narrative return to images of light. She notes: "Light also enables the look, the male gaze—it makes the woman specularizable. The doctor's light legitimates scopophilia."[28] The light introduced by Sims's speculum allowed for an entirely new medical specialty premised on the vaginal spectacle. Sims drew the labial curtains, propped open the vaginal walls, and revealed an entirely new vision; this accounts for his epithet Architect of the Vagina. Making the internal structures of the live woman visible with the speculum allowed the enlightened knowledge of medical science to enter; physicians could now see and, therefore, manipulate this previously invisible zone. In this respect, the creation of the speculum participated in a Western medical tradition that was founded on visibility.[29] As in Luce Irigaray's notion of the speculum, the light thrown into the dark space is then reflected back onto the prestigious image of Sims himself, whose name flashed "over the medical world like a meteor in the night." Illuminating the inside of the vagina lit up his own career in the process, making him a guiding light to those physicians who had previously labored in the dark.

Baldwin, Sims's eulogizer, proceeds to compare the speculum to other great inventions: "It has been to diseases of the womb what the printing press is to civilization, what the compass is to the mariner, what steam is to navigation, what the telescope is to astronomy, and grander than the telescope because it was the work of one man."[30] In Baldwin's account, Sims alone discovered the instrument that would help organize the uncharted female landscape. This man-made invention was construed as yet another example of science's triumph over nature. The speculum served as yet another instance of man's progress in that it made visible the inner recesses of the female body, just as the telescope enabled a view of the outer depths of space. The speculum was like a compass in that it helped guide the physician into this unknown terrain. In this rhetorical construction, the female body is metaphorically produced as raw natural territory awaiting discovery and cultivation by the hands of male medical culture. On first using the speculum and viewing the inside of the vagina, Sims himself wrote, "I felt like an explorer in medicine who first views a new and important territory."[31] Without science the female body was unruly and nonsensical; the speculum helped organize and establish the female body, particularly the female reproductive organs, as a place suitable for, and open to, medical intervention.

The narrative formulas used to describe Sims's medical adventures present classic scenarios: a hero triumphantly overcoming trial and tribulation, fighting battles in order to conquer new lands, build new spaces, and create new orders.[32] Under all of this lies the female body, serving at once as obstacle and as object in need of discovery, conquering, and restructuring. Thus in historic writings about Sims, the female body, particularly the Black female body, becomes what Teresa de Lauretis refers to as a "plot-space," marking the landscape that Sims, the medical hero, traverses in order to find fame, knowledge, and wealth.[33]

Bearing the Pain

After Sims's first use of the pewter spoon and his view of what "no man had ever seen before," he asked Lucy to stay and requested that Anarcha and Betsey be sent back to him. Believing he was "on the eve of a great discovery," he asked their masters for consent: "I agree to perform no experiment or operation . . . to endanger their lives and will not charge a cent for keeping them, but you must pay their taxes and clothe them. I will keep them at my own expense."[34] Since Sims had already argued that these women could not properly perform their duties as servants due to their "disgusting condition," his offer must have seemed a good deal to the owners. He would not deplete their slave capital but would sustain their lives himself and might even repair them and thus return them to their original value. The backyard hospital for slaves was enlarged, and Sims set about inventing instruments, setting the stage for a show that would be extended time and time again, finally closing after a four-year run.

Who were the slave women on whom Sims experimented? We know them from Sims's autobiography and subsequent biographical writings only by their first names. Did they have husbands, partners, children, and loved ones whom they were made to leave for four years while Sims worked on them? Did they agree to his experimentation? Were they given any choices? Under what terms? What were their feelings toward their condition? Did they ever leave Sims's backyard hospital over the course of their tenure there? It is impossible to know. They did not write their own histories. Thus the ways in which Sims's surgeries related to these women's lives are left unknown; the documentation of their performances is subject to surviving writings mainly unconcerned with such incidental facts.

Lucy was the first to undergo surgery to suture together the edges of the fistula. With a patronizing flourish, Sims remarked on her fortitude: "That was before the days of anesthetics, and the poor girl, on her knees, bore the operation with great heroism and bravery."[35] The pain these women must have experienced during and following these operations is inconceivable. And as if the pain of unanesthetized vaginal surgery were not traumatic enough, after this first operation, Lucy nearly died from infection due to a sponge Sims had left in her urethra and bladder.

Sims and Harris depict the slave women as inherently more durable than white women. About one hundred years after the surgeries, Harris echoes Sims's racist patronizing: "Sims's experiments brought them physical pain, it is true, but they bore it with amazing patience and fortitude—a grim stoicism which may have been part of their racial endowment or which possibly had been bred into them through several generations of enforced submission."[36] Causing the slave women great pain did not deter Sims from proceeding with the operations. Not only were the painful punishments administered to slave women by masters and overseers seen as a kind of "preparation" for the rigors of unanesthetized surgery, but slaves were viewed as genetically more predisposed than whites to the kind of domestication that trained them to bear pain.[37]

Pathologizing Difference

Other cultural and historical factors allowed Sims to believe that slave women were appropriate subjects for such painful experimentation. It was possible for Sims to operate repeatedly and unabashedly on slave-women subjects in part because these women were viewed as abundantly symptomatic and pathological. Given a cultural backdrop that pathologized race and Black female sexuality alike, slave women with vesico-vaginal fistulas were triply symptomatic. Their first pathological symptom was their primary racial characteristic: their skin color. In a medical world that categorized life as either normal or pathological, people of the African diaspora were continually condemned to the category of pathological, their "abnormal" skin color serving as a foil for "normal" white skin. Pathological causes for this condition were concocted in order to explain its prevalence. Sander Gilman explains: "Medical tradition has a long history of perceiving this skin color as the result of some pathology. The favorite theory, which reappears with some frequency in the early nineteenth century, is that skin color and attendant physiognomy of the black are the result of congenital leprosy."[38] Such medical arguments, in collusion with racist and stereotypic scientific and cultural explanations and excuses, provided the grounds for differential "treatment."

The slave woman's second symptom was her sex, taken in combination with her skin color. Black female sexuality and sex characteristics were the site of great attention by a nineteenth-century scientific community that systematically found them to be pathological.[39] Black female sexuality, constructed as heathen, lascivious, and excessive, was used by dominant nineteenth-century scientific culture to counter its constructions of fragile and frigid (and also pathological) white female sexuality.[40] These differing constructions of white and Black female sexualities may account for the fact that Mrs. Merrill, the white woman who had been thrown from a horse, was covered with a sheet during examination, whereas unanesthetized Lucy underwent Sims's first experimental surgery while "about a dozen" male spectators watched. The spectacle of Lucy's genital display did not require limiting the number of spectators or providing an obscuring sheet. In this way, slave women may have been seen as more appropriate objects of study, for the experimenting physician believed that he need not worry about protecting the slave's modesty.

In the early nineteenth century, white European researchers documented physical evidence to provide proof of pathology. Black female genitals and "steatopygia" (protruding buttocks) were singled out as telling sites of difference and pathology. In their trips to Africa, researchers commented on the "primitive" genitalia of African women, particularly Bushman and Hottentot. Named the "Hottentot Venus," Saartjie Baartman (also referred to as Sarah Bartmann) was exhibited in Europe for over five years. She was clothed during live exhibitions, so her buttocks were of greater interest than the hidden genitalia. But following her death in 1815 in Paris, her genitalia took the spotlight: "The audience that had paid to see Sarah Bartmann's buttocks and fantasized about her genitalia could, after her death and dissection, examine both."[41] Following her death, Georges Cuvier, a pathologist, presented "the Academy the genital organs of this woman prepared in a way so as to allow one to see the nature of the labia."[42] The postmortem museum display of the Hottentot Venus's genitalia is reminiscent of Barnum's orchestration of Joice Heth's theatricalized autopsy. The surgical theater and museum display, spaces often reserved for serious scientific investigation, become Barnum sideshows. In both cases, public display of what is normally private—the genitals or the inside of the body—was used as evidence of freakish abnormalities. The genitalia of the Hottentot woman became the marker of her inherent pathology, her sex parts serving as a metonym for her pathological sexuality and therefore as fitting representatives for inclusion in an anatomical museum.

Given this historical context of the continual pathologizing of Black women, the third pathological symptom and only legitimate abnormality, the vesico-vaginal fistula, made these slave women ideal subjects for study. The vesico-vaginal tears, located in the mysterious inner cavity, were only accessible by a physician's probing fingers and tools. There were persistent questions regarding the moral and ethical appropriateness of examining white women's genitals and reproductive organs; Western society questioned the suitability of a physician penetrating such a private place traditionally reserved for the patient's husband.[43] Yet with the slave, these questions were laid to rest. Not only was she white man's property, but because of her racially legitimized pathological "nature," she was considered promiscuous and sexually voracious. The need to manipulate the slave's genitals in search of the vesico-vaginal fistula made her an apt surgical recipient.

Utilizing Sameness

Difference was vital to Sims's experiments. The slave's triple pathology allowed him to perform multiple operations. Western medical and scientific men in the nineteenth century tried to prove Black female difference, as is evidenced in the actual display of Sarah Bartmann's external genitals. Yet Sims's experiments were also premised on an internal sameness, his invention of the speculum providing the tool that allowed such sameness to be examined. If he could successfully mend a slave woman's fistula, then it was assumed that he would be able to repair *any* woman's fistula. This simultaneous sameness and difference is what made the slave women such fitting "human guinea pigs."[44] Slavery provided the ideal conditions for Sims's surgical experimentation. As we have seen, convenient racial pathologies legitimated surgical manipulation and unabashed pelvic observation of the slave women, while their palpably (and now visibly) analogous insides made them suitable white female correlates.

In Baldwin's eulogizing of Sims, he proclaims, "The time was ripe when Sims patiently began to work out problems which were essential to operative gynaecology. Even slavery had its uses in the pursuit of his ends. Who can tell how many more years the progress of the art might have been delayed if the humble Negro servitors had not brought their willing sufferings and patient endurance to aid in the furthering of Sims's purpose."[45] "The time was ripe" indeed, but not necessarily for the reasons that Baldwin asserts. Who was actually offering the slaves' "willing sufferings . . . to aid in the furthering of Sims's purpose"? Of course, it was the slave owners rather than the slaves themselves who initiated contact with Sims and who had the final say as to whether their slaves could remain in Sims's care. "The time was ripe" because Sims, an already reputable body mechanic, offered these masters a promising proposition: he would repair their laborer, making her fit for her duties. In a slave economy, this surgery held particular value. Not only did it repair the slave capital so she could work, but by ridding her of the fistula's "loathsome" and "disgusting" attributes the surgery also affected her likelihood to reproduce, a vital aspect of her role as slave.

Harris suggests that there were even greater risks to having a fistula. He maintains that some slave women were led to suicide by their "loathsome" condition. Harris's statement suggests that Sims's experimentation was really for the slave women's benefit. However, we may further ask, as Diana Axelsen has in an essay on Sims, how severe a disorder a vesico-vaginal fistula truly is and whether it merited such extreme attention: "While certainly a source of chronic discomfort and possible secondary irritation, and while obviously embarrassing in many contexts, vesico-vaginal fistula is not a disorder involving chronic or severe pain . . . the discomfort of vesico-vaginal fistula, in comparison to the effects of excessive beatings, chronic malnutrition, and other forms of physical and psychological aggression, hardly constitutes a probable motive for suicide."[46] Not to mention the tremendous agony of unanesthetized vaginal surgery. The pain and suffering these women endured was hardly a break from hardship. While none of the women undergoing Sims's experimentation committed suicide, four years of unanesthetized surgery on one's vagina might have been a much more likely motive than the vesico-vaginal fistula itself.

Lucy did not die following Sims's first surgical attempt but survived the infection, healing in due course for her subsequent operations. More slaves came to live in Sims's backyard: "Besides these three cases, I got three or four more to experiment on, and there was never a time that I could not, at any day, have had a subject for operation."[47] Sims rotated operations on his slave patients but could not make the operation work. Each time he would make adjustments to the procedure, but there was always a small fistula remaining, and a small fistula had the same result as a large fistula: it leaked. As one patient was healing, he would operate on the next (who would have just finished healing from her last operation), incorporating his latest surgical innovation.

Those physicians and students who had initially attended the operations, eagerly awaiting Sims's great success, lost interest. Without assistants, he trained the slave women to assist in each other's operations.[48] Thus the slave's role shifted throughout the surgical process: slave as laboring assistant or stagehand, slave as repairable capital, and slave as medical guinea pig. Women, particularly women of color, have been cast most often in similar roles throughout Western medical history: as either nurse, technician, or nonphysician assistant; and as subject of experimentation and manipulation particularly with regard to reproductive organs.[49] Their power in the medical apparatus has reflected the roles they have been assigned. However, since the abolition of slavery, the nature of the experimentation and manipulation of African American women's reproductivity has shifted with the changing status of African American women as reproductive capital.

Three years after Sims's experiments began, his brother-in-law, Dr. Rush Jones, visited Sims and implored him to discontinue his work on the slaves. He told Sims that he was working too much, that the cost of supporting the slaves was high, and that he was being unfair to his family. According to Sims's and Harris's accounts, Jones did not raise concerns about the slaves' welfare. However, Harris does note that there was talk in the community: "And socially the whole business was becoming a marked liability, for all kinds of whispers were beginning to circulate around town—dark rumors that it was a terrible thing for Sims to be allowed to keep on using human beings as experimental animals for his unproven surgical theories."[50] Nowhere else in Sims's biography or autobiography is there mention of the possible ways in which his treatment of the slaves was unethical. Rather, it is continuously emphasized that the slaves were there out of desperation and in the hope that Sims might rid them of their condition. In response to the townspeople's uneasiness with Sims's practice, Harris emphasizes that "the human guinea pigs themselves, however, made no complaints on this score." He uses the term "human guinea pigs" ironically here to imply the slave women's willing acceptance of their role as experimental animal, even though "dark rumors" were being spread around town. However, in an article on Sims in the *Journal of Medical Ethics,* Durrenda Ojanuga asserts that the women "were in no way volunteers for Dr. Sims's research." In fact, "the evidence suggests that Sims's use of slave women as experimental subjects was by no means the order of the day!"[51] Thus Sims's practices cannot be viewed as historically acceptable or commonplace. Yet it is important to remember that these practices, nonetheless, instituted the foundation of gynecology as a distinct specialty.

Sims's tenacity in battling the fistula despite criticism from his relatives, friends, and colleagues is highlighted by both Sims and his biographer. He is rhetorically placed on a research team with the slaves in a dedicated search for a cure for their ailments. In the writings, it is as though no power differential existed between Sims and his experimentees. But the slaves themselves would not become famous; it was Sims who would wear the honors. According to Harris, Sims was so driven that when Jones begged him to stop the experimentation, Sims was steadfast in his commitment. As Harris describes: "It was like advising a dog that he will be out of breath if he doesn't stop chasing a squirrel—like advising Columbus to turn back because the voyage is long and there is no land in sight. Sims, once aroused, was a zealot."[52] Even eighty years later the characterization of the slave woman as "dark continent" had not died out. Metaphors similar to the ones used to remark on Sims's speculum in 1883 were used by Harris to remark on Sims's actions. Once again, the slave body is metaphorized as an unruly, uncharted, dark continent containing rich mysteries and spicy secrets. While the explorer utilizes the telescope or compass, the physician dealing in female disorders will make use of the speculum. Sims, like Columbus, was determined to conquer a naturalized resource (the Americas or the female body), civilizing the previously "uncivilized" territory. Fame was at stake for both, dependent on brutality, racist notions of entitlement, and the institution of slavery. However, less glamorous than the comparison to Columbus, Sims is also referred to as a dog chasing the wild squirrel of surgical success. With the Columbus and dog metaphors, ideas of driven and instinctual behavior, exploration, conquest, and domestication are joined as a means of legitimizing racial and sexual domination.

Throughout his experiments, Sims made adjustments in the hopes of successful surgery. Each time he was frustrated by the small fistula that remained. Deciding he needed a different type of suture, he traded in his silk thread for a silver-wire suture that he had had specially made, and the fistula was repaired. He considered his silver sutures to be "the greatest surgical achievement of the nineteenth century."[53] In the summer of 1849 he operated on Anarcha, the first fistula case he had ever seen, and the operation was a success. It was Anarcha's thirtieth operation.

Master Showman's Second Act

In 1855 Sims founded the Woman's Hospital in New York, a place where women could go despite their economic circumstances. The hospital was the first ever dedicated to female disorders, and its wards were largely filled with destitute Irish immigrant women.[54] It would appear that this was a charity hospital for the good of the poor. But as was the case with the slaves in Sims's backyard, patients at the Woman's Hospital were frequently kept there "indefinitely" and underwent multiple surgeries.

From 1856 to 1859, an early indigent Irish visitor to the Woman's Hospital, Mary Smith, survived thirty operations, the same number Anarcha endured in Sims's backyard. It must not be forgotten that these women, unlike the slaves, had the benefits of anesthetics. Before Sims was aware of the existence of anesthetics he had attempted surgery on white women, "but they seemed unable to bear the operation's pain and discomfort with the stoicism shown by the Negroes."[55] The widespread use of anesthetics finally allowed Sims to bring his surgeries to white women and allowed for the establishment of places such as the Woman's Hospital. The Woman's Hospital continually provided Sims with bodies on which he could experiment with new surgeries and instruments. Discoveries he made at the hospital were then utilized in his private practice in exchange for high fees.[56]

Sims moved to Europe during the Civil War, retaining his position as a "loyal southerner."[57] With the help of anesthetics, Sims operated on numerous wealthy European women, including a countess in France; he often had large audiences filling his operating theater to capacity. He stayed in Paris, where he was a "hit": "Here I performed in the amphitheatre, in which Joubard de Lamballe had performed all his operations."[58] Thus he clearly measured his success by the surgeon stars who had frequented the same stage.

When Sims returned to New York with his European fame and confidence, he took center stage, making the Woman's Hospital into his own private experimentation theater—scores of medical men came to observe Sims's performance of daring surgeries. Here he performed controversial surgeries as well, including Battey's operation, which Sims helped "make respectable." In the 1870s Battey's operation, or bilateral ovariotomy (removal of both ovaries), became a fashionable surgery to "treat" a variety of illnesses including insanity, epilepsy, and nervous disorders that were believed to originate in the female reproductive organs.[59] The operation had the additional effect of sterilization.

On his return from Europe with his new titles, Knight Commander of the Legion of Honor of France, Knight of the Order of Isabella the Catholic of Spain, and Knight of the Order of Leopold I of Belgium, there was new concern about Sims's practices. His biographer attributes this to his contemporaries' jealousy of and weariness over Sims's success: "He was too cocksure, they felt, too reckless, too much inclined to hold the spotlight in a one-man starring part." The Board of Lady Managers, a group of rich white women who oversaw the "moral and domestic management" of the Woman's Hospital and whose help Sims himself had solicited in order to afford his hospital legitimacy, recognized that Sims was experimenting on his patients and objected to the large audiences Sims allowed into his operating theater. A Lady Managers' memorandum asks, "Is the Woman's Hospital to be made a public school or is it to be a Private Hospital where our afflicted Sisters can come without fear?"[60] They limited to fifteen the number of spectators allowed during operations. Outraged, Sims resigned from the hospital in 1875 and a few months later was elected president of the AMA, his well-publicized resignation apparently rewarded by this esteemed organization. In his presidential address he attacked the AMA's code of ethics, which oversees and disciplines physicians' practices. Sims asked his colleagues, "Did it ever occur to you that [the AMA's code of ethics] is capable of being used as an engine of torture and oppression?" Sims felt that the code was too strict, as reflected by the medical establishment's unease with some of Sims's practices.[61]

Throughout the latter part of his career Sims invented new tools and techniques for "treating" women. Contemporaneous with sterilizing the mentally disordered, Sims was seeking out innovative solutions to correct private patients' infertility. For example, he invented and used an instrument for the amputation of the cervix that he called the "uterine guillotine." A pioneer in artificial insemination, Sims was also taken with the practice of "splitting the cervix," supposedly in order to ease the travel of semen and menses through the cervical canal. Many gynecologists considered the practice "butcherous."[62] Coining the term *vaginismus* to refer to female "frigidity," a condition that disallows penetration by the penis into the vagina, Sims proceeded to invent a number of methods to remedy the situation, including hymenotomy, incising the vaginal orifice, and dilating the vagina with various-sized wedges. In "treating" vaginismus, Sims would sometimes simply anesthetize the woman so that her husband could have intercourse with her in order to impregnate her. This procedure asserted the compatibility of the passive, anesthetized female body with gynecological as well as sexual manipulation. This relationship was mirrored one hundred years later in the use of anesthetized women for teaching medical students how to perform pelvic exams. The passive, powerless female pelvis is thus situated as a model receptacle for medical intervention.

Sims continued to enlist such passive female bodies in order to prove his master showmanship. In 1879, four years prior to his death, Sims threw a gala event, something between a trade show and a circus. For four days, he performed a series of varied operations on different women, ending in a dinner at Sims's house for fifty or sixty physicians.[63]

As if in response to the Board of Lady Managers' reprimand of Sims for his large audiences at the Woman's Hospital, the gala event openly defied the Lady Managers' protocol for proper surgical performance.

Between Sims and the Board of Lady Managers, the staging of the operative performance had been called into question. The Lady Managers disputed Sims's previously unlimited power over the type of gaze and manipulation practiced on his patients' bodies. The gaze he wished to have control over, however, was not only his own but also that of his audience-followers. Throughout his medical career, Sims was always in the spotlight; after Sims enlisted anesthetics, his patients were even more proplike than before. The fact that the patients at the Woman's Hospital were white undoubtedly influenced the Lady Managers' idea of appropriate modesty. Because of their race and position within antebellum southern society, the slave women had been more appropriate objects for exhibition.

The appropriateness of the slave women for exhibition and unanesthetized experimentation served as a legitimation of the institution of slavery, as is evident in Sims's eluogist's statement that "the time was ripe" for Sims's experimentation. Implicit in this statement is the idea that the ends, gynecology and the furtherance of medicine, justified the means, slavery. The implication is that it is fortunate for humanity in general that slavery existed if only because it helped foster medical innovation. And as we can see from Sims's practices following slavery, his attitudes toward women, their bodies, and reproductivity were undoubtedly affected by his longtime experimentation on slave women. Gynecology in the United States evolved through the bodies of slave women. While slavery was eventually abolished, inequality and institutionalized racism flourish. Certain populations, particularly poor women of color, are still viewed as more fitting experimentees for, and more fitting recipients of, new technologies than other populations. Unfortunately, the time is still ripe, and medical innovation is still the excuse.

Sims continues to be praised in the introductions to gynecology texts and medical-history books without reference to his questionable practices. When his practices are questioned, as they were in a 1970s article that appeared in the *American Journal of Obstetrics and Gynecology* titled "Reappraisals of James Marion Sims," many physicians were outraged and defended Sims. The author, Irwin H. Kaiser, M.D., was not particularly critical of Sims and even responded to Barker-Benfield's chapter on Sims in *Horrors of the Half-Known Life* that although "Sims was insensitive to the status and needs of women," he was simply a "product of his era" and that one must "be skeptical of judging 1850 decisions by 1975 norms." Kaiser's colleagues, as evidenced by their discussion following his piece, were outraged by *any* questioning of Sims's practices. Dr. Denis Cavanagh responded, "Lest this distinguished Society degenerate into just another social club, we all have a responsibility to supply the program committee with good scientific papers. In my opinion this paper damns Sims with faint praise and is one of the least impressive papers that I have heard before this society." Dr. Lawrence L. Hester Jr. concurred: "I rise not to reappraise J. Marion Sims, but to praise him—to praise him as the father of gynecology and not to condemn him as an exploiter of women." These responses illustrate the vehemence with which Sims's work has been supported.[64]

While such a staunch defense of Sims might not commonly be found in print today, it is significant that the evolution of the specialty of gynecology is not openly considered and questioned in medical texts and medical-history books. If gynecology is premised on such practices, might the entire specialty be reconsidered in this light? If it were, we would surely find that the racism and misogyny underlying Sims's practices still flourish in contemporary medicine and its applications, particularly with regard to women and their reproductive organs. The decisions made in the mid–nineteenth century continue to directly and indirectly influence the lives of women today. This does not mean that practitioners have studied Sims or are aware of his historic importance. Rather the medical apparatus continues to accommodate and even reward such racism and misogyny.

Sims's experiments on slave women, his practice of ovariotomy on the mentally disabled, and his pioneering work in artificial insemination and infertility helped institute the idea that it was appropriate for medical professionals to seek out new ways of both limiting and fostering female reproductivity. Forever in search of a new tool or surgical technique, Sims was one of the earliest physicians to link female reproductivity with a kind of technophilia, publishing extensively on each new innovation. Sims's work also linked experimentation on the female reproductive organs to race and power, since his earliest experiments were executed on female slaves.

In order to explore the legacy of Sims's work, I will consider the contraceptive technology Norplant. Experiments with Norplant were conducted almost exclusively on poor third world women, and since its FDA approval in 1990 it has been coercively and even legislatively aimed at poor women of color in the United States and abroad as a solution to the threat of their reproductivity. Whereas new technologies that limit reproductivity are often aimed at poor women of color, con-

Fig. 41. Norplant advertisement. In the *Nurse Practitioner*
(June 1992).

currently new reproductive technologies that extend or promote fertility (e.g., in vitro fertilization) are largely aimed at wealthy, white
women. The impetus to enhance or contain reproductivity on the basis
of race or social status can be traced to Sims's early practices.

Whereas Sims's vesico-vaginal fistula operations can be viewed as
one of the earliest reproductive technologies, enhancing slaves' reproductive capacities and thus allowing them to continue their "duties" as

Fig. 42. Norplant advertisement. In the *Nurse Practitioner* (July 1992).

"breeders," Norplant is a form of temporary sterilization that prevents re-productivity. The historical conditions out of which each technology arose explain their opposite aims. Sims conducted his experiments at a time when the ruling southern whites could benefit from the reproductivity of slave women; Norplant has been developed as a response to the alleged need for new ways of controlling poor women's reproductivity given the rhetorical backdrop of welfare crises and overpopulation.

While arising out of very different historical conditions, Norplant and Sims's crude reproductive technologies are cousins. Both in Sims's time and today, certain women's reproductivity is valued over others', and new technologies are demanded in order to foster and prevent reproduction.

"Welcome to a New Era in Contraceptive Technology"

Approved by the FDA in 1990, Norplant is a subdermal contraceptive consisting of six small silicone-rubber capsules that are surgically implanted in a woman's arm.[65] The capsules diffuse a synthetic progesterone, levonorgestrel, that effectively inhibits ovulation and thickens cervical mucus, preventing pregnancy for up to five years. Because it is surgically implanted and removed, Norplant is physician controlled and "user soft." Theoretically, the user cannot designate when to start and stop Norplant; rather a health practitioner must insert and remove the capsules, making Norplant particularly prone to institutional abuse. Norplant has been especially attractive to the international population-control industry, for whom technologies that are effective, low maintenance, and provider dependent are valued. Norplant is mainly used in developing countries in Asia, Latin America, and Africa. The majority of Norplant's clinical or preintroduction studies were conducted in developing countries as well. Some fifty-five thousand women were included in these studies.[66]

This seemingly science-fictive technology confirms the medical industry's presumption, asserted if not established by Sims, of the compatibility of the female body, particularly the female reproductive organs, with new technologies. Norplant, yet another case of science triumphing over nature, has been heralded throughout the world as a panacea technology. From Egypt, where the national press referred to Norplant as "the magic capsule," to the United States, where it has been heralded as "a birth control breakthrough," Norplant has received praise for its remarkable possibilities.

Its high-tech appeal was taken up by Norplant's advertising agents when they constructed a series of ads that pictured women meeting the viewer's gaze while responding to the question "Why do you choose Norplant?" White women and white families are dressed in white on a white background, constructing users as overwhelmingly modern, wealthy, and white (see figs. 41 and 42). Often, a contraceptive is at the center of the frame in pharmaceutical advertising (see fig. 44); that is, the product itself is pictured. However, because Norplant is placed

Fig. 43. Norplant advertisement. In the *Nurse Practitioner* (May 1992).

within the body, it is absent from the image, indicating that the woman shown has already securely incorporated Norplant into her modern body. One ad does picture an African American woman (see fig. 43). She too is dressed in the uniform white and set against a white background. Her reasons for choosing Norplant are not those of her white counterparts, who have either temporarily reached optimal family size or are taking a break between children. Rather, the woman represented wishes

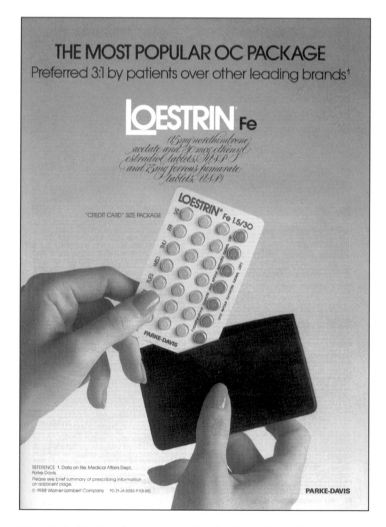

Fig. 44. LoEstrin advertisement. In the *Nurse Practitioner*
(May 1989).

to finish school; she wishes to enter into a viable socioeconomic space
that would allow her to support her future baby. Issues of supporting the
young white children pictured in the ads previously shown are left un-
addressed. It is assumed that personal, not economically motivated,
choice is the reason a white woman or white family would decide to
stop reproducing. The single African American woman, pictured child-
less, is given an economic reason, and a societally acceptable one at that.

Both technological innovations, Norplant and Sims's vesico-vaginal surgeries, are proposed as ways of helping Black women be more "fit for their duties." Sims's vesico-vaginal fistula reparations would make the slave women more fit for their duties as breeders. In a slave economy, it is economically beneficial to those in power to repair slave capital so that she and her future progeny may provide labor. The slave woman's reproductivity must be reclaimed *from* pathology. In a capitalist welfare economy, the reproductivity of the poor woman of color *is* her pathology. In the former case, reproductivity is economically beneficial to those with capital; in the latter reproductivity is believed to deplete economic resources. Whereas the slave women Sims experimented on were attributed a triple dose of pathology—race, sex, fistula—poor women of color today are still pathologized for the first two (race and sex), but reproductivity replaces the fistula as the third pathology.

Slave masters encouraged adolescent slave girls to have children; now "teenage pregnancy," predominantly associated with poor women of color, is linked with gangs and drugs as an evil of modern society.[67] Norplant is seen as a new technology that can help put an end to teenage pregnancy and restore racial "balance" to the U.S. population. In December 1992, the front page of the *New York Times* told the story well. An article with the headline "Population Growth Outstrips Earlier U.S. Census Estimates" showed projections into the year 2050, where "white" population growth would remain steady while Black, Asian, and Hispanic populations would double at the very least.[68] Bedfellows with this front-page article was another piece titled "Baltimore School Clinics to Offer Birth Control by Surgical Implant."[69] It is no surprise that the large majority of young women affected by this decision in the Baltimore area are poor African Americans. Norplant will not protect these teens from sexually transmitted diseases or educate them about their bodies and pregnancy, nor had any medical research addressed the health risks of Norplant in women under the age of twenty at the time such decisions were made. Norplant is used as a "quick fix" to the high teen birthrate in the Baltimore area and as a means of remedying uneven population growth.

Poor African American women who do have many children, women that ex-senator Russell B. Long referred to as "Black Brood Mares," are often disdained for leeching tax dollars.[70] The duties of African American women today are viewed by the dominant culture as opposite to those of her slave ancestors. No longer is the African American woman in the Norplant ad expected to breed for her oppressors; now, new technologies such as Norplant aid her in becoming an educated, income-earning member of society *before* she has children. The narrative of these ads suggests that Norplant in fact serves a purpose similar to Sims's reparative surgeries, playing into current dominant constructions of proper African American women's reproductive identity.

If poor women, particularly poor African American women, are not "fit for their duties," securing proper earning potential before they have children, Norplant has been seen as a technology that can remedy such misbehavior. The *Philadelphia Inquirer* published an editorial two days following FDA approval in December 1990, suggesting readers think about using Norplant as a "tool in the fight against African-American poverty."[71] A few weeks later, California judge Howard Broadman ordered Darlene Johnson, a twenty-seven-year-old pregnant African American mother of four who had been convicted of child abuse, to have Norplant inserted or to serve a jail sentence.[72] In 1993 Washington State, Arizona, Colorado, Ohio, Tennessee, North Carolina, South Carolina, and Florida all proposed incentive-based or mandate-based welfare reform linked to Norplant. For example, the proposal in Ohio would increase monthly Aid to Families with Dependent Children (AFDC) payments and offer a $500 incentive for Norplant insertion or $1,000 for sterilization. If a woman chose not to use Norplant and subsequently became pregnant, her benefits might be discontinued entirely or they might not be increased with the birth of the child. In Florida, the proposed reform set AFDC benefits at $258 per month regardless of the number of children in the family, but a recipient with an effective implant would receive $400 per month.[73] As the National Black Women's Health Project's newsletter asserts, "the line between incentive and coercion is fuzzy. The incentives are only being offered for one contraceptive—Norplant—to one class of women—poor, single, mothers on welfare—who are more likely women of color—what happened to choice?"[74]

Women on welfare receive incentives for temporary or permanent sterilization; slave women received incentives such as better rations for prolific reproduction. It is unclear, however, what the slaves' "incentives" were for submitting to Sims's repeated surgeries. In their writings, Sims and Harris altogether disavow questions of the slaves' choice or consent by maintaining that the slave women were eager to be cured, willingly submitted to surgery, and even participated in the surgeries as Sims's assistants. Their positions as slaves authorized their "willingness" and consent, as they already had few legitimate choices regarding their bodies and everyday activities.[75] Similarly, we might consider how much "choice" a poor woman on welfare has when faced with such options regarding Norplant. And this "choice" is not as clear-cut as it may seem. Norplant does not serve as a simple on-and-off switch for fertility: there are a host of side effects that may accompany its use. The most common is a change in menstrual bleeding patterns. A significant number of women will bleed on and off throughout their cycle for the first year of use.[76] Other side effects include dizziness, headaches, nervousness, weight gain, weight loss, ovarian cysts, acne, infections at the implant site, nipple discharge, inflammation of the cervix, mood changes, depression, general malaise, itching, and hypertension.[77] The term *side effect* belittles the crushing impact any one of these symptoms may have on an individual's life.

Despite these foreboding possibilities, internal Population Council documents show that women in Indonesia, Bangladesh, and numerous other countries had difficulties getting Norplant removed due to resistant trial investigators whose scientific data "would be rendered incomplete."[78] Likewise, in early clinical trials done with Norplant, many cases of abuse regarding informed consent have been noted in numerous countries, including Indonesia, Brazil, Thailand, and Egypt. Medical innovation and experimentation are again used to legitimate oppression and control over the bodies of poor women of color. As in the case of Sims's experiments, it is "difference"—in this case, poor women of color's pathological race, sexuality, and reproductivity—that legitimates Norplant experiments and the product's continued use. And yet such studies are premised on a convenient user "sameness"—since Norplant will work identically on all female bodies, women of color will be adequate testing grounds for technologies to be potentially used on higher-valued white bodies in the future, if they so choose. Balanced between Western pharmaceutical companies, the medical establishment, and assorted governmental bodies, one finds a distinct colonialist attitude at work, not dissimilar to the rhetoric underlying writings about Sims. Dominant white forces go to faraway lands to identify their sameness with the exotic "other," while simultaneously establishing and maintaining the other's difference and reaping the benefits of the new land and culture.

In many states in the United States a woman on public aid who has received free Norplant is in a position similar to that of third world women facing resistant trial investigators: she can only have Norplant removed if a practitioner deems it medically necessary.[79] Changes in menstrual bleeding patterns, the most common Norplant side effect, are not considered by the medical establishment to be a reason to discontinue its use. And yet this single side effect may deeply affect the cultural performance of some women, particularly Native American and Muslim women. A report on Norplant issued by the Native American Women's Health Education Resource Center reads: "For Native American women, the bleeding restricts their daily activity and prohibits them from participation in many traditional practices and religious cere-monies. . . . They do not attend sundances, sweats, or other spiritual cer-emonies or go to any place where the pipe is used or to meetings of the Native American church. They also refrain from sexual activity. Ironi-cally, the primary purpose of contraception—the ability to be sexually active without fear of pregnancy—then becomes a moot point."[80] Nor-plant users are from a variety of ethnic backgrounds and engage in a va-riety of cultural practices that are not factored into the statistical and bi-ological studies conducted by the pharmaceutical and medical institutions. Such "difference" is not considered significant alongside the benefits of Norplant as an effective, ethnicity-blind technology for "controlling" populations.

"It's Your Choice"

Temporary sterilization in the form of hormonal contraceptives is a common visitor to foreign lands.[81] Norplant is not the first contracep-tive to be tried on women of color in its early stages of development. Poor women of color in developing countries are used consistently as experimental subjects in order to test new hormonal contraceptive tech-nologies before they are used on North American women.[82] The high-dose birth control pill and Depo-Provera, an injectable contraceptive, have each undergone these contraceptive trials, presenting women with a host of side effects and unknown long-lasting effects all under the aus-pices of population control.

　　Norplant, a form of temporary sterilization, is a participant in a form of eugenics deeply indebted to older, cruder technologies such as perma-nent sterilization. Norplant's newness and technological sophistication help mask its appropriation for the same racist patterns of behavior that resulted in the systematic coercive and abusive sterilization of huge num-bers of women of color in Puerto Rico, the continental United States, and abroad beginning in the 1940s. By 1968, one-third of the women of child-bearing age on the island of Puerto Rico had been sterilized. Most women sterilized had not been informed that the operation was, for all intents and purposes, irreversible.[83] Once again, one of the reasons these women were sterilized was so they could "fulfill their duties" as defined by U.S. manufacturing industries who needed cheap labor: "sterilization was per-ceived as a way to help 'free' them for employment, as opposed to, for ex-ample, providing good child-care facilities."[84]

Funds from the United States were often involved in sterilization campaigns. For example, in the early 1980s the World Bank Project funded a program in Bangladesh that would give starving women relief wheat if they would be sterilized. Women also received monetary awards and a sari and sarong. In addition, physicians and staff received incentives for each woman who agreed to sterilization.[85] At that time, the director of obstetrics and gynecology at a New York municipal hospital explained, "In most major teaching hospitals in New York City, it is the unwritten policy to do elective hysterectomies on poor black and Puerto Rican women, with minimal indications, to train residents."[86] Sterilization abuse has been widespread and disastrous, affecting the lives of many women who have had to live with choiceless futures.

In the United States, the most flagrant abuses took place between 1970 and 1976.[87] Alabama, the home of Sims's backyard hospital, was also the state in which, more than a century later, two Black teenagers were sterilized without their consent or knowledge. This incident, known as the Relf case, was tried in the early 1970s; the court found "uncontroverted evidence in the record that minors and other incompetents have been sterilized with federal funds and that an indefinite number of poor people have been improperly coerced into accepting a sterilization operation under the threat that various federally supported welfare benefits would be withdrawn unless they submitted to irreversible sterilization."[88] The "incompetents" referred to here include mentally retarded and imprisoned women. These practices harken back to those of the Father of Modern Gynecology. As noted earlier, Sims himself practiced "female castration" on the "mentally disordered." Now such practices are taken up by Norplant. When introduced into Finland, its birthplace, Norplant was viewed as an inappropriate method for the majority of women but was targeted at very specific populations, one of them being "asocial women" (incarcerated, mentally ill, etc.). The category "asocial women" was "included in a commercial list of possible users given out by the manufacturer."[89] Though Norplant was viewed as an inappropriate method for most Finnish women, it was pushed as a first choice for many women of color. Certain women are deemed to be more fit users than others. As Purvis asks, "Are the women deemed 'unfit for motherhood' deemed fit for Norplant use?"[90] Whether subject to temporary or permanent sterilization or surgical reparation, the kinds of women targeted for medically sanctioned social control of their reproductivity—poor women, women of color, "asocial women"—are historically echoed.

Hidden Visibility

In the rhetoric surrounding Sims's practices, the importance of making visible the inner recesses of the female body is clear. It was necessary for Sims to invent the speculum so that he could visualize the vagina in order to ply his instruments. The speculum made Sims famous, his future practices dependent on such visibility. As a technology, Norplant displaces the vagina or pelvis as the site of intervention. Norplant is not about spectacular visual display. Rather it is about spectacular miniature technology, a modern means of mastering the female pelvis. It is heralded because it is hidden. In addition, practitioners do not have to "get their hands dirty" by viewing or manipulating the reproductive organs themselves. Norplant enlists a different theater of operations. The inner arm becomes a control booth for the reproductive organs, from which the six silicone satellites release their hormones. Sims's daring and spectacular surgical feats are met today by technologies that regulate the female reproductive organs from afar.

Norplant's manufacturer's claims about its invisibility have come under fire. There is concern that Norplant, particularly in thin women, *does* mark the body. The capsules are indeed visible, serving as a sort of contraceptive tattoo or brand. The implications of these markings for population control are ominous.[91] In addition, scarring, particularly among women prone to keloids (African, African American, Middle Eastern, Mediterranean, etc.), has been a problem for many women using Norplant and one of the factors that led to a class-action suit originating in Chicago on behalf of scarred users.[92] The women involved in this suit stated that they were not properly informed before insertion. Although Norplant's distributors claim that it may be surgically removed in twenty minutes, some users have had a string of removal attempts, resulting in broken capsules (with large amounts of hormones flooding the body), excruciating pain, and significant scarring.

Besides the many cases of inadequate preinsertion counseling and informed consent, one of the worst problems associated with Norplant use abroad as well as in this country is the woman's difficulty having Norplant removed.[93] Many women, particularly poor women, have trouble finding practitioners who will agree to its removal: either practitioners are trained in insertion and not removal or they do not deem the woman's removal request medically necessary.[94] Having control over when and how one has surgery is largely a factor of a woman's social status, thus directly related to race, class, and economics. This was as true in Sims's time as it is today. After Sims had operated twice on a white woman, Miss C., for a harelip, he "was eager to perfect his handiwork with a third" operation.[95] However, Miss C. refused, satisfied after two operations. The slaves in Sims's backyard hospital and the indigent women at the Woman's Hospital in New York did not have such clear options.

Nor do poor women today. In my work at a women's health clinic, I have heard stories—horrifying but not unexpected stories—of women so pained by Norplant's effects on their bodies and frustrated by the unwillingness of medical practitioners that they attempted to remove the implanted capsules from their own arms. For them, freedom from Norplant was worth the pain of self-surgery without anesthetics.

There is no need for "sentimental reverie" over lost history in looking at the speculum, as J. Chassar Moir romantically suggests in the epigraph to this chapter. If we do gaze at the "curious speculum," we will catch much more than "a fleeting glimpse of an old hut in Alabama and seven Negro women who suffered, and endured, and had rich reward." Not only will we see that slavery served medicine, but we will also see that poor women, particularly poor women of color, continue to serve medicine. Meanwhile medical technologies serve those in power, be they slave owners or concerned taxpayers. By gazing into the "curious speculum," we might consider just how gynecology positions poor women of color and women in general and how it is decided just who is a fitting subject for medical experimentation and display. Gazing into the speculum reminds us to question the politics of visibility, of what is made visible—heroes and obstacles, ringmasters and silver sutures, cervixes and vaginas for surgical manipulation—and what is left invisible—pain and suffering, power differences, slave identities, questionable origins, semivisible contraceptive technologies. By gazing into the speculum, we may consider how this tool may have solidified the medical institution's involvement in racist, eugenicist practices concerned with the reproductive capacities of poor women.

Gaze into the "curious" speculum. Look again and again and again and reflect on the formation of the medical specialty called gynecology.

NOTES

1. See Jessica Mitford, *The American Way of Birth* (New York: Dutton, 1992), 39. Mitford's discussion of Sims is largely based on G. J. Barker-Benfield, *The*

Horrors of the Half-Known Life (New York: Harper and Row, 1976), chap. 10: "Architect of the Vagina."

2. Mitford, *American Way of Birth*, 39. Irwin H. Kaiser, M.D., states that "Sims and the other gynecological surgeons made their money by applying the hospital discoveries [made on slaves and poor white women] in private practice, where they charged stupendous fees." See his article, "Reappraisals of J. Marion Sims," *American Journal of Obstetrics and Gynecology* 132 (1978): 878.

3. Seale Harris, M.D., *Woman's Surgeon: The Life Story of J. Marion Sims* (New York: Macmillan, 1950), 107.

4. Historically, there has been a connection between circus freaks and medical institutions. In London, for example, physicians were sought after to bless new freak shows with reviews declaring the verity of their freakishness. Often medical men would denounce the show, but then later they would purchase the skeletons of dead freaks in order to display them at the medical school. See Richard Daniel Altick, *The Shows of London* (Cambridge: Harvard University Press, 1978), 260.

5. A. H. Saxon, *P. T. Barnum: The Legend and the Man* (New York: Columbia University Press, 1989), 79.

6. Saxon, *P. T. Barnum*, 76, 99.

7. Saxon, *P. T. Barnum*, 68.

8. Saxon, *P. T. Barnum*, 71.

9. J. Marion Sims, M.D., *The Story of My Life*, ed. H. Marion-Sims, M.D. (New York: D. Appleton and Company, 1886), 231.

10. J. Chassar Moir, *The Vesico-Vaginal Fistula*, 2d ed. (London: Bailliere Tindall and Cassell, 1967), 2.

11. Elizabeth Fox-Genovese, *Within the Plantation Household: Black and White Women of the South* (Chapel Hill: University of North Carolina Press, 1988), 171. Also see Deborah Gray White, *Ar'n't I a Woman?: Female Slaves in the Plantation South* (New York: W. W. Norton, 1985), 124–25.

12. W. O. Baldwin, "Tribute to the Late James Marion Sims, November, 1883," in *The Story of My Life*, by J. Marion Sims, M.D. (New York: D. Appleton and Company, 1886), 429.

13. Harris, *Woman's Surgeon*, 95.

14. Sims, *Story of My Life*, 23.

15. Sims, *Story of My Life*, 277.

16. John D'Emilio and Estelle B. Freedman, *Intimate Matters: A History of Sexuality in America* (New York: Harper and Row, 1988), 99–100. D'Emilio and Freedman cite Angela Davis's discussion of the value slave women placed on motherhood for their own reasons. See Angela Davis, "The Black Woman's Role in the Community of Slaves," *Black Scholar* 3 (Dec. 1971): 2.

17. White, *Ar'n't I a Woman?*, 79–80.

18. D'Emilio and Freedman, *Intimate Matters*, 94.

19. While an undeniably unpleasant condition for women to have, it is important to note that fistulas usually do not affect a woman's ability to conceive.

20. White, *Ar'n't I a Woman?*, 80. Todd L. Savitt, "Black Health on the Plantation: Masters, Slaves, and Physicians," in *Science and Medicine in the Old South*, ed. Ronald L. Numbers and Todd L. Savitt (Baton Rouge: Louisiana State University Press, 1989), 345.

21. White, *Ar'n't I a Woman?*, 82.

22. Sims, *Story of My Life,* 230.

23. Many of the normal positions of the uterus were considered pathological in the early practice of gynecology; thus "replacing the uterus" was a common procedure. For example, in Henry T. Byford's *Manual of Gynecology* (Philadelphia: P. Blakiston, 1897), there is a description of the maneuver that Sims learned as a medical student: "The uterus may be replaced by putting the patient in the knee-chest position (Campbell), admitting air to the vagina, and pushing the fundus toward the promontory of the sacrum with a blunt instrument like a drumstick. . . . When the fundus is dislodged from the hollow of the sacrum, gravity completes the replacement. This is a good method for the replacement of the pregnant uterus" (246). A number of physical and mental disorders were linked to the uterus. "Local treatments" to the uterus consisting of manual relocation, leeches, and "injections" of various substances were common practice. See Ann Douglas Wood, "'The Fashionable Diseases': Women's Complaints and Their Treatment in Nineteenth-Century America," in *Women and Health in America,* ed. Judith Walzer Leavitt (Madison: University of Wisconsin Press, 1984), 222–38.

24. Sims, *Story of My Life,* 234–35.

25. See Harold Speert, M.D., *Obstetric and Gynecologic Milestones* (New York: Macmillan, 1958), 447–49.

26. Baldwin, "Tribute," 434.

27. See Mary Ann Doane, "Dark Continents: Epistemologies of Racial and Sexual Difference in Psychoanalysis and the Cinema," in *Femmes Fatales: Feminism, Film Theory, Psychoanalysis* (New York: Routledge, 1991), 209–48.

28. Mary Ann Doane, *The Desire to Desire* (Bloomington: Indiana University Press, 1987), 61.

29. See Michel Foucault, *The Birth of the Clinic: An Archaeology of Medical Perception,* trans. A. M. Sheridan Smith (New York: Random House, 1973).

30. Baldwin, "Tribute," 434.

31. Sims, *Story of My Life,* 235.

32. Donna Haraway locates this trope of the "hero-scientist" in an immunology textbook from 1987. She maintains that "science remains an important genre of Western exploration and travel literature." See Haraway, "The Biopolitics of Postmodern Bodies: Constitutions of Self in Immune System Discourse," in *Simians, Cyborgs, and Women: The Reinvention of Nature* (New York: Routledge, 1991), 205.

33. Teresa de Lauretis, *Alice Doesn't: Feminism, Semiotics, Cinema* (Bloomington: Indiana University Press, 1984), 127–28.

34. Sims, *Story of My Life,* 236.

35. Sims, *Story of My Life,* 237.

36. Haris, *Woman's Surgeon,* 99.

37. Diana E. Axelsen, "Women as Victims of Medical Experimentation: J. Marion Sims' Surgery on Slave Women, 1845–50," *Sage* 2, no. 2 (1985): n. Axelsen questions "Sims' continued failure to use ether or to seek out current research in the area of anesthesiology." She implies that no attempt was made on Sims's part to help alleviate the slave women's pain.

38. Sander L. Gilman, "Black Bodies, White Bodies: Toward an Iconography

of Female Sexuality in Late Nineteenth-Century Art, Medicine, and Literature," *Critical Inquiry* 12 (autumn 1985): 231. Winthrop D. Jordan, *White over Black: American Attitudes toward the Negro, 1550–1812* (New York: W. W. Norton, 1968), 517–21.

39. Black *male* sexuality was undeniably constructed as pathological too. But the link between Black female sexuality and genitalia was repeatedly drawn, whereas Black male genitalia were left out of the discussion. When Gilman examines autopsy reports from the late nineteenth century, he finds that Black female genitalia are discussed but that there is no discussion of Black male genitalia whatsoever. See Gilman, "Black Bodies, White Bodies," 218.

40. For a discussion of this dichotomy, see Hazel Carby, "Slave and Mistress: Ideologies of Womanhood under Slavery," in *Reconstructing Womanhood: The Emergence of the Afro-American Woman Novelist* (New York: Oxford University Press, 1987), 20–39.

41. Sander L. Gilman, *Difference and Pathology: Stereotypes of Sex, Race, and Madness* (Ithaca: Cornell University Press, 1985), 88.

42. Gilman, *Difference and Pathology,* 88 n. 19. For a contemporary take on the Hottentot Venus, see Lisa Jones, "Venus Envy," in *Bulletproof Diva: Tales of Race, Sex, and Hair* (New York: Anchor Books, 1994), 73–77.

43. Ludmilla Jordanova, *Sexual Visions: Images of Gender in Science and Medicine between the Eighteenth and Twentieth Centuries* (Madison: University of Wisconsin Press, 1989), 138–39.

44. See Harris, *Woman's Surgeon,* 98. Historically, Africans and in turn African slaves were considered to be beasts, thus making them particularly fitting "guinea pigs." See Jordan, *White over Black,* 228–34. See also Todd L. Savitt, "The Use of Blacks for Medical Experimentation and Demonstration in the Old South," *Journal of Southern History* 48, no. 3 (1982): 332.

45. Sims, *Story of My Life,* 470.

46. Axelsen, "Women as Victims," 12.

47. Sims, *Story of My Life,* 241.

48. Sims, *Story of My Life,* 241.

49. This is not to belittle the great achievements of Black female health-care professionals regardless of their role, but rather to point to the fact that Black women have often been excluded from positions of power within the medical establishment. Black women have had to fight tremendously hard for inclusion even as assistants. See Darlene Clark Hine, "Mabel K. Stauper and the Integration of Black Nurses into the Armed Forces," in *Women and Health in America,* ed. Judith Walzer Leavitt (Madison: University of Wisconsin Press, 1984), 497–506. For exceptions to the idea of limited roles for Black women in the health professions, see Sheila P. Davis and Cora A. Ingram, "Empowered Caretakers: A Historical Perspective on the Roles of Granny Midwives in Rural Alabama," in *Wings of Gauze: Women of Color and the Experience of Health and Illness,* ed. Barbara Bair and Susan E. Cayleff (Detroit: Wayne State University Press, 1993), 191–201; and Melissa Blount, "Surpassing Obstacles: Pioneering Black Women Physicians," in *The Black Women's Health Book: Speaking for Ourselves,* ed. Evelyn C. White (Seattle: Seal Press, 1990), 44–51.

50. Harris, *Woman's Surgeon,* 99.

51. Durrenda Ojanuga, "The Medical Ethics of the 'Father of Gynaecology,'

Dr. J. Marion Sims," *Journal of Medical Ethics* 19 (1993): 28–31. See also Todd L. Savitt, *Medicine and Slavery: The Diseases and Health Care of Blacks in Antebellum Virginia* (Urbana: University of Illinois Press, 1978), 293.

52. Harris, *Woman's Surgeon*, 92.

53. Cited in Barker-Benfield, *Horrors of the Half-Known Life*, 96.

54. Barbara Ehrenreich and Deirdre English, *For Her Own Good: 150 Years of the Experts' Advice to Women* (New York: Doubleday, 1978), 125.

55. Harris, *Woman's Surgeon*, 109.

56. Barker-Benfield, *Horrors of the Half-Known Life*, 102–3.

57. Barker-Benfield, *Horrors of the Half-Known Life*, 98.

58. Sims, *Story of My Life*, 295.

59. See Lawrence D. Longo, "The Rise and Fall of Battey's Operation: A Fashion in Surgery," in *Women and Health in America*, ed. Judith Walzer Leavitt (Madison: University of Wisconsin Press, 1984), 270.

60. See Harris, *Woman's Surgeon*, 298.

61. Harris, *Woman's Surgeon*, 129, 135, 288.

62. See Barker-Benfield, *Horrors of the Half-Known Life*, 110.

63. Barker-Benfield, *Horrors of the Half-Known Life*, 105.

64. Kaiser, "Reappraisals of J. Marion Sims," 878. See also S. Buford Word, M.D., "The Father of Gynecology," *Alabama Journal of Medical Science* 9, no. 1 (1972): 33–39.

65. The front cover of Wyeth-Ayerst Laboratories' Norplant information booklet for consumers reads: "Would you like up to 5 years of continuous birth control that is reversible? Welcome to a new era in contraceptive technology."

66. I find one volume on Norplant particularly helpful. See Barbara Mintzes, Anita Hardon, and Jannemieke Hanhart, eds., *Norplant: Under Her Skin* (Amsterdam: Women's Health Action Foundation, 1993), 90.

67. White, *Ar'n't I a Woman?*, 98.

68. Robert Pear, "Population Growth Outstrips Earlier U.S. Census Estimates," *New York Times*, Dec. 4, 1992.

69. Tamar Lewin, "Baltimore School Clinics to Offer Birth Control by Surgical Implant," *New York Times*, Dec. 4, 1992.

70. Thomas M. Shapiro, *Population Control Politics: Women, Sterilization, and Reproductive Choice* (Philadelphia: Temple University Press, 1985), 118. This very term was used during slavery to refer to slave women who could reproduce efficiently. See White, *Ar'n't I a Woman?*, 105.

71. See Faye Wattleton, "Using Birth Control as Coercion," *Los Angeles Times,* Jan. 13, 1991.

72. See Stacey L. Arthur, "The Norplant Prescription: Birth Control, Woman Control, or Crime Control?" *UCLA Law Review* 40, no. 1 (1992): 1–101; and Gretchen Long, "Norplant: A Victory, Not a Panacea for Poverty," *National Lawyers Guild Practitioner* 50, no. 1 (1993): 11–13. The attempt to control African American reproduction by means of the judicial system has a long and sordid history. See Dorothy E. Roberts, "Crime, Race, and Reproduction," *Tulane Law Review* 67 (1993): 1945–77.

73. Shana Morrow, "Welfare Reform and Reproductive Freedom," Planned Parenthood, Chicago Area, "Political Affairs Perspective" (fall 1993): 2–3, 7.

74. National Black Women's Health Project, "Facts: Norplant" (newsletter) 1992.

75. Issues of "choice" and informed consent haunt another set of medical experiments that occurred about eighty years following Sims's experiments and less than forty miles from Montgomery. These experiments, which happened in and around Tuskegee County, were nontherapeutic, meaning no new technology (e.g., surgery or device) was being tried. This time poor, illiterate African American men were the subjects, not slave women. Men were chosen who had been infected with syphilis but who were never told that they had syphilis. Instead the white Public Health Service (PHS) practitioners told them they had "bad blood." In exchange for being part of the study, the men received free physical exams, lunch on the day of the exam, and burial insurance. No treatment was ever given; instead their slow physical and/or psychological deterioration was monitored over the course of forty years (1932–72). This study has been superbly documented by James H. Jones in his book *Bad Blood: The Tuskegee Syphilis Experiment*.

At first sight, it might seem as though Sims's work and the PHS study have little in common other than geographical proximity. Yet both projects are founded on similar attitudes regarding Black bodies, Black sexuality, and the relationship of these bodies and sexualities to pathology. Both syphilis and vesicovaginal fistulas are conditions related to genitalia and therefore sexuality. Syphilis is a sexually transmitted disease that is often associated with sexual promiscuity. The contraction and transmission of the disease were therefore readily associated with African Americans. As Jones notes, "No disease seemed more suited to blacks than syphilis, for physicians were certain that exaggerated libido and sexual promiscuity had led to a high incidence of the disease among blacks." Both Sims's and the PHS's experiments are symptomatic of a pathological, white-dominated medical mindset that devalues Black bodies. Why not let these societally less powerful people experience prolonged suffering and pain? Suffering and pain might lead either to reparation or to death depending on the desires of those officiating the "treatments." The slave woman would be more helpful repaired; the poor Black man after slavery would be more useful dead.

76. Robert A. Hatcher, M.D., M.P.H. et al., *Contraceptive Technology 1990–1992*, 15th rev. ed. (New York: Irvington, 1994), 307.

77. Mintzes, Hardon, and Hanhart, *Norplant*, 10.

78. The Population Council, "Norplant Worldwide" no. 16 (Nov. 1991): 2.

79. American Health Consultants, "Clinicians, Patients, Medicaid: Is Anyone to Blame for Norplant Removal Dilemma?" *Contraceptive Technology Update* 14, no. 10 (1993): 152.

80. Native American Women's Health Education Resource Center, *The Impact of Norplant in the Native American Community* (June 1992): 13.

81. The back cover of Wyeth-Ayerst Laboratories' Norplant information booklet for consumers reads: "Ask your doctor if the Norplant System is right for you. . . . It's your choice."

82. Mintzes, Hardon, and Hanhart, *Norplant*, 90.

83. Betsey Hartmann, *Reproductive Rights and Wrongs: The Global Politics of Population Control and Contraceptive Choice* (New York: Harper and Row, 1987), 232.

84. Hartmann, *Reproductive Rights and Wrongs*, 232.

85. Hartmann, *Reproductive Rights and Wrongs*, 213.

86. Hartmann, *Reproductive Rights and Wrongs*, 241.

87. See Shapiro, *Population Control*, 107.

88. Cited in Hartmann, *Reproductive Rights and Wrongs*, 241.

89. Eeva Ollila, Kristiina Kajesalo, and Elina Hemminki, "Experience of Norplant by Finnish Family Planning Practitioners," in *Norplant: Under Her Skin,* ed. Barbara Mintzes, Anita Hardon, and Jannemieke Hanhart (Amsterdam: Women's Health Action Foundation, 1993), 61.

90. Ollila, Kajesalo, and Hemminki, "Experience of Norplant," 61. Here the authors cite A. Purvis, "A Pill That Gets under the Skin: Norplant Could Spur Birth Control—and Stir Controversy," *Time,* (Dec. 24, 1990), 45.

91. Hartmann, *Reproductive Rights*, 200.

92. *Jane Doe, Annrita Garcia, Mary Roe, and Leticia Walker v. Wyeth-Ayerst Laboratories*, 93 L 11096. See Heather M. Little, "No Panacea: Norplant Suit Charges Failure to Educate Patients," *Chicago Tribune,* Oct. 31, 1993.

93. Inadequate counseling and informed consent as well as the practice of inserting Norplant in women who are medically at risk have been well documented within the Native American community. See Native American Women's Health Education Resource Center, *Impact of Norplant.* An overview of this study was printed as "Native American Women Uncover Norplant Abuses," *Ms.,* Sept./Oct. 1993, 69.

94. See American Health Consultants, "Too Much or Too Little—Access to Norplant Implants Fuels Ethics Debate," *Contraceptive Technology Update* 14, no. 9 (1993); and "Clinicians, Patients, Medicaid: Is Anyone to Blame for Norplant Removal Dilemma?" *Contraceptive Technology Update* 14, no. 10 (1993).

95. Barker-Benfield, *Horrors of the Half-Known Life,* 95.

Evelynn Hammonds

Black (W)holes and
the Geometry of
Black Female Sexuality

> The female body in the West is not a unitary sign. Rather,
> like a coin, it has an obverse and a reverse: on the one
> side, it is white; on the other, not-white or, prototypically,
> black. The two bodies cannot be separated, nor can one
> body be understood in isolation from the other in the
> West's metaphoric construction of "woman." White is
> what woman is; not-white (and the stereotypes not-white
> gathers in) is what she had better not be. Even in an
> allegedly postmodern era, the not-white woman as well as
> the not-white man are symbolically and even theoretically
> excluded from sexual difference. Their function continues
> to be to cast the difference of white men and white
> women into sharper relief.
> —Lorraine O'Grady, "Olympia's Maid"

When asked to write on queer theory I must admit I was at first hesitant
even to entertain the idea. Though much of what is now called queer theory I find engaging and intellectually stimulating, I still found the idea of
writing about it disturbing. When I am asked if I am queer I usually answer yes even though the ways in which *I* am queer have never been articulated in the *body* of work that is now called queer theory. Where
should I begin? I asked myself. Do I have to start by adding another adjective to my already long list of self-chosen identities? I used to be a
Black lesbian, feminist, writer, scientist, historian of science, and activist.
Now would I be a Black, queer, feminist, writer, scientist, historian of science, and activist? Given the rapidity with which new appellations are

301

created I wondered if my new list would still be up to date by the time the article came out. More importantly, would this change or any change I might make to my list convey to anyone the ways in which I am queer?

Even a cursory reading of the first issue of the journal *differences,* on queer theory, or a close reading of *The Lesbian and Gay Studies Reader* (Abelove, Barale, and Halperin)—by now biblical in status—would lead me to answer no. So what would be the point of my writing on queer theory? Well, I could perform that by-now-familiar act taken by Black feminists and offer a critique of every white feminist for her failure to articulate a conception of a racialized sexuality. I could argue that while it has been acknowledged that race is not simply additive to, or derivative of, sexual difference, few white feminists have attempted to move beyond simply stating this point to describe the powerful effect that race has on the construction and representation of gender and sexuality. I could go further and note that even when race is mentioned it is a limited notion devoid of complexities. Sometimes it is reduced to biology and other times referred to as a social construction. Rarely is it *used* as a "global sign," a "metalanguage," as the "ultimate trope of difference, arbitrarily contrived to produce and maintain relations of power and subordination" (Higginbotham 255).

If I were to make this argument, I wonder under what subheading such an article would appear in *The Lesbian and Gay Studies Reader?* Assuming, of course, that they would want to include it in the second edition. How about "Politics and Sex"? Well, it would certainly be political, but what would anybody learn about sex from it? As I look at my choices I see that I would want my article to appear in the section "Subjectivity, Discipline, Resistance." But where would I situate myself in the group of essays that discuss "lesbian experience," "lesbian identity," "gender insubordination," and the "Butch-Femme Aesthetic"? Perhaps they wouldn't want a reprint after all, and I'd be off the hook. Maybe I've just hit one of those "constructed silences" that Teresa de Lauretis writes about as one of the problems in lesbian and gay studies ("Queer" viii).

When *The Lesbian and Gay Studies Reader* was published, I followed my usual practice and searched for the articles on Black women's sexuality. This reading practice has become such a commonplace in my life I have forgotten how and when I began it. I never open a book about lesbians or gays with the expectation that I will find some essay that will address the concerns of my life. Given that on the average most collections don't include writers of color, just the appearance of essays by African Americans, Latinos, and Native Americans in this volume was welcome. The work of Barbara Smith, Stuart Hall, Phillip Brian Harper,

Gloria Hull, Deborah McDowell, and, of course, Audre Lorde has deeply influenced my intellectual and political work for many years, as has the work of many of the other writers in *The Lesbian and Gay Studies Reader.*

Yet, despite the presence of these writers, this text displays the consistently exclusionary practices of lesbian and gay studies in general. In my reading, the canonical terms and categories of the field, *lesbian, gay, butch, femme, sexuality,* and *subjectivity,* are stripped of context in the works of those theorizing about these very categories, identities, and subject positions. Each of these terms is defined with white as the normative state of existence. This is an obvious criticism that many have expressed since the appearance of this volume. More interesting is the question of whether the essays engaging with the canonical terms have been in any way informed by the work of the writers of color that do appear in the volume. The essays by Hull and McDowell both address the point I am trying to make. Hull describes the life of Angelina Weld Grimké, a poet of the Harlem Renaissance whose poetry expressed desire for women. This desire is circumscribed, underwritten, and unspoken in her poetry. McDowell's critical reading of Nella Larsen's *Passing* also points to the submersion of sexuality and same-sex desire among Black women. In addition, Harper's essay on the death of Max Robinson, one of the most visible African Americans of his generation, foregrounds the silence in Black communities on the issue of sexuality and AIDS. "Silence" is emphasized as well in the essay by Ana Maria Alonso and Maria Teresa Koreck on the AIDS crisis in "Hispanic" communities. But the issue of silence about so-called deviant sexuality in public discourse and its submersion in private spaces for people of color is never addressed in theorizing about the canonical categories of lesbian and gay studies in the reader. More important, public discourse on the sexuality of particular racial and ethnic groups is shaped by processes that pathologize those groups, which in turn produces the submersion of sexuality and the attendant silence(s). Lesbian and gay theory fails to acknowledge that these very processes are connected to the construction of the sexualities of whites, historically and contemporaneously.

Queer Words and Queer Practices

I am not by nature an optimist, although I do believe that change is possible and necessary. Does a shift from lesbian to queer relieve my sense of anxiety over whether the exclusionary practices of lesbian and gay studies can be resolved? If queer theory is, as de Lauretis notes in her introduction to the first special issue of *differences*, the place where "we [would] be willing to examine, make explicit, compare, or confront the respective histories, assumptions, and conceptual frameworks that have characterized the self-representations of North American lesbians and gay men, of color and white," and if it is "from there, [that] we could then go on to recast or reinvent the terms of our sexualities, to construct another discursive horizon, another way of thinking the sexual," then *maybe* I had found a place to explore the ways in which queer, Black, and female subjectivities are produced (iv–v). Of course, I first had to gather more evidence about this shift before I jumped into the fray.

In her genealogy of queer theory, de Lauretis argues that the term was arrived at in the effort to avoid all the distinctions in the discursive protocols that emerged from the standard usage of the terms *lesbians* and *gay*. The kind of distinctions she notes includes the need to add qualifiers of race or national affiliation to the labels "lesbian" and "gay." De Lauretis goes on to address my central concern. She writes:

> The fact of the matter is, most of us, lesbians and gay men, do not know much about one another's sexual history, experiences, fantasies, desire, or modes of theorizing. And we do not know enough about ourselves, as well, when it comes to differences between and within lesbians, and between and within gay men, in relation to race and its attendant differences of class or ethnic culture, generational, geographical, and sociopolitical location. *We do not know enough to theorize those differences.* (viii, emphasis added)

She continues:

> Thus an equally troubling question in the burgeoning field of "gay and lesbian studies" concerns the discursive constructions and constructed silences around the relations of race to identity and subjectivity in the practices of homosexualities and the representations of same sex desire. (viii)

In my reading of her essay, de Lauretis then goes on to attribute the problem of the lack of knowledge of the experiences of gays and lesbians of color to gays and lesbians of color. While noting the problems of their restricted access to publishing venues or academic positions, she concludes that "perhaps, to a gay writer and critic of color, defining himself gay is not of the utmost importance; he may have other more pressing

304

priorities in his work and life" (ix). This is a woefully inadequate char-acterization of the problem of the visibility of gays and lesbians of color. Certainly institutional racism, homophobia, and the general structural inequalities in American society have a great deal more to do with this invisibility than personal choices. I have reported de Lauretis's words at length because her work is symptomatic of the disjuncture I see between the stated goals of the volume she edited and what it actually enacts.

Despite the presence of writers of color, the authors of the essays in the *differences* volume avoid interrogating their own practices with re-spect to the issue of difference—that is to say, to differences of race, eth-nicity, and representation in analyzing subjectivity, desire, and the use of the psychoanalytic in gay and lesbian theory. Only Ekua Omosupe ex-plicitly addresses the issue of Black female subjectivity, and her essay foregrounds the very issue that queer theory ostensibly is committed to addressing. Omosupe still sees the need to announce her skepticism at the use of the term *lesbian* without the qualifier "Black" and addresses the lack of attention to race in gay and lesbian studies in her analysis of Adrienne Rich's work (108). For her, the term *lesbian* without the racial qualifier is simply to be read as "white" lesbian. Despite her criticism, however, she too avoids confronting difference within the category of Black lesbian, speaking of "the" Black lesbian without attention to or ac-knowledgment of a multiplicity of identities or subject positions for Black women. She notes that the title of Audre Lorde's collected essays is *Sister Outsider,* which she argues is "an apt metaphor for the Black les-bian's position in relation to the white dominant political cultures and to her own Black community as well" (106). But metaphors reveal as much as they conceal, and Omosupe cannot tell us what kind of out-sider Lorde is—that is to say, what sexual practices, discourses, and sub-ject positions within her Black community she was rebelling against. As with the Hull and McDowell essays, Omosupe's article acknowledges si-lence, erasure, and invisibility as crucial issues in the dominant dis-courses about Black female sexuality, while the essay and the volume as a whole continue to enact this silence.

Thus, queer theory as reflected in the *differences* volume has so far failed to theorize the very questions that de Lauretis announces the term *queer* will address. I disagree with her assertion that we do not know enough about one another's differences to theorize differences between and within gays and lesbians in relation to race. This kind of theorizing of difference, after all, isn't simply a matter of empirical examples. And we do know enough to delineate what queer theorists *should* want to know. For me it is a question of knowing specifically about the production of Black female queer sexualities: if the sexualities of Black women have been shaped by silence, erasure, and invisibility in dominant discourses, then are Black lesbian sexualities doubly silenced? What methodologies are available to read and understand this perceived void and gauge its direct and indirect effects on that which is visible? Conversely, how does the structure of what is visible, namely white female sexualities, shape those not-absent-though-not-present Black female sexualities that, as O'Grady argues, cannot be separated or understood in isolation from one another? And, finally, how do these racialized sexualities shaped by silence, erasure, and invisibility coexist with other sexualities, the closeted sexualities of white queers, for example? It seems to me that there are two projects here that need to be worked out. White feminists must refigure (white) female sexualities so that they are not theoretically dependent upon an absent-yet-ever-present pathologized Black female sexuality. I am not arguing that this figuration of (white) female sexuality must try to encompass completely the experiences of Black women but that it must include a conception of the power relations between white and Black women as expressed in the representations of sexuality (Higginbotham 252).[1] This model of power, as Judith Butler has argued, must avoid setting up "racism and homophobia and misogyny as parallel or analogical relations," while recognizing that "what has to be thought through, is the ways in which these vectors of power require and deploy each other for the purpose of their own articulation" (18). Black feminist theorists must reclaim sexuality through the creation of a counternarrative that can reconstitute a present Black female subjectivity and that includes an analysis of power relations between white and Black women and among different groups of Black women. In both cases I am arguing for the development of a complex, relational, but not necessarily analogous conception of racialized sexualities (JanMohamed 94). In order to describe more fully what I see as the project for Black feminist theorists, I want to turn now to a review of some of the current discussions of Black women's sexuality.

The Problematic of Silence

To name ourselves rather than be named we must first
see ourselves. For some of us this will not be easy. So
long unmirrored, we may have forgotten how we look.
Nevertheless, we can't theorize in a void; we must have
evidence.

—Lorraine O'Grady, "Olympia's Maid"

Black (W)holes and the Geometry of Black Female Sexuality

Black feminist theorists have almost universally described Black women's sexuality, when viewed from the vantage of the dominant discourses, as an absence. In one of the earliest and most compelling discussions of Black women's sexuality, the literary critic Hortense Spillers wrote, "Black women are the beached whales of the sexual universe, unvoiced, misseen, not doing, awaiting *their* verb"("Interstices" 74). For writer Toni Morrison, Black women's sexuality is one of the "unspeakable things unspoken" of the African American experience. Black women's sexuality is often described in metaphors of speechlessness, space, or vision, as a "void" or empty space that is simultaneously ever visible (exposed) and invisible and where Black women's bodies are always already colonized. In addition, this always already colonized Black female body has so much sexual potential that it has none at all (Spillers, "Interstices" 85). Historically, Black women have reacted to this repressive force of the hegemonic discourses on race and sex with silence, secrecy, and a partially self-chosen invisibility.

Black feminist theorists, historians, literary critics, sociologists, lawyers, and cultural critics have drawn upon a specific historical narrative that purportedly describes the factors that have produced and maintained perceptions of Black women's sexuality (including their own). Three themes emerge in this history: first, the construction of the Black female as the embodiment of sex and the attendant invisibility of Black women as the unvoiced, unseen everything that is not white; second, the resistance of Black women both to negative stereotypes of their sexuality and to the material effects of those stereotypes on their lives; and, finally, the evolution of a "culture of dissemblance" and a "politics of silence" by Black women on the issue of their sexuality. The historical narrative begins with the production of the image of a pathologized Black female "other" in the eighteenth century by European colonial elites and the new biological scientists. By the nineteenth century, with the increasing exploitation and abuse of Black women during and after slavery, U.S. Black women reformers began to develop strategies to counter negative stereotypes of their sexuality and their use as a justification for the rape, lynching, and other abuses of Black women by whites. Although some of the strategies used by Black women reformers might have initially been characterized as resistance to dominant and increasingly hegemonic constructions of their sexuality, by the early twentieth century Black women reformers promoted a public silence about sexuality that, it could be argued, continues to the present.[2] This "politics of silence," as described by historian Evelyn Brooks Higginbotham, emerged as a political strategy by Black women reformers who hoped by their silence and by the promotion of proper Victorian morality to demonstrate the lie of the image of the sexually immoral Black woman (262). Historian Darlene Clark Hine argues that the "culture of dissemblance" that this politics engendered was seen as a way for Black women to "protect the sanctity of inner aspects of their lives" (915). She defines this culture as "the behavior and attitudes of Black women that created the appearance of openness and disclosure but actually shielded the truth of their inner lives and selves from their oppressors" (915). "Only with secrecy," Hine argues, "thus achieving a self-imposed invisibility, could ordinary Black women acrue the psychic space and harness the resources needed to hold their own" (915). And by the projection of the image of a "super-moral" Black woman, they hoped to garner greater respect, justice, and opportunity for all Black Americans (915). Of course, as Higginbotham notes, there were problems with this strategy. First, it did not achieve its goal of ending the negative stereotyping of Black women. And second, some middle-class Black women engaged in policing the behavior of poor and working-class women and any who deviated from a Victorian norm in the name of protecting the "race."[3] My interpretation of the conservatizing and policing aspect of the "politics of silence" is that Black women reformers were responding to the ways in which any Black woman could find herself "exposed" and characterized in racist sexual terms no matter what the truth of her individual life and that they saw this so-called deviant individual behavior as a threat to the race as a whole. Finally, one of the most enduring and problematic aspects of the "politics of silence" is that in choosing silence Black women also lost the ability to articulate any conception of their sexuality.

Without more detailed historical studies we will not know the extent of this "culture of dissemblance," and many questions will remain to be answered.[4] Was it expressed differently in rural and in urban areas, in the North, West, or South? How was it maintained? Where and how was it resisted? How was it shaped by class? And, furthermore, how did it change over time? How did something that was initially adopted as a political strategy in a specific historical period become so ingrained in Black life as to be recognizable as a culture? Or did it? What emerges from the very incomplete history we have is a situation in which Black women's sexuality is ideologically located in a nexus between race and gender, where the Black female subject is not seen and has no voice. Methodologically, Black feminists have found it difficult even to fully characterize this juncture, this point of erasure where African American women are located. As legal scholar Kimberlé Crenshaw puts it, "Existing within the overlapping margins of race and gender discourse and the empty spaces between, it is a location whose very nature resists telling" (403). And this silence about sexuality is enacted individually and collectively by Black women and by Black feminist theorists writing about Black women.

It should not surprise us that Black women are silent about sexuality. The imposed production of silence and the removal of any alternatives to the production of silence reflect the deployment of power against racialized subjects, "wherein those who could speak did not want to and those who did want to speak were prevented from doing so" (JanMohamed 105). It is this deployment of power at the level of the social and the individual that has to be historicized. It seems clear that we need a methodology that allows us to contest rather than reproduce the ideological system that has up to now defined the terrain of Black women's sexuality. Spillers made this point over a decade ago when she wrote: "Because black American women do not participate, as a category of social and cultural agents, in the legacies of symbolic power, they maintain no allegiances to a strategic formation of texts, or ways of talking about sexual experience, that even remotely resemble the paradigm of symbolic domination, except that such a paradigm has been their concrete disaster" ("Interstices" 80). To date, through the work of Black feminist literary critics, we know more about the elision of sexuality by Black women than we do about the possible varieties of expression of sexual desire.[5] Thus what we have is a very narrow view of Black women's sexuality. Certainly it is true, as Crenshaw notes, that "in feminist contexts, sexuality represents a central site of the oppression of women; rape and the rape trial are its dominant narrative trope. In antiracist discourse, sexuality is also a central site upon which the repression of blacks has been premised; the lynching narrative is embodied as its trope" (405). Sexuality is also, as Carol Vance defines it, "simultaneously a domain of restriction, repression, and danger as well as a domain of exploration, pleasure, and agency" (1). The restrictive, repressive, and dangerous aspects of Black female sexuality have been emphasized by Black feminist writers while pleasure, exploration, and agency have gone underanalyzed.

I want to suggest that Black feminist theorists have not taken up this project in part because of their own status in the academy. Reclaiming the body as well as subjectivity is a process that Black feminist theorists in the academy must go through themselves while they are doing the work of producing theory. Black feminist theorists are themselves engaged in a process of fighting to reclaim the body—the maimed immoral Black female body—which can be and still is used by others to discredit them as producers of knowledge and as speaking subjects. Legal scholar Patricia Williams illuminates my point: "No matter what degree of professional I am, people will greet and dismiss my black femaleness as unreliable, untrustworthy, hostile, angry, powerless, irrational, and probably destitute" (95). When reading student evaluations, she finds comments about her teaching and her body: "I marvel, in a moment of genuine bitterness, that anonymous student evaluations speculating on dimensions of my anatomy are nevertheless counted into the statistical measurement of my teaching proficiency" (95). The hypervisibility of Black women academics and the contemporary fascination with what bell hooks calls the "commodification of Otherness" (21) mean that Black women today find themselves precariously perched in the academy. Ann duCille notes:

> Mass culture, as hooks argues, produces, promotes, and perpetuates the commodification of Otherness through the exploitation of the black female body. In the 1990s, however, the principal sites of exploitation are not simply the cabaret, the speakeasy, the music video, the glamour magazine; they are also the academy, the publishing industry, the intellectual community. (592)

In tandem with the notion of silence, Black women writers have repeatedly drawn on the notion of the "invisible" to describe aspects of Black women's lives in general and sexuality in particular. Lorde writes that "within this country where racial difference creates a constant, if unspoken distortion of vision, Black women have on the one hand always been highly visible, and on the other hand, have been rendered invisible through the depersonalization of racism" (91). The hypervisibility of Black women academics means that visibility too can be used to control the intellectual issues that Black women can and cannot speak about. With Black women already threatened with being sexualized and rendered inauthentic as knowledge producers in the academy by students and colleagues alike, this avoidance of theorizing about sexuality can be read as one contemporary manifestation of their structured silence. I want to stress here that the silence about sexuality on the part of Black women academics is no more a "choice" than was the silence practiced by early twentieth-century Black women. This production of *silence* instead of *speech* is an effect of the institutions such as the academy that are engaged in the commodification of Otherness. While hypervisibility can be used to silence Black women academics, it can also serve them. Lorde has argued that the "visibility which makes us most vulnerable," that of being Black, "is that which is the source of our greatest strength." Patricia Hill Collins's interpretation of Lorde's comment is that "paradoxically, being treated as an invisible Other gives black women a peculiar angle of vision, the outsider-within stance that has served so many African-American women intellectuals as a source of tremendous strength" (94).

Yet, while invisibility may be somewhat useful for academicians, the practice of a politics of silence belies the power of such a stance for social change. Most important, the outsider-within stance does not allow space for addressing the question of other outsiders, namely Black lesbians. Black feminist theorizing about Black female sexuality, with a few exceptions—Cheryl Clarke, Jewelle Gomez, Barbara Smith, and Audre Lorde—has been relentlessly focused on heterosexuality. The historical narrative that dominates discussion of Black female sexuality does not address even the possibility of a Black lesbian sexuality, or of a lesbian or queer subject. Spillers confirms this point when she notes that "the sexual realities of black American women across the spectrum of sexual preference and widened sexual styles tend to be a missing dialectical feature of the entire discussion" ("Interstices" 91).

At this juncture, then, I cannot cast blame for a lack of attention to Black lesbian sexuality solely on white feminist theorists. De Lauretis argues that female homosexualities may be conceptualized as social and cultural forms in their own right, which are undercoded or discursively dependent upon more established forms. They (and male homosexualities) therefore act as "an agency of social process whose mode of functioning is both interactive and yet resistant, both participatory and yet distinct, claiming at once equality and difference, and demanding political and historical representation while insisting on its material and historical specificity" ("Queer" iii). If this is true, then theorizing about Black lesbian sexuality is crucially dependent upon the existence of a conception of Black women's sexuality in general. I am not arguing that Black lesbian sexualities are derivative of Black female heterosexualities but only that we cannot understand the latter without understanding it in relation to the former. In particular, since discussions of Black female sexuality often turn to the issue of the devastating effects of rape, incest, and sexual abuse, I want to argue that Black queer female sexualities should be seen as one of the sites where Black female desire is expressed.

Discussions of Black lesbian sexuality have most often focused on differences from or equivalencies with white lesbian sexualities, with "Black" added to delimit the fact that Black lesbians share a history with other Black women. However, this addition tends to obfuscate rather than illuminate the subject position of Black lesbians. One obvious example of distortion is that Black lesbians do not experience homophobia in the same way as do white lesbians. Here, as with other oppressions, the homophobia experienced by Black women is always shaped by racism. What has to be explored and historicized is the specificity of Black lesbian experience. I want to understand in what way Black lesbians are "outsiders" within Black communities. This, I think, would force us to examine the construction of the "closet" by Black lesbians. Although this is the topic for another essay, I want to argue here that if we accept the existence of the "politics of silence" as a historical legacy shared by all Black women, then certain expressions of Black female sexuality will be rendered as dangerous, for individuals and for the collectivity. From this it follows then that the culture of dissemblance makes it acceptable for some heterosexual Black women to cast Black lesbians as proverbial traitors to the race.[6] And this in turn explains why Black lesbians who would announce or act out desire for women—whose deviant sexuality exists within an already preexisting deviant sexuality—have been wary of embracing the status of "traitor" and the attendant loss of community such an embrace engenders.[7] Of course, while some Black lesbians have hidden the truth of their lives, there have been many forms of resistance to the conception of lesbian as traitor within Black communities. Audre Lorde is one obvious example. Lorde's claiming of her Black and lesbian difference "forced both her white and Black lesbian friends to contend with her historical agency in the face of [this] larger racial/sexual history that would reinvent her as dead" (Karla Scott, qtd. in de Lauretis, *Practice* 36). I would also argue that Lorde's writing, with its focus on the erotic, on passion and desire, suggests that Black lesbian sexualities can be read as one expression of the reclamation of the despised Black female body. Therefore, the works of Lorde and other Black lesbian writers, because they foreground the very aspects of Black female sexuality that are submerged—that is, female desire and agency—are critical to our theorizing of Black female sexualities. Since silence about sexuality is being produced by Black women and Black feminist theorists, that silence itself suggests that Black women do have some degree of agency. A focus on Black lesbian sexualities, I suggest, implies that another discourse—other than silence—can be produced.

I also suggest that the project of theorizing Black female sexualities must confront psychoanalysis. Given that the Freudian paradigm is the dominant discourse that defines how sexuality is understood in this postmodern time, Black feminist theorists have to answer the question posed by Michele Wallace: "Is the Freudian drama transformed by race in a way that would render it altered but usable?" (*Invisibility* 231) While some Black feminists have called the psychoanalytic approach racist, others, such as Spillers, Mae Henderson, and Valerie Smith, have shown its usefulness in analyzing the texts of Black women writers. As I am not a student of psychoanalytic theory, my suggested responses to Wallace's question can only be tentative at best. Though I do not accept all aspects of the Freudian paradigm, I do see the need for exploring its strengths and limitations in developing a theory of Black female sexualities.

It can readily be acknowledged that the collective history of Black women has in some ways put them in a different relationship to the canonical categories of the Freudian paradigm, that is, to the father, the maternal body, to the female-sexed body (Spillers, "Mama's"). On the level of the symbolic, however, Black women have created whole worlds of sexual signs and signifiers, some of which align with those of whites and some of which do not. Nonetheless, they are worlds that always have to contend with the power that the white world has to invade, pathologize, and disrupt those worlds. In many ways the Freudian paradigm implicitly depends on the presence of the Black female other. One of its more problematic aspects is that in doing so it relegates Black women's sexuality to the irreducibly abnormal category in which there are no distinctions between homosexual and heterosexual women. By virtue of this lack of distinction, there is a need for Black women, both lesbian and heterosexual, to, as de Lauretis describes it, "reconstitute a female-sexed body as a body for the subject and for her desire" (*Practice* 200). This is a need that is perhaps expressed differently by Black women than by white women, whose sexualities have not been subjected to the *same* forces of repression and domination. And this seems to me to be a critical place where the work of articulating Black female sexualities must begin. Disavowing the designation of Black female sexualities as inherently abnormal, while acknowledging the material and symbolic effects of the appellation, we could begin the project of understanding how differently located Black women engage in reclaiming the body and expressing desire.

What I want to propose requires me to don one of my other hats, that of a student of physics. As I struggled with the ideas I cover in this essay, over and over again I found myself wrestling with the juxtaposed images of "white" (read normal) and "Black" (read not white and abnormal) sexuality. In her essay "Variations on Negation," Michele Wallace invokes the idea of the black hole as a trope that can be used to describe the invisibility of Black creativity in general and Black female creativity

313

specifically (*Invisibility* 218). As a former physics student, I was immediately drawn to this image. Yet it also troubled me.[8] As Wallace rightfully notes, the observer outside of the hole sees it as a void, an empty place in space. However, it is not empty; it is a dense and full place in space. There seemed to me to be two problems: first, the astrophysics of black holes, in other words, how do you deduce the presence of a black hole? And second, what is it like inside of a black hole? I don't want to stretch this analogy too far, so here are my responses. To the first question, I suggest that we can detect the presence of a black hole by its effects on the region of space where it is located. One way that physicists do this is by observing binary star systems. A binary star system is one that contains two bodies that orbit around each other under mutual gravitational attraction. Typically, in these systems one finds a visible apparently "normal" star in close orbit with another body such as a black hole, which is not seen optically. The existence of the black hole is inferred from the fact that the visible star is in orbit and its shape is distorted in some way, or it is detected by the energy emanating from the region in space around the visible star that could not be produced by the visible star alone.[9] Therefore, the identification of a black hole requires the use of sensitive detectors of energy and distortion. In the case of Black female sexualities, this implies that we need to develop reading strategies that allow us to make visible the distorting and productive effects these sexualities produce in relation to more visible sexualities. To the second question— what is it like inside of a black hole?—the answer is that we must think in terms of a different geometry. Rather than assuming that Black female sexualities are structured along an axis of normal and perverse paralleling that of white women, we might find that for Black women a different geometry operates. For example, acknowledging this difference I could read the relationship between Shug, Celie, and Mister in Alice Walker's *The Color Purple* as one that depicts desire between women and desire between women and men simultaneously, in dynamic relationship rather than in opposition. This mapping of the geometry of Black female sexualities will perhaps require Black feminist theorists to engage the Freudian paradigm more rigorously, or it may cause us to disrupt it.

Can I Get Home from Here?

I see my lesbian poetics as a way of entering into a dialogue—from the margins—with Black feminist critics, theorists and writers. My work has been to imagine an

historical Black woman-to-woman eroticism and living—
overt, discrete, coded, or latent as it might be. To imagine Black women's sexuality as a polymorphous erotic
that does not exclude desire for men but also does not
privilege it. To imagine, without apology, voluptuous
Black women's sexualities.

—Cheryl Clarke, "Living the Texts Out"

So where has my search taken me? And why does the journey matter? I
want to give a partial answer to the question I posed at the beginning of
this chapter. At this juncture queer theory has allowed me to break open
the category of gay and lesbian and begin to question how sexualities
and sexual subjects are produced by dominant discourses and then to
interrograte the reactions and resistances to those discourses. However,
interrogating sites of resistance and reaction did not take me beyond
what is generally done in gay and lesbian studies. The turn to queer
should allow me to explore, in Clarke's words, the "overt, discrete,
coded, or latent" and "polymorphous" eroticism of differently located
Black women. It is still not clear to me, however, that other queer theorists will resist the urge to engage in a reranking, erasure, or appropriation of sexual subjects who are at the margins of dominant discourses.

Why does my search for Black women's sexuality matter? Wallace
once wrote that she feared being called elitist when she acted as though
cultural criticism was as crucial to the condition of Black women as
health, the law, politics, economics, and the family. "But," she continued,
"I am convinced that the major battle for the 'other' of the 'other' [Black
women] will be to find voice, transforming the construction of dominant
discourse in the process" (*Invisibility* 236). It is my belief that what is
desperately needed is more rigorous cultural criticism detailing how
power is deployed through issues like sexuality and the alternative forms
that even an oppressed subject's power can take. Since 1987, a major part
of my intellectual work as a historian of U.S. science and medicine has
addressed the AIDS crisis in African American communities. The AIDS
epidemic is being used, as Simon Watney has said, to "inflect, condense
and rearticulate the ideological meanings of race, sexuality, gender, childhood, privacy, morality and nationalism" (ix). The position of Black
women in this epidemic was dire from the beginning and worsens with
each passing day. Silence, erasure, and the use of images of immoral sexuality abound in narratives about the experiences of Black women with
AIDS. Their voices are not heard in discussions of AIDS, while intimate
details of their lives are exposed to justify their victimization. In the "war

of representation" that is being waged through this epidemic, Black women are victims that are once again the "other" of the "other," the deviants of the deviants, regardless of their sexual identities or practices. While white gay male activists are using the ideological space framed by this epidemic to contest the notion that homosexuality is "abnormal" and to preserve the right to live out their homosexual desires, Black women are rendered silent. The gains made by queer activists will do nothing for Black women if the stigma continues to be attached to their sexuality. The work of Black feminist critics is to find ways to contest the historical construction of Black female sexualities by illuminating how the dominant view was established and maintained and how it can be disrupted. This work might very well save some Black women's lives. I want this epidemic to be used to foment the sexual revolution that Black Americans never had (Giddings 462). I want it to be used to make visible Black women's self-defined sexualities.

Visibility in and of itself, however, is not my only goal. Several writers, including bell hooks, have argued that one answer to the silence now being produced on the issue of Black female sexuality is for Black women to see themselves, to mirror themselves (61). The appeal to the visual and the visible is deployed as an answer to the legacy of silence and repression. As theorists, we have to ask what we assume such reflections would show. Would the mirror Black women hold up to themselves and to each other provide access to the alternative sexual universe within the metaphorical black hole? Mirroring as a way of negating a legacy of silence needs to be explored in much greater depth than it has been to date by Black feminist theorists. An appeal to the visual is not uncomplicated or innocent. As theorists we have to ask how vision is structured, and, following that, we have to explore how difference is established, how it operates, how and in what ways it constitutes subjects who *see* and *speak* in the world (Haraway, "Promises" 313). This we must apply to the ways in which Black women are seen and not seen by the dominant society and to how they see themselves in a different landscape. But in overturning the "politics of silence" the goal cannot be merely to be seen: visibility in and of itself does not erase a history of silence, nor does it challenge the structure of power and domination, symbolic and material, that determines what can and cannot be seen. The goal should be to develop a "politics of articulation." This politics would build on the interrogation of what makes it possible for Black women to speak and act.

Finally, my search for Black women's sexuality through queer theory has taught me that I need not simply add the label queer to my list as another naturalized identity. As I have argued, there is no need to re-produce Black women's sexualities as a silent void. Nor are Black queer female sexualities simply identities. Rather, they represent discursive and material terrains where there exists the possibility for the active pro-duction of speech, desire, and agency.

NOTES

My thanks to Joan Scott, Mary Poovey, Donna Penn, and Geeta Patel for their support and for their thoughtful and incisive critiques of the ideas in this essay.

1. Here I am referring to the work of Stuart Hall and especially Hazel Carby: "We need to recognize that we live in a society in which dominance and sub-ordination are structured through processes of racialization that continuously interact with other forces of socialization. . . . But processes of racialization, when they are mentioned at all in multicultural debates are discussed as if they were the sole concern of those particular groups perceived to be racialized sub-jects. Because the politics of difference work with concepts of individual iden-tity, rather than structures of inequality and exploitation, processes of racializa-tion are marginalized and given symbolic meaning only when subjects are black" (Carby, "Multicultural" 193).

2. See Higginbotham, Hine, Giddings, Carby (*Reconstructing*), and Brown ("What").

3. See Carby, "Policing." Elsa Barkley Brown argues that the desexualization of Black women was not just a middle-class phenomenon imposed on working-class women. Though many working-class women resisted Victorian notions of womanhood and developed their own notions of sexuality and respectability, some also, from their own experiences, embraced a desexualized image ("Ne-gotiating" 144).

4. The historical narrative discussed here is very incomplete. To date there are no detailed historical studies of Black women's sexuality.

5. See analyses of novels by Nella Larsen and Jessie Fauset in Carby (*Recon-structing*), McDowell, and others.

6. I participated in a group discussion of two novels written by Black women, Jill Nelson's *Volunteer Slavery* and Audre Lorde's *Zami,* where one Black woman remarked that while she thought Lorde's book was better written than Nelson's, she was disturbed that Lorde spoke so much about sex and "aired all of her dirty linen in public." She held to this even after it was pointed out to her that Nel-son's book also included descriptions of her sexual encounters.

7. I am reminded of my mother's response when I "came out" to her. She asked me why, given that I was already Black and that I had a nontraditional profession for a woman, I would want to take on one more thing that would make my life difficult. My mother's point, which is echoed by many Black women, is that in announcing my homosexuality I was choosing to alienate my-self from the Black community.

8. I was disturbed by the fact that the use of the image of a black hole could

also evoke a negative image of Black female sexuality reduced to the lowest possible denominator, in other words, just a "hole."

9. The existence of the second body in a binary system is inferred from the periodic Doppler shift of the spectral lines of the visible star, which shows that it is in orbit, and by the production of X-ray radiation. My points are taken from the discussion of the astrophysics of black holes in Wald, chaps. 8 and 9.

REFERENCES

Abelove, Henry, Michèle Barale, and David Halperin, eds., *The Lesbian and Gay Studies Reader.* New York: Routledge, 1993.

Alonso, Ana Maria, and Maria Teresa Koreck. "Silences, 'Hispanics,' AIDS, and Sexual Practices." In Henry Abelove, Michèle Barale, and David Halperin, eds., *The Lesbian and Gay Studies Reader,* 110–26. New York: Routledge, 1993.

———. " 'What Has Happened Here': The Politics of Difference in Women's History and Feminist Politics." *Feminist Studies* 18, no. 2 (1992): 295–312.

Busia, Abena, and Stanlie James. *Theorizing Black Feminisms: The Visionary Pragmatism of Black Women.* New York: Routledge, 1993.

Butler, Judith. *Bodies That Matter: On the Discursive Limits of "Sex."* New York: Routledge, 1993.

Carby, Hazel. "The Multicultural Wars." In Michele Wallace and Gina Dent, eds., *Black Popular Culture,* 187–99. Seattle: Bay, 1992.

———. "Policing the Black Woman's Body in the Urban Context." *Critical Inquiry* 18 (fall, 1992): 738–55.

———. *Reconstructing Womanhood: The Emergence of the Afro-American Woman Novelist.* New York: Oxford University Press, 1987.

Clarke, Cheryl. "Living the Texts Out: Lesbians and the Uses of Black Women's Traditions." In Abena Busia and Stanlie James, eds., *Theorizing Black Feminisms: The Visionary Pragmatism of Black Women,* 214–27. New York: Routledge, 1993.

Collins, Patricia Hill. *Black Feminist Thought, Knowledge, Consciousness, and the Politics of Empowerment.* Cambridge: Unwin Hyman, 1990.

Crenshaw, Kimberlé. "Whose Story Is It Anyway?: Feminist and Antiracist Appropriations of Anita Hill." In Toni Morrison, ed., *Rac(e)-ing Justice, En-gendering Power: Essays on Anita Hill, Clarence Thomas and the Construction of Social Reality,* 402–40. New York: Pantheon, 1992.

de Lauretis, Teresa. *The Practice of Love: Lesbian Sexuality and Perverse Desire.* Bloomington: Indiana University Press, 1994.

———. "Queer Theory: Lesbian and Gay Sexualities: An Introduction." *differences* 3 (summer, 1991): iii–xviii.

duCille, Ann. "The Occult of True Black Womanhood: Critical Demeanor and Black Feminist Studies." *Signs* 19, no. 3 (1994): 591–629.

Giddings, Paula. "The Last Taboo." In Toni Morrison, ed., *Rac(e)-ing Justice, Engendering Power: Essays on Anita Hill, Clarence Thomas and the Construction of Social Reality,* 441–65. New York: Pantheon, 1992.

Gomez, Jewelle. "A Cultural Legacy Denied and Discovered: Black Lesbians in Fiction by Women." In Barbara Smith, ed., *Home Girls: A Black Feminist Anthology,* 110–23. New York: Kitchen Table, 1983.

Haraway, Donna. "The Promises of Monsters: A Regenerative Politics for Inappropriate/d Others." In Laurence Grossberg, Cary Nelson, and Paula Treichler, eds., *Cultural Studies,* 295–337. New York: Routledge, 1992.

———. "Situated Knowledges: The Science Question in Feminism and the Privilege of Partial Perspective." In *Simians, Cyborgs, and Women: The Reinvention of Nature,* 183–201. New York: Routledge, 1991.

Harper, Philip Brian. "Eloquence and Epitaph: Black Nationalism and the Homophobic Impulse in Responses to the Death of Max Robinson." *Social Text* 9 (fall, 1991): 183–201.

Henderson, Mae Gwendolyn. "Speaking in Tongues: Dialogics, Dialectics, and the Black Woman Writer's Literary Tradition." In Cheryl Wall, ed., *Changing Our Own Words: Essays on Criticism, Theory, and Writing by Black Women,* 16–37. New Brunswick, N.J.: Rutgers University Press, 1989.

Higginbotham, Evelyn Brooks. "African-American Women's History and the Metalanguage of Race." *Signs* 17, no. 2 (1992): 251–74.

Hine, Darlene Clark. "Rape and the Inner Lives of Black Women in the Middle West: Preliminary Thoughts on the Culture of Dissemblance." *Signs* 14, no. 4 (1989): 915–20.

hooks, bell. "Selling Hot Pussy: Representations of Black Female Sexuality in the Cultural Marketplace." In *Black Looks: Race and Representation,* 61–76. Boston: South End, 1992.

Hull, Gloria T. "'Lines She Did Not Dare': Angela Weld Grimké, Harlem Renaissance Poet." In Henry Abelove, Michèle Barale, and David Halperin, eds., *The Lesbian and Gay Studies Reader,* 453–66. New York: Routledge, 1993.

JanMohamed, Abdul. "Sexuality on/of the Racial Border: Foucault, Wright, and the Articulation of 'Racialized Sexuality.'" In Donna Stanton, ed., *Discourses of Sexuality: From Aristotle to AIDS,* 94–116. Ann Arbor: University of Michigan Press 1992.

Lorde, Audre. *Sister Outsider: Essays and Speeches.* Trumansburg, N.Y.: Crossing Press, 1984.

———. *Zami: A New Spelling of My Name.* Trumansburg, N.Y.: Crossing Press, 1982.

McDowell, Deborah E. "'It's Not Safe. Not Safe at All': Sexuality in Nella Larsen's *Passing.*" In Henry Abelove, Michèle Barale, and David Halperin, eds., *The Lesbian and Gay Studies Reader,* 616–25. New York: Routledge, 1993.

Morrison, Toni, ed. *Rac(e)-ing Justice, En-gendering Power: Essays on Anita Hill, Clarence Thomas and the Construction of Social Reality.* New York: Pantheon, 1992.

Nelson, Jill. *Volunteer Slavery: My Authentic Negro Experience.* Chicago: Noble, 1993.

O'Grady, Lorraine. "Olympia's Maid: Reclaiming Black Female Subjectivity." *Afterimage* (1992): 14–23.

Omosupe, Ekua. "Black/Lesbian/Bulldagger." *differences* 3 (summer, 1991): 101–11.

Smith, Barbara. "Towards a Black Feminist Criticism." *Conditions* 2 (1977): 25–44.

———, ed. *Home Girls: A Black Feminist Anthology.* New York: Kitchen Table, 1983.

Smith, Valerie. "Black Feminist Theory and the Representation of the 'Other.' " In Cheryl Wall, ed., *Changing Our Own Words: Essays on Criticism, Theory, and Writing by Black Women,* 38–57. New Brunswick, N.J.: Rutgers University Press, 1989.

Spillers, Hortense. "Interstices: A Small Drama of Words." In Carole Vance, ed., *Pleasure and Danger: Exploring Female Sexuality,* 73–100. London: Pandora, 1989.

———. "Mama's Baby, Papa's Maybe: An American Grammar Book." *Diacritics* 17 (summer 1987): 65–81.

Vance, Carole, ed. *Pleasure and Danger: Exploring Female Sexuality.* London: Pandora, 1989.

———. "Pleasure and Danger: Toward a Politics of Sexuality," In *Pleasure and Danger: Exploring Female Sexuality,* 1–24. London: Pandora, 1989.

Wald, Robert. *Space, Time, and Gravity: The Theory of the Big Bang and Black Holes.* 2d ed. Chicago: University of Chicago Press, 1992.

Walker, Alice. *The Color Purple.* New York: Harcourt, 1982.

Wall, Cheryl, ed. *Changing Our Own Words: Essays on Criticism, Theory, and Writing by Black Women.* New Brunswick, N.J.: Rutgers University Press, 1989.

Wallace, Michele. *Invisibility Blues: From Pop to Theory.* New York: Verso, 1990.

Wallace, Michele, and Gina Dent, eds. *Black Popular Culture.* Seattle: Bay, 1992.

Watney, Simon. *Policing Desire: Pornography, AIDS and the Media.* Minneapolis: University of Minnesota Press, 1989.

Williams, Patricia J. *The Alchemy of Race and Rights: Diary of a Law Professor.* Cambridge: Harvard University Press, 1991.

CONCLUSION

Bridgett Davis

Directing the Gaze

An Inside Look at Making *Naked Acts*

> "When, I ask, do we start to see images of the black
> female body by black women made as acts of auto-
> expression . . . ? When, in other words, does the present
> begin?"
>
> —Lorraine O'Grady, visual artist, "Olympia's Maid:
>   Reclaiming Black Subjectivity"

If we are our bodies, then who are we as Black women? And further, how do we form a sense of sexuality out of whatever it is our bodies reveal us to be? This complex question is the one I posed for myself as a Black feminist back in 1992 when I set out to write a screenplay that would focus on a Black woman's journey to explore her own sexuality. The film that emerged from that screenplay, *Naked Acts,* was completed four years later and tells the story of Cece, a contemporary African American actress who does everything in her power to avoid doing a nude scene in a movie and almost gets away with it. But to everyone's surprise, Cece ends up revealing herself in ways she never imagined. Emotional nakedness, she finds, is much harder than just taking your clothes off.

Naked Acts ultimately became much more than, and much less about, one woman's sexual coming-of-age. I soon discovered that in my efforts to explore a Black woman's sexual identity, I needed to first explore the myriad influences—personal, familial, communal, and societal—that have an impact on her sense of herself as a sexual being. Then and only then did it make sense for me to deal with her having a healthy sex life. Besides, what I loathe most about so many Black film characters is that they seem to fall out of the sky onto the screen, with no context for who they are or where they come from; I was determined to give Cece a rich backstory.

I reached for a historical context out of which to create this prototypical contemporary Black woman. I started by acknowledging that we've had a markedly different *sexualized* experience in this country than that of white women. I knew that as a justification for acts of brutality, white slave owners had created myths about Black women's abnormal sexual appetites; had made us out to be sexually aggressive exoticas, forever lascivious, forever "asking for it." I knew too that considering this historical baggage, it was no wonder that Black mothers had admonished their daughters over the years to "keep your dress down and your panties up" in an effort to counteract the whorish image laid unfairly upon us.

Extending the context, I looked to the dominant film portrayals of Black women in this country's cinematic history. Much, after all, of how we see ourselves is shaped by how we have been represented. No other image was more ubiquitous, of course, than that of the Mammy. The Mammy image had haunted my psyche since my college days, when I wrote a research paper on Hattie McDaniel, whose 1940 Oscar for Best Supporting Actress in *Gone with the Wind* seemed to forever immortalize the overweight, subservient, yet bull-strong Negro woman in popular culture—what Hollywood Black actress Sheryl Lee Ralph calls in a *New York Times* article the "Fat Mama on the Couch Syndrome" Joy Horowitz, "Black Actresses Still Waiting for Star Roles," (May 28, 1992).

My challenge with *Naked Acts* was to provide some subjectivity, to tell the rest of the story. Without that, I strongly felt Black women on screen would forever stay relegated to the two extremes—asexual mule or oversexed jungle bunny. To be sure, there is a third stop on the continuum of extremity in terms of our image within popular culture—that of the nagging bitch, the ball-buster, the castrator. Actress Ralph has a name for those portrayals as well. She calls them examples of the "Sassy Sister on the Corner Syndrome." It's interesting to note that no matter how demure and sexually repressed Black women have been in real life, we've never been portrayed as pure women, as the Virgin Madonna. That image has been reserved for our white counterparts.

And so, I knew that with *Naked Acts,* I wanted the present to begin—that is, I wanted us to get beyond the limitations placed on our bodies by our racialized past. Namely, I wanted the Black woman's body to be a source of beauty, an "object" of desire. But this is a tricky slope to climb, as the line between celebration and exploitation can be thin—especially in a medium as powerful as film and particularly with all the baggage we carry around this subject as Black women. It was further complicated by a radical decision on my part to showcase Black female nudity in the film. I believed it would be a cowardly act to tell a story about a Black woman learning to accept her own body and yet never reveal her nude body at any time on screen. Still, I knew it would be tough to avoid the very stereotyping I was critiquing. I ultimately decided that none of the women characters' nudity would be used in any sexual contexts, but rather in natural, everyday settings. (I had a little fun with the main male character's body. He gets to take *his* clothes off during love scenes.) Too, the audience would anticipate seeing Cece's body as she strove to keep it covered but would go on this journey with her, as she slowly peeled off more and more layers, shedding cultural baggage along with her clothing and wigs, until finally viewers would see her body only as she revealed it to herself, for herself. The effect, I hoped, would be for audiences to feel that they were witnessing a private moment, a private yet empowering moment that had nothing to do with sex but everything to do with self-awareness and the individual's own sexuality—because we are our bodies. Still, I knew this was risky.

I knew that for this woman, Cece, to be a genuine African American woman of the 1990s, she would have to embody all of those women who were influences upon her, who helped shape and form what her sexual image of herself would become. I also knew that this character's sexual identity would have to evolve out of my personal research, my effort to gather and look at the stories of contemporary women within my own life. I started with my siblings.

All three of my sisters were overweight, two of them obese. I saw how each made life choices, sometimes destructive ones, that I now feel were highly influenced by their relationship to their own bodies—and, in effect, by how they felt about themselves as Black women. I was equally influenced by a close friend from my days as a newspaper reporter in Philadelphia who had just lost fifty pounds when I met her. A beautiful Puerto Rican woman, she once told me that the two biggest changes she had to get used to after her weight loss were the flirtations from men who had barely noticed her before she lost weight and accepting what she now saw in the mirror; or as she put it, "In my head, I'm still fat."

Another influence, also stemming from my early reporting days, was my memory of being in an Atlanta newsroom the day "cropped" photos of Vanessa Williams posing nude came across the news wire. I'll never forget the glee with which the white reporters rushed out to buy copies of *Penthouse Magazine,* then clustered around the pictures, feigning shock and shaking their heads yet drinking in every photo nevertheless. So close in age to Vanessa Williams, and as another Black woman, I took the public and media denunciation of her personally. I felt that a naive young woman exploring her sexual power and her liberation had stumbled into a quagmire of stereotypes swarming around Black women's bodies, societal roles for women, and men's exploitation of those women. I felt she was a symbol of the schizophrenic attitudes toward sex and race and gender that America embraces (the Good Negress became the Bad Nigger-Girl). The fact that Williams overcame the debacle, rising in fame with her sexy image intact, only highlights the hypocrisy with which she was publicly denigrated and "punished" in the first place.

Finally, there was Oprah. Watching her over the years go through a public battle with her weight, which in effect has really been a private battle to conquer low self-esteem, has provided an extraordinary metaphor for Black women in this country. So many of us don't have the features or the figures that the dominant culture embraces, which naturally leads a lot of Black women to feel inferior. Luckily for us, here was a national figure, a woman who looked like us, working through her own similar issues on a public stage. Oprah is another symbol of America's darker-hued daughters triumphing over the damage done to the Black female psyche.

Because I always envisioned *Naked Acts* as a historical, iconographic story told through a contemporary lens, I incorporated all of these various Black women's lives and stories and portrayals into both the characterizations and the plot of the film. Cece became a twenty-seven-year-old actress who has just lost fifty-seven pounds when you meet her. Her mother, Lydia Love, is a former Blaxploitation Queen who now owns a video store. And her grandmother is a former Black actress from the 1950s. Imagine that your grandmother was Dorothy Dandridge, your mother was Pam Grier, and you wanted to be an actress. Who would you be? How to combine the smoldering-yet-nice-girl sensuality of one influence with the buxom, afro-haired, in-your-face sexiness of the other to emerge with something that is uniquely you? That is Cece's struggle.

The other women populating the film are Winsome, Randi, and Diana. Winsome represents a rarely seen type of Black woman—one who suffers from the belief that she can't be thin enough, one who sees her body as a tool for her work as a dancer/art model/actress. Randi is the full-figured character who flaunts her body, overcompensating for the asexual image usually laid upon Black women her size by relying on an over-the-top sexiness. Finally there is Diana, the "sistah spirit" who eases Cece through her struggles to regain control of and love for her own body. Diana is the emotionally centered female character of the story; she embodies what the others would be if the best parts of each of them were integrated into one woman.

The two male characters in the film represent the complex roles that Black men have played in helping to define what Black women feel about themselves as sexual beings. Joel, Cece's old flame and the first-time director of the film she is cast in, is the man who both loved her when she was heavier and wants her to show off her newly svelte body in his film. His character speaks to the ambiguous agendas of Black men in the entertainment business who genuinely love Black women and yet willingly compromise them for their own success. Marcel, as an older Black actor and producer, represents the voice of integrity and uncompromising principles. He is Cece's father figure—the man who tells her what's good for her, who pushes her to be honest, who will settle for nothing less than the best of herself.

I chose to make Cece's actual father someone whom she idolized, a man who loved her but who left her mother when Cece was a little girl. Shortly after his departure, Cece became the victim of sexual abuse at the hands of one of her mother's boyfriends.

Three major factors influenced my decision to give the main character this particular history: (1) I knew that many experts believe there is a correlation between childhood sexual abuse and eating disorders—which for Black women often result in obesity. Oprah is our most prominent example of that. (2) As an English professor, I often gave a writing assignment to my students: describe in detail your first childhood memory. I'd given this assignment at least twenty times, and without fail, in every class, I found young women writing about sexual abuse. I teach at an institution with a large population of students from other countries, and what affected me so profoundly was that these brave women were from Eastern Europe, Asia, the Caribbean, and South America, as well as the United States. I couldn't help but believe that this random sampling was representative of a silent epidemic. Herein lay the universality of the story. Women around the world, I realized, suffer from sexual abuse as young girls. I wanted in some small way to comment on that. (3) I felt Cece needed a motivation for resenting her mother as she did. Surely, if she felt her mother had not protected her as a child, she would grow to feel abandoned by her and would be struggling more with defining herself, with "stepping out of her mother's well-endowed shadow," to quote Marcel, the producer.

Finally, I made the decision not to show a "before" picture of Cece when she was fat nor to begin the film before she lost the weight. Some people have questioned me on that decision—feeling that perhaps seeing Cece struggling with her weight would help explain her problems. But I strongly believe that obesity is often a symptom of an internal, psychological battle, and I felt it important to show that Black women's body issues are not corrected simply by "losing weight"; I didn't want viewers to subconsciously think that Cece's problems could be solved if she just learned some discipline and ate less—a bad rap placed on so many overweight women. I wanted to show viewers that here was a woman whose problems *began* after she shed the pounds—because she hadn't yet shed the mental weight of her poor sense-of-self.

Casting a film that would include the nudity of Black women—even if it *was* nonsexualized—turned out to be its own major challenge. I wrote the screenplay with the lead actress in mind, so I was thrilled when she, Jake-ann Jones, agreed to do the part. I only found out days before shooting that the issues facing her character were in fact issues Jake-ann Jones had faced in her own life. She'd been overweight as a child and teenager, and she too had been sexually abused as a girl. I knew too that she was taking a professional as well as emotional risk by agreeing to be in a film that required complete frontal nudity by story's end. At one point, I entered our production office just before the shoot began and found her standing at the top of the stairs, completely naked.

"You have to see what I look like," she said. "You have to know what you're getting."

It was a powerful, defining moment. I understood then that she was entrusting me with her career, her body, her image. She needed to feel she was literally in good hands. After all, here she was, a Black actress, willingly exposing her nude body in a film. In my journal, dated 23 July 1994, I wrote: "Jake has to be treated very tenderly throughout this shoot. . . . She is laying herself open for this role. She has to be protected."

I assured her not only that her body was perfect for the film but that I would see to it that it was photographed in a sensitive way. And thanks to my cinematographer, Herman Lew—a feminist Chinese American man—it was. Shooting that final scene of the film, in which Cece strips while taking photos of herself, required several preparations. First, I insisted upon a closed set, so that only myself, Jake-ann, and the cinematographer were allowed on. Next, I made sure the scene was shot at the end of the first week of production—just long enough for the actress to feel accustomed to the shoot but not so far in that her anticipation and anxiousness about the scene would have worn her out emotionally. Finally, I told her to think of the undressing as a dance, one she would perform only for herself. And so, with a cassette player on set, we played an evocative song by Annie Lennox chosen by Jake-ann, and I let her do the entire scene as one long take. That meant that she was able to get through it without stopping. This was important for the pacing that I was after and for her own comfort. This way, we only filmed the scene twice. I felt it would be too trying if I forced her to take her clothes off over and over and over again just so I could get the "coverage" I needed as the director. Subsequently, I simply used jump cuts to move the scene along.

In trying to cast for the part of Diana, the "sistah spirit" in the film, I initially couldn't find the right actress to play the part. The problem was that Diana had to do a nude scene in the sauna room. I auditioned several actresses, and when they found that the part required nudity, they refused it. This I found both understandable and ironic. Understandable because Black actresses feel fully the double standard placed on them in the industry: a white actress can disrobe in a film and launch a career (e.g., Sharon Stone and Annette Bening); a Black actress is tainted by it and relegated forever to "those" kinds of parts (note Tracy Camilla Johns, *She's Gotta Have It*). Therefore most Black actresses make it a rule not to take their clothes off in a film. Ironic because this need to "cover up" to compensate for historical stereotyping, to avoid societal punishment, was the very issue I was attempting to explore in the film—attempting to show how it cost us a true relationship with our own bodies. Yet the situation I wanted to examine on film was potentially thwarted by the reality of that very situation. Real life was imitating art.

Luckily, I was saved by a chance meeting with a Black woman art photographer, Renee Cox, whom I met while still writing the screenplay.

"I'm creating this woman character who takes nude photographs of Black women," I said to her. "But I don't think such a person really exists."

"That's what I do," she said. I couldn't believe my good luck, but in fact, Renee has built a career out of doing self-portraiture photography of herself in arresting, self-affirming and challenging nude poses. In fact, former New York City Mayor Rudolph Giuliani went on a censorship rampage against the Brooklyn Museum of Art for showing one of her pieces in a February '01 exhibit. The piece, entitled "Yo Mama's Last Supper," depicts a revised version of The Last Supper, with a nude Renee portraying Christ at the head of the table surrounded by her disciples, who are all Black men. Seemingly so outraged by the temerity of a Black woman representing Christ in her own naked image, Giuliani threatened to create a Decency Commission to review art that would be shown in publicly financed institutions. We subsequently used one of her most stunning pieces in the film (a large-format photo of herself, nude, holding her son in her arms). More importantly, Renee was completely comfortable with the concept of nudity within artistic contexts, and she agreed with me that we as Black women needed to get beyond our own reticence about revealing our bodies. Although she was not a professional actress, I ultimately cast her as Diana because I believed the comfort she felt with her own body would transcend performance. And it did. And fortunately for the film, she had no problem with the sauna scene.

The themes of the film continued to play themselves out in the making of it. Most notable to me was the intensity with which the actresses playing Cece and Winsome worked out with a trainer throughout preproduction so that their bodies would "look good" on film. This again seemed like an irony. Here I was trying to comment on how visual media forces Black women to conform to a prescribed body type, and my film was prompting these two women to do just that. It was both enlightening and unsettling.

Since its completion, *Naked Acts* has gone on to screen in more than two dozen film festivals throughout the United States, Europe, Africa, Cape Verde, and Brazil. The film also enjoyed a one-month theatrical run in New York City in 1998, where more than 600 ticket buyers showed up for the opening night screening. Audience response has been consistently supportive and, in many cases, effusive. Men express gratitude over the chance to view women's bodies from a fresh perspective. As a male colleague said to me, "Here I am, a man who's not opposed to the male gaze, finding myself watching Cece strip from *her* point of view. That's a first for me."

Women, of course, have offered the most emotional responses to *Naked Acts,* many shedding cathartic tears by the film's ending. Black women especially seem to appreciate the emotionally raw journey taken by an African American woman struggling with an internal, personal issue. One friend, who brought her eighteen-year-old daughter to see *Naked Acts,* said to me afterward that she was glad her daughter saw the film because "she doesn't like breasts, even though she has large ones herself, and this was the first time she didn't say 'ugggh!' when she saw a woman's breasts on the screen."

Too, many seem relieved that the main character is *not* a lighter-skinned woman. As one Spelman College student said to me after a screening, "It was so good to see a dark-skinned, *thin* Black woman as the heroine for a change." She and her fellow Spelmanites talked back to the screen when Cece refused to take her clothes off in a love scene and insisted that her lover take his clothes off instead. "You go, girl!" they yelled.

White women have embraced the film's body image themes as well—finding a universality in Cece's character. In one instance, after a screening in New York, a young white woman approached me in tears. She was crying so hard, she couldn't speak. Finally, she just hugged me, said "thank you," and walked away.

Similarly, after another festival screening, a heavyset white woman ran up to me and said, "I understand Cece!" She began to recount in breathless detail how once, when extremely depressed, she'd picked up an Instamatic camera and begun snapping photos of her nude self. "I needed to do it," she said. "It made me feel valuable again."

Nowhere was the audience response to the film more intense and complex than on the African continent. *Naked Acts* was invited to be the opening-night film for the 1996 Southern African Film Festival in Harare, Zimbabwe. The film showed before a full auditorium of four hundred people, including African dignitaries, U.N. representatives, and African filmmakers, as well as hundreds of local residents. I was not prepared for the responses.

As soon as the lights came up, an older African woman came up to me and said, "Why did you have to show her body like that? Something so private?"

"Have you ever seen your own body in a mirror?" I asked.

She walked away in anger.

I then met a woman, a UNESCO representative, who quietly approached me after the screening and—referring to the flashback scene in which Cece is abused by her mother's boyfriend—explained that the rape of young girls in Zimbabwe was rampant. In fact, she told me that many African men from that region falsely believed that the cure for AIDS was to have sex with virgins, the younger the better. South African Bishop Desmond Tutu is now bringing that issue to light as the continent faces decimation from the epidemic.

Later, during a reception, another Zimbabwean woman whispered to me that she really liked my film but that I would have to understand that the love scenes in my film were disturbing because Africans don't kiss. "Well, we know that we do, but no one has ever seen it," she explained. Certainly not, I realized, on the big screen in Africa or in recycled black sitcoms exported to the continent from America.

I subsequently discovered that the Zimbabwean culture is a very modest, conservative one, and so the nudity in the film was disturbing for obvious reasons. Yet equally disturbing were the sex scenes between Cece and Joel—because they weren't married.

By the time a Zimbabwean man launched into an intense discussion with me, insisting that the sexual abuse Cece suffered had nothing to do with her problems, I at least knew enough to receive his comments within the context of an African perspective. Not surprisingly, my film, which was to have screened two more times during the festival, was quietly pulled from the screening schedule.

That hypocrisy arose again for me when I showed the film in, of all places, our nation's capital. Invited by the Women Make Movies film festival in Washington, D.C., I sent the standard promotional picture to the festival coordinators. The photo shows Cece's nude body covered up by rolls and rolls of film. To my surprise, one of the coordinators of the festival—a white woman—called to ask if I had alternative photos I could send. "Cece's nipple is showing on the photo," she said.

I looked and looked at this publicity still that had been printed in newspapers and magazines in numerous U.S. cities and at least seven other countries. What nipple? I never found it, but she was insistent that it was there. Another example of America's schizophrenia about the Black woman's body.

In contrast, the same photograph was displayed in full color as part of a centerpiece article in a weekly magazine in Milan, Italy. Attitudes toward women's bodies are so different in Italy that the female programmer of *that* festival fell in love with the image and wanted to showcase it wherever she could.

Industry response to the film has been a completely different matter. Critics have lauded it, calling the film, "Fresh, funny and original," "smartly written and charmingly neurotic," and "a rewarding and invigorating find." Yet while many film distributors—from the biggest Hollywood studio to the smallest independent label—saw *Naked Acts*, none trusted that it had marketing potential. For one, it's not easily categorized, isn't "like" something else they've seen. (The best label I could come up with has been, "It's a weak cross between *All About Eve, Cinema Paradiso,* and *Hollywood Shuffle.*") The most consistent response I've heard from distributors is, "We don't know who the audience is for this film."

That ludicrous comment no longer surprises me. Without realizing it, I made more than a progressive film; I made a radical film with a Black woman at its center, a context for her complex life, and a multilayered plot. I've learned that the more textured a story by a Black film-maker, the more troubling it is to mainstream marketers—especially if that texture is not directly exploring the race issue but instead is exploring the humanity (rather than pathology and stereotypes) in contemporary Black life. If the story is neither a comedy nor a dramatization of history, that's even more troubling. That is why we ultimately chose to self-distribute the film.

What impresses me most as I reflect back on the life of *Naked Acts* is that considering all of the times it has screened—at festivals, in museums, at community centers, in classrooms, at conferences—people have asked me innumerable questions about the film but have rarely asked about the final scene—when Cece strips for herself before the still camera. That scene I expected to create the most controversy, and yet people don't mention it. I've come to view the silence as success, because it suggests that viewers have lived with this character in such a way for ninety minutes that by the time they witness her unveiling, they feel less like voyeurs, more like allies. They are, I would like to believe, cheering Cece as she finally liberates herself and lets go. The silence suggests to me that I've done what I set out to do with *Naked Acts*: I've presented a Black woman who embraces and celebrates her own nakedness—and gets away with it.

Contributors

Rachel Adams specializes in nineteenth- and twentieth-century American literature, media studies, theories of race, gender, and sexuality, and disability studies. For three years she served as Managing Editor of *Camera Obscura: Feminism, Culture, and Media Studies.* She is author of *Sideshow U.S.A.: Freaks and the American Cultural Imagination* (2001) and coeditor (with David Savran) of *The Masculinity Studies Reader* (2002). Her articles have appeared in journals such as *American Literature, Camera Obscura, GLQ,* and *Signs,* as well as the edited collection *Freakery: Cultural Spectacles of the Extraordinary Body* (1996).

Elizabeth Alexander is Assistant Professor in the Department of English Language and Literature at the University of Chicago. An acclaimed poet-scholar, her distinctive poems combine a luminously personal, often lyrical voice with a keen sense of the ways in which individuals bear and know the weight of history. In these poems, filaments of emotion connect the domain of intimate pleasures and losses with the larger cultural universe in which the agonies and inspirations are collective—issues she also addresses in scholarly publications devoted to nineteenth-century African American literature and culture. She is the author of several volumes of poetry, *Venus Hottentot* (1990), *Body of Life* (1996), and most recently *The Antebellum Dream Book* (2001).

Lisa Gail Collins received her Ph.D. in American Studies from the University of Minnesota. Currently Assistant Professor in Art History and Africana Studies at Vassar College, she is author of *The Art of History: African American Women Artists Engage the Past* (2002). Her other writings appear or are forthcoming in *Exposure, Chicago Art Journal, Rutgers Art Review, Colors,* and *The International Review of African American Art.*

Bridgett Davis is Associate Professor of English at City University of New York, Baruch College, where she teaches writing and film. Her original film *Naked Acts* received national attention in 2000. She is completing her first novel, *Shifting through Neutral.*

335

Lisa Farrington is an art historian teaching at the New School/Parsons Institute. She was co-narrator of the 1999 film *Howardena Pindell: Atomizing Art* and served as curator of "Art & Identity: the African-American Aesthetic" (1999) and "Women as Inspiration: The Paintings of Gaye Ellington" (2001). A 2001–2002 Ford Foundation Fellow, she was recently appointed to the College Board's AP Art History Test Development Committee. Her most recent publication is the textbook *Creating Their Own Image: A History of African-American Women Artists* (2002).

Anne Fausto-Sterling is Professor of Biology and Women's Studies in the Department of Molecular and Cell Biology and Biochemistry at Brown University. In addition to having served on the Brown faculty for more than 25 years, she has been a visiting professor at a number of institutions both here and abroad. She is a Fellow of the American Association for the Advancement of Science and has been the recipient of grants and fellowships in both the sciences and the humanities. Professor Fausto-Sterling has also written more broadly (and critically) about the role of race and gender in the construction of scientific theory and the role of such theories in the construction of ideas about race and gender. Her book *Myths of Gender: Biological Theories about Men and Women* (1985, 1992) analyzes research about the biological basis of behavior among women and men; *Sexing the Body: Gender Politics and the Construction of Sexuality* (2000) examines the social nature of biological knowledge about animal and human sexuality. Professor Fausto-Sterling is also the general editor for a book series published by Indiana University Press entitled "Race, Gender and Science."

Beverly Guy-Sheftall is Founding Director of the Women's Research and Resource Center and Anna Julia Cooper Professor of Women's Studies at Spelman College. She is also an adjunct professor at Emory University Institute for Women's Studies, where she teaches graduate courses in their doctoral program. She has published a number of texts in African American and Women's studies, including the first anthology on Black women's literature, *Sturdy Black Bridges: Visions of Black Women in Literature* (1979), coedited with Roseann P. Bell and Bettye Parker Smith; *Daughters of Sorrow: Attitudes Toward Black Women, 1880–1920* (1991); and *Words of Fire: An Anthology of African American Feminist Thought* (1995). Her most recent publication is an anthology coedited with Rudolph P. Byrd, *Traps: African American Men on Gender and Sexuality* (2001). She has been involved with the national women's studies movement since its inception and provided leadership for the first women's studies major at a historically Black college. Beyond the academy, she has been involved in a number of advocacy organizations, such as the National Black Women's Health Project, the National Council for Research on Women, and the National Coalition of 100 Black Women, on whose boards she serves. She teaches women's studies courses, including feminist theory, African American women, and global Black feminisms.

Evelynn M. Hammonds is Professor of the History of Science and Afro-American Studies at Harvard University. Her publications include *The MIT Reader on Race and Gender in Science,* coauthored with Rebecca Herzig and Abigail Bass (forthcoming); *The Logic of Difference: A History of Race in Science and Medicine in the United States, 1850–1990* (forthcoming); *Encyclopedia of Science, Technology, and Society,* consulting editor (forthcoming); and *Childhood's Deadly Scourge: The Campaign to Control Diphtheria in New York City, 1880–1930* (1999). Hammonds was co-organizer of the historic 1994 Black Women in the Academy Conference held at MIT. During 1994-95 she was National Endowment for the Humanities Fellow and member of the School of Social Science at the Institute for Advanced Study in Princeton. Her research is in the history of science, medicine, and public health in the United States and in race and gender in science studies. Hammonds obtained dual undergraduate degrees from Spelman College in physics and from the Georgia Institute of Technology in electrical engineering in 1976. She obtained a master's degree in computer software from the Massachusetts Institute of Technology in 1980 and her doctoral degree in history of science from Harvard University in 1993.

Terri Kapsalis is a performer and health educator. Her work has appeared in *Lusitania, New Formations, Public,* and the *Drama Review.* She has taught at Northwestern University in the Department of Performance Studies and has been a gynecology teaching associate in various medical schools. She is the author of *Public Privates: Performing Gynecology from Both Ends of the Speculum* (1997).

Jennifer L. Morgan is Assistant Professor of History and Women's and Gender Studies at Rutgers, the State University of New Jersey, New Brunswick. She is currently completing a manuscript on reproduction and slavery in the American colonies. Her work appears in the *William and Mary Quarterly, Social History, Money, Trade, and Power: The Evolution of Colonial South Carolina's Plantation Society* (2000), and *TransAtlantic Slavery: Against Human Dignity* (1994).

Contributors

Siobhan Somerville is Associate Professor of English and Women's Studies at Purdue University, where she also teaches American Studies. Her publications include *Queering the Color Line: Race and the Invention of Homosexuality* (2000) and articles in the *Journal of the History of Sexuality* and *American Literature*. She edited a special issue of *Modern Fiction Studies* on "Queer Fictions of Race" (2002). Her fields of specialization are late nineteenth- and early twentieth-century American literature, queer studies, feminist theory, African American studies, film, and Women's studies.

Kimberly Wallace-Sanders is Assistant Professor in the Institutes of Liberal Arts and Women's Studies at Emory University. She teaches courses on cultural representations of the female body, representations of race and gender in American culture, gender and American identity, advertising stereotypes, and African American material culture. Her work appears in *American Quarterly, Initiatives, SAGE: A Scholarly Black Woman's Journal,* the *Oxford Companion to African American Literature,* and *Burning Down the House: Recycling Domesticity* (1996). She is completing the book *Motherlove Supreme: Maternal Obsessions and the Black Mammy Figure in America.*

Carla Williams is a writer and photographer. She is coauthor, with Deborah Willis, of *The Black Female Body: A Photographic History* (2002). Her writings and images can be found on her website at <www.carlagirl.net>.

Doris Witt teaches and writes about twentieth-century literature and culture, particularly post–World War II African American literature and culture. Her first book, *Black Hunger* (1999), explores the sociological significance of debates over soul food during the Black Power era. While continuing to teach and publish studies of food, Professor Witt is also researching a book project that reconceives the history of space exploration and the cosmological imagination from a postcolonial perspective. She is Associate Professor of English at the University of Iowa.

Index

Index

American Museum, 265
Amerindian, 6, 41–42, 45–46
Am I Not a Man and a Brother?, 102
   fig. 17
Am I Not a Woman and a Sister?, 102
   fig. 18
Ammons, Elizabeth, 209
Amos, Emma, 6, 112–15, 122; *Creatures of the Night*, 113 fig. 24
Amsterdam, 128, 191
anatomy, 67, 70–72, 88, 189
ancestors, 119, 142
anesthesia, 8
Angola, 50, 255
Angelou, Maya, 182, 195
animalism, 25
Ann-Margret, 241
anorexia nervosa, 242–44, 246, 254
Antigua, 54
antislavery, 101–2
apartheid, 255
apes, 21
Appel, Toby, 70–71
Arizona, 289
art, 99, 114, 128–29, 141, 196;
   African American folk, 114; Afro-
   Cuban, 114; of the Black Diaspora,
   114; collectors, 107; Haitian, 114;
   history, 100–101, 109, 143; pre-
   Columbian, 114
Asia, 285, 327
Atkins, John, 55
Auguste, Jules-Robert, *Les amies*,
   103–4, 104 fig. 19
Aunt Jemima, 133–37, 134–36 figs.
   30–32, 182, 239–41, 244, 254
Axelsen, Diana, 276, 296–97

Baartman, Saartjie (or Bartmann,
   Sarah), 2, 9, 18–19, 19 figs. 3, 4,
   66, 67, 69, 74–82, 84, 86–87,
   89–92, 103, 112, 225, 247, 274
Bailey, Thomas, 25
Baillei, Dr. M., 85
Baker, Houston, 216
Baker, Josephine, 110–16, 111 fig. 23,
   113 fig. 24, 248
Bakhtin, M. M., 167–68, 209

Baldwin, W. O., M.D., 270–71, 275
Ballet Theatre, 189
Baltimore, 159, 288
Bangladesh, 290, 292
Barbados, 37
Barbot, John, 53
Barker-Benfield, Graham, *Horrors of
   the Half-Known Life*, 281, 298, 300
Barnum, P. T., 156, 158, 160, 162–63,
   178, 265, 266
Bartmann, Sarah. *See* Baartman,
   Saartjie
Bass, Maudelle, 189–91
Battell, Andrew, "Strange Adventures," 50, 51
Beale, Frances, 132
Bearden, Romare, 221–22
Beavers, Louise, 246–47
Bening, Annette, 329
Benois, Marie-Guilhelmine, *Portrait
   d'une négresse*, 15–16, 16 fig. 2
Benzoni, Girolamo, *History of the
   New World*, 42–44, 61
Berger, James, 180–81
Berger, John, 143
Berlin, 159
Bernhard, Sandra, 201
Berzon, Judith, 203
bestiality, 17, 49, 55, 165
biomythography, 219, 227
Bird, Calvin, 159
Black actresses. *See* actresses, Black
Black artists, 132–33, 148
Black Arts Movement, 133
Black Atlantic, 119
Black body, 1, 15. *See also under*
   Black female; Black men; Black
   women
Black Brood Mares, 288
Black church, 26
Black community, 25
Black Diaspora, 116
blackface, 201, 203–5, 208, 212
Black female, 310; appetite(s), 8,
   241–42, 246, 250; body or bodies,
   1, 6, 9, 19, 26, 103, 105, 113, 114,
   118, 120, 122, 182–84, 191, 194,
   247, 309–10, 312; construction of,

Index